THE HISTORY OF PARLIAMENTARY BEHAVIOR

The History of Parliamentary Behavior

Edited by William O. Aydelotte

Princeton University Press

Princeton, New Jersey

Series Preface

THIS is the fifth volume in a series sponsored by the History Advisory Committee of the Mathematical Social Science Board in order to encourage the application of mathematical methods to historical analysis. The series is being published by the Princeton University Press under the general title "Quantitative Studies in History." Other volumes in the series, both those already published and those forthcoming, are listed on page ii. The introductory volume, *The Dimensions of Quantitative Research in History,* was an attempt to show the scope of the quantitative methods that are today being applied in history and the variety of issues for which they are appropriate. Each of the other volumes is centered around a single major historical problem. The history of parliamentary behavior, the topic of the essays in this book, is not only a subject of enormous interest in itself but also one for which the use of mathematical methods has proved particularly rewarding.

The Mathematical Social Science Board (MSSB) was established in 1964 under the aegis of the Center for Advanced Study in the Behavioral Sciences "to foster advanced research and training in the application of mathematical methods in the social sciences." The following fields are each represented on MSSB by one member: anthropology, economics, history, geography, linguistics, political science, psychology, and sociology. The three methodological disciplines of mathematics, statistics, and computer science are also represented. Members of MSSB are appointed, subject to the approval of the Board of Trustees of the Center, for a term of four years. At the present time the members of MSSB are:

William K. Estes, Department of Psychology, Rockefeller University (Chairman)

Preston S. Cutler, Center for Advanced Study in the Behavioral Sciences

Edward A. Feigenbaum, Computer Science Department, Stanford University

Samuel Goldberg, Department of Mathematics, Oberlin College

Eugene A. Hammel, Department of Anthropology, University of California, Berkeley

Gerald Kramer, Cowles Foundation

Kenneth C. Land, Department of Sociology, University of Illinois, Urbana

Marc Nerlove, Department of Economics, Northwestern University

Stanley Peters, Department of Linguistics, University of Texas, Austin

Thomas W. Pullum, Department of Sociology, University of California, Davis

Herbert A. Simon, Department of Psychology, Carnegie-Mellon University

Charles Tilly, Departments of History and Sociology, University of Michigan

Waldo Tobler, Department of Geography, University of Michigan

MSSB has established advisory committees to plan its activities in the various substantive fields with which it is concerned. The current members of the History Advisory Committee are listed on page ii above.

Supported by grants from the National Science Foundation, MSSB has organized five major classes of activities.

(1) *Training Programs,* which last from two to eight weeks during the summer, are designed to provide young pre- and post-Ph.D.s with intensive training in some of the mathematics pertinent to their substantive fields and with examples of applications to specific problems.

(2) *Research and Training Seminars,* which last from four to six weeks, are composed of both senior social scientists and younger people who have already received some training in mathematical applications. The focus is on recent research, on the intensive exploration of new ideas, and on the generation of new research. The training is less formal than in (1); it has the apprentice nature of advanced graduate work.

(3) *Advanced Research Workshops* last from four to six weeks, but they are almost exclusively restricted to senior social scientists and are devoted to fostering advanced research. They afford the possibility of extensive and penetrating contact over a prolonged period, which would otherwise probably not be possible, of men deeply steeped in research.

(4) *Preparation of Teaching Materials.* In some areas, the absence of effective teaching materials—even of suitable research papers—is a limiting factor in the development of research and teaching activities within the university framework. The Board has, therefore, felt that it could accelerate the development of such materials, in part, by financial support and, in part, by help in organizing their preparation.

(5) *Special Conferences.* Short conferences, lasting a few days, are organized to explore the possibilities of the successful development of mathematical theory and training in some particular area that has not

previously been represented in the programs, or to review the progress of research in particular areas when such a review seems warranted.

Charles Tilly, CHAIRMAN

Ann Arbor, Michigan   History Advisory Committee, MSSB
November, 1975

Contents

Preface

THIS collection of essays is designed to illustrate the ways in which a variety of mathematical tools can be used to attack several general problems relating to the history of parliamentary behavior. The papers were originally presented at a conference which met at the University of Iowa, in Iowa City, March 13–15, 1972. The group of slightly over forty scholars who participated, and whose names are listed at the end of the volume, included members of departments, not only of History, but also of Political Science and Sociology. Most of these essays have been extensively recast since their first appearance and, in their revised versions, reflect many of the criticisms and arguments brought forward in the discussions at the sessions of the meeting.

The conference was financed by a generous grant from the National Science Foundation, operating through the History Advisory Committee of the Mathematical Social Science Board. The grants for this and other conferences that have resulted in volumes in this series have been handled by the Center for Advanced Study in the Behavioral Sciences. I am grateful to Preston S. Cutler, a member of the MSSB and Associate Director of the Center, for his efficient administration of the grant. I am indebted also to Robert W. Fogel and Charles Tilly, former and present Chairmen of the History Advisory Committee, for assistance and encouragement. I wish to thank Natalie Brody, my editorial assistant, who made a major contribution to the task of getting the book in shape for publication, Mary E. Strottman, who did the necessary re-typing of a large part of the manuscript, Julia Mears, my research assistant, who helped me with the final checking and proofreading, and Miriam Gallaher, who prepared the index.

My greatest obligation is to Allan G. Bogue and Samuel C. Patterson, who served with me as members of a committee to plan the conference and the book. Their immense knowledge of the state of current research on legislative behavior was of great assistance in working out a program, and they have given support and counsel throughout the enterprise.

The format of the book has been based on *A Manual of Style*, 12th ed. (Chicago: University of Chicago Press, 1969), © 1969 by the University of Chicago. The University of Chicago Press kindly gave permission for Chapters 15 and 17 of this manual to be Xeroxed and distributed to the contributors.

A Spanish translation of a shorter, preliminary version of Peter H.

Smith's paper has been published in *Historia Mexicana*, 22, no. 3 (1973): 363–395. A French translation of the paper by Antoine Prost and Christian Rosenzveig has been published in the *Revue Française de Science Politique*, 23, no. 4 (1973): 701–728. In both cases, permission was secured in advance both from the editor and from the Princeton University Press, and appropriate arrangements were made.

W. O. A.

THE HISTORY OF PARLIAMENTARY BEHAVIOR

Introduction

WILLIAM O. AYDELOTTE

ALTHOUGH parliaments or legislatures are central to representative, democratic government, and although they have been extensively studied by historians and political scientists, the ways in which they function are still only imperfectly understood. Uncertainty and disagreement persist with regard to such important matters as how members of a parliament are recruited, how they behave, and why they behave as they do. Recent research has called into question interpretations that once seemed plausible but that do not fit with new evidence that has been uncovered.

Modern investigations have raised questions not only about how parliaments work but also about their effectiveness. The view that they constitute a principal instrument of popular control has become qualified as students have noted developments that appear to limit their influence upon political decisions or upon the initiation of policy. James Bryce in his *Modern Democracies* (1921) welcomed the great increase in the number of representative assemblies in the world in the hundred years before his book was published,[1] but also had something to say about the "decline of legislatures" and the assumption of their powers by the administrative or executive branches of the government.[2] Valerie Cromwell, in a paper read before the Royal Historical Society in 1967, "The Losing of the Initiative by the House of Commons, 1780–1914"—a reversal of the title of Wallace Notestein's famous Raleigh Lecture in 1924—argued that, in the period she covered, the freedom of action of private Members of Parliament became more restricted while the influence of the cabinet was correspondingly enlarged.[3] Jean Blondel, assessing the current state of knowledge and problems of research in the study of parliaments in his recent book, *Comparative Legislatures* (1973), borrowed Bryce's expression and examined the "decline of legislatures" and the ways in which their performances and

[1] James Bryce, *Modern Democracies*, 2 vols. (London: Macmillan & Co., 1921), 1: viii, 3–5.

[2] Bryce, *Modern Democracies*, 1:367–377; 2: 53–54, 64, 335, 346, 356, 410–412, 560, 576.

[3] Wallace Notestein, *The Winning of the Initiative by the House of Commons* (London: Oxford University Press, 1924); Valerie Cromwell, "The Losing of the Initiative by the House of Commons, 1780–1914," *Transactions of the Royal Historical Society*, 5th ser. 18 (London: Royal Historical Society, 1968), pp. 1–23.

WILLIAM O. AYDELOTTE

achievements have disappointed the expectations of observers, though he also expressed an interest in the phenomenon which he described as the "resilience of legislatures." [4] Questions have been raised, as well, about how far or in what fashion parliaments are "representative"— the word has been used in different senses—of the constituents who elect them.[5]

Such reservations must be made, but the enormous importance of legislatures in the politics of most Western countries remains clear enough. Even the considerations that make it necessary to qualify this statement raise questions about the location of power in a modern state that are worth investigating and may, as some scholars have suggested, lead to fruitful reformulations of the objectives of research.[6] Parliaments are influential political elites, and it is imperative to understand how they have developed and functioned, and the circumstances in which their members have performed their duties and made their decisions. Beyond this, parliamentary history raises questions not only about the maneuvers and strategies of political leaders but also about the conditions out of which these actions emerged or with which they were designed to cope. A legislature that deals with major questions reflects the society behind it, public tensions and disagreements, in the sense that general social and political problems are dealt with and settled in parliament, whether adequately or not. It is sometimes argued that the study of representative assemblies, in view of the kind of work they did and in view of the great amount of information we have about them, constitutes one of our principal windows upon the political history of the past, an effective means of learning how politics actually worked.

The scope and interest of the problems arising in parliamentary history and the wealth of materials available for studying them have long attracted the attention of scholars. Although quantitative research on these problems, at least on the present scale, is new, the study of the

[4] J. Blondel, *Comparative Legislatures* (Englewood Cliffs, New Jersey: Prentice-Hall, 1973), pp. 2–10.

[5] Gerhard Loewenberg provides a convenient summary of these arguments in "The Role of Parliaments in Modern Political Systems," his introductory chapter to the collection of selections that he has edited, *Modern Parliaments: Change or Decline?* (Chicago and New York: Aldine-Atherton, 1971), pp. 1–20.

[6] Samuel C. Patterson and John C. Wahlke, "Trends and Perspectives in Legislative Behavior Research," in Patterson and Wahlke, eds., *Comparative Legislative Behavior: Frontiers of Research* (New York: John Wiley & Sons, 1972), pp. 289–303; John C. Wahlke, "Policy Demands and System Support: The Role of the Represented," in Loewenberg, ed., *Modern Parliaments,* pp. 141–171; David Easton, *A Framework for Political Analysis* (Englewood Cliffs, New Jersey: Prentice-Hall, 1965); Sir Cecil Carr, *Delegated Legislation: Three Lectures* (Cambridge: At the University Press, 1921); Ronald Butt, *The Power of Parliament* (London: Constable, 1967), pp. 1, 5, 10–13.

4

history of representative institutions by other methods for some time has been a major enterprise in the historical profession. Much valuable work was done before the advent of the quantifiers, and the earlier investigations have produced a large accumulation of information and insights on which those experimenting with new methods can still draw, to their great advantage, if they are alert to pick up these intellectual leads.

Yet the use of mathematical tools for parliamentary history, the development which this book is designed to reflect, has made great differences. These tools have given access to important classes of information that, without them, would, for practical purposes, have been unavailable. They have also made possible the manipulation of this information in ways that greatly further the purposes of scholars. They will not do everything, of course, and it is absurd to introduce them when they are inappropriate. Their special value for parliamentary history is that they provide a highly efficient means of summarizing and analyzing information about the behavior of large numbers of individuals. In view of the changing interests and concerns of political historians in the mid-twentieth century, this service is an exceptionally useful one.

Modern research on political history has tended to emphasize not merely the description of laws and institutions but also and still more the study of behavior. In politics the formal arrangements do not tell the whole story. Popular control is not achieved inevitably by constitutional devices, and the ostensible purposes of legislation may be altered in practice by the actions of individuals. As Walter Lippman observed, "Democracy has put an unfounded faith in automatic contrivances." [7] Political practices are shaped not only by legal provisions but also by the culture, habits, and traditions of a country. Sir Lewis Namier suggested something of this in his epigram: "England knows not democracy as a doctrine, but has always practiced it as a fine art." [8] A. Lawrence Lowell put almost the same point more simply but more clearly twenty years earlier when he wrote that the attempts of certain other European countries to adopt the English parliamentary system had yielded results of varying merit and that, elsewhere, the system "has not worked as it does in England, because the environment which determines the real functions of the organs of government could not be reproduced." [9] Lowell was interested in this problem and, in his book on European governments published in 1896, he noted a number of

[7] Quoted in David E. Butler, *The Study of Political Behaviour* (London: Hutchinson & Co., 1958), p. 16.

[8] Sir Lewis Namier, *England in the Age of the American Revolution* (London: Macmillan & Co., 1930), p. 6.

[9] A. Lawrence Lowell, "The Physiology of Politics," *American Political Science Review* 4 (1910): 3.

cases in which the reality did not fit the blueprint.[10] To understand politics it is necessary to study not merely what it was legally possible for people to do but also what they actually did, the ways in which prescriptions or intentions were implemented or modified in practice.

Furthermore, in research on parliamentary history, it is necessary to consider the behavior of a large number of individuals. It would be feasible, without resorting to mathematics, to examine the actions of a few eminent politicians, whose careers are apt to be documented extensively, and to discuss their attitudes, preferences, and decisions. This is the form that political history traditionally has taken, and many explanations of the course of the events have been in these terms. Yet for parliamentary history, as well as for some other kinds of history, this is not enough, and modern parliamentary historians would be much dissatisfied with so restricted a definition of their assignment. An account that describes only the leaders can be misleading since the rank and file may behave differently. Research that deals with a whole legislature raises questions of broader interest. General statements about a large body cannot, however, be based on information about only a few individuals in it. It is necessary to study the entire group under consideration or, if it is too big to be manageable, a carefully selected sample of it. The procedures that sufficed for the examination of small elites will not be adequate for the analysis of the behavior of large numbers.[11] It is an indication of Sir Lewis Namier's stature that he understood this need for getting the picture of a whole parliament and planned his researches accordingly; that he appreciated the importance of studying the backbenchers as well as the leaders; and that he had the imagination to see the value of the information about such men that could be extracted from their correspondence in the Duke of Newcastle's papers.

Research that permits generalizations about all, or almost all, members of a parliament is often feasible. The documentation, though far from covering everything we might wish to know, is plentiful. Data

[10] A. Lawrence Lowell, *Governments and Parties in Continental Europe* (Cambridge, Mass.: Harvard University Press, 1896); cited by Blondel, *Comparative Legislatures,* p. 5.

[11] Lee Benson, *Toward the Scientific Study of History: Selected Essays* (Philadelphia: J. B. Lippincott Company, 1972), pp. 112–113; David S. Landes and Charles Tilly, eds., *History as Social Science* (Englewood Cliffs, New Jersey: Prentice-Hall, 1971), pp. 71–72; Samuel C. Patterson, "Review Article: The British House of Commons as a Focus for Political Research," *British Journal of Political Science* 3, part 3 (July 1973): 370–375; S. E. Finer, H. B. Berrington, and D. J. Bartholomew, *Backbench Opinion in the House of Commons, 1955–59* (Oxford: Pergamon Press, 1961); Hugh Berrington, *Backbench Opinion in the House of Commons, 1945–55* (Oxford: Pergamon Press, 1973).

can be assembled about many aspects of the political behavior of members of a legislature and about many circumstances that have been conjectured to affect it: their political careers, their public actions, their party or factional affiliations, their attitudes on issues of the day so far as these are revealed by votes in roll calls, their personal backgrounds, and the kinds of constituencies they represented. It might be objected that such information, in the summary form in which it can be obtained for all members of a legislature, will not permit the kind of intimate treatment possible in an account of one or a few major statesmen whose papers can be studied in detail. What must be said on the other side is that these materials can be used for the study of an entire parliament and that, for such a purpose, they are much better than what historians ordinarily get. They are not trivial, they relate to important matters, and on many points they permit a full account.

What is particularly important is that this information comes close to being complete. It often can be procured for the whole or almost the whole legislature, the entire "population" that is to be studied. This is a signal advantage, and one that historians seldom have. Detailed data about all members of a large or significant group in the past is usually hard to come by. Murray G. Murphey has identified this as a major obstacle to the verification of explanatory historical generalizations. "It is, in fact, rare," he writes, "that any record can be found which is complete—i.e., where the probability is one that the entire set of responses of a given sort were recorded." A historian, he says, cannot test his hypotheses by specifying what observations would confirm or disconfirm them, since the "chances are that the predicted observations cannot be made." [12] For parliamentary history, however, the problem of missing data is less formidable than in some other historical enterprises. On many important points generalizations can be made and hypotheses tested for the whole legislature, or something close to it.

It is an additional advantage that this information is available for each member of a legislature, which makes it possible to describe the actions of legislators in terms of concepts of individual behavior, and to examine the relation between different variables on an individual basis instead of attempting to deal with aggregates. The "ecological" problem outlined by W. S. Robinson in his famous essay [13] does not often arise; certainly far less frequently than in the study of electoral behavior. Although ingenious methods now have been worked out for

[12] Murray G. Murphey, *Our Knowledge of the Historical Past* (Indianapolis and New York: The Bobbs-Merrill Co., 1973), pp. 142, 147.

[13] W. S. Robinson, "Ecological Correlations and the Behavior of Individuals," *American Sociological Review* 15 (1950): 351–357.

coping with this problem under certain conditions,[14] it is still a help not to be faced with it.

The use of these materials for historical research is difficult, however, because of their bulk and complexity. They could not be exploited effectively until the development of methods, largely mathematical in character, of systematic summation and analysis. Fortunately, much of the information about parliaments lends itself to such treatment. A parliament is to a high degree a data-producing entity. Many of the things that can be found out about members of such bodies can be quantitatively handled, provided that due precautions are taken not to do violence to the evidence. Quantitative methods have made it possible to describe and summarize information on the attributes and behavior of large numbers of persons, and to appraise the general structure and trend of the findings. They have afforded a means of coming to grips with the masses of data about parliaments and have enabled scholars, at long last, to begin to dig out of these materials the great wealth that is in them. Such methods also have permitted a more searching and more precise treatment of several questions that formerly had to be discussed in general terms and have made it possible to reach, with regard to these questions, firmer and more assured ground.

These advances have involved more than simply adding up figures and producing a few percentages and averages, although even such elementary procedures sometimes can reveal a great deal in an area where there has been little previous formal work. In addition, however, the means now available for analyzing the data have, in turn, made possible the creation and use of more refined and exact theoretical concepts that have proved central to many investigations. An example that is often given is the working out of better methods for defining and measuring political attitudes by Guttman scales or by factor analysis, devices that have been used in a number of these papers. Another illustration is the attempt by Mogens N. Pedersen in Chapter 2 to analyze what variables are relevant to the study of the circulation of a legislative elite, and how they can be measured. Still another is the examination by Gudmund Hernes in Chapter 9 of what is involved in the exchange of favors in a legislature and how measurable variables reflecting this can be created. Such explorations are not to be dismissed

[14] Leo A. Goodman, "Some Alternatives to Ecological Correlation," *American Journal of Sociology* 64 (1959): 610–624; E. Terrence Jones, "Ecological Inference and Electoral Analysis," *Journal of Interdisciplinary History* 2 (1972): 249–262; J. Morgan Kousser, "Ecological Regression and the Analysis of Past Politics," *Journal of Interdisciplinary History* 4 (1973): 237–262.

as nothing more than arithmetic. They consist, rather, in attempts to think through the meaning of certain commonly used terms and to redefine these terms more clearly and precisely. They entail also the attempt to make these redefined concepts "operational" and to devise tests, using the kinds of information that still can be obtained, to measure the attributes or the behavior to which they refer.

The application of quantitative methods in parliamentary history, though it has recently been accelerated, is not entirely a novelty. For some time parliamentary historians occasionally have resorted to counting—there is an example as far back as 1867—and their efforts have produced useful results. Much of this work, however, was restricted to accounts of the composition of legislatures in terms of the presonal backgrounds of their members. In general, it is only after the development, within the last several decades, of techniques for analyzing roll calls that scholars have been able to use quantitative methods to study behavior.[15] One interesting exception to this, an early effort in the direction of behavioral research, is A. Lawrence Lowell's ambitious investigation (1901) of the relation between party and vote in the British House of Commons and in the United States Congress over a large part of the nineteenth century.[16] Lowell was restricted by the limited technical resources at his disposal and his analysis, though it must have involved tremendous labor, is crude by modern standards. It was, nevertheless, a bold and imaginative effort that anticipated several features of the kind of historical research that was to develop fifty years after he published.

This collection of essays brings together some examples of recent quantitative research on parliamentary history. Among the scholars who were induced to contribute are a number who have been pathbreakers along this line and have already, in earlier books and articles, made significant contributions. The essays deal with seven different countries. Collections of analytical papers on political history are often heavily concentrated on the United States. Yet much interesting research is now under way elsewhere. This work is reflected here, and the volume has a strong international slant. Two chapters deal with the United States, two with Britain, and one each with Denmark, France, Sweden, Mexico, and Norway. Of the thirteen authors of the nine papers (four have joint authorship), seven are Europeans attached

[15] Bernard Cracroft, "The Analysis of the House of Commons, or Indirect Representation," in G. C. Brodrick and others, *Essays on Reform* (London: Macmillan & Co., 1867), pp. 155–190; Butler, *The Study of Political Behavior*, pp. 57–58.

[16] A. Lawrence Lowell, "The Influence of Party Upon Legislation in England and America," in *Annual Report of the American Historical Association for the Year 1901*, 2 vols. (Washington, D.C.: 1902), 1: 319–542.

to European universities, while six are attached to universities in the United States. In time, the papers range through the nineteenth and twentieth centuries. These are the centuries for which evidence is most abundant, particularly roll-call evidence, on which the majority of the papers are based. Quantitative analysis of behavior in earlier periods is also possible, however, as has been shown, for example, in the interesting article on Parliament in the late seventeenth century by Henry G. Horwitz and Kelly Moore.[17] Assembling figures on the composition of legislatures before the nineteenth century is, of course, a simpler task, and a great deal of such research has been done. Three of the essays in this book treat the most recent period, the 1960s. Some might regard them, on this ground, as "unhistorical." There is, however, a long tradition, extending from Thucydides to William L. Langer, that permits historians to write about recent events which they have themselves observed.[18] All three of these papers pursue questions that are of interest to historians and that are taken up in other essays in the book, and whatever additional light they can cast on these large issues is welcome.

There are three subjects, among others, about which much more detailed information is needed before it will be possible to attempt extensive generalizations about parliamentary behavior. These topics, around which this book has been organized, are by no means unfamiliar. They are basic to research in this field, and have already received attention, although the development of new tools of analysis has made it possible to attack them in different ways. The first, treated in Chapters 1 and 2, is the recruitment of legislatures: not, in this case, the personal and political backgrounds of members, but the patterns of circulation and of political careers that led to these configurations or apparently were connected with them. The second topic, which is the concern of Chapters 3, 4, and 5, is the description, in a fashion more precise and more comprehensive than has hitherto been possible, of the behavior of legislators: their actions and decisions. The third, treated in the last four papers, is the explanation of this behavior: the formulation and testing of hypotheses that may help to account for it. On these matters the contributors have sought to obtain and present conclusions that are based not on impressions but on hard data, and not on illustrative anecdotes about a few prominent individuals but on the study of the entire membership of a legislature.

[17] T. K. Moore and H. Horwitz, "Who Runs the House? Aspects of Parliamentary Organization in the Later Seventeenth Century," *Journal of Modern History* 43, no. 2 (1971): 205–227.

[18] The "great" historians of antiquity "did in fact tend to write either exclusively or prevalently about facts of the near past." (Arnaldo Momigliano, "Tradition and the Classical Historian," *History and Theory* 11, no. 3 [1972]: 280.)

Much early research on the recruitment of parliaments took the form of collective biography: the summarizing of information on the occupations of legislators, their social backgrounds, and their previous political experience. This line of research was recognized, twenty-five years ago, as a major intellectual lead. Sir John Neale, in a paper delivered in 1950, presented a vigorous argument for compiling biographies of Members of Parliament which, he insisted, should be uniform and comparable, and based on attempts to answer, for each individual, a set of questions previously enunciated.[19] The efforts of Neale, Sir Lewis Namier, and other forward-looking historians of that generation led to the establishment of the History of Parliament Trust, under an annual grant set up by the British Government in 1951, which is assembling and publishing an immense collection of short biographies of Members of Parliament that, it is hoped, will be useful for research of this kind. There has been interest elsewhere in gathering such materials. Plans are under way to establish at Princeton University an institution to assemble collective biographical data in machine-readable form, though its program will not be restricted to members of legislatures. The Inter-University Consortium for Political Research at Ann Arbor is collecting biographical information for members of both Houses of the U. S. Congress throughout the history of the American republic. Unquestionably the use of collective biography constituted a great step forward in the study of parliamentary history. Many investigations of this type have now been completed, for Britain and for other countries. The results are fascinating, and these inquiries have brought to light a great deal that was not clear before. More of such work is needed.[20] Yet collective biography by itself has limitations. There is a danger that it may become a mere description and summary in which the wider implications of the evidence are not taken into account, and apparently this has happened in some recent studies.[21] Nor is it clear how far information about personal background can help to explain the behavior of legislators, a subject that has been discussed by Peter H. Smith in Chapter 6.

Some scholars have recently attempted to raise a more general question and to examine by systematic means, not the composition of parliaments, but the processes that helped to produce these results or were associated with them: the patterns of circulation in such a body, of

[19] J. E. Neale, "The Biographical Approach to History," *History* 36, no. 128 (October 1951): 193–203.

[20] Landes and Tilly, *History as Social Science*, pp. 48, 74–75.

[21] Patterson, "The British House of Commons as a Focus for Political Research," pp. 363–381.

movement in or out of it, and the career patterns of its members. Douglas Price and Mogens N. Pedersen in the first two chapters discuss problems of this kind in two widely removed legislatures, the United States Congress and the Danish Folketing. Both authors seek to show changes over time and each deals with an extended period, more than a century. These are the only two chapters that cover anything like so long a span.

Mathematical tools make it possible to treat the rate of turnover or circulation of members of a legislature as a measurable variable—or, as Pedersen prefers, following some leads from Pareto and Mosca, as a composite of several measurable variables—so that the changes over the periods surveyed can be charted exactly. This information, of great interest in itself, then can be compared with changes in other variables, for example, the social composition of a legislature, a matter that Pedersen has discussed. Price, following a different tack, has devised ingenious tests to measure the extent of career satisfaction and the extent of electoral competition, which allow him to say something about how far discontinuity of service in the House of Representatives in the nineteenth century is attributable to a disinclination to serve or to a failure to be elected. He also has examined the development of strict seniority in appointments to committee chairmanships in both Houses of Congress, and has sought to clear up the conceptual confusion surrounding the discussion of this subject.

In these two chapters patterns emerged that, despite minor exceptions, were unmistakable, and that might not have been expected. In both Denmark and the United States, in the periods surveyed, there has been a marked increase in continuity and a decrease in turnover. Careers have become more stable and more secure. This was true, in Denmark, even when domination by a narrow upper-class group was disappearing and the legislature was becoming in its social make-up more like the population as a whole. Such findings raise interesting questions. If re-elections to a legislature become more frequent, more a matter of course, does this weaken the impact of general elections upon legislative policy, and does it limit the extent to which constituents can exercise control over their representatives? The emergence of closed political elites also may bear on the question of the development of a professional political class, conscious of a role of its own, with its own norms and expectations, a subject that recently has attracted much interest among students of parliaments.

In the investigation of parliamentary behavior the basic task is to define and measure the behavior that is the subject of study. This is the problem attacked in Chapters 3, 4, and 5. To the uninitiated this may seem a simple undertaking, but in fact it is not. Members of a legislature cannot be simply classified as either conservative or liberal. Those who support similar lines of policy may differ in the strength of their support and in the lengths to which they are willing to go. Issues are not on an equal footing: a man may be progressive on one question and reactionary on another. Patterns of voting may prove surprising: subjects that seem to us connected may have appeared unconnected to men living at the time while other issues, between which we at first see no obvious relation, may have been treated at the time as if they were different facets of some larger general question. To puzzle all this out and to produce a set of satisfactory descriptive generalizations about voting in a legislature is difficult, and it is only recently that we have had the means to make some headway with this task.

The study of legislative behavior has been revolutionized by the development of effective methods for the analysis of roll calls, which have proved to be an extremely illuminating source of information about the political attitudes and preferences of members of legislative bodies. Roll calls are, of course, not the whole of the political behavior of legislators, who may make important decisions on other occasions: in committees, for example, or in private conferences with their colleagues. They do, however, constitute the final actions taken on controversial issues, at least on those that were allowed to reach the floor.

Roll-call votes also have the virtue that they are answers to sets of uniform questions. This permits comparisons between individuals. It is an additional help, for purposes of comparison, that it is possible to obtain this information not merely for a few prominent men but for all members of a legislature so far as they voted, a major advantage in a systematic inquiry for reasons already explained. There may have been abstentions, many in some cases, but these also can be regarded as political decisions or political behavior, and a clever scholar can often make something out of them. In any case a division list, if a complete one was kept, provides information about all the votes that were cast. A set of abstentions, though it may create problems for the student, does not constitute missing data in the sense that an imperfect record does. Roll-call evidence is also, ordinarily, extremely accurate, particularly so when, as happened in many cases, the record was watched by participants and corrections, when needed, were made quickly. Its abundance, its reliability, and its close relation to major questions of contemporary political controversy make possible the examination of the attitudes of members of a legislature on issues of the day with a thoroughness and exactness that, in most historical research about large numbers of men, would be utterly out of the question.

13

WILLIAM O. AYDELOTTE

The problem of what roll calls measure and what inferences may legitimately be drawn from them is more intricate than it might at first appear. A vote in a roll call is not simply an expression of a legislator's private opinion. It is a political act, publicly recorded, and may reflect his view of his responsibilities toward any of a variety of groups whose opinions may not be in accord with his own. It also may reflect considerations of political strategy. Yet such policy positions, once formed, were ordinarily consistently maintained and, as Aage R. Clausen has argued in his recent book, the portrait of a legislator who uses the roll-call vote to project an image for public consumption, but takes a different line in the "important" decisions made offstage, is not really convincing.[22]

Unfortunately roll-call evidence is available only for a limited period. It is hard to get much information of this kind before the late eighteenth century. Earlier accounts of votes or divisions, though extremely useful, are apt to be incomplete or sporadic and ordinarily do not permit the same fullness of coverage or the same elasticity and freedom in designing variables and making tests. For some countries there is an additional restriction. The period for which it is possible to make maximum use of roll calls not only began late but also ended early. The increased amount of party voting in many legislatures over the last century has made this evidence less informative about the attitudes of individuals. The growth of party cohesion in the modern age is doubtless in itself an important finding. Furthermore, politicians have, legitimately, other objects in view than providing data that will be convenient for scholars to analyze. The fact remains, however, that roll calls are revealing particularly when parties do not vote unanimously and thus publicly display their internal disagreements. When members of each party vote together the analysis of votes inevitably will be more restricted. To illustrate from the essays in this volume, there is far more detailed evidence on the opinions of individuals, regardless of party, for Britain in the 1840s (Chapter 7) than for Britain in the early twentieth century (Chapter 4) or for Sweden in the 1960s (Chapter 5). Important findings can emerge even from a study of a highly disciplined party system, as these last two papers show. Yet, in general, the development of party cohesion has increasingly concealed a great deal of information about men's opinions that historians would much like to have and, in this way, has impaired the value of this once incomparable source.

[22] Aage R. Clausen, *How Congressmen Decide: A Policy Focus* (New York: St. Martin's Press, 1973), pp. 14, 19–20; see also Warren E. Miller and Donald E. Stokes, "Constituency Influence in Congress," *American Political Science Review* 57 (1963): 45–56.

14

Even so, the possibilities of the analysis of roll calls are enormous. Yet these materials are so voluminous that they are difficult to handle and until recently they have seldom been used on a large scale. Over the last generation, and particularly since World War II, means to exploit them have been provided by a series of remarkable conceptual and technical advances in methods of describing and measuring political attitudes. These advances have taken place mostly in other fields and were designed for other purposes: the study of the attitudes of members of the armed services; or the study of the political opinions of members of the electorate in survey research. These concepts and methods, however, once ways had been worked out to apply them to legislatures, have proved extremely useful to political historians as well. Progress has been rapid and techniques have been improved and refined. By now a number of these paths are fairly well trodden. Procedures which, a decade ago, seemed to most historians too outlandish to be worthy of serious consideration now have become widely accepted and—so quickly does opinion change—almost might be described today as conventional or traditional. Increasingly, it has become clear what can be done with such standard methods as clustering, scaling, or factor analysis: what are their advantages and disadvantages, what assumptions they entail, and what kinds of inferences may legitimately be drawn from the findings they produce.[23] New methodological departures are also possible, however, as is exemplified in Chapter 3.

The use of modern techniques of attitude measurement has permitted asking questions of a different kind about legislative behavior. It is now feasible to examine not merely votes in a single roll call but broader patterns extending through many roll calls, and to describe the relations of these patterns to other variables that might help to explain them. A scholar beginning his study of a legislature today might inquire about: the consistency of the votes of individuals on issues; the extent to which all the votes on a single issue constitute a continuous or a dichotomous variable; how far dimensions appear that embrace several issues; whether there is only one such dimension, or whether the voting pattern is multi-dimensional; the relation of voting on these dimensions to parties or to other political groups; as well as other, more complex, matters.

We do not, of course, have simple answers to these questions, universally applicable in all cases. Although the structure of voting in most

---

[23] On the dangers of improper assumptions in scaling see Allan G. Bogue, "The Radical Voting Dimension in the U.S. Senate During the Civil War," *Journal of Interdisciplinary History* 3 (1973): 451–455; and Murphey, *Our Knowledge of the Historical Past*, pp. 188–189.

legislatures has turned out to be far more consistent than previously was supposed, the larger patterns can take extremely different forms in different cases, as this book illustrates. In almost every investigation special circumstances appear that give an unusual twist to the findings or that present new problems of interpretation. A great deal of further work—many more case studies—will be needed before it will be possible to attempt, with some hope of success, ambitious cross-national or cross-temporal generalizations.

These are, however, questions that it often has proved profitable to investigate. They are not empty speculations but, on the contrary, have been formulated as the result of prolonged and energetic wrestling with the problem of characterizing legislative behavior and with the classes of evidence that are available for this purpose. They may seem obvious to many modern students. Yet to students of parliamentary history a generation ago they would not have seemed obvious and might not, at least in the way we now put them, even have been intelligible. The fact that it has now become possible to formulate such questions and the fact that doing this has become common practice represent a set of changes in our thinking about the legislative process that makes earlier discussions of the subject seem to belong to a different and unfamiliar world.

As methods have been worked out to exploit roll-call evidence, and as its value for the study of political behavior has become understood, scholars increasingly have turned to it. This source is so important that it will, for the periods for which it can be obtained, clearly be central to future investigations. Chapters 3, 4, and 5, which deal with the nature of legislative behavior, and the four remaining papers, which try to account for it, draw heavily upon this kind of evidence.

The authors of Chapters 3, 4, and 5 have attempted the complex task of the analysis of votes in a representative body. They have sought to identify the major patterns of choices, decisions, and disagreements in the legislatures they treat, the relations of these patterns to parties or to other factional groups, and the ways in which the findings can be interpreted in the light of what else is known about the surrounding political circumstances. The chapters deal with different situations and use different methods. Antoine Prost and Christian Rosenzveig in Chapter 3, "Measurement of Attitude Changes Among the Members of the French Chamber of Deputies, 1882–1884," have rejected attitude scales, as inappropriate to the special circumstances of French politics in this period, and have, instead, following the lead of Jean-Paul Benzécri,[24] presented an "analysis of correspondences" by which they

---

[24] Jean-Paul Benzécri, *L'Analyse de Données:* tome 1, *La Taxonomie;* tome 2, *L'Analyse des Correspondances* (Paris: Dunod, 1973).

try to measure the "slidings" ("glissements") of individuals from one position to another in the attitude universe created by the votes of Members of the Chamber. Their chapter is of considerable methodological interest. It carries further the analysis in their highly innovative article, "La Chambre des Députés (1881–1885): Analyse Factorielle des Scrutins," which was published in the *Revue Française de Science Politique* in 1971. Geoffrey Hosking and Anthony King in Chapter 4, "Radicals and Whigs in the British Liberal Party, 1906–1914," have attempted to find out how far the break-up of the Liberal Party after the First World War was foreshadowed by disagreements on issues in the last eight years before the war. They have used scale and factor analysis to identify the principal lines of cleavage in the party in these years, and have tried to ascertain how far voting against the Government was consistent and how far it could reasonably be regarded as foreshadowing the later break. Aage R. Clausen and Sören Holmberg in Chapter 5, "Legislative Voting Analysis in Disciplined Multi-Party Systems: The Swedish Case," have examined the relation of party to attitudes on issues in an almost contemporary legislature, the Swedish Riksdag in 1967. They found that party cohesion, even in modern Sweden, was by no means complete, and they have shown how it varied between different parties and between different issues. They also have raised some interesting questions about the dimensional ordering of parties and about the distances between parties on the principal left-right dimension that they discovered.

There have been changes, too, in ideas about the explanation of legislative behavior, the subject of the last four chapters. Motivation is, in any case, an obscure subject, and some regard it as one largely closed to historical investigation.[25] Historians who have generalized freely about the motives of large groups have been taken to task for failing to produce evidence to support their assertions. On this refractory problem quantitative methods sometimes can help. "One of the achievements of quantification," Richard Jensen contends, "has been to demonstrate that motivations can be deduced from numbers."[26] The last four essays take up different aspects of this problem and attempt to test, by quantitative methods, several alternative ways of accounting for legislative behavior.

An explanation of the political choices of legislators in terms of their personal backgrounds is plausible, and traces of this view have long

[25] Martin Duberman, *The Uncompleted Past* (New York: E. P. Dutton & Co., 1971), pp. 42–59.

[26] Richard Jensen, "Quantitative American Studies: The State of the Art," *American Quarterly* 26, no. 3 (August 1974): 226. Jensen's further discussion of this important point is extremely useful.

appeared in scholarly controversy and also in public arguments over political reform. It seems only natural that individuals with different kinds of economic interests or coming from different social origins would vote accordingly when questions arise that appear to affect their own welfare, defined in these terms. The social and occupational backgrounds of legislators have received a great deal of attention from scholars, particularly in Europe, and much of this research would seem to envisage at least the possibility of an explanation of this kind. Yet this reasonable expectation has not always been supported by the evidence. Peter H. Smith in Chapter 6, "The Making of the Mexican Constitution,"[27] has considered how far attitudes on the principal lines of controversy in the Mexican Constitutional Convention of 1916–1917 can be explained in terms of the social, occupational, and political backgrounds of the delegates. This was a considerable undertaking since it was necessary first to investigate the composition of the Convention and the principal patterns of voting in it, tasks that heretofore had not been attempted by modern methods. The largely negative findings emerging from Smith's sophisticated analysis of the relation between these two sets of variables fit only too well with the evidence accumulated in much other work on representative assemblies. It has proved difficult to account for the behavior of members of such bodies in terms of their personal backgrounds, and the more exact methods of modern research repeatedly have tended to qualify such explanations.[28]

An attractive alternative is to attribute the behavior of members of a legislature to the influence exerted upon them by their constituents. A statistical relationship often has been observed between the political preferences of legislators and the demographic attributes of the constituencies they represent. This seems easy to understand. It is reason-

[27] Peter H. Smith's chapter is the only one in the volume that does not deal with a legislature. He presents, instead, an analysis of a constitutional convention, the famous one of 1916–1917 that produced the constitution of modern Mexico. There might be some question—Smith raises the point himself—about whether a constitutional convention is comparable to a legislature. Yet many of the questions raised about legislatures may also be raised about conventions, as Smith has done. Duncan MacRae surely is correct when he includes constitutional conventions in his list of other bodies and groups about which it is possible to make the same general inferences that we make about legislatures and when he states that "the work of any group concerned with common issues, and recording disagreements about them, involves processes and data similar to those of legislatures." (Duncan MacRae, Jr., *Issues and Parties in Legislative Voting: Methods of Statistical Analysis* [New York: Harper & Row, 1970], pp. 1–2.)

[28] William O. Aydelotte, "The Country Gentlemen and the Repeal of the Corn Laws," *English Historical Review* 82, no. 322 (January 1967): 47–60. This is only one example out of many that could be cited. The general problem is discussed in Loewenberg, "Comparative Legislative Research," pp. 14–15.

able to suppose that voters in different kinds of constituencies had different kinds of demands which they enforced upon their representatives at election time. By this view, elections were the critical process for making parliaments responsive to the voters, the mechanism that ensured a link between citizens' views and the public policies followed by their representatives.[29] A stimulus-response theory of this kind, though perhaps not quite so crudely or simply presented, has commonly served both as an explanation of the behavior of legislators and also as a rationale or justification of representative institutions. In Chapter 7, "Constituency Influence on the British House of Commons, 1841–1847," I tried to summarize certain classes of information that might throw light on the question whether constituents exercised pressure on their representatives. The results were negative. Although there was a clear relationship between the political choices of Members of Parliament and the kinds of constituencies for which they sat, the evidence tells against the hypothesis that this behavior was enforced by pressure at elections. These results, like those of Chapter 6, can be fitted into a wider context. In their general news they are consistent with and help to confirm what has emerged from a great deal of research on legislatures and electorates in the mid-twentieth century. It is hard to demonstrate that constituents influence the detailed decisions of their representatives, and some students tentatively have concluded that such an explanation of legislative behavior can be accepted no longer. Though there is frequently a correlation between the votes of legislators and the demographic circumstances of their constituencies, it is still by no means clear how this result is produced.[30]

If research along these lines has not yielded adequate explanations of behavior it may help to examine instead a different part of the decision-making process: not how a representative's original preferences or wishes are formed, but how he attempts to put them into effect. This is the problem attacked by the authors of the last two chapters, although they have taken quite different lines and proposed for consideration two highly dissimilar mechanisms. Donald R. Matthews

[29] Wahlke, "Policy Demands and System Support," p. 144.

[30] Loewenberg, "The Role of Parliaments in Modern Political Systems," pp. 15–17; Wahlke, "Policy Demands and System Support," pp. 143–144; Chapters 29–33 (largely by Dexter) in Raymond A. Bauer, Ithiel de Sola Pool, and Lewis Anthony Dexter, *American Business and Public Policy: The Politics of Foreign Trade* (1963; 2nd ed., Chicago: Aldine-Atherton, 1972). The authors of several recent monographs have, however, suggested that this argument may have been pushed too far. See John W. Kingdon, *Congressmen's Voting Decisions* (New York: Harper & Row, 1973); Morris P. Fiorina, *Representatives, Roll Calls, and Constituencies* (Lexington, Mass.: D. C. Heath and Company, 1974); and Frank J. Sorauf, *Party and Representation: Legislative Politics in Pennsylvania* (New York: Atherton Press, 1963).

and James A. Stimson in Chapter 8, "Cue-Taking by Congressmen: A Model and A Computer Simulation," have attempted to explain how a legislator decides what kind of a vote in a given roll call will best advance his own general objectives. It is difficult for him to obtain enough knowledge to do this because of the amount and variety of the business transacted in a legislature and because of the complex, technical, and specialized nature of many of the questions on which he must register his preference. The authors of this paper have argued that legislators ordinarily meet this problem by accepting cues from trusted colleagues, and they have worked out this theory in detail and supported it by a computer simulation. This essay carries further their earlier research on this subject and constitutes a more extended statement of the results of an investigation that has already attracted wide attention. They have incorporated additional evidence and have recast their conceptual scheme in what they regard as a more advanced and satisfactory form. Their simulation model is the most recent of three that they have developed.

Gudmund Hernes in Chapter 9, "Interests and the Structure of Influence: Some Aspects of the Norwegian Storting in the 1960s," has discussed how a legislator deals with circumstances that may, unless he takes steps to prevent it, limit his ability to influence decisions on matters in which he is interested. He accomplishes this, it is suggested, by an exchange of favors, helping others to achieve their goals in return for their helping him to achieve his. Hernes, taking as his starting-point the theory of collective decisions proposed by James S. Coleman, has developed an elaborate theoretical analysis to show how transactions of this kind could take place in a legislature. His chapter, though it ventures into some uncharted territory, is a thoughtful and impressive attempt to develop a satisfactory model of legislative behavior.

There was, at the conference where these essays were first presented, some discussion of the implied disagreement between the last two chapters, which propose quite different mechanisms of decision making, and of how far or by what means this difference of opinion could be adjudicated. Obviously this could not be done from the information presented here since each chapter naturally explores its own hypothesis and does not discuss or present evidence bearing upon the contention of the other. In principle it should be possible to set up a project in which the two hypotheses could be compared to see which accounts for the larger amount of the variance. On closer inspection, however, questions arise about how far such a comparison would be feasible or legitimate. Not only are the theoretical structures of the arguments different, but also the chapters describe different kinds of situations. Hernes analyzes committee decisions in a legislature where much of the work was done in standing committees, whereas Matthews and Stimson examine actions taken in the whole house. Matthews and Stimson, for the most part, use roll-call evidence, which is also available to historians, and the majority of their contentions could be tested for a legislature in the past. This would not be possible with the model presented by Hernes since he relies heavily on interview data, a kind of information that historians cannot get. Beyond this, the two chapters deal with attempts of legislators to achieve different goals. For Matthews and Stimson, the problem that a representative faces is understanding what are the implications, for his own general objectives, of complex or technical proposals. For Hernes, the main problem for a legislator is to get the leverage he needs in order to influence decisions, on issues about which he cares and on which he presumably already has an opinion, that will be made by committees of which he is not a member. Matthews and Stimson deal with the gaining of knowledge and Hernes with the gaining of power. These are different questions, and it could be argued that the answer to one is only loosely related to the answer to the other.

The findings in this book and more generally the results of much recent research have large implications for the way in which we think about representative government. Certain standard assumptions regarding this form of government do not fit what has been learned in the last twenty years about its actual workings, and many hold that these assumptions can no longer be made. Nor is it clear what will take their place. We still do not understand what the representative relationship is and what explains it. The present state of knowledge on this subject has provoked Heinz Eulau to declare that "our common conceptions of representative government are obsolete!" and to speak of a "crisis in orientation" in the study of legislatures.[31]

The complaint occasionally is made that quantitative research reveals only the obvious, what everybody knew already. This objection can scarcely be directed against the quantitative study of legislative behavior. This is one line of investigation that clearly has *not* demonstrated the obvious but has, on the contrary, raised serious doubts about a number of the things that "everybody knew already" and that, at an earlier stage in the game, seemed so obvious that they could be taken for granted. Quantitative methods have revealed the extent of our ignorance, though this in itself may be regarded as an intellectual gain.

[31] Heinz Eulau, *Micro-Macro Political Analysis: Accents of Inquiry* (Chicago: Aldine Publishing Company, 1969), pp. 76, 80.

The essays in this book have made concrete contributions to the study of several problems, and those doing further research on these questions will have to take their evidence and their arguments into account. Much, however, remains to be done. The new findings raise new questions or point the way toward further investigations. It is useful to have, for Denmark and the United States, this information on changes in recruitment and career patterns and on their relation to other developments. Similar tests should, however, be made for other countries—there is reason to conjecture that the patterns might in some cases be different—and it is also necessary to explore further what can account for these relationships. Systematic analysis has brought out unexpected regularities in legislative voting, but further research is needed to identify their limits, their special character in different situations, and their relations to other political and social variables. We know more about the relation of party to vote in legislatures and how its extent varied with different kinds of circumstances,[32] but the picture is not complete and more case studies are required to verify or to refine the generalizations that are now being adumbrated. Nor are the reasons for party voting, when it did occur, clearly established. Old views about party discipline are under a cloud, and more complex explanations are being discussed. We can identify with more assurance what were *not* the causes of the behavior of legislators, but what *were* the causes of their behavior is less clear.

Little would be gained by an attempt to offer a set of specific agenda for further work in a field where the directions and objectives, as well as the methods, of inquiry are changing so rapidly. Predictions of research goals in the past have not always been confirmed by the further progress of investigation, and some have come to look rather bizarre after a few years. Intellectual advance sometimes is achieved not by carrying out a program but by questioning its assumptions: by showing that the proposed scheme involved misapprehensions, or that it did not address itself to the most important matters.

It may be useful, however, to say something in more general terms about the arguments over new research procedures in parliamentary history. Historians who try to use formal or quantitative methods not

---

[32] William O. Aydelotte, "Parties and Issues in Early Victorian England," *Journal of British Studies* 5 (1966): 95–114; John R. Bylsma, "Political Issues and Party Unity in the House of Commons, 1852–1857: A Scalogram Analysis," (Ph.D. diss., University of Iowa, 1968); William A. Speck, *Tory & Whig: The Struggle in the Constituencies, 1701–1715* (London: Macmillan & Co., 1970), pp. 1–12, 31–32, 111–112. A different line on some of these questions has been presented by Lawrence Dodd in *Party Coalitions and Parliamentary Government* (Princeton, New Jersey: Princeton University Press, 1975).

only expose themselves to abuse from those who do not welcome the new approaches but also open themselves to attack from those at the other end of the methodological spectrum, who argue that their efforts are only half-hearted and that they have fallen far short of being as systematic as they ought to be. Two general lines of research strategy for the study of the history of parliamentary behavior have been particularly recommended: the organization of comparative investigations, the results of which will be cumulative and will add to general knowledge; and a more formal and explicit elaboration of theory, so that historians will have a clearer idea of what should be their objectives and of how to interpret their findings.

To answer general questions about legislative behavior and to find out what can be said not just about one parliament but about several or many, it is necessary to resort to comparisons. This means not the comparison of individual legislators with each other, which we have learned to do pretty well, but the comparison of different legislatures, across time or across national boundaries. Ideally, such investigations should be strictly parallel in that, for each of the legislatures being compared, the same issues should be considered and, so far as the evidence permits, the same questions asked. Lee Benson regards comparative research as the principal task facing the historical profession and one so urgent that he has, half-humorously, proposed a gigantic administrative apparatus to encourage it.[33] Comparative research is described by Landes and Tilly as one of the three major research strategies of history as social science. They define it as "the systematic, standardized analysis of similar social processes or phenomena (for example, slavery) in different settings in order to develop and test general ideas of how these processes or phenomena work."[34] This method has been strongly urged for parliamentary history.[35]

Many recommend comparative research on legislative behavior but few attempt it. Most undertakings, even when systematic in their methods, are case studies of a single instance. One distinguished exception, the book of John C. Wahlke and his three associates, deals with state legislatures, not national ones.[36] The essays in this volume, though several groups of them treat similar topics and a few comparisons

[33] Lee Benson, "Explanations of American Civil War Causation: A Critical Assessment and a Modest Proposal to Reorient and Reorganize the Social Sciences," in *Toward the Scientific Study of History*, pp. 225–340.

[34] Landes and Tilly, *History as Social Science*, p. 73.

[35] Blondel, *Comparative Legislatures*, pp. xi, 28, and *passim*.

[36] John C. Wahlke, Heinz Eulau, William Buchanan, and LeRoy C. Ferguson, *The Legislative System: Explorations in Legislative Behavior* (New York and London: John Wiley & Sons, 1962).

between them were possible, are not strictly parallel in the sense described. Some students have complained that, because of the failure of scholars to use this potentially powerful method of analysis, the findings of different research projects have not been cumulative and have made only limited contributions to general knowledge.[37] Comparative research might be difficult. Team work, which it probably would require, could be hard to organize, and comparable data are not always available. Also, it is not a simple matter to decide what kinds of comparisons are legitimate or useful, and this question would require preliminary thought and discussion. Yet these difficulties are not necessarily insuperable and we have as yet so little experience that it is not easy to judge how formidable they will prove. The substantial achievements of Bryce and Lowell, though they used the methods and concepts of an earlier generation, may give some general idea of the feasibility of comparisons and of the kinds of intellectual leads that they can furnish.[38]

The situation with regard to comparative research is actually, however, not so bad as it sometimes is represented. It would be absurd to argue that the findings of every project have been totally irrelevant to the findings of every other project. On the contrary, the results of different investigations often have been comparable in some respects, and it is simply not true that there have been no cumulative gains. Most of what general knowledge we do have about legislative behavior has resulted from accretions of this sort, from comparison of the findings of case studies which, if seldom exactly parallel, do corroborate each other on some points. The cumulative effect of these results may in the course of time amount to a revolution as there has been, for example, in our thinking about the nature of patterns of voting in legislatures, the relation of personal background to political attitude, or the ways in which constituencies affect or do not affect the behavior of their representatives.

Yet it is certainly arguable that historians have been unnecessarily individualistic in formulating their research goals. Authors of monographs on comparable topics frequently address themselves to slightly different issues or ask slightly different questions, and sometimes it is hard to see what they would have lost by concerting their efforts. These eccentric and unprofitable divergences often make it difficult to summarize the existing state of knowledge on a particular question, and drive those who attempt the task into a state of exasperation. Though historians have contributed to cumulative knowledge, their contributions have tended to be tentative, fumbling, and sometimes uninten-

[37] Lowenberg, "Comparative Legislative Research," pp. 5–6.
[38] Blondel, *Comparative Legislatures,* pp. xi, 22–25, 27, 133.

tional. Even so, the results have been so profitable as to suggest that more deliberate and more carefully planned efforts would be rewarding. This would not exclude case studies of individual legislatures, which are more feasible than extended comparative inquiries and which are still greatly needed. Such studies, however, should be brought into closer relation with each other. Each should be designed to bear on general issues and to test hypotheses that are also of interest to other historians. It would be even better if some agreement on common objectives could be achieved at the outset between scholars who are preparing to investigate comparable problems in different settings.

Comparative research would require careful preliminary clarification of assumptions and agreement about what hypotheses should be investigated. This is the other major point on which concern has been expressed: the present state of theoretical discussion of legislative behavior. The criticism is that scholars have not thought through the implications of their findings and have not formulated adequately, in the light of present knowledge, the research questions that it will be most useful to ask. The complaint has been made that the current state of theory about legislative behavior is unimpressive and that much of the research on this subject shows a low level of conceptualization or abstraction.[39] The skillful use of statistical methods provides no safeguard against this danger, since research can be technically expert but still deficient in ideas. It is a common criticism of work in this field that theoretical advances have not kept up with the development of technical skills. Some investigations of parliamentary behavior have been described as "methodologically sophisticated but theoretically unstructured."[40] Historical generalizations in this field, it is also said, tend to be empirical. Historians first assemble and marshal the evidence on a topic, though they may do this by technically advanced methods, and then try to dream up a theory and to assign meanings to the patterns discovered. Hence their conclusions are merely the impressions they get, the things they happen to notice, when they look at the collected data, but are derived without the guidance of prior hypotheses. A sounder procedure, it is argued, would be to set up in advance hypotheses or models to be tested, in mathematical terms if possible, specifying the conditions that will satisfy them, and then to collect the relevant data and ascertain how far they meet the stipulated conditions.

These are serious matters, particularly for historians, since the neglect of general problems of interpretation for some time has been identified

[39] Patterson, "The British House of Commons as a Focus for Political Research," p. 376.
[40] Wahlke, "Policy Demands and System Support," p. 152.

as a major weakness of much modern historical scholarship.[41] On this point too, however, complaints sometimes have been pushed too far. It cannot be maintained seriously that thinking on the subject of legislative behavior has not advanced. On the contrary it has, in several respects, been revolutionized. There have been major changes in the interpretation of certain phenomena, as well as in the direction of research interests. There are still unsolved problems, in this area as in others, but this does not mean that the discussion of them has been intellectually innocent. Even the realization of ignorance, as I have argued earlier, is in itself an advance, particularly when, as in this case, it involves the jettisoning of simplistic theories. The value of negative findings as a path to knowledge should not be underestimated. Nor is formal theory, the development and testing of hypotheses, wholly lacking. No research, of course, proceeds entirely without hypotheses; the alternative would be chaos. All investigators begin with at least some general ideas, some loosely organized and perhaps even unstated model, and could hardly come to terms with their materials if they did not. On a higher level, a number of scholars, including some of the contributors to this volume, have set up hypotheses or formal models and attempted to verify them, sometimes by complicated means. There might be argument over whether all these schemes are elaborate or technical enough to be properly described as models, but this objection is formalistic. Models can come at different levels of abstraction and complexity. Judgment of their serviceability should depend, not on a uniform and rigid standard, but on the existing state of knowledge of the subject and on whether they serve to advance the study of it. The gains of theoretical explorations so far, which have pointed the way to the discovery and description of larger patterns in the evidence, have been so considerable as to suggest that further efforts would be extremely useful.

There is always the danger that an abstract discussion of procedures will oversimplify or distort what actually goes on in research. The prescription that models be formulated *a priori* and then tested may not, unless properly qualified and elaborated, get at the essence of what is needed. It is more usual, and more useful, to take the line that theory and empirical investigation proceed together, each depending upon but also helping to guide the other. Furthermore, in a new and still devel-

[41] M. I. Finley, "Generalizations in Ancient History," in Louis Gottschalk, ed., *Generalization in the Writing of History: A Report of the Committee on Historical Analysis of the Social Science Research Council* (Chicago: University of Chicago Press, 1963), pp. 19–35; David M. Potter, "Explicit Data and Implicit Assumptions in Historical Study," in Gottschalk, pp. 178–194.

oping field, an emphasis in the direction of empiricism may be a wise precaution. Too rigid a definition of research problems at the outset can divert attention from unexpected but profitable intellectual leads, or block the approach to other kinds of formulations that may ultimately prove more useful. One should handle the theory with a loose rein, and be prepared to modify or refine it as knowledge advances and as the results may suggest.

The general thrust of both these lines of criticism is so powerful that they cannot be ignored, and some reconsideration of research objectives in the light of these arguments is clearly in order. The other side is that these objections, if pushed too far, grossly misrepresent the present state of work in the field. More comparisons would be fine, and I hope we can get them, but they may be harder to make than is always realized, and some comparisons are feasible even on the basis of the findings that have been produced already. Certainly we need to think our way more carefully into these problems, and much more can be done by the formal and conscious organization of our ideas, but we have been turning these questions over in our minds already and have made at least some headway with them. The recommendations of the purists are a little too sweeping and their diagnoses are a little too neat to be wholly persuasive to those who have to do the work of confronting the evidence and trying to interpret it.

In any case these concerns should not be allowed to obscure the gains that have been made already, the dramatic increases in knowledge that have taken place over the last twenty-five or thirty years. It is true that there are problems on which it is still hard to see our way. On the other hand, we are not wholly in the dark either. Research up to this time has not only excluded certain hypotheses but also has made possible a sharper definition of objectives. It is now feasible to identify more precisely the topics to be investigated and the questions to be answered. The accumulation of evidence and the development of thinking about legislative behavior, though still inadequate, are sufficient to afford at least some general guidance, and the prospects for further work in the field are promising. These essays may serve to show what can be done by an attempt to achieve clarity and precision through a prudent use of the tools of analysis now available.

1

Careers and Committees in
the American Congress:
The Problem of Structural Change

DOUGLAS PRICE

I
INTRODUCTION

OVER the past two decades a great deal of research has been done on the post-World War II House and Senate. Obviously our understanding is still by no means complete, but we have come a long way. Capitol Hill is no longer a mysterious, virtually unexplored domain. We now have, if not a full-fledged paradigm, at least a more or less consistent set of conclusions about the structure and functioning of the post-New Deal House and Senate. What has remained until very recently mysterious and virtually unexplored is the time dimension: how have these systems changed or evolved, and how did they function in different eras?

A serious concern with the time dimension soon brings one to the question of when, if at all, there have been basic structural changes so sharp as to suggest the emergence of a new system of organization requiring a new analytic paradigm. Put another way, how far back in time can our current set of generalizations about the House and Senate be safely extended? If the features of the House Appropriations Committee as described by Richard Fenno [1] can be traced back to 1925, how about 1905; if Ralph Huitt's Senate majority leader [2] can be found in Woodrow Wilson's presidency, how about McKinley's presidency? If most House districts have been relatively "safe" in the twentieth century, how many were "safe" in the nineteenth century?

Most books dealing with the history of the House and Senate shed

The research for this chapter has been supported by National Science Foundation Grant GS–2428.

[1] Richard F. Fenno, Jr., "The House Appropriations Committee as a Political System: The Problem of Integration," *American Political Science Review* 56 (1962): 310–324.

[2] Ralph K. Huitt, "Democratic Party Leadership in the Senate," *American Political Science Review* 55 (1961): 333–344.

little light on such questions; rather they belong to what one might term the parliamentary rules paradigm. My interest in the development of the nineteenth-century House and Senate has centered around the tremendous impact of parties and changes in the party system on Congress. This is *not* a perspective of prime importance for understanding the functioning of the contemporary Congress. The modern House and Senate are committee-centered, with parties in the background helping to provide a very modest infusion of new members who automatically go to the bottom of the committee seniority lists. But it was not always so. It seems to me that the current view of the House and Senate can be extrapolated back, with rather minor modification, to around 1920. But as one moves further backward in time most of the familiar congressional landmarks drop from sight, one by one, until 1890 when the House and Senate appear as very different structures from their modern counterparts.

Long-run careers and stable committees, the twin pillars of the modern Congress, are largely missing in the pre-1896 House or the pre-1876 Senate. To comprehend how these bodies functioned in their absence requires a major readjustment of ideas and mental habits, as in the case of non-Euclidean geometry (to which Sir Lewis Namier once compared parliamentary politics not based on parties). The purpose of this chapter is to explore, in a comparative House-Senate perspective, the emergence of the long-run congressional career, and its crucial consequences for the subsequent development of strict committee seniority practices.

II

PROFESSIONALIZATION OF CAREERS: SENATE AND HOUSE

The so-called Clay Congresses (1811–25) mustered at no time more than twenty members who had served five terms each, while from 1789 to 1860 only forty exceeded six terms.

DeAlva S. Alexander [3]

WE know that for the modern "professionalized" Senate and House resignations are extremely rare, that efforts at re-election are the norm, and that successful re-election is overwhelmingly the case for the House and quite frequent for the Senate. But what are some of these magnitudes for past periods, and when did they begin to approach modern levels? We shall begin with the Senate.

The distinguished senators of the very first Congress set the early career pattern for that chamber: they fled the capitol, not yet in Wash-

---

[3] DeAlva S. Alexander, *History and Procedure of the House of Representatives* (Boston: Houghton Mifflin Co., 1916), p. 306.

ington, almost as fast as was humanly possible. Five of the original 26 hastened to resign even before completing their initial terms, most of which were for only two or four years (they had drawn lots to determine who would serve two-, four-, or six-year terms). One died in office, and 2 who had been selected for short terms had the unusual misfortune to seek re-election and fail. Eight were re-elected, but 6 of these had been on short terms. The remaining 10 managed to serve out their term (or sentence to obscurity), but did not seek another round. By the time the capitol was moved from Philadelphia to the swamps of Washington only 2 of the original 26 senators remained, and in two more years they were gone.

Career data on the early Senate is a morass of resignations, short-term appointments, elective replacements, and more resignations. There are *no* notable careers in terms of long service. Rather, records are set by the same senator resigning the same seat in the same term twice (by coming back to it for a time after his initial replacement resigned), or by a single man's serving as a state's replacement for each of the state's two senate seats and quitting from each. From 1789 to 1801 the amazing total of 94 individuals (or 95, if one counts Albert Gallatin, who was admitted but then held ineligible) had warmed senatorial seats for varying times.

In its initial decades, of course, the Senate was an honorific nothing. Everyone was for a second chamber in theory, but no one could figure out what, if anything, it should do in actual practice. Some states used their senatorships as a sinecure for defeated House members, and ambitious young politicians—Madison or Clay—were unanimous in their determination to avoid being stuck in the "do-nothing" chamber. How and why this came to change is itself an exciting story, but cannot be pursued here. That it was a long time before it did change, however, is obvious from the careers of successive Senate cohorts.

Senate "cohorts" are a bit more awkward to define than are House "cohorts." There is the problem of the three classes of seats, with one-third coming up for election every two years. And there is the much greater role played by appointive or elective replacements. Many of the appointive replacements did not seek or expect election, and including them with the regularly elected senators tends to confuse the picture. For explanatory purposes I have adopted the simple, though hardly ideal, expedient of taking as a "cohort" all those senators who were on hand at the beginning of a given Congress. I have then pursued their careers through to the end of their current terms, about one-third coming up for election every two years. This should not affect the probability of their seeking re-election or not, but it does somewhat reduce (to an average of about four years) the time in which they might

TABLE 1-1. SENATORIAL CAREERS IN NINETEENTH CENTURY: PERFORMANCE IN OFFICE OF COHORTS CONSISTING OF MEMBERS ON HAND AT OPENING OF CONGRESSES INDICATED. (NOTE: SOME OVERLAP OF CASES MAY EXIST BETWEEN CONGRESSES LESS THAN SIX YEARS APART.)

	Number of Cases from Senate Cohort Indicated									
Congress Year	8th 1803	9th 1805	11th 1809	24th 1835	27th 1841	29th 1845	31st 1849	32nd 1851	33rd 1853	49th 1885
1. Entering Cohort	34	34	34	52	51	56	62	62	62	76
2. Serve Out Term	19	20	20	34	31	33	45	46	51	68
3. Resign in Term	12	12	11	14	13	15	12	12	6	5
4. Die during Term	3	2	3	4	7	7	5	4	4	3
5. Unseated	–	–	–	–	–	1	–	–	–	–
6. Seek Re-election	11	15	7	21	14	20	20	18	27	55
7. Do not run for Re-election [a]	8	5	13	13	17	13	25	28	24	13
8. Re-elected	10	14	6	16	10	10	15	17	22	42
9. Defeated [a]	1	1	1	5	4	10	5	1	5	13

[a] Some of the "Do not run" category actually may have desired and/or sought re-election, but biographical data are limited and do not always show "defeats" that take place within state legislatures, not at the polls.

resign from office. The advantage is that most of the very temporary interim appointees are thus eliminated and we can concentrate on more or less "regular" senators. This also means that looking at such a "cohort" for a given Congress gives us data not only on the one-third elected to that Congress but also on those (or their replacements) who were elected to the previous two Congresses. Conversely, data on Congresses less than six years apart include some overlap.

Using the categories of Table 1-1 I have hand tabulated the career patterns of such cohorts for ten different pre-Civil War Congresses. For comparison I present the post-Civil War picture as of the 49th Congress (1885). There is, of course, extensive published material on later senatorial careers in Rothman (1869–1901) [4] and Donald Matthews (1947–1957). [5] My preliminary findings are presented in Table 1-1.

Perhaps the most salient point of the data is that, for most of the pre-Civil War cohorts, almost one-third resigned *before* their terms were up; another one-third finished their terms but did *not* seek re-election; while only slightly over one-third finished their terms *and* sought re-election. This ignores the 10 percent who died in office, with unknown career intentions. (See Figure 1-1.)

[4] David J. Rothman, *Politics and Power: The United States Senate 1869–1901* (Cambridge, Mass.: Harvard University Press, 1966).
[5] Donald R. Matthews, *U.S. Senators and their World* (Chapel Hill: University of North Carolina Press, 1960).

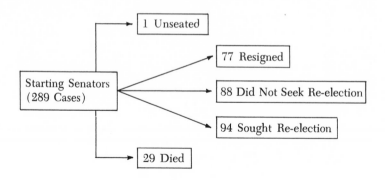

FIGURE 1–1.

Summary of Data for All Senators of Six Early Congresses (8th, 11th, 24th, 27th, 29th, and 31st) with Some Overlap

The massive level of senatorial resignations—often exceeding the number of senators willing to stand for re-election—is an unexpected finding. There is, however, some shift in the nature and reasons for resigning between the period before 1830 and the one from 1830 to 1850. For the whole period down to the election of Jackson the Senate was barely existing, or was in a sort of political limbo. The galvanizing effects of the organization of the first American party system (Republicans versus Federalists) had worked to magnify the decision-making role of the House. The Republicans had made little headway in the Senate during the 1790s, and in 1800 the Federalists threw away their chance to use the Senate as a citadel of Federalism. (John Adams took good Federalists *out* of the Senate and appointed them to the Judiciary.)

For a generation there was continuing confusion over the intended role of the Senate. Colonial second chambers usually had been "councils" which advised or restrained the governor.[6] The Senate had been grafted onto the proposed Constitution largely as a sop to the small states, but political conflict had *not* developed on small state versus large state lines. Moreover, the Senate had failed to achieve any effective position as a "council" to the President—this function had rapidly devolved on the cabinet. In Madison's administration the Senate showed some fight over major appointments, and finally in 1816 it

[6] See the discussion in Jackson Turner Main, *The Upper House in Revolutionary America, 1763–1788* (Madison: University of Wisconsin Press, 1967).

set up a system of standing committees. But it was still widely regarded as a rather inconsequential body, substantially inferior to the House.[7] Small wonder that aspiring politicians like Henry Clay spurned it. As Henry Jones Ford put it: "Presidential timber was not grown in the Senate." [8]

The development of the second American party system in the 1830s brought about a virtual revolution in the position of the Senate. As the first American party system was built largely on House opposition to the Federalists, the second American party system was built on Senate opposition to the Jacksonians. Jackson's major appointments could be fought, and sometimes beaten, only in the Senate; routine patronage also could be controlled from the Senate. Public attention was focused on the Senate, and presidential hopefuls were concentrated there (though it was still considered good form to resign one's seat when launching a presidential campaign). As the Senate waxed in importance the attractions of a House career waned; [9] from Jackson to Wilson the traffic from top House positions to the Senate was substantial.

Resignations from the Senate continued to be numerous in the 1830s and 1840s, but now they were more likely to reflect movement into the cabinet, the launching of a presidential campaign, or perhaps refusal to obey "instructions" from a state legislature.[10] The changes in the ratio between senators resigning their seats and those seeking re-election are dramatic. Table 1–2 presents this information for six separate Congresses, in which resignations were roughly as frequent as efforts at re-election. By contrast, the post-Civil War 49th Congress had only 5 resignations from the Senate, while 55 members sought re-election. The shift is from a one-to-one ratio to a one-to-ten ratio.

Up to about 1840 those in each cohort who sought and won an additional term did not behave very differently, in this respect, from the others. Of the 8 senators re-elected from the original 26, no less than 4 (including John Carroll of Carrollton) resigned in the course of their new terms. From the cohort of the 9th Congress (1805) 14 were re-elected, but 5 of these resigned. From the 24th Congress (1835) 16 were

[7] Henry Jones Ford, *The Rise and Growth of American Politics* (New York: Macmillan Co., 1898), p. 266.

[8] See the interesting comments in ibid., p. 262.

[9] Under the Federalists (and in Jefferson's administration) the House was a relatively small and quite elite body. Turnover was less than at almost any other time prior to the twentieth century, and an ambitious member might expect to move from the House to either the cabinet or a major ambassadorship. By the time de Tocqueville visited this country the House was a large and generally undistinguished body with extremely high turnover.

[10] William H. Riker, "The Senate and American Federalism," *American Political Science Review* 49 (1955): 452–469.

TABLE 1–2. Senate Careers: Proportion of Senators Resigning and Proportion Seeking Re-election for Six Selected Pre-Civil War Senate Cohorts.

Senate Cohort:	Total Number:	Percent of Cohort:	
		Resigning	Seeking Re-election
8th Congress (1803)	34	35 (12)	32 (11)
11th Congress (1809)	34	32 (11)	20 (7)
24th Congress (1835)	52	26 (14)	40 (21)
27th Congress (1841)	51	25 (13)	27 (14)
29th Congress (1845)	56	26 (15)	35 (20)
32nd Congress (1851)	62	19 (12)	29 (18)

re-elected but 9 resigned. The Civil War precludes this analysis for the 1850s, but a marked shift was evident in the 1840s. The cohorts of 1841, 1845, and 1849 show with some overlap a total of 35 members re-elected, but only 3 of these resigned in their subsequent terms. Here we have a glimmer of hope for the emergence of career senators. Indeed, in the 1850s the dominant Southern Democrats tended to pursue long-run careers in the Senate. As a result even average terms of service show a modest gain.[11]

Prior to the Civil War most senators did not make a long-run "career" out of continuous Senate service.[12] Since no positions in the Senate rested on any form of seniority (in the chamber, or on committees) major political figures drifted in and out of the Senate as convenience dictated. Cabinet posts were a major attraction, luring both Clay and Webster for a time. The less well-known John J. Crittenden served *four* separate, non-consecutive terms in the Senate between 1817 and 1861, interspersing them by twice serving in the cabinet as Attorney-General, by a term as governor of his state, by an appointment to the Supreme Court (for which his former colleagues refused confirmation), and by some other posts, including membership in the House of Representatives. Lateral movement from Senate to cabinet and then *back* to the Senate was particularly important in the nineteenth century, but was a practice that could *not* be combined easily with a strict committee seniority system.

In the twentieth century one can pick almost any year and then turn

[11] Randall B. Ripley, *Power in the Senate* (New York: St. Martin's Press, 1969), p. 43.

[12] Thomas Hart Benton is the exception that proves the rule; his unusually long service reflected the failure of his ambitions for military command during the Mexican War or for the White House.

to the Senate of a decade earlier and find at least one–fourth, sometimes one-third, and recently almost one-half, of the same individual members serving for continuous long-term periods. Put another way, the political "half life" of a Senate cohort over the past decade has been close to ten years. But for the pre-Civil War Senate it is rare to find more than two or three Senators who might be continuously on hand over a ten-year period. Thus Table 1–3 contrasts the number of such ten-year veterans for selected Congresses in the nineteenth and the twentieth centuries:

The long-term survivors in the earlier periods do include such historically important figures as Webster (from 21st to 26th), Clay and Calhoun (both from 26th to 31st), and Stephen A. Douglas (31st to 36th). But three of these four served "broken" Senate careers.

After the Civil War and Reconstruction the Senate was at a peak of influence. The executive branch was in a long eclipse, and senators extended their effective control of state party machines (or vice versa). The national government was by then of vital importance in regard to tariff policy, monetary policy, and, for the South, race policy. Senators controlled the allocation of federal patronage, and increasingly lorded it over the House. Thus by the 49th Congress (our 1885 cohort in Table 1–1) resignations were only one-third the number for 1845 though the Senate was larger by 20 members. The ratio of members seeking re-election to those not doing so is no longer half and half, but stands at 55 to 13. By this time most states were predominantly either Democratic or Republican, so that electoral hazards were reduced. By this time, as we shall see, Senate committee chairmanships were being han-

TABLE 1–3. SENATE VETERANS SERVING OVER TEN CONTINUOUS YEARS
FOR PARTICULAR CONGRESSES INDICATED

Period of Service	Number Surviving	From Total in Base Year
1st to 6th Congress	3	26
6th to 11th Congress	2	32
11th to 16th Congress	3	34
16th to 21st Congress	9	44
21st to 26th Congress	4	48
26th to 31st Congress	8	52
52nd to 57th Congress	22	88
62nd to 67th Congress	29	96
72nd to 77th Congress	28	95 (plus a vacancy)
82nd to 87th Congress	42	96
86th to 91st Congress	52	100

dled quite rigorously in terms of continuous committee service. The Senate was, as Rothman's book makes clear, a good place for a politician to be. And the longer he stayed there, the better it would be. For the Senate, career stability led to irresistible demands for adherence to seniority norms for committees.

But let us turn to the House of Representatives. Richard Morningstar collected data on the careers of all members who left the House in three different periods.[13] The crucial importance of distinguishing between *alternative reasons* for turnover is evident in Morningstar's comparisons between the periods 1811–1820 and 1887–1896. Both are marked by very high turnover. But for the earlier period *only* 49 of 465 departures could be attributed to electoral defeat; for the latter period electoral defeat accounted for 309 of 750. What the early House lacked was not safe seats, but a desire and incentive to retain one's seat. In the late nineteenth century the desire for re-election was up somewhat, but re-election had become more risky.

The difference between the nineteenth and twentieth centuries in regard to House careers has been evident ever since Stuart Rice assembled his materials on first-term members (and on age) in 1929.[14] Recently a trio of political scientists at the University of Rochester [15] has developed a somewhat more refined time series which distinguishes continuous service from prior non-continuous service and also separates out members occupying newly created House seats. In only two of 50 cases (1804 and 1898) do the *highest* nineteenth-century re-election rates reach the *lowest* figures for the twentieth century (1932, which combines a presidential landslide with an extensive reapportionment of seats, and 1914).

In a paper in 1964 [16] I argued that changes in the structure of the House career were crucially linked to the massive political realignment of the 1890s. This decade was marked by the emergence of the really solid Democratic South, by the rapid spread of ballot reform and registration systems, but above all by the collapse of the Democrats in the 1896 Bryan campaign. Democratic gains in the silver states and some

[13] Richard Morningstar, "Congress as a Closed System: Its Characteristics and Implications" (Senior honors thesis, Harvard University, 1967). The author analyzed House careers for the three periods 1811–1822, 1887–1896, and 1951–1960.

[14] Stuart A. Rice, *Quantitative Methods in Politics* (New York: Alfred A. Knopf, 1929), chap. 21.

[15] Morris P. Fiorina, David W. Rohde, and Peter Wissel, "Historical Change in House Turnover," in Norman J. Ornstein, ed., *Congress in Change: Evolution and Reform* (New York: Praeger, 1975), pp. 24–57.

[16] Douglas Price, "The Congressional Career: Then and Now," reprinted in Nelson Polsby, ed., *Congressional Behavior* (New York: Random House, 1971).

farming states proved temporary, but massive Democratic losses in the Northeast and Midwest were to last until Al Smith and the Great Depression. As a result, re-election became more probable and more incumbents came to seek re-election. A record for years of prior service in the House was set in 1900, then a higher record in 1904, then a yet higher record in 1906, and that one was broken in 1908. Successive new all-time low records for proportion of new members were set in 1898, again in 1900, again in 1904, and yet again in 1908.

A number of scholars are now working on the problems posed by House career data. But the data on sheer turnover are inherently ambiguous like much other political data. The non-voting of constituents may be the result of satisfaction *or* the result of alienation. Continuity of members of a committee may be attributed to a seniority norm *or* to a wide variety of other causes. A 50 percent turnover in the House may be the consequence of a situation in which everyone wants to stay and pursue a House career but a competitive electorate defeats half the incumbents, *or* of a situation in which every single House district is safe but service in the House is so unattractive that half the incumbents choose not to run for re-election.

The proportion of incumbents who in fact seek re-election is a much more useful indicator of career satisfaction. Similarly, the proportion of incumbents running who are defeated gives precise insight into the extent of electoral competition. In a previous paper I have compiled such data for a variety of widely separated periods,[17] and these are presented in Table 1–4. The impact of the realignment of the 1890s is evident in the differences between the 49th Congress and the 59th. The proportion of incumbents *not* running for re-election declined from 27.2 percent to 15.7 percent in states outside the South, and dropped from 33.8 percent to 8.2 percent in the South. Despite this, the proportion of *incumbents defeated* was down from 22.5 percent to an insignificant 3.5 percent in the South, and from 19.4 percent to 16.5 percent elsewhere.

The more or less obvious impact of the changes of the 1890s can be presented in the form of a rather simple causal model (which eventually can be estimated by the use of path analysis), shown in Figure 1–2.

The extent to which the realignment and other changes of the 1890s reduced two-party competition can be seen by comparing the number of Congressional districts that changed hands in the course of a post-census decade. Paul Hasbrouck calculated such figures for the 1914–

---

[17] Douglas Price, "Computer Simulation and Legislative 'Professionalism': Some Quantitative Approaches to Legislative Evolution" (Paper presented at meeting of American Political Science Association, Los Angeles, 1970).

TABLE 1–4. HOUSE CAREERS: PERFORMANCE IN OFFICE OF HOUSE MEMBERS ELECTED TO CONGRESSES INDICATED, FOR SOUTH AND NON-SOUTH

Members Performance	2nd Congress	12th Congress	24th Congress	34th Congress	49th Congress	59th Congress	89th Congress
Members from Outside the South:							
Number Elected	45	93	166	163	240	288	329
Resigned	2	4	7	4	4	5	2
Died	–	–	3	2	7	9	2
Unseated	–	–	–	–	1	1	–
Served Term	43	89	156	157	228	273	325
Ran for Re-election	31	55	84	106	180	236	310
Did Not Run	12	34	72	51	49	37	15
Re-elected	31	47	66	76	145	197	272
Defeated	–	8	18	30	35	39	38
Resigned (after re-election)	–	3	–	–	1	1	–
Died (after re-election)	–	1	–	–	–	–	–
Members from the South:							
Number Elected	23	50	76	66	85	98	106
Resigned	–	1	6	2	1	3	1
Died	1	1	2	1	1	3	3
Unseated	–	1	–	–	–	–	–
Served Term	22	47	68	63	83	92	102
Ran for Re-election	12	37	53	46	62	85	95
Did Not Run	10	10	15	17	21	7	7
Re-elected	12	33	48	39	48	82	83
Defeated	–	4	5	7	14	3	12
Resigned (after re-election)	–	–	–	–	–	–	–
Died (after re-election)	–	–	–	–	–	–	–

1926 period,[18] and Charles Jones has carried the analysis up to 1960.[19] Table 1–5 gives the same information for the 1882–1890 decade and, for contrast, for the 1902–1910 decade. Even though the latter decade includes the atypical 1910 Democratic sweep, the differences between the periods are striking.[20] The proportion of House seats changing

[18] Paul Hasbrouck, *Party Government in the House of Representatives* (New York: Macmillan Co., 1927), chap. 9.

[19] Charles Jones, "Inter-Party Competition for Congressional Seats," *Western Political Quarterly* 17 (1964): 461–476.

[20] For the Democrats the number of "standpat" (unchanging) districts is almost the same for the 1900s decade and the 1880s, but the number of Southern seats jumps from 63 to 92. For the Republicans the number of unchanging districts is almost tripled.

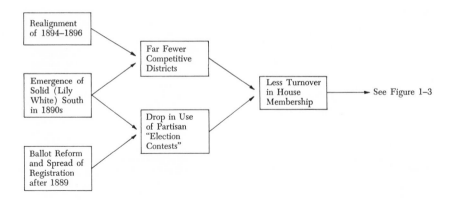

FIGURE 1–2.

Causal Model Showing Impact of Changes of 1890s on Turnover in
House Membership

party hands is cut almost in half, with reductions in every major census region except the Border states. (There, the strengthening of the Republicans in an area where the Democrats were the traditional majority produced a modest increase in competition.)

The more important point, however, is a bit more subtle. As the possibility of winning repeated elections went up (and the likelihood of an unfair "contested election" case sank to virtually zero) the *desire* to pursue a career in the House also went up. This is apparent for both South and North. This set up an important feedback loop, indicated by arrows A, B, C, and D, which *further* reduced turnover and increased within-chamber stability. Indeed this process has continued ever since 1896. This indirect effect of 1896 can be added to our previous causal model as shown in Figure 1–3. Note that this model is non-recursive (because of the A-B-C-D loop) and can be estimated only by means of a simultaneous equation approach.

III

SENATE COMMITTEES: FROM CONTINUITY TO SENIORITY

My long service here and the custom which has obtained almost from the beginning of the Government entitles me to select from among the committees of which I am a member a chairmanship. I am senior Democrat on three important committees and can select

TABLE 1–5. PARTY REGULARITY OF CONGRESSIONAL DISTRICTS: PRE–1890s
AND POST–1890s CONTRASTED

Census Region	Number of Districts with Stable Boundaries [a]	Districts with No Change in Party Control:		Switching Districts by Frequency of Party Change				Rate of Party Turnover for House Districts [b] (Percent)
		Dem.	Rep.	1	2	3	4	
1882–1890								
New England	26	2	10	8	3	1	2	24.0
Middle Atlantic	69	17	19	16	8	8	1	21.7
Central	65	16	8	19	16	6		25.6
West Central	35	1	9	10	8	6	1	34.3
Border	36	23	0	4	7	2		16.7
South	85	63	2	7	10	3		10.6
Mountain & Pacific	9	1	5	2	1			11.1
Total, U.S.	325 [a]	123	53	66	53	26	4	20.5
1902–1910								
New England	29	3	21	3	2			6.0
Middle Atlantic	79	13	38	15	10	3		13.9
Central	71	4	29	27	11			17.3
West Central	49	1	37	6	5			8.2
Border	40	14	4	8	6	4	4	30.0
South	98	92	3		2	1		2.2
Mountain & Pacific	21	0	13	7	1			9.3
Total, U.S.	387 [a]	127	145	66	37	8	4	11.6

[a] Districts with little or no apportionment change in decade.
[b] Percent of elections involving change in party control of district.

the chairmanship of either one of them: Appropriations, Interstate Commerce, and Naval Affairs.

> Senator Benjamin R. Tillman
> (in personal letter to Woodrow
> Wilson, January 21, 1913) [21]

DATA about the membership of congressional committees have long been available in the *Congressional Record* (and its predecessors) and in *Congressional Directories*.[22] For the modern House and Senate

[21] *Congressional Record,* 63 Cong., spec. sess., 17 March 1913, pp. 26–36.

[22] Use of the *Congressional Record* for this purpose is not as difficult as sometimes suggested. The exact dates on which committee appointments were made from 1861 on appear in *Hinds' Precedents* (1906), vol. 4, sec. 4454, p. 891. For more recent Congresses the date of appointment of committees is usually the first reference in the index under the name of any given committee.

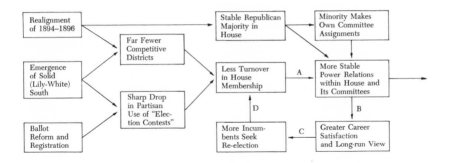

FIGURE 1–3.

Causal Model for Direct and Indirect Effects of Realignment of 1890s on Careers of House Members

(down to 1975) seniority has been the norm which underlies the data. But when did seniority become the rule, and why? Various writers have suggested that the Senate may have been using seniority as early as the 1850s, and that the House may not have adopted a full seniority system until some time after 1946. Analysis of the subject is difficult since the data are, in fact, hard to locate and hard to interpret. The historical record is muddied by the fact that the term "senior" member often has been used in a loose sense to refer to age or total experience and not to the more technical concept of continuous service on a party's list of members of a given committee. The statistical record is difficult to interpret since substantial continuity of committee members and chairmen is frequent, even in the absence of a strict seniority system.

Fortunately for the researcher, a strict seniority system is a dichotomous variable. It is either present or absent, and hence ordinarily can be distinguished from situations of varying continuity. But even where strict seniority usually holds, as in the modern House and Senate, there is the exceptional case, such as "Pitchfork" Ben Tillman in the Senate of 1913 or Adam Clayton Powell in the recent House. Ideally the proof of the reliance on a systematic seniority norm should rest on a combination of contemporary testimony (e.g., newspaper accounts) to such a norm plus statistical evidence that year after year committee posts do represent, with near 100 percent accuracy, the workings of such a rule.

The most obvious effect of increased congressional tenure is increased stability of committee memberships. This is reflected in the Senate after 1876 and in the House after 1896. Such *de facto* stability typically generates demands for *de jure* acceptance of committee "seniority" for determining rank and chairmanships.[23] Indeed, Southern senators had hinted at such a system in the 1850s, but in fact were unwilling to abide by it when it did not serve their interests (as in the demotion of Stephen A. Douglas from the Committee on Territories in 1859). From 1816 to 1845 the Senate generally had engaged in open floor balloting for chairmanships (a majority being required) and committee memberships (ranked by plurality vote).[24] With small committees—typically five members—and a very high turnover of members there was little continuity and no hint of any overall "seniority" norm.

Since 1846 the Senate generally has left the preparation of committee slates to be worked out by the major political parties.[25] In the absence of a powerful presiding officer, around whose selection bargaining over committees could be carried on, the Senate tended to drift in the direction of very substantial continuity of committee chairmen, but still subject in the 1860s and 1870s to occasional non-seniority practices. Thus the Radical Republicans demoted three chairmen who refused to vote for the removal of Andrew Johnson, the chairmanships of the Appropriations Committee and Finance Committee deviated from seniority, some Liberal Republican bolters were deposed after 1872, and in 1871 President Grant's supporters engineered the removal of Charles Sumner as chairman of the prestigious Foreign Relations Committee. Though Sumner's removal was highly controversial, neither his supporters nor his opponents discussed it in terms of seniority.

Such removals in the Senate clearly establish the lack of any absolute seniority norm, but they leave a pattern of continuity vastly more stable than that found for the turbulent House in the same period. The Senate pattern suggests a sort of halfway house on the way to complete seniority based not on degree of continuity (a continuous variable) but rather on the extent of the domain within which seniority will be respected. In effect, this amounts to a sort of conditional seniority in which a chairmanship is secure so long as the incumbent abides by a variety

[23] If one had asked in 1910 who held the all-time record for longest service as chairman of 14 of the most important substantive committees of the House (DeAlva S. Alexander's list of 15, minus the Elections Committee) in 13 of the 14 cases the all-time record would have been set (or in 2 cases only tied) by chairmen of the 1895–1910 era.

[24] See George H. Haynes, *The Senate of the United States,* 2 vols. (Boston: Houghton Mifflin Co., 1938), 1: 273–277.

[25] For a full account of the specific circumstances which brought about the change in procedure, see Frederick Merk, *The Oregon Question: Essays in Anglo-American Diplomacy and Politics* (Cambridge, Mass.: Harvard University Press, Belknap Press, 1967), pp. 374–376.

of behavioral norms. This sort of conditional seniority seems to have operated in the Senate from the 1850s through the 1870s, and also fits the House pattern for roughly the first two decades of the twentieth century. In both cases, when the power to punish violations of desired behavioral norms declined, a fully developed seniority system was the result. House changes in the 1970s, however, in effect have narrowed the domain within which seniority will be respected.

When the Democrats found themselves in a majority in the Senate in 1879—for the first time since the South had seceded—they *explicitly* agreed to make assignments and chairmanships on the basis of committee seniority.[26] At the time this would seem to have had advantages for the party as a whole as well as for both Southern and non-Southern senators. Since the Southerners only recently had replaced the Reconstruction Republicans, use of seniority temporarily worked to the advantage of non-Southern Democrats (who headed Appropriations, Finance, and Foreign Relations). The party thus avoided any open conflict, the non-Southerners did better than their numbers would have warranted, and the party as a whole presented an appearance which minimized Republican chances for criticism of Southern influence. The numerically dominant Southern Democrats, in turn, had given up some short-run advantage to set a precedent which gave them a substantial advantage in years to come. Indeed, this has been the case for over 90 years.

In general the history of the Senate from 1861 to 1911 is the story of the Republican party. When the Republicans returned to the majority in 1881 there was an extensive shake-up of committee assignments. Perhaps more important, the Republicans soon took the opportunity to admit five sparsely settled Western states, thus fortifying their position in the Senate with ten additional members. This major infusion made it advantageous to the already incumbent Republicans to adhere to committee seniority as much as possible. The presence of a substantial Democratic minority also made it more important to maintain Republican harmony. Finally, there was no unifying office (such as the House speakership), ideology, or individual figure around which to organize any systematic challenge to the general reliance on committee seniority.

By the 1880s the Senate rules still said (as they do today) that committees would "be elected," but in fact the Senate merely ratifies the slates submitted by the parties. In turn, the party committees usually consider only new assignments and requests for transfers to available vacancies, leaving incumbent members to rise on the committee ladders

[26] David Rothman, *Politics and Power*, pp. 298–299.

by strict seniority of continuous committee service. Woodrow Wilson (who visited Washington only once while writing his *Congressional Government*) merely penetrated to the rules, irrelevant at least since 1846, which indicated that senate committees were "elected." If Wilson had bothered to ask a senator, whether Republican or Democrat, he could have become the academic discoverer of Senate seniority. And what added scorn such a peculiar system could have generated in Wilson's criticism of the disadvantages of "government by committee" as contrasted to "government by debate"! Senate seniority was accurately described in 1895 by Clara H. Kerr in her *Origin and Development of the U.S. Senate*,[27] and in even more detail in Lauros G. McConachie's *Congressional Committees*, published in 1898:

> Where the upper classmen [non-freshmen] have constantly a two-thirds majority, the control of the machinery will always be firmly within their grasp. If the House of Representatives is a presbytery [hierarchical], the Senate is a college of cardinals [equally important]. Out of the claims of the majority to the chairmanships has been evolved as nice a system of seniority as could be devised. In 1845 and thereafter, when the five members of a committee had been elected by ballot, their names were on motion arranged as follows:—

> 1. Democrat
> 2. Democrat
> 3. Whig
> 4. Democrat
> 5. Whig

> If there were but one Whig on the committee, he stood third. . . . But the hold of the custom grew, until finally all the members from the majority were grouped first, with the distinct understanding that names were to be pushed forward as vacancies occurred in their front, and that new Senators were to "take their places at the bottom of the ladder." Men who find themselves at the head of two or more committees when a new Congress opens, make a choice, and relinquish all but one chairmanship.[28]

McConachie captures most of the crucial points about the detailed workings of a completely developed seniority system in the Senate. The seniority ladder is a *party* ladder of *continuous* service on a *given*

[27] Clara H. Kerr, *Origin and Development of the U.S. Senate* (Ithaca, N.Y.: Andrus and Church, 1895).

[28] Lauros G. McConachie, *Congressional Committees* (New York: Thomas Y. Crowell, 1898), pp. 325–326.

committee. A senator loses his place if he leaves his party (the LaFollette Progressives of 1924, or Wayne Morse in 1953), or if he leaves the Senate (Edward Cary Walthall in 1894–1895 or Alben Barkley in 1953). None of these cases "violate" seniority, they serve to define the conditions that in fact *are* seniority: continuous party standing on a given committee. Moreover, with rare and usually minor exceptions both the House and Senate have long imposed a one chairmanship limit. Finally, seniority is a right which can be waived, either as to a chairmanship (T. F. Green stepped aside for J. William Fulbright on Foreign Relations) or as to member rank (several Republicans volunteered to permit Strom Thurmond to switch from a high Democratic seat on Armed Services to roughly comparable standing on the Republican side of the committee).

IV

HOUSE COMMITTEES: DISCRETION, CONTINUITY, AND SENIORITY

The appointment and constitution of the committees of the lower house make up the chief prerogative of the Speaker. . . . The power given him is, indeed, immense and practically irresponsible. It constitutes Mr. Speaker the most powerful functionary in the government of the United States. . . . Has he friends whose influence was powerful in bringing about his elevation to the chair? Who will be surprised if he gives those friends the coveted chairmanships?

Thos. Woodrow Wilson (1882) [29]

Responsibility vanished. The conditions made almost inevitable a strict adherence to the seniority rule, whereunder the Representative who had served longest on a committee became its chairman, with the result that some important chairmanships fell to men whom a Speaker with the appointing power could have undoubtedly placed somewhere else.

Congressman Robert Luce (1922) [30]

To discover how committees were constituted in the nineteenth-century House we can turn to a variety of sources. There are general descriptions by Woodrow Wilson for the 1880s and Lauros McConachie for the 1890s. There are contemporary accounts by participants and newspapermen, and more recent particular accounts by biographers.

[29] This quotation is from Wilson's unpublished 1882 manuscript on "Government by Debate." See Arthur S. Link, ed., *The Papers of Woodrow Wilson,* 19 vols. to date (Princeton: Princeton University Press, 1966–), 2 (1967): 177.

[30] Robert Luce, *Legislative Procedure* (Boston: Houghton Mifflin Co., 1922), p. 109.

Finally, there is the overall statistical record. We shall briefly review each of these, concentrating on the following two questions: (1) what is the causal process at work in the appointment of committees? and (2) is there any evidence at all for the existence of a general norm requiring that all appointments be made in accord with length of continuous service on a given committee?

From the early development of standing committees down to the Democratic change of procedure in 1911, in form at least, the appointment of committees and their chairmen was solely the responsibility of the Speaker. Moreover, it would appear that the reality accorded to the form, subject only to normal political considerations. That is, nineteenth-century Speakers made their committee choices subject to the same problems and constraints as a President in making a cabinet. In both cases there were various expectations to be considered and a price for removing someone once appointed. But for neither was there any norm of perpetual tenure or of automatic promotion of the next in line. As we shall see, in point of fact continuity was relatively high in the appointment of House chairmen, but no higher than for most other groups of political leaders, such as state legislative chairmen,[31] British cabinet members,[32] or even members of a Communist Party Central Committee.

Woodrow Wilson, in his *Congressional Government*, had earlier noted the central role of the Speaker in naming the committees:

It is highly interesting to note the extraordinary power accruing to Mr. Speaker through this pregnant prerogative of appointing the

---

[31] See, for example, William Buchanan, *Legislative Partisanship: The Deviant Case of California* (Berkeley: University of California Press, 1963). Buchanan points out that the percentage of committee chairmen retained in successive terms in the California Assembly, 1945–1961, varied with the extent of political change as follows:

	Percent of Chairman Retained
Same Assembly Speaker in Office:	69
Change in Speaker and in Majority:	23

For the U.S. House of Representatives, Polsby et al. calculate that for 1881–1910 "seniority" was respected in 69 percent of the cases where the same Speaker continued, and in only 25 percent where Speaker and majority were different. (Nelson W. Polsby, Miriam Gallaher, and Barry Spencer Rundquist, "The Growth of the Seniority System in the U.S. House of Representatives," *American Political Science Review*, 63[1969], 787–807.) Everyone knows that the California assembly does *not* operate on a seniority system. I would suggest the same for the nineteenth-century House.

[32] For the importance of long experience and continuity in Britain (which obviously does not have a systematic seniority rule), see Philip W. Buck, *Amateurs and Professionals in British Politics, 1918–1959* (Chicago: University of Chicago Press, 1963).

Standing Committees of the House. That power is, as it were, the central and characteristic inconvenience and anomaly of our constitutional system, and on that account excites both the curiosity and the wonder of the student of our institutions. The most esteemed writers upon our Constitution have failed to observe, not only that the Standing Committees are the most essential machinery of our governmental system, but also that the Speaker of the House of Representatives is the most powerful functionary of that system. So sovereign is he within the wide sphere of his influence that one could wish for accurate knowledge as to the extent of his power.

After an historical excursus Wilson concludes:

It is plain, therefore, that the office of Speaker of the House of Representatives is in its present estate a constitutional phenomenon of the first importance, deserving a very thorough and critical examination. If I have succeeded, in what I have already said, in making clear the extraordinary power of the Committees in directing legislation, it may now go without the saying that he who appoints those Committees is an autocrat of the first magnitude. There could be no clearer proof of the great political weight of the Speaker's high commission in this regard than the keen strife which every two years takes place over the election to the Speakership, and the intense interest excited throughout the country as to the choice to be made.[33]

Wilson does, however, make the statement that "by custom, seniority in *congressional* service determines the bestowal of the principal chairmanships." Here we have two clear hints that Wilson is *not* referring to any systematic seniority system. In the first place he refers to "congressional service," not to continuous committee service; in the second place he limits the scope to "principal chairmanships." His meaning becomes fully clear when one considers the congressional scene from which he was generalizing—he was writing in 1884—and looks at the entire passage: "I know not how better to describe our form of government in a single phrase than by calling it a government by the chairmen of the Standing Committees of Congress. This disintegrate ministry, as *it* figures on the floor of the House of Representatives, has many peculiarities. In the first place, *it* is made up of the elders of the assembly; for, by custom, seniority in congressional service determines the bestowal of the principal chairmanships; . . . and, in the fourth place, *it* is instituted by appointment from Mr. Speaker. . . ."[34]

[33] Woodrow Wilson, *Congressional Government* (1885; reprint ed., New York: Meridian Books, 1956), pp. 82–83, 84–85.
[34] Wilson, *Congressional Government*, p. 82. My italics.

What Wilson is saying, which would have been obvious to anyone familiar with the House of the early 1880s, is that, if one considered *all* the chairmen of the major standing committees as constituting a government or ministry (as Wilson did), then this collective ministry would consist largely of members with considerable total prior service. By custom the Speaker would not appoint freshman members—who made up over half of the House after the 1882 election—as major committee chairmen. Indeed, the heads of the major committees usually would consist of relatively experienced members. But there was no custom or expectation that a *particular* committee chairman necessarily would be reappointed to the *same* committee. Quite the opposite; it was widely understood that successful experience as head of a minor committee should put one in a position to assume the leadership of a more important one and that success there should enable one to advance to candidacy for the chairmanship of Appropriations or Ways and Means. Again McConachie summarized the nineteenth-century experience when he wrote in 1898: "The rare qualities demanded in these respects make Speakers increasingly cautious in placing their subordinates, and in shifting them from one part of the field to another as occasion may require. The line of promotion has led from headship of some one of the others to headship of the finance committee . . . Garfield advanced from the Military Affairs, 1867–1869, to the Banking and Currency, 1869–1871, then to the Appropriations, 1871–1875 . . . William S. Holman held three different chairmanships of two terms each. . . . The most striking record of all is that of William M. Springer, successively head of seven different committees." As if in reply to Wilson's lament of lack of evidence for limits on the Speaker's power McConachie concluded: "It is time that the Speaker's limitations were thoroughly outlined, as a corrective to broad assertions concerning his arbitrary authority. Before his election powerful caucus combinations exact from him pledges as to office and policy. That man who can command the largest block of votes thus secures in advance the chairmanship of Appropriations. The leader of the second powerful coterie obtains very likely a minor set of Appropriations, or the headship of Judiciary and second place on the Rules." [35]

Here McConachie penetrated much more deeply into the workings of the House than had Wilson a decade earlier. Wilson was ambiguous (or plain confused) in pairing the unlimited power of the Speaker with the idea of a completely disintegrated collection of committee chairmen. Similarly he was ambiguous (or confused) in contrasting the

[35] McConachie, *Congressional Committees*, pp. 159–160, 165.

Speaker's discretionary power to appoint whom he would with the idea that chairmen came from a pool of elders. In fact, neither continuity of service nor total length of service ensured any position in either the House or any of its committees.

There remains the paradox that the chairmen of the leading committees usually were among the more senior members of the chamber, even though they often came to head committees with no prior service on the particular committee. There was indeed an association between length of congressional service and committee chairmanships, but the first was not the cause of the second. On the contrary, in the absence of any species of strict committee seniority, the only clear incentive for remaining in the House was the possibility of obtaining (by commanding important blocks of votes) major chairmanships. It was the holding of chairmanships (often a bewildering variety of them, as with William S. Springer) that led to the accumulation of more chamber seniority, and *not* vice versa.

This is obvious in a career such as Joseph Cannon's. Cannon was a key figure from a large-state delegation (Illinois) and was able to obtain attractive committee positions. This encouraged him to remain in the House, and his seniority (which was irrelevant) increased. Then in 1890 Cannon was defeated. But he returned in 1892, and when the Republicans captured the House in 1894 Cannon was installed as chairman of Appropriations. His lack of continuous committee service was irrelevant. By all the nineteenth-century norms of the House this was right, proper, and expected. Indeed, it fits Wilson's criteria, as well as McConachie's, if one just recognizes that being "senior" in age and experience did *not* mean continuous service or service on a particular committee. But these *are* the two touchstones of the modern seniority system. The nineteenth-century House did *not*, then, operate on anything even vaguely resembling the modern seniority system.

This view is reinforced by looking at accounts of the selection of slates of committee chairmen and members by various post-Civil War Speakers. The following, which attest to the Speaker's discretion but *not at all* to continuous committee service, are typical:

Speaker Blaine in 1869: "Blaine's experience throws a flood of light on the difficulties encountered in framing committees. 'Your father,' wrote a member of the Speaker's family, 'left for New York on Wednesday. He had cotton and wool manufacturers to meet in Boston, and, over and above all, pressure to resist or permit. As fast as he gets his committees arranged, just so fast some other consideration comes up which overtopples the whole list like a row of bricks.'

49

The construction of committees, having regard for harmony and the effect upon legislation as a whole, requires much patience, rare skill, and a thorough knowledge of the views and fitness of members. There must also be more or less bargaining." [36]

Speaker Kerr in 1875: "He asked Marble [NYC Democratic editor and publisher] for help in the selection of chairmen for major committees and even 'peremptorily' insisted that Marble come to Washington to help draw up the slate. Kerr placed Randall (his rival for Speaker) at the head of Appropriations but was in a quandary as to Ways and Means since both Wood and Cox felt that their services to the party and to Kerr in the caucus merited the assignment. Eventually he made William H. Morrison of Illinois head of Ways and Means, Cox of Banking and Currency, and ignored Wood's claims to a position of honor." [37]

Speakers Randall and Keifer in the 1870s: "[Congressman] Orth knew that many members of both parties regarded with suspicion the tremendous power of such a piece of patronage as committee appointments. For five years Randall had ignored Democrats who stood for a tariff for revenue only, while the gossip of the cloak-room and of the press indicated that several Republicans, resenting Keifer's method of securing votes in exchange for desirable appointments, were ripe for a change." [38]

Speaker Carlisle in the 1880s: "Committee arrangement would have been far easier had not each member of the party been so sure of his especial fitness for a leading position. Carlisle had always allowed every member to express in writing his first and second choices, but he had never contemplated [such] a demand for positions. The Speaker struggled through the entire Christmas recess on the composition of the committees and had not completed them when Congress reassembled on January 5. Shortly afterward some strange grapevine telegraph diffused the news of the various assignments, and immediately the Speaker's room was the scene of many a furtive visit by Congressmen who felt that the country could better be served if they were placed on more important committees. . . . The Speaker had slapped no one; he had simply formed the committees in conformity with his ideas of Democracy. A great majority of the chair-

[36] Gail Hamilton, *Biography of James G. Blaine* (Norwich, Conn.: Henry Bill Co., 1895), pp. 260, 263.
[37] Albert V. House, "The Speakership Contest of 1875: Democratic Response to Power," *Journal of American History* 52 (1965): 272.
[38] Alexander, *House of Representatives*, p. 78.

manships went to Representatives from the South and West, nineteen to the former and twenty to the latter, while the Middle Atlantic States received eight and New England only one." [39]

Speaker Reed in 1889: "On December 9, the Speaker announced the first of his committee appointments. McKinley received the chairmanship of Ways and Means, Cannon and Henderson were both placed on the Appropriations Committee, and Burrows became head of the Committee on Manufacturers. The Speaker's late competitors were thus taken care of, according to the usual precedents of congressional politics. . . .

"On December 21, the remaining committees were announced . . . and there was some criticism of the Speaker's generosity to his Western supporters. New York, however, had also been generously rewarded for the support its delegation had given, receiving seven chairmanships. In spite of the inevitable criticism that there was unfair discrimination, the appointments were regarded as unusually good." [40]

Speaker Crisp in 1891: "On the first ballot in the caucus only a few votes separated Mills and Crisp, the leaders, and it was regarded as certain that one of them would be named. Then the dickering began among the managers of the candidates for high committee places, and the Crisp men outgeneraled the Mills' forces in that line of work. Judge Springer withdrew his name and voted for Crisp and that settled it. Mr. Crisp was nominated, and Judge Springer secured the chairmanship of the Ways and Means Committee and, as the floor leadership went with it as usual, he was satisfied with the outcome. The other Crisp managers got important committee assignments." [41]

And so it went, at least to the 1890s. The process should be familiar to anyone who has watched the wheeling and dealing involved in making committee assignments in a twentieth-century state legislature. By and large in state legislatures the big chairmanships also go to relatively senior members. But it should be noted that in the nineteenth-century

[39] James A. Barnes, *John G. Carlisle: Financial Statesman* (New York: Dodd, Mead & Co., 1931), pp. 97–98.

[40] William A. Robinson, *Thomas B. Reed: Parliamentarian* (New York: Dodd, Mead & Co., 1930), pp. 199–201.

[41] O. O. Stealey, *Twenty Years in the Press Gallery* (Washington: published by author, 1906), p. 106. This fascinating collection, by a variety of leading Washington reporters, includes chapters on eleven Congresses (48th to 58th), plus biographical studies of over a score of leading House members. In all of these there is not a single reference to any such thing as a committee seniority system, although there is a great deal of discussion of the "making" of committe slates.

House major chairmanships, and in 1875 even the Speakership, went to experienced members with *zero continuous service* at the time of their selection. In their "furtive visits" to the Speaker's office nineteenth-century congressmen, like modern-day state legislators, might dwell on their age, experience, and length of service, but they could point to no general norm that sanctified automatic reappointment or promotion on a given committee. Taken *as a group* the more experienced members (including those with non-continuous experience) could be regarded as somewhat "favored claimants" to the more important chairmanships or committee seats. But there was no semblance of any prescriptive right to any *particular* post. The disposition of members' claims, which were as often for promotion to new posts as for retention of old ones, was left entirely to the Speaker. In the ordinary course of events a Speaker would reward, often by promotion to a new chairmanship, the claims of his principal rivals (especially when they headed major blocs of votes), and also the claims of members whose abilities he respected or whose policies he approved. Chairmen of minor committees, of which the House had a great number, had little significance. Clearly the pressures were concentrated on the important chairmanships and on seats on the two leading committees, Ways and Means and Appropriations.

The fate of chairmen who would not cooperate with a Speaker was usually the same, regardless of age, gray hair, or alleged senior standing. DeAlva S. Alexander, a long-time House member, stated in 1916: "Ordinarily a chairman who gets in the way is promptly put out of the way." [42] But when did this cease to be the case? And how are we to know whether a chairman "gets in the way" or not?

In considering the statistical record on appointments of chairmen it is crucial to distinguish between relative degrees of continuity and the presence or absence *of a norm* requiring total adherence to seniority. If such a norm exists it applies to a right to a chairmanship, which can be waived; this right is limited to one committee; it pertains to party standing on a given committee; and it can be lost by loss of party standing or by switching to another committee. Of course there is no

[42] Alexander, *History and Procedure, House of Representatives*, p. 242. I have found Alexander an especially useful source on the House, in which he served from 1897 to 1911 (he lost in 1910 by a single-vote margin). He was a close personal friend of Speaker Reed (both served on the Board of Trustees of Bowdoin College), and he made a remarkable effort to interview leading House figures and members who had known leading House figures back into the pre-Civil War period. In his final term in Congress he was a committee chairman, complete with appropriations jurisdiction, for the crucial area of rivers and harbors. Hence his views are not to be taken lightly.

violation where a member voluntarily gives up one position because he prefers another (e.g., as majority leader, or on another committee). Seniority protects the member's *right* to a position (not the position) so long as the member wants to exercise that right *and* meets all the eligibility criteria.

In analytic terms the degree of continuity is a dependent variable, and the presence or absence of a seniority norm is a possible independent variable. But we know that other independent variables, chiefly bargaining, were involved in Speakers' appointment decisions. How can we infer whether the Speaker, up to 1911, was restrained by a general seniority norm? The relative extent of continuity in chairmanships seems the obvious piece of evidence, but how can it be interpreted? Polsby et al. simply take the percent of continuity of previous chairmen or of those survivors next in line and interpret this as the *extent* to which "seniority" was being used. This is not satisfactory since the major committees, around which bargaining concentrated, are lost in a myriad of trivial ones. Moreover, we know that in many cases the person who was next in line only managed to receive or retain a post after a vigorous effort, and was rewarded because of *this effort* and *not* because of his length of service.

Perhaps worst of all, once a Speaker made his appointments, all of which might have been discretionary, he ordinarily would tend to reappoint most of those leaders. He would do this not because of any alleged norm but because he would continue to have the same incentives to reappoint an able or a powerful figure as he originally had. Thus Speaker Carlisle appointed Samuel Randall, his opponent for the speakership, as chairman of the Appropriations Committee. At the time Randall had zero continuous service on the committee, but was leader of a powerful bloc of Northern Democrats. Carlisle's subsequent reappointment of Randall was also because of his factional strength and should not be taken to indicate adherence to a norm of seniority.

Michael Abram, in an earlier attempt at measuring House use of seniority, made a useful distinction between the sheer "statistical" extent of continuity and a *corrected* "historical" measure.[43] The latter consists of the initial (Polsby-type) measure *minus* those known examples where the continuity was obviously due to other *known* causes. This is a useful step in the right direction, but is still dangerous in that it

---

[43] Michael E. Abram, "The Rise of the Modern Seniority System in the U.S. House of Representatives" (Senior honors thesis, Harvard University, 1966). The distinction is also used in the article by Michael Abram and Joseph Cooper, "The Rise of Seniority in the House of Representatives," *Polity* 1 (1968): 52–85.

literally treats the total residual use of continuity as a measure of one specific thing, seniority.[44] The "historical" measure may thus reflect our ignorance of factional contests and other factors.

A more basic objection to either the Polsby or Abram measures is that they confuse a *dichotomous variable*, presence or absence of a general seniority norm, with a continuous variable, the degree of continuity.[45] To be sure that a seniority *norm* is present one might well require that continuity be 100 percent (with a very occasional exception), *and* that there be independent corroborative evidence from participants and contemporary observers that such was indeed the case. Of course, one does not want to lean over backward—there are Type I errors as well as Type II errors. So it is equally vital *not* to classify as seniority "violators" members who voluntarily request another assignment or waive their seniority or lose their party standing. All such cases are quite compatible with a 100 percent reliance on seniority, as that norm is understood and as related to other norms (such as the limitation to one chairmanship at a time). In short, there is no need for a category of "compensated violation." What is needed is careful definition of the changing qualitative scope of a seniority rule, which is either followed or not.

The scope of such a rule need not be always the same. Thus in the Senate for several decades transfers of members between committees were allowed on the basis of total chamber seniority, an extension of the reliance on seniority never accepted by the House. It may be useful to view the Congressional definition of "seniority" as an evolving norm rather like the Supreme Court's definition of "due process" or "interstate commerce." One does not define the latter by a simple batting average of the percent of cases in which Congressional power is upheld; rather one seeks to determine the scope of the power as interpreted by the Court in a particular period. Similarly a seniority *norm* exists only if there is some defined scope within which the norm clearly prevails.

For the nineteenth-century House the comments of observers, rank and file members, committee chairmen, and speakers are in overwhelming agreement on the absence of any norm of seniority that would guarantee 100 percent continuation of those members behaving in a given

[44] The problem is analogous to that encountered in the analysis of the extent of party voting in a legislative body. This dependent variable cannot be taken as a reliable indicator of strength of party loyalty (as an independent variable) since the overall degree of party voting rests on a variety of factors (and may be quite high even in the absence of any party loyalty).

[45] A seniority system is like cabinet government, one either has it or one does not. Varying degrees of party voting do not indicate varying degrees of having cabinet government.

way. A committee chairman might do precisely what the Speaker appointing him desired but find himself exiled to a lesser post by a new Speaker. There seems to have been no way that a member could insulate himself from periodic shake-ups of committee appointments. Particular chairmen might retain a post for several Congresses but this usually resulted from inertia (there was little competition for the chairmanship of the Committee on Ventilation and Acoustics) or from the continuation in office of the same Speaker. The real test of any normative restraint comes in the case of important committees and especially at the election of a new Speaker.[46]

The lack of reliance on committee seniority in the nineteenth century is particularly clear for the House's two leading committees, Ways and Means and Appropriations. Thaddeus Stevens was the last chairman of the old Ways and Means Committee that also had appropriations jurisdiction. When a separate Appropriations Committee was set up, at the end of the Civil War, Stevens chose to head it rather than to continue as chairman of Ways and Means. (This illustrates the standard limitation to one chairmanship.) Table 1–6 lists the chairmen of these two committees from the Civil War to 1910. Those who became chairmen in clear violation of seniority are denoted by asterisks. Of the 13 Ways and Means chairmen after Stevens only 4 could be said to have been appointed according to seniority (and even for these seniority was usually not the causal factor). Of the 12 Appropriations chairmen after Stevens only 2 fit the seniority pattern, and one of these is known to have been appointed for reasons other than alleged seniority.

The statistics of continuity in chairmanships are more useful for confirming the *absence* of a seniority norm than for indicating its presence. Thus in 1825 the *National Intelligencer* noted: "The last chairmen of all the principal committees (they being now members) are the same as at the last session, except one; and that one (Mr. Crowninshield) is understood to have been transferred with his own consent." [47] Continuity was almost 100 percent, but so far no one has suggested that

[46] The author has compiled directly from the *Congressional Record* (and its predecessors) the chairmen and members for the 12 leading committees of the House and Senate from 1861 to 1945. The record for minor committees is confusing since House members in the post-World War I period often served simultaneously on five, six, or seven of the trivial committees, but subject to the usual limitation of one chairmanship (at least so far as legislative committees were concerned). By 1922 it was common practice for newspapers to print, immediately after the election, the names of impending new chairmen who had reached the top of the seniority ladder. By contrast, the official announcement of committee chairmen, which had been front-page news throughout the nineteenth century, was by the 1920s a routine item to be recorded along with ship arrivals and departures.

[47] Haynes, *The Senate of the United States.*

TABLE 1–6. HOUSE FLUIDITY: CHAIRMEN OF TOP TWO COMMITTEES, AND THEIR ASSIGNMENTS IN THE PREVIOUS CONGRESS, 1861–1910.

Year	Ways and Means	Appropriations
1861	T. Stevens (*ranking* Rep.)	–
1863	T. Stevens	–
1865	J. Morrill (*ranking* Rep.)	T. Stevens (new committee)
1867	*R. C. Schenck (Military Affairs)	T. Stevens
1869	R. C. Schenck	*H. L. Dawes (Elections)
1871	*H. L. Dawes (Approp.)	*J. A. Garfield (Banking-Currency)
1873	H. L. Dawes	J. A. Garfield
1875	*W. R. Morrison (War Claims)	*S. J. Randall (Banking-Currency)
1877	*F. Wood (#2 Dem.; displaced Morrison)	J. D. C. Atkins (*ranking* Dem.)
1879	F. Wood	J. D. C. Atkins
1881	W. D. Kelley (*ranking* Rep.)	*F. Hiscock (jumped from low rank)
1883	*W. R. Morrison (#4 Dem. promoted over Tucker)	*S. J. Randall (Rules; ex-Speaker)
1885	W. R. Morrison	S. J. Randall
1887	R. Q. Mills (*ranking* Dem.)	S. J. Randall
1889	*W. McKinley (jumped from low rank)	J. Cannon (*ranking* Rep.)
1891	*W. M. Springer (Territories)	*W. S. Holman (Public Lands)
1893	*W. L. Wilson (jumped from #4)	*J. D. Sayers (#3 Dem.; displaced Holman)
1895	*N. Dingley (Approp.)	*J. Cannon (bottom-ranked Rep.; not in House 1891–1893)
1897	N. Dingley	J. Cannon
1899	S. E. Payne (*ranking* Rep.)	J. Cannon
1901	S. E. Payne	J. Cannon
1903	S. E. Payne	*J. Hemenway (jumped over Bingham)
1905	S. E. Payne	*J. A. Tawney (Ways & Means)
1907	S. E. Payne	J. A. Tawney
1909	S. E. Payne	J. A. Tawney

Note: Asterisk denotes members who became chairmen in violation of seniority.

seniority was the rule in the House of 1825! Continuity, like the additive pattern of the Guttman scale, is a useful test to disconfirm a hypothesis, but needs to be supplemented by additional information.

The real test of the putative influence of seniority obviously comes at the time a new Speaker assumes office. Once in office a given Speaker ordinarily continues to support most of his initial choices of chairmen, thus producing high continuity. His new appointments are based, however, on his prior exercise of discretion, not on any normative constraint. When a Speaker is re-elected there is almost perfect collinearity between continuity (which may be of *no* causal significance) and the real grounds for the Speaker's initial choice of chairmen (policy agreement, bargaining, etc.).

Given the sharp differences between the situations of same Speaker and new Speaker most of the talk about alleged nineteenth-century "seniority" would appear to rest on a spurious interpretation of situations where a Speaker tended to reappoint the chairmen he had picked previously with utter discretion. But the Reed chairmen were, by and large, continued in office by Speakers Henderson and Cannon, though Cannon did *not* rely heavily on promotion in the naming of key replacement chairmen. Statistically there would appear to be three periods. The nineteenth-century situation, which prevailed until the 1896 realignment, was one of utter discretion in appointments. When a Speaker continued in office he would tend to exercise his discretion in a similar manner over time, but obviously could do differently if he so desired. The problem here is simply not to confuse relative stability of a particular Speaker's desires with alleged constraints on what any Speaker could do if he wished.

By 1919 the sway of seniority in the House was, as Cooper and Abram rightly concluded, virtually complete.[48] But what is one to make of the interim period, roughly from 1896 to 1919? With more and more House members serving longer and longer terms there was increased pressure to adhere to seniority-type practices, even though the modern norm could not be said to exist. Neither the Republican Speakers from 1897 to 1910 nor the Democratic committee on committees from 1911 to 1918 felt constrained to reappoint or move up the committee ladder all senior members. Thus Speaker Cannon named chairmen of both Appropriations and of Ways and Means who were not next in line and, for the latter, a member who was not even on the committee.

In the period of unusually strong party ties [49] the one claim that could

[48] An adequate study of the role of seniority in the 1920–1921 re-establishment of a single integrated House Committee on Appropriations remains to be done. The *New York Times* for July 19, 1921, states: "Representative James W. Good of Iowa has resigned as chairman. His natural successor, if the seniority rule is followed, as is customary, would be Representative Charles R. Davis of Minnesota. . . ." But Davis, like Tillman in the Senate, was regarded by his party's leaders as inadequate for the job, especially given the great importance placed on the "new Budget Committee" (as it was often referred to at the time) in strengthening the position of the House vis-à-vis the Senate. The Republican Committee on Committees met, and agreed to pass over Davis, giving the chairmanship to the then-second ranking member Representative Martin Madden. Madden's high rank, in turn, depended upon the manner in which the respective parties treated prior committee service on the committees which were losing their appropriations jurisdiction to the new integrated committee, which was to gain one Republican and one Democrat from each such affected committee. Madden had been handling appropriation bills on the Post Office Committee.

[49] On the influence of party see David W. Brady and Phillip Althoff, "Party Voting in the U.S. House of Representatives: Elements of a Responsible Party System," *Journal of Politics*, 36 (August 1974): 753–775.

be used to counter efforts to legitimize standing by seniority was that of party. Both Speaker Cannon and the Democratic caucuses from 1911 to 1918 sought to base most of their removals of members or committee chairmen, as well as non-seniority promotions, on grounds that the members had failed to cooperate with the party.[50] Since most members and most chairmen did cooperate, the committee listings began to show very marked stability. In turn this fed member expectations of regular movement up the committee rankings. But the respective party leaderships clung to their belief in their right to intervene, though this no longer rested on the necessities of bargaining for the Speakership but rather on rationales of party.

But where bargaining previously had been unconstrained and provided no sure haven for the member seeking to stabilize his position, the narrowed leadership discretion from 1896 to 1918 did provide such a haven in party regularity. Here we seem to have the germ of a true seniority norm, not a statistical artifact, with a defined scope. The practices of this transitional period increasingly came to reflect adherence to seniority, subject to "good party behavior." But the contingent requirement of "good party behavior" was to be interpreted by the respective party leaderships and could be construed to apply across most of a member's activities. This, of course, is vastly different from the post-1919 norm of nominal party membership (rather than behavior), which typically rests on declared party label plus support for the Speaker on the opening day of a new Congress.

From 1911 to 1919 the Democrats operated with a committee on committees making appointments, as the Republicans did after their return to power in 1919. As in the case of the Senate, the committee device appeared much less resistant to seniority demands than had the Speaker as a single appointing authority. The Democrats rather explicitly followed a pattern of retention subject to good behavior, where "good behavior" was interpreted as willingness to go along with the Democratic caucus. But after 1917 even this limitation faded as many chairmen, and even the House floor leader, were opposed to Wilson's war measures but retained their posts.

If the caucus failed to lay down a party line then nothing would be left as a test of party acceptability *except* nominal classification and how one voted to organize the House. And this was precisely what

---

[50] "Deviant forms of behavior, by marking the outer edges of group life, give the inner structure its special character and thus supply the framework within which the people of the group develop an orderly sense of their own cultural identity." Kai T. Erikson, *Wayward Puritans: A Study in the Sociology of Deviance* (New York: John Wiley & Sons, 1966), p. 13.

happened. Seniority was operationally dominant, if not universally desired, among the Democrats in the House by 1918. The Republicans had criticized Democratic reliance on seniority in the 1918 elections, but the Republican organization of the House in 1919 did not challenge the senior standing of Republican ranking members. The outcome of the 1919 speakership contest and acceptance of a committee for making appointments (at least of new members and to fill vacancies at the bottom of committee lists) suggest that by then a majority of the Republicans favored the principle. At any rate they behaved as if that were the case, subject to the one exception of the reorganization of the Appropriations Committee in 1921. And even this involved appointment of a new chairman for a substantially reorganized committee, not the deposing of a chairman nor the question of promotion in an unchanged committee.

Demands for a *de jure* seniority principle depended upon the emergence of *de facto* continuity of membership in the House and on major committees. Acceptance of these demands depended upon the absence both of a strong single appointing officer and of any potent party unifying ideology. The Democratic dismantlement of the speakership in 1911 removed the single figure. General adherence to the virtues of party government and party loyalty were abandoned as the direct primary and ballot reform made it both possible and necessary for each member to paddle "his own political canoe." [51] The Wilsonian Democrats' agreement on substantive policy was exhausted by 1916, and issues of World War I split the party sharply. Small wonder that by 1920 *neither* party caucus in the House amounted to much, and that, as a consequence, seniority became, as it had for the Senate, irresistible for both parties. With the decline of party feeling and the caucus the domain of enforceable "good behavior" shrank so as to include little more than the matter of voting with one's party on opening day. Thus for the House, as for the Senate, professionalization of careers led to demands for stability, and plural appointing bodies, the respective committees on committees, were not strong enough to resist these demands for long. The process is summarized in Figure 1–4.

One little noticed consequence of the acceptance of an absolute seniority norm (subject to party standing) in the House was that it established a powerful incentive for straight party voting in the vote for Speaker at the beginning of each Congress. Even in the era of strongest party loyalty and of most powerful (and willful) Speakers it

---

[51] This apt phrase is from George Rothwell Brown, *The Leadership of Congress* (Indianapolis: Bobbs-Merrill Co., 1922), p. 246.

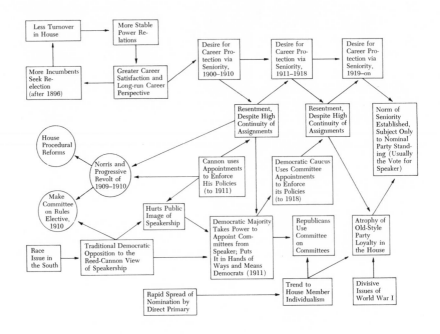

FIGURE 1-4.

Summary Causal Model for Final Triumph of House Seniority Norm:
Careerism Unrestrained After Switch to Appointments by Committee
on Committees and Atrophy of Party Caucuses

had been difficult to generate a straight party vote. Indeed, at the state
level even Mayor Daley's Illinois Democrats have found that the task
may exceed their "clout." [52] But by tying seniority in committee to the
slim requirement of party standing the party leaders, so long as they
did not interfere with seniority, at least after the lesson of 1924, could
look forward to an absolutely perfect, automatic party vote on the
matter of organizing the House!

This should not be overlooked in considering the advantages to be
gained by a break with seniority. By the 1970s seniority influence has

[52] See, for example, Thomas B. Littlewood, "Bipartisan Coalition in Illinois"
(Eagleton Institute: Cases in Practical Politics, 1960). In the absence of a commit-
tee seniority rule linked to the vote for Speaker, liberal Democrats would have to
worry not only about defections of Southern Democrats but also about possible
splinter candidacies from the Black Caucus or Women's Caucus.

become much attenuated by development of committee rules that permit a majority of the committee to work its way, even over the head of a resisting chairman. But in a period in which party is of declining influence seniority helps to guarantee a straight party vote on the choice of Speaker. This is not a minor point, and liberal Democrats in particular might well contemplate what they might lose should a break of seniority also open the Pandora's box of cross-party coalitions, independent candidacies, and commitments as to chairmanships in the now automatic election of a Speaker.

V
POSTSCRIPT: 1975

IN the wake of the Watergate scandals, Nixon impeachment proceedings, sweeping Democratic gains in the 1974 elections, and the sudden fall from power of former Ways and Means chairman Wilbur Mills, reform-oriented Democrats sought major modification of the House seniority norm at the opening of Congress in 1975. For over a decade liberal House Democrats had wanted to give the Democratic caucus a more active role in defining the minimum range of "good party behavior" that would be required for a member to have his committee seniority in party rankings recognized. This would move the House Democratic treatment of seniority back to something very like that of the 1911–1918 period: seniority would be respected unless a member's party standing and performance were questioned, but such standing would no longer be assumed automatically. This would amount to a narrowed scope for the norm but members could still secure their positions by demonstrating a record of acceptable party regularity.

The actual outcome of House Democratic changes in 1975 went considerably beyond this.[53] The power to prepare the party slate of committee posts was taken from the Democratic members of the Ways and Means committee and given to the Democratic Policy Committee. Approval of this party slate was to be given by the Democratic caucus, where several chairmen were challenged. Most of these indeed were conservatives who had hardly evinced "good party behavior." But challenges also were made against Wayne Hays, an abrasive personality but hardly a member of the conservative coalition, and against Wright Patman, a certified liberal for decades but by 1975 suffering the effects of age and illness. Hays narrowly survived, but Patman was thrust aside.

[53] This development is reflected in successive issues of the *Congressional Quarterly* for 1975.

The successful challenges required both vulnerability of the presumptive chairmen and the presence of an alternative candidate among the senior members of the committee. But the challenges to Hays and Patman obviously went beyond a narrowing of the seniority norm to members displaying reasonable party regularity. One might add physical capacity to do the job (involved in the Patman challenge),[54] but the Hays challenge resembled a nineteenth-century power struggle. Since Hays was sustained the Democratic caucus still has the opportunity to spell out the criteria that are expected of members who seek to claim their seniority rights via the party. Of course, some of the conservatives who were challenged threatened to bolt the party and to protect their positions by a floor coalition of Republicans and conservative Democrats. In 1975 the liberal Democratic contingent was so large as to make this step unattractive, but in future Congresses this is likely to be a more viable alternative.

In 1975 serious concern over the workings of seniority was largely limited to House Democrats. Senate Democrats agreed that chairmanships should indeed be confirmed by the caucus, but displayed no desire to challenge anyone. Republicans in both chambers have tended to stick to their established ways with a minimum of cosmetic changes. But House Democrats have presented the biggest challenge to seniority in over half a century. Just how lasting and how extensive a change this will produce will depend upon the response to it by subsequent Congresses.

[54] This question of physical capability had been at issue in the Tillman dispute in the Senate in 1913; was raised in the House fight of 1921 over the chairmanship of the newly reorganized and expanded Appropriations Committee; and had motivated Lyndon Johnson's successful effort to have the elderly Theodore Francis Green waive his seniority on the Senate Foreign Relations Committee.

2

The Personal Circulation of a Legislature: The Danish Folketing, 1849–1968

MOGENS N. PEDERSEN

I

INTRODUCTION

THIS chapter presents an account of a political process which hitherto has not adequately been subjected to detailed, systematic analysis. This is the process by which legislatures are renewed: by which they recruit new members and part with old members.

Using diachronic data relating to the Danish Folketing, I propose to describe the long-term changes in the recruitment and the derecruitment patterns of this legislature.[1] The description will be given by means of a simple conceptual scheme which makes it possible to depict the major changes that have taken place during the 120-year period since the introduction of a legislature into the Danish political system. This scheme, furthermore, permits the discussion of various hypotheses relating to the general trend toward institutionalization and professionalization of legislatures in Western political systems.

The growing literature on political recruitment deals, of course, with renewal phenomena: both recruitment to and derecruitment from legislatures.[2] Modern recruitment research, however, has not treated the renewal of the legislature on the analytic level of the legislature itself, and has also failed to study it as a process that goes on in time as well as in space.[3]

The legislative renewal process can be seen as part of the more gen-

---

[1] The term derecruitment is an invention of Marion J. Levy, Jr., see his *Modernization and the Structure of Societies* (Princeton: Princeton University Press, 1966), p. 441. Frederick Frey has used the term *release* about the same phenomenon. See his *The Turkish Political Elite* (Cambridge, Mass.: The M.I.T. Press, 1965), pp. 392–393.

[2] Probably the best book-length introduction to the problems of recruitment theory is Kenneth Prewitt, *The Recruitment of Political Leaders: A Study of Citizen-Politicians* (Indianapolis: Bobbs-Merrill Co., 1970). See also Dwaine Marvick, "Political Recruitment and Careers," *International Encyclopedia of the Social Sciences* 12 (New York: Macmillan Co. and Free Press, 1968): 273–282.

[3] Kenneth Prewitt, "Political Socialization and Leadership Recruitment," *Annals of the American Academy of Political and Social Science* 361 (1965): 111.

eral problem of elite renewal processes and, as such, was once a matter of central concern to certain social scientists. Vilfredo Pareto and Gaetano Mosca opened up this field with their discussions of the causes, the mechanisms, and the effects of the *circulation of elites.* Their pupils, successors, and antagonists took up the challenge and did empirical work along the lines laid out, especially those suggested by Pareto in his *Trattato di Sociologia Generale.*[4]

Although the names of Pareto, Mosca, Mannheim, and Schumpeter are always mentioned with reverence by recruitment theorists, their line of inquiry nevertheless has not been carried on in the behavioral era.[5] Research on the issues they identified requires a willingness to deal with political phenomena in dynamic terms, to make use of historical, process-generated data of often doubtful reliability, and to work on the macro-level. None of these commitments is in line with the behavioral research tradition, which until recently has favored static analysis on the basis of project-generated data, collected and analyzed at the level of the individual.

It is possible to put forward at least three reasons for a reintroduction of empirical studies of the legislative renewal processes or what I will term the *personal circulation of the legislature.* All of them have something to do with recent lines of development in legislative research.

Since the publication of the report from the State Legislative Research Project,[6] a distinction has been made between two interrelated aspects of the legislative career: the career as an *objective* sequence of experiences, and the career as a *subjective* "moving perspective in which a person sees his life as a whole and interprets . . . the things which happen to him."[7] This dual concept, which is borrowed from the sociology of the professions, implies that it is possible to understand how and why individuals are recruited to the legislature only if their total careers and their changing perceptions are taken into consideration. In

[4] Vilfredo Pareto, *Trattato di Sociologia Generale* (Florence, 1916), [*The Mind and Society. A Treatise on General Sociology* (New York: Dover Publications, 1963)]. Summaries and discussions of the elite theories of Pareto and others can be found, for example, in Thomas B. Bottomore, *Elites and Society* (London: C. A. Watts & Co., 1964), esp. chap. 3; and in Wolfgang Zapf, *Wandlungen der Deutschen Elite* (Munich: R. Piper & Co., 1965).

[5] For a recent stock-taking, see Richard L. Merritt, *Systematic Approaches to Comparative Politics* (Chicago: Rand McNally & Co., 1970), pp. 110–111.

[6] John C. Wahlke, et al., *The Legislative System: Explorations in Legislative Behavior* (New York: John Wiley & Sons, 1962).

[7] Everett Hughes, "Institutional Office and the Person," in his book *Men and Their Work* (Glencoe, Ill.: Free Press, 1958), p. 63; quoted in Wahlke, *Legislative System,* p. 69; cf. Kenneth Prewitt, *Recruitment,* p. 20. See also Heinz Eulau and John D. Sprague, *Lawyers in Politics* (Indianapolis: Bobbs-Merrill Co., 1964).

order to do this, it is necessary to examine how and why the general structure of political opportunity changes over time,[8] since it is this structure that presumably determines the perceptions of the individual. If the opportunity structure changes during the lifetime of an aspiring or incumbent individual, and if different generations of politicians are given different opportunities, this makes it difficult to estimate the chances and the risks of a political career. In many contexts it is legitimate to assume that the opportunity structure is stable or at most only subject to "glacial changes."[9] It is, however, a central theme in the writings of many students of political recruitment that it is primarily the number of "openings" that determines the political opportunity structure and hence the perceptions of the politically ambitious,[10] and, since this variable may change over time, personal circulation is a phenomenon that is relevant for an understanding of legislative recruitment, past and present.

A second reason for a renewal of the interest in personal circulation is to be found in recent trends in the study of the social background of legislators. One of the new approaches to the study of social background consists in the analysis of change over time. This approach assumes that, primarily by means of a description and comparison of sequences of statistical frequency distributions for relevant variables, a better understanding will be developed not only of the social background variables themselves but also of the relations between societal context, elite characteristics, and legislative decisions and policies.[11] To reach the obvious goal of this approach, an understanding of the old Paretian theme of the circulation of the political elite, it is essential to study the narrower concept of personal circulation. This variable is critical because its variations over time tend to constitute the limiting value for the variations in the social background variables proper and possibly for other legislative variables.[12]

Finally, the introduction of the concept of *political institutionaliza-*

---

[8] The concept of a structure of political opportunity has been used in various ways in the literature on political recruitment. I prefer to define it simply as the set of probabilities that in a given period determine or describe what kinds of persons and social categories will come to function as candidates and legislators.

[9] Joseph A. Schlesinger, *Ambition and Politics: Political Careers in the United States* (Chicago: Rand McNally & Co., 1966), pp. 19–20.

[10] Ibid., chap. 1; see also Joseph A. Schlesinger, "Political Party Organization," in James G. March, ed., *Handbook of Organizations* (Chicago: Rand McNally & Co., 1965), pp. 768–769.

[11] The theme is further developed in Mogens N. Pedersen, *Political Development and Elite Transformation in Denmark*, (Beverly Hills: Sage Corporation, 1976).

[12] This argument is well developed, although scattered, in Pareto's *Mind and Society*. See, in particular, sec. 1734.

tion in recent studies of political development has made an analysis of legislative renewal processes more profitable, because this general notion provides us with a variable that links the recruitment variables to other variables in the political development syndrome.[13]

Scholars are far from agreement as to the content of this concept. Nevertheless, however it is defined, in most studies of the institutionalization of representative bodies it is assumed that a crucial aspect of this process is a change in recruitment practices by means of which the impact of new men, new groups, and new viewpoints is restricted and moderated. Thus, in the legislative context, institutionalization means the creation of "filters" that protect the legislature from certain kinds of external influence, the establishment of boundaries between the organization and its environment.[14]

Two tasks must be performed if empirical research is going to cumulate around this concept. First, since at the present stage the boundaries of the concept of political institutionalization are vague, the future use of this concept will require the formation of a consensus with regard to its delineation.[15] Second, comparisons must be made both between organizations at different levels within the same culture and between functionally equivalent organizations in different cultures, in order to test the various theoretical assumptions about political institutionalization and in order to get knowledge about the sequences and the timing of the process.

This chapter represents a modest attempt to move forward along these paths. It describes the personal circulation of the Danish Folketing since the introduction of representative, democratic government in 1849. The Danish political system changed rather abruptly in that year from a variant of bureaucratic and monarchial absolutism to a representative system based upon almost universal male suffrage. This system has survived and developed without interruptions or reversals. The pattern of personal circulation in the Folketing can be followed from the early days of groping experimentation with representative princi-

[13] Samuel P. Huntington, *Political Order in Changing Societies* (New Haven: Yale University Press, 1968).

[14] For definitions and discussions of the concept, see Huntington, *Political Order*, p. 12; Shmuel N. Eisenstadt, "Social Institutions," *International Encyclopedia of the Social Sciences* 14 (New York: Macmillan Co. and Free Press, 1968), p. 414; Nelson Polsby, "The Institutionalization of the U.S. House of Representatives," *American Political Science Review* 62 (1968): 144–145.

[15] Cf., for example, the narrow concept used in E. Spencer Wellhofer and Timothy M. Hennesey, "Political Party Development: Institutionalization and Leadership Recruitment" (Paper presented at the Annual Meeting of the American Political Science Association, Chicago, 1971), and the all-comprehending concept used in Huntington, *Political Order*.

ples and procedures to the modern, party-based system of representa-
tion.[16] The data are adequate for mapping the trends in the develop-
ment of the circulation variables over the whole 120-year period. It is
possible to examine how far the pattern of personal circulation consti-
tuted a fairly stable and slowly changing or, on the other hand, a highly
unstable feature of the political system. The materials can also be used
to throw light on the causes that produced this pattern and on the
effects that resulted from it. In particular it will be feasible to deal with
political institutionalization, a concept that can be translated fairly
easily into the language of personal circulation.

There are certain preliminary tasks. It is necessary to define the
concept of personal circulation and to explore its implications. Beyond
this, operational indicators must be devised that will make it possible
to describe in detailed, quantitative terms the patterns of personal cir-
culation throughout the period. The next sections will deal with these
matters, and will present the main findings. The last parts of the
chapter return to the more general problems of explanation.

II
THE CONCEPTS OF PERSONAL CIRCULATION

THE concept of personal circulation has never been given adequate
attention in legislative behavior and recruitment research. In most of
the descriptive studies of national legislatures only two variables have
been considered: *turnover* and *seniority*. A few attempts have been
made to analyze these phenomena in a wider context by relating them
to other legislative variables.[17]

These two variables, however, describe only partially the phenome-
non of personal circulation. What is implied in the use of this term
here is something broader and more comprehensive.

The personal circulation of a legislature should be understood to sig-
nify the total process of exchange of persons between the legislative
positions and their societal environment. This process involves at least
three distinguishable sub-processes: (1) the flow of personnel into the
legislature (*legislative recruitment*); (2) the flow of personnel within
the legislature (*legislative career*); and (3) the flow of personnel out of

[16] See Kenneth E. Miller, *Government and Politics in Denmark* (Boston:
Houghton Mifflin Co., 1968) for an introduction to the Danish political system. A
discussion of the transformation of the Danish Folketing in terms of the socio-eco-
nomic recruitment patterns can be found in Pedersen, *Political Development and
Elite Transformation.*

[17] See in particular Schlesinger, *Ambition and Politics;* idem, "Political Careers
and Party Leadership," in Lewis J. Edinger, ed., *Political Leadership in Industrial-
ized Societies* (New York: John Wiley & Sons, 1967), pp. 266–293.

the legislature *(legislative derecruitment)*. To understand the nature of personal circulation it is necessary to examine each of these processes and the interplay between them.

As soon as we begin to look upon the personal circulation of an elite as an exchange between the elite and its environment, we need concepts that make it possible for us to differentiate the various aspects of this exchange without losing sight of the phenomenon as a whole.

In the following pages I will propose a conceptual framework which, because of the context in which it is put forth, is primarily applicable to an analysis of legislative elites, but which, nevertheless, is sufficiently general to warrant application in the analysis of the circulation of any societal elite. I will define four concepts, each of which can be used to characterize an elite at a given point in time in dynamic terms. By comparing a sequence of characterizations it becomes feasible to describe in detail the various aspects of the exchange process between the elite and its environment.

First, we can talk about the *permeability* of the elite, by which is meant quite simply *the ease with which aspiring individuals can become members of the elite.*[18] Elites differ strongly with regard to permeability. Some are impossible or difficult to enter for all persons except those who possess certain distinctive characteristics, ascriptive or achieved. Some elites are immediately accessible for all who want to enter. Some require that the aspirants follow a *cursus honorum*, which fits them more or less easily for entrance into the elite, while other elites acquire at least some of their members through some sort of lateral entry. The various principles of selection that are used by established elites for filling vacant positions, such as hereditary succession, appointment from the top, or selection from below, tend to condition the extent of permeability, but do not determine it. Formal requirements, such as eligibility requirements, form only a minor part of the total sum of obstacles to the commencement of a legislative career, and a measure of formal requirements therefore cannot function as a substitute for the broader concept of permeability. In the following discussion, I will call an elite highly permeable if aspiring individuals do not meet any obstacles or meet only few obstacles to entering the elite. Conversely, the more obstacles and requirements there are, the less permeable the elite will tend to be. It is important to note that this concept describes a property of the collectivity, even if its definition and even more so its measurement build on information per-

[18] Harold D. Lasswell and Abraham Kaplan, *Power and Society: A Framework for Political Inquiry* (New Haven: Yale University Press, 1950), p. 35.

taining to individual members. Like the other concepts put forward in this section, permeability is defined at the level of the elite by means of *construction* from the individual level.[19]

Next, the term *volatility* of the elite will be used to denote the *extent of irrevocable change in the composition of the elite over time*.[20] An elite is volatile if a large portion of its members at time t_1 has left the elite definitely at a subsequent time, t_2, i.e., when a large amount of the members is *irrevocably* replaced during a given period. Conversely, the elite is non-volatile if its members tend to stay in the elite for a prolonged period.

Again, elites differ strongly with regard to volatility. Some elites, such as hereditary ones, will tend to be non-volatile, while many elective elites are characterized by an extraordinary degree of volatility. It is easily seen that the principles of selection condition the degree of volatility, but, just as was the case with permeability, do not determine it.

The third concept is the *continuity* of the elite. Members of an elite may stay in the elite for a shorter or longer period, but they will differ with regard to the degree to which their careers in the elite are continuous or discontinuous. In some elites membership is continuous, but in others and especially in elective elites a member has to calculate the risk that his career may be interrupted, if not terminated, by election defeats or by severe sanctions on the part of the nominating body. As is well known, this aspect of the personal circulation becomes especially important in legislative systems that are characterized by rigid norms of seniority. On the basis of the observation of differences in individual careers we can formulate the corresponding concept at the level of the elite: *an elite is continuous if its members tend to have stable positions in relation to the legislature and the electorate after they have acquired the positions the first time.* Conversely, elites characterized by a highly unstable relationship will be called discontinuous.

Finally, the concept of *security of tenure* will refer to *the extent to which replacement of members of the elite happens due to "natural"*

---

[19] The level-of-analysis problem in political science is discussed most profoundly in the introductory chapter, "On Units and Levels of Analysis," in Heinz Eulau, *Micro-Macro Political Analysis* (Chicago: Aldine Publishing Co., 1969), pp. 1–19.

[20] The term, but not the concept, of volatility was borrowed from Heinz Eulau and Kenneth Prewitt, "Social Bias in Leadership Selection, Political Recruitment and Electoral Context" (International Political Science Association, 8, World Congress, Munich 1970, Paper No. B–X/3). The two authors used it to characterize a specific type of electoral context. It is easily seen that my concept is related to what Lasswell and Kaplan call *circulation* (see Lasswell and Kaplan, *Power and Society*, p. 35), and to the concept of *rate of opportunities* in Schlesinger, *Ambition and Politics*, pp. 38–41. Cf. Pareto, *Mind and Society*, p. 1426, in which the term *velocity in circulation* is used (sec. 2044).

causes such as the death or physical aging of the members.[21] A secure elite thus is one from which members depart primarily because of death or because they have grown so old that they either themselves prefer to leave or are required to leave by organizational, formal, or informal norms. In a hereditary elite in which entrance is signaled by birth, exits are signaled by death. Conversely, many elites, for example the top echelons of the Communist Party of the Soviet Union, are characterized by extreme insecurity.

These four concepts have been designed in order to distinguish between various aspects of the personal circulation; they are clearly related, but they are not conceptually equivalent. An elite may, to mention just one example, be extremely permeable, and at the same time non-volatile, continuous, and secure. Any combination is logically possible, if not empirically plausible. One of the concepts, permeability, describes the recruitment process; another, security of tenure, taps the derecruitment process. Volatility and continuity are related to the career patterns in the elite, and the notion of volatility also reflects the volume of flow between environment and elite. Taken together, these concepts circumscribe the more general concept of personal circulation.

It is appropriate to think of the four concepts as dimensional constructs: an elite is more or less permeable, volatile, continuous, and secure. We can easily think of many different combinations of values for the variables, of different *profiles* of an elite over time, and of different profiles of various elites at a given point in time or over a shorter or longer span of time. As long as we remain at the purely conceptual level and do not bother about the empirical referents, we can move quite freely in space and time. For those who like the spatial vocabulary, we can say that any elite at any given point in time will be located in a position in a four-dimensional space; we can trace the movement of the elite in this space over time, just as well as we can compare the positions and the movements of several elites simultaneously.

As long as focus is on the concepts and not on their operational indicators, it is feasible to treat the variables as polar concepts. The personal circulation of an elite can then be characterized by means of four of the following eight characteristics:

permeable	non-permeable
volatile	non-volatile
continuous	discontinuous
secure	insecure

[21] In Suzanne I. Keller, *Beyond the Ruling Class* (New York: Random House, 1963), p. 213, it is argued that elite status has grown less rather than more secure. The concept, but not the argument around it, has been borrowed from this source.

70

TABLE 2–1. THE PROFILES OF OPEN AND CLOSED ELITES

The Character of the Elite	Permeability	Volatility	Continuity	Security of Tenure
Open	High	High	Low	Low
Closed	Low	Low	High	High

These characteristics can be combined in 16 different ways, none of which can be ruled out *a priori* as impossible. At the very best, we will have access to hypotheses that may guide the search for patterns, but as we have seen there are no logical linkages between the four concepts.

Two types of circulation pattern, however, do stand out as theoretically interesting in the sense that they may function as yardsticks for the searching process. These two types also happen to correspond fairly well to categories which are familiar to students of political recruitment and legislative behavior. What I have in mind are the concepts of *open* and *closed* elites.[22]

In this paper I will characterize an elite as *open* if it is permeable, volatile, discontinuous and insecure. If the elite has these properties, it follows that the personal exchange between elite and environment takes its maximum value: it is easy to enter the elite; the velocity of circulation is high; the risks of dropping out of the elite, temporarily or for good, are high; and it is seldom that a member stays in the elite until the time of death or voluntary retirement. In short, in the case of the open elite it is easy to become a member of the elite, but on the other hand it is also easy to lose the position.

In contrast, an elite is *closed* if it is difficult to become a member, but at the same time it is also seldom that members of the elite lose their positions involuntarily. The closed elite is non-permeable, non-volatile, continuous, and secure.

If we treat the four concepts as continuous variables instead of dichotomies, we get the conceptual profiles for the two types of elites that are depicted in Table 2–1.

Until now the argument has been quite general: it is postulated that the concepts of personal circulation, and the typology based upon these concepts, are applicable to the analysis of the personal exchange be-

[22] This distinction between open and closed elites, recruitment systems, etc. comes up in many contexts, but the definitions differ and are seldom made unambiguous. See, e.g., William Kornhauser, *The Politics of Mass Society* (London: Routledge & Kegan Paul, 1960), p. 52; Samuel C. Patterson, "Comparative Legislative Behavior: A Review Essay," *Midwest Journal of Political Science* 12 (1968): 606; cf. Keller, *Beyond the Ruling Class*, p. 58, and Zapf, *Wandlungen der Deutschen Elite*, p. 64.

tween any elite and its environment, provided that it is possible to describe the attributes of the elite in an unambiguous way. In this chapter, however, the concepts will be used only in connection with a description of a legislative elite, and comments on the typology will be confined to the process of exchange occurring in this context.

The legislative elite differs from many other politically significant elites because of its fundamental mechanism of exchange, the election. However intricate and "invisible" the recruitment processes, and however complex the post-entrance career histories may be, it is an important characteristic of the legislative elite that its members have entered their positions of authority by means of an election and that most of them will have their legislative careers terminated in an election. Therefore, the election forms a meaningful point of reference for mapping legislative career patterns: it constitutes the foundation for a distinction between the pre-legislative and the legislative career, or between the legislative career and the post-legislative career.

Open and closed legislative elites appear to differ with regard to the effect of the election upon personal circulation. The distinctive property of the open elite is the critical role of the election and the campaign in the exchange process: the election is the *moment of truth* both for aspirants to legislative office and for incumbents. In contrast, the closed elite is marked by the down-playing of the election as an exchange mechanism. Aspirants are screened well before election day, and after election they are by means of various devices safeguarded against defeat in later elections. In the open elite system the chances of success and survival for aspirants and incumbents alike are difficult to predict, while in the closed elite the predictability of the career is high.

If this is so—and no one can be sure about it before much more empirical research has been done—then it is plausible to suggest that different types of personnel are recruited under the two conditions. We need not use the obliging Paretian terms of *speculators* and *rentiers*; it is enough to say that certain types of social backgrounds are suitable for the open elite for reasons of, for example, dispensability, or—in Weber's term—"Betriebstechnischen Gründen," while other types are attracted and visible in a closed elite situation. In the same way recruitment and career systems, depending upon their predictability and risk, will probably tend to attract individuals with different personality traits. This argument also can be phrased thus: the type of personal circulation is probably determined by the type of individuals who dominate the legislature. This possibility of an inversion of the propositions has created a real dilemma for research since Pareto invented the concept of the *circulation of elites*.[23]

These arguments are, however, only hypothetical. To test them we need: first, clearcut examples of open and closed elites; and, second, elaborate controls for other, possibly confounding, variables. This task is beyond the scope of this chapter, and only a few suggestions and hypotheses will be discussed in sections v and vi.

III
FROM CONCEPTS TO MEASUREMENTS

THE four concepts of personal circulation, if they are to be used as descriptive and analytical tools, must be given operational definitions. In one sense this is an easy job. Data will be available for most legislatures on entries and exits of legislators, and these data do not present the same kind of troublesome problems of reliability as do most of the data on socio-economic background. In the Danish case several reliable sources exist from which one can pick up the information about the careers of individual legislators that is necessary to create indicators for the legislature.[24]

Three problems have to be solved in order to link the data and the concepts. First, it has to be decided what sort of *periodization* should be used. As we have seen, the personal circulation consists of a continuous flow of personnel into, through, and out of the legislature, and consequently any attempt to describe this flow at a given moment will describe a situation, but will not provide us with information about the direction and the rates of change in the flow. This kind of information has to be inferred from sequences of descriptions, and consequently the sequencing to be used becomes an important problem of design.

The use of the life of the legislature, the period between two elections, as a time unit was ruled out from the beginning. Although this solution would have had several advantages, it would also have resulted in serious difficulties of interpretation, because the various time series

[23] The most thorough attempt to separate and conceptualize the personal and the social aspects of circulation is probably the one found in Zapf, *Wandlungen der Deutschen Elite*, pp. 60ff.

[24] Main standard biographical sources are Victor Elberling, *Rigsdagens Medlemmer gennem 100 aar*, 3 vols. (Copenhagen: J. H. Schultz, 1949–1950); Magnus Sorensen and Svend Thorsen, *Folketinget* (Copenhagen: J. H. Schultz, 1956–); J.P. Jensen, *Valgene til Rigsdagen i 80 Aar, indbefattet Valgene til den grundlovgivende Rigsforsamling 1848* (Roskilde: Nordgaard, 1929), and the successive volumes of the electoral statistics are the principal sources for career data. The best guide to this type of data is found in Stein Rokkan and Jean Meyriat, eds., *International Guide to Electoral Statistics* (The Hague and Paris: Mouton, 1969), pp. 58–76.

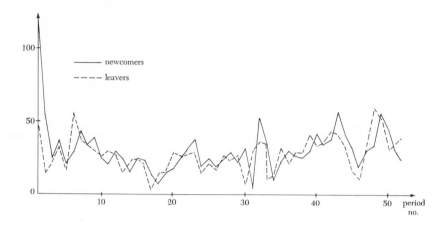

FIGURE 2–1.

The Absolute Number of Newcomers and Leavers 1849–1968

would have tended to become unstable due to the smallness of the Danish legislature. In Figure 2–1 the oscillatory movements in the data come out clearly in the two time series for the newcomers and the leavers: the absolute number of newcomers to the Folketing varies from 4 to 115, and the corresponding numbers of members who left the legislature for good are 4 and 60.

As the primary aim of this chapter is to map the long-term change in the recruitment and the derecruitment variables, a manageable approach, if not the only possible one, to the problem of handling the data consists in reporting them by means of a method of moving averages, designed to remove most of the oscillations. Accordingly, a five-period moving average technique has been used to bring out the secular trend in the data.[25]

It may puzzle the reader that the number of newcomers and the number of leavers in each election period differ, and that in some periods they differ considerably. This apparent discrepancy results from the concepts of the legislative career, and of *newcomers* and *leavers,* which have been used. Newcomers are those who in a given period entered the parliament for the first time, embarking upon a career as elected representatives; occasional proxies who never were

[25] A standard textbook dealing with the descriptive analysis of time series is Frederick E. Croxton and Dudley J. Cowden, *Applied General Statistics,* 2nd ʾd. (London: Pitman and Sons, 1955), chaps. 11–16.

elected are left out, and no attention is given in this definition to those individuals who entered the legislature again after disruptions of their careers. This principle also bears on the concept of leavers, which is defined so as to comprise only those legislators who permanently left the legislature. In other words, behind these definitions stands a particular concept of the legislative career which should be kept in mind: *the legislative career is seen as the total sequence of events that come between the first election of the individual and his final and definitive exit from the legislature.*

Apart from the fact that this definition of the career makes data collection much more manageable, it is in accordance with the concepts of continuity and security of tenure as defined earlier. This operationalization has its costs in terms of the possibilities for cross-national comparisons, but these costs are not prohibitive.[26]

The third and most important problem is to choose indicators for the four concepts and to choose an effective method of using data, collected at the level of the individual *legislators*, as a basis for descriptions and comparisons of *legislatures*.

Just as the concept of personal circulation has several dimensions that must be considered, so it can be argued that each of its components can and should be measured in various ways, in order to probe the validity of the single indicator, in order to use as much as possible the information available, and in order to explore the multi-dimensional character of the concepts.

It is, of course, possible to think of more than one indicator of *permeability*. In fact, a thorough understanding of the permeability of a legislature would require analysis of the total pre-legislative recruitment process with all of its "screening" processes.[27] Since this could not be undertaken here, partly because of the scarcity of data, it was necessary to select a few indicators all of which tap the phenomenon of permeability. These indicators could be interpreted as measuring some of the obstacles that the prospective individual meets on his way to the legislature, although they cannot cover more than a few aspects of the theoretical concept, nor are they exclusive measures of permeability. As they stand, some of them are quite debatable on grounds of both reliability and validity. It is, for example, not safe to use an index of pre-legislative activity (see Table 2–2) throughout the period, partly because data from the nineteenth century are relatively unreliable, but

---

[26] Due to the restrictive definitions of newcomers and leavers, the Danish figures for some of the variables will tend to be somewhat deflated. Direct comparison of the levels of volatility, continuity, and security of tenure is, therefore, not permissible without correction.

[27] See, e.g., Prewitt, *Recruitment*, chap. 1.

TABLE 2-2. INDICATORS OF PERSONAL CIRCULATION: DEFINITIONS AND DESCRIPTIONS

Indicator No.	Theoretical Concept	Description of Indicator	Universe	Type of Metric	Unit of Measurement	Supplementary Remarks
I		The average number of electoral campaigns and nominations the legislators had to participate in, before they entered the legislature.	Newcomers	Arithmetic mean	No. of nominations	Minimum value: 1.0.
II		The average number of constituencies the legislators had to run for office in, before they entered the legislature.	—	—	No. of constituencies	Minimum value: 1.0.
III	Permeability	Index of pre-legislative activity.	—	—	Value of index	The index takes its minimum value 0 for legislators who, before entering the legislature, had held neither elective positions in local government, nor major leadership positions in party and principal interest organizations. The maximum value 2 is obtained by legislators who had held at least two such positions.
IV		The proportion of legislators whose index of pre-legislative activity value exceeded 0.	—	Proportion of universe	%	
V		The average age at first election.	—	Arithmetic mean	Years, rounded	
VI		Turnover, reversed:	Total no. of legislative positions	Proportion of universe	%	The reverse value of the proportion of newcomers has been chosen in order to ease comparisons with indicators VII–IX.

		Description	Base	Statistic	Unit	Notes
VII	Volatility	The average total seniority of departing legislators, in years.	Leavers	Arithmetic mean	Years, rounded	
VIII		The average total seniority of departing legislators, in election periods.	–	–	Election periods, rounded	
IX		The proportion of legislators who stayed in the legislature longer than to the end of their first election period.	–	Proportion of universe	%	
X	Continuity	Index of membership discontinuity.	–	Arithmetic mean	Value of index	The index takes the value 1 for members who had no interruptions in their legislative career, and the value $p+1$ for members with p interruptions. Minimum value: 1.0
XI		The average number of constituencies in which members were nominated during their legislative career.	–	–	No. of constituencies	
XII		Index of absence during legislative career.	Leavers, whose legislative career was discontinuous	–	Years, rounded	The index is a simple additive index: from age at final departure are subtracted age at first entrance and total seniority in years, rounded values.
XIII	Security of Tenure	The average age at final departure from legislature.	Leavers	–	Years rounded	
XIV		The proportion of members who left the legislature at age 65 years or older.	–	Proportion of universe	%	
XV		The proportion of members who left the legislature due to death, retirement, etc.	–	–	%	The exact definition is: members who terminated their legislative career due to death, transfer to the upper chamber, or who left at age 65 years or older due to other reason than electoral defeat.

mostly because opportunities for pre-legislative political activities have expanded tremendously as the political system has developed a specialized political infra-structure. In the case of this and other questionable indicators other measures were defined that may function as complements or correctives to the first one. Although it is possible through this strategy to control for some of the invalidations arising from the comparison of political phenomena over time, I am painfully aware that the single time series are often open to criticism. Whatever conclusion one wants to draw, therefore, should preferably be based upon the four sets of indicators: to the extent that the findings inside the sets tend to corroborate each other, it becomes safer to draw a conclusion.

This kind of logic lies behind the selection of all four sets of indicators. For *volatility* the central measure is the simple turnover rate, which tells us the extent of change in the personal composition over time, independent of change in the size of the legislature.[28] This measure has been supplemented with various measures based on individual seniority in order to give further insights into the "length of life" of the legislature, which, of course, is partly dependent upon the turnover rate. *Continuity* has been measured in three independent ways, each tapping a different aspect of this concept. A legislative career may be discontinuous in the sense that it becomes interrupted one or several times due to, for example, electoral defeats. Discontinuity, however, could be seen as a discontinuity vis-à-vis the represented, for example, when legislators move from constituency to constituency, trying eventually to stabilize their own legislative careers; or it could be treated as a situation that creates shorter or longer periods of absence from the legislature. Finally, *security of tenure*, perhaps the most vague of the four concepts, was measured by a series of indicators each of which describes an aspect of derecruitment. Essentially, what should be measured is the extent to which the patterns of departure from the legislature resemble the patterns of departure from certain other political elites, such as the judiciary and the civil service, both of which—at least in the Danish case—can be depicted as having a bureaucratic pattern.[29]

[28] It is somewhat simplistic to speak about "the simple turnover rate," because several different definitions can be thought of. Normally, turnover rates are computed from a comparison of the legislature at times t_1 and t_2; other possible measures are based on the number of newcomers or leavers between t_1 and t_2; dependent on the definition of these two concepts, various concepts of turnover will emerge, cf. notes 20 and 26. When both chronological and electoral time are taken into consideration, several problems of comparison arise. Cf. Schlesinger, *Ambition and Politics*, pp. 37–41. Wherever the concept of turnover is introduced or used, one should, therefore be cautious before comparisons are made.

[29] See the discussion of the judicial and the administrative career in Mogens N. Pedersen, "Lawyers in Politics: The Danish Folketing and American Legislatures,"

The various indicators, their definitions, and properties are summarized in Table 2–2. Two comments should be made on this table. First, it is easily seen that the method which has been used in order to condense a large amount of factual information about individual political careers is quite simple, and not at all new. The aim was to find time series pertaining to the legislature rather than to the individual legislator; the most simple solution, in most cases, was to summarize information by means of central tendency statistics of frequency distributions. This type of metric, in some cases, was supplemented by proportion measures to gauge the amount of dispersion and skewness in the distributions.

These unsophisticated statistical tools which, when used to measure variations along a time continuum, have been called *comparative frequency metrics* [30] have certain advantages in this context. First, they focus attention on the attributes of the aggregate, not of the single legislator; they provide an easy way of comparing and ordering data and of interpreting changes over chronological or parliamentary time in terms of rapidity, extension, and duration; and the assumptions about the data set that they involve are not necessarily less rigorous than they would be if more complex statistical methods of dynamic analysis had been applied.

Second, a look at Table 2–2 shows that this technique of description is essentially a special kind of cohort analysis.[31] Whereas cohort analysis, when used in recruitment analysis and other types of political analysis, ordinarily tends to be future-directed, in that it follows in statistical terms an entering cohort through its subsequent life cycle, the cohort approach used here faces backward, in the sense that the collective biographical histories of newcomers and leavers respectively have been mapped at a moment when the theoretically relevant segment of the total career was already a thing of the past. This property of the technique should be kept in mind, as it follows from it that the frequency metrics relate to two distinct subsets of the legislature and thus do not lend themselves to direct comparison or to inferences about the

in Samuel C. Patterson and John C. Wahlke, eds., *Comparative Legislative Behavior Research* (New York: John Wiley & Sons, 1972).

[30] Harold D. Lasswell, Daniel Lerner, and C. Easton Rothwell, *The Comparative Study of Elites*, Hoover Institute Studies, Series B: Elites, no. 1 (Stanford: Stanford University Press, 1952), pp. 27–29.

[31] About cohort analysis, see, e.g., Norman Ryder, "The Cohort as a Concept in the Study of Social Change," *American Sociological Review* 30 (1965): 843–861. An application on legislative data can be found in Frey, *Turkish Political Elite*, pp. 212–223.

career patterns of individual legislators either by simple techniques or by means of any kind of regression analysis.

IV
THE FINDINGS: FROM OPEN TO CLOSED ELITE

BY means of these concepts and these empirical indicators it is possible to describe the personal circulation in the Danish Folketing from 1849 to 1968.

We may as well start with the conclusion: with regard to the distinction outlined earlier between open and closed elites, it is clear from the data summarized in Figures 2–2, 2–3, 2–4, and 2–5 that the Danish legislative elite moved from relative openness to relative closedness during the 120-year period. This, of course, can be demonstrated only by means of an inspection of fifteen, partly independent, indicators, so that generalizations beyond that universe of variables must be highly provisional. But, as will be seen shortly, the various findings tend to corroborate each other and thus strengthen the general proposition.

Because of the considerable number of fluctuations in the series, the use of a method of five-period moving averages has not removed entirely the oscillatory movements in the raw data, but it has on the other hand performed sufficiently well to allow descriptions of the trends in the data, and to distinguish periods of rapid change from periods of relative stability. The reader should, however, be warned against over-interpretation of the graphs.

From Figure 2–2 it appears that the members of the legislature have tended to be older and older when they first entered the chamber. Their pre-electoral experiences have tended to be more extensive and diversified, and it is the exception if a newcomer to the legislature has not held an elective position in local politics or an important leadership position in one of the various political and semi-political organizations. The M.F. has had to invest more and more of his energy in preparatory positions, which have come to function as *cursus honorum* positions for aspiring politicians.

An over-all view of the indicators of permeability leads to the first conclusion: *the permeability of the Danish legislative elite has decreased over time*. This development, however, has not taken the form of a linear, incremental decrease. The general trend in the development is one of growth in the values of the five indicators, and this can only be interpreted as meaning that the elite has become less permeable over time. But in all of the five graphs we find the same pattern of change, which is that the most significant decrease in permeability

80

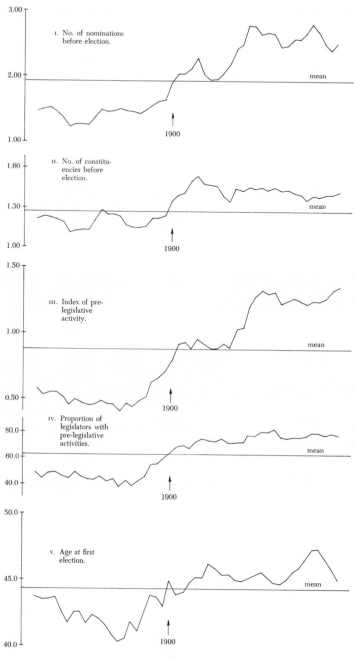

3.00

I. No. of nominations before election.

2.00   mean

1900

1.00

1.60   II. No. of constitu-encies before election.

1.30   mean

1.00   1900

1.50

III. Index of pre-legislative activity.

1.00   mean

0.50   1900

IV. Proportion of legislators with pre-legislative activities.

80.0

60.0   mean

40.0   1900

50.0   V. Age at first election.

45.0   mean

1900

40.0

FIGURE 2-2.

Indicators of Permeability

occurred in the decades around the turn of the century. With some qualifications we may even say that one, relatively high, level of permeability is characteristic for the nineteenth century, and another, much lower one, for the twentieth century.

The next set of time series in Figure 2–3 tells a partly similar, partly

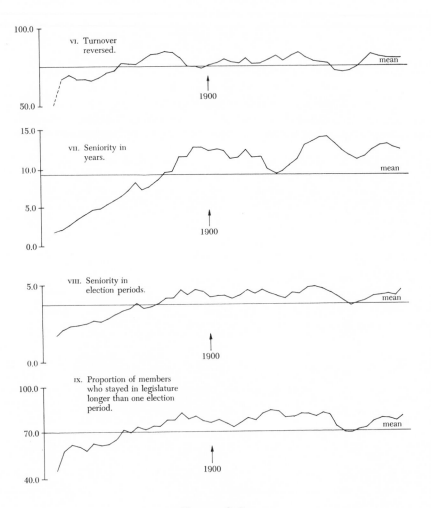

FIGURE 2–3.

Indicators of Volatility

different story. Again the values tend to increase, and do so for all the indicators, thus indicating decreasing volatility. This time, however, the recurring general trend is one of dramatically increasing values during the first couple of decades, followed by a tendency toward stability. In terms of the theoretical concept, this is equivalent to a decreasing volatility until a certain level is reached. We may conclude that *the volatility of the Danish legislative elite decreased sharply throughout the first 20 to 30 years of democratic government and that thereafter it has remained fairly stable.*

In the indicators of continuity shown in Figure 2–4 a more diffuse picture appears. In this case it is not possible to describe the trend as simply unilinear or curvilinear. From an artificially low point of departure the curves rise steeply to a peak and then tend to show decreasing values. In the conceptual language of this chapter, the continuity of

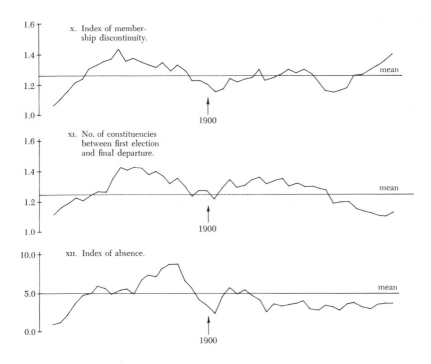

FIGURE 2–4.

Indicators of Continuity

the legislative elite tended to decrease during the first decades of democratic government, regardless of which aspect of continuity is chosen for inspection. Continuity reached its lowest point between 1864 and 1890—the exact date depends upon which indicator is used—after that period continuity increased again. The oscillations, however, are so pronounced as to prohibit general statements. With reference to the dichotomy between open and closed elites it seems permissible to state that *over the entire 120-year period continuity has at least not decreased.*

Finally, Figure 2–5 shows that security of tenure increased throughout the period. Not only did the average age of departing members tend to become higher, but also an increasingly large proportion of

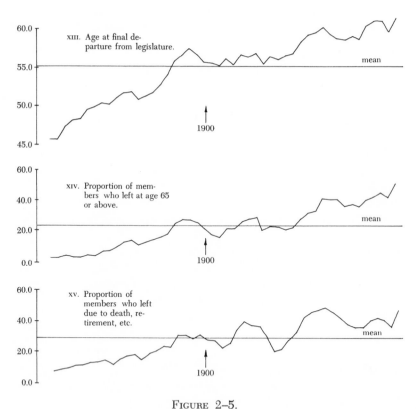

FIGURE 2–5.

Indicators of Security of Tenure

members left the legislature at a relatively old age. Even more important is the fact that the proportion of members whose careers were terminated for non-political reasons changed from less than 10 percent to almost 50 percent. A retirement pattern like the one found either in the civil service or in other bureaucratic public sectors has not materialized as yet, but the trend of the available data is clearly one of long-term growth, indicating that *the security of tenure in the Danish legislative elite has been increasing ever since the introduction of a legislature into the Danish political system.*

In conclusion, the various patterns described here support the general contention sketched above about the over-all pattern of personal circulation. During the first decades of democratic selection of legislators, the elite was relatively open. Members did not go through a particular *cursus honorum* before their election; many legislators were elected when they first ran. A legislator's career, once he was elected, generally turned out to be relatively short with only few interruptions; the career terminated in many cases a long time before the individual had reached the normal age of retirement. For the legislature this meant a quick renewal of the membership.

This open legislative elite rapidly disappeared during the latter half of the nineteenth century. First, there was a decrease in the volume of personnel flow between environment and elite. This decrease was paralleled by a transient instability in legislative careers. Although there were fewer newcomers, more incumbents served non-consecutive terms and changed constituency affiliation.

The closing of the elite accelerated when the permeability of the elite began decreasing rather sharply in the decades around the turn of the century; at that time the volatility of the elite already had reached a considerably lower level than at the beginning of the period. Meanwhile security of tenure grew steadily, and continuity tended to increase somewhat. In relative terms these patterns are compatible with the view that the Danish legislative elite has changed from an open elite to a much more closed elite. This process started as early as 1849, and still goes on, although the critical changes in the pattern occurred before the First World War.

V

SOME EXPLANATORY HYPOTHESES

THE conclusions that have been reached in the preceding section certainly do not constitute the final word about the personal circulation of the Danish legislature. At best they provide a starting point for the researcher by raising a great many questions about the causes and consequences of the closing of the legislative elite.

The remaining part of this chapter will be devoted to the problem of explaining this phenomenon. There are also important questions about the effects of the gradual closing of the legislature upon the political system, but I will not attempt to discuss these here. It seems reasonable to argue that an explanation of the emergence of the phenomenon should be undertaken before an effort is made to map its effects in a wider context. This is the more desirable since previous research has been unsatisfactory on this point. Social scientists, so far as they have dealt at all with the phenomenon of the circulation of elites, have tended to mix and confuse various aspects of the phenomenon and, furthermore, have been prone to offer speculations and metaphors instead of substantive analysis.[32]

A good starting point for the discussion is provided by Vilfredo Pareto, who was probably the first scholar in modern times who attempted to deal systematically with personal circulation on the basis of a model of elite renewal processes. He never made an explicit distinction between personal and other forms of circulation, but wrote in his glittering style that "in virtue of class-circulation, the governing *élite* is always in a state of slow and continuous transformation. It flows on like a river, never being today what it was yesterday. From time to time sudden and violent disturbances occur. There is a flood— the river overflows its banks. Afterwards, the new governing *élite* again resumes its slow transformation. The flood has subsided, the river is again flowing normally in its wonted bed." [33]

In this, as well as in other metaphors used to characterize various aspects of the elite circulation phenomenon, the slowness and the incremental character of the process are stressed.[34] Even if disturbances may occur, due to revolutionary events or to *critical elections*, it is assumed that the best prediction of the circulation pattern of tomorrow is provided by an inspection of that of today and yesterday. For a good many countries, including the United States and various Western European nations, there exists at least rudimentary evidence supporting this view; in most cases the developmental trend is probably identical to

[32] See also the critique by Thomas B. Bottomore in his *Elites and Society*, p. 61.
[33] Pareto, *Mind and Society*, p. 1431, sec. 2056.
[34] See Carl J. Friederich, *Man and His Government* (New York: McGraw-Hill, 1963), p. 318; Mattei Dogan, "Political Ascent in a Class Society: French Deputies 1870–1958," in Dwaine Marvick, ed., *Political Decision Makers* (New York: Free Press, 1961), pp. 58–59; and Philip W. Buck, *Amateurs and Professionals in British Politics, 1918–1959* (Chicago: University of Chicago Press, 1963), p. 10 for three other metaphors which tap different dimensions of the concept of elite circulation.

86

that found in Denmark.[35] We, therefore, in the search for explanatory factors pertaining to the case under inspection, should look out for factors that are universal rather than concentrating exclusively on factors apparently specific and unique to Danish history.

The first and most important observation to make is that recruitment to the legislature, the legislative career itself, and derecruitment from the legislature take place in the context of political parties. Parties have developed and have tended to become salient agencies for the renewal of political elites. This simple fact should guide the formulation of hypotheses.

In the case of Denmark it has, since the rise of the modern party system in the last quarter of the nineteenth century, become increasingly difficult for an aspiring individual to run for office as an independent candidate without the endorsement of a party organization. The parties have thus become the gatekeepers of the legislature, and the legislative career has become tied to the fate of the party, especially in the sense that the defeat of the party may ruin the legislative career of even the most competent legislator.

Any attempt to understand the closing of the legislature will have to start with this observation. The central question, in the Danish, as well as in many other cases, is: to what extent is this closing of the legislative elite as a whole primarily a result of changes in the renewal processes in the parties and/or changes in the distributions of the legislative positions among parties, which display different internal circulation patterns?

Behind the formulation of this question stands the assumption that what really matters, if we want to understand the personal circulation of a legislature, are the renewal processes within the participating parties. For explanatory purposes we can simply choose to look upon the time series as artificial summations of party-based time series. This point of view, however, has only a limited scope: when accounting for the changes in the personal circulation of the legislative elite we also should be prepared to broaden the search to include more general causal factors, such as those related to the system of representation and to the wider political system. To push matters to the extreme, it is possible to conjecture either that the closing was the result of a substitution in the legislature of parties with different recruitment and derecruitment patterns, or that it was the result of a general trend toward the simultaneous closing of all the parties in the party system.

[35] Consult, e.g., the sequence of articles by nine contributors under the general heading, "The Parliamentary Profession," in *International Social Science Journal* 13 (1961): 513–649.

There are several properties of parties that might influence the re-newal process and cause the closing of a party's parliamentary group over time. One such factor is the *age of the party*. The older the party, the more complex and routinized its organizational structure often tends to become; the party develops auxiliary and socialization organi-zations with leadership positions, which can function as stepping stones to higher office for ambitious individuals; it develops institutionalized career paths in the sense that norms about the proper conduct of office-seeking individuals and nominating bodies crystallize. The general pat-tern of leadership recruitment in organizations has been demonstrated to be closely related to the key tasks performed by leaders; [36] as a party grows older these tasks will tend to change and, presumably, so will the recruitment pattern. The direction of change is toward favoring those types of individuals who have made substantive personal invest-ments in the organization; who identify with it; and who specialize in running the organization with all its routinized administrative tasks—in short the professional politician in contrast to the Weberian *nebenberu-fliche Politiker*.[37]

Another, probably important, factor is the *class-relation* of the party, because this relation will tend to determine the educational require-ments with which a legislator-to-be will have to cope. Without much evidence and without taking a strictly functionalist stand, it can be argued that, for an individual to live up to the legislator role, not only ambitions but also a large number of physical and psychological skills are required. Many of the skills are exactly those that are learned in a system of formal education, though most of them also can be learned in other contexts.

In the recruitment process within the party, the individuals who present themselves as candidates or who are asked to run are, pre-sumably, those who match the description of the ideal representative. This screening of the ambitious probably will tend to have diverse effects in the different parties, depending upon their positions in the class structure. Middle- and upper-class based parties will tend to have a larger pool of formally educated and occupationally trained party activists than will parties dominated by lower-stratum voters and mem-bers.[38] This suggests the hypothesis that the low-stratum-based party

[36] Philip Selznick, *Leadership in Administration* (White Plains, N.Y.: Row, Peterson and Co., 1957).

[37] Wellhofer and Hennesey in "Political Party Development" have done impor-tant empirical research along these lines. The argument can be traced back to Max Weber, Robert Michels, and Maurice Duverger.

[38] This theme is developed and investigated in Stein Rokkan and Angus Camp-bell, "Citizen Participation in Political Life: A Comparison of Data for Norway and

88

will make up for this "deficiency" by becoming more prone to establishing its own training and *cursus honorum* than will the other parties. This latter hypothesis can be seen as a complement to the one concerned with the age of parties, but it, of course, can be discussed independently and eventually can be given a dynamic formulation.

Two other factors pertaining to the class producing static differences among parties are the *size of the party* and the *rate and direction of growth*. It is a plausible hypothesis that, since safe seats are a scarce commodity for each party, the smaller the number of such openings, the more intense the competition will tend to be, and this will mold the pattern of personal circulation in the party. In the same way, steadily growing and declining parties can be assumed to differ with regard to their patterns of personal circulation.[39]

Finally, *the degree of centralization in a party* and the *degree of openness of the selection process* proper have been assumed to be important conditioning factors with regard to the renewal of parliamentary groups.[40] These factors, however, are only mentioned here for the sake of completeness; as the Danish parties do not, and have never differed fundamentally on these variables, we need not consider them in this context.

The hypothesis underlying this enumeration of factors is that various structures in the individual party will tend to develop in such a way that the result may be a closing of the renewal process in that party. This closing, which is primarily a result of the party's growing older, is conditioned and mediated by the position of the party in the party system, by its size, and by whether it is growing or shrinking. Under some circumstances these factors may reinforce the effect of aging, but they may be neutral or even work against it. The effect upon the personal circulation of the legislature as a whole is a function of the effect

---

the United States of America," *International Social Science Journal* 12 (1960): 69–99; rpt. in Stein Rokkan, *Citizens, Elections, Parties* (Oslo: Universitetsforlaget, 1970), pp. 362–396.

[39] Size as well as direction and rate of growth are properties that presumably influence the pattern of renewal in the single party. Their eventual effect upon the personal circulation of the legislature as such is very complicated. If they were the only effective causes of variations in the patterns of renewal of the parties, these effects would of course tend to cancel out each other at the level of the legislature.

[40] These hypotheses have been forwarded in Maurice Duverger, *Political Parties* (London: Methuen & Co., 1954), see esp. pp. 162ff., and in Lester G. Seligman, *Recruiting Political Elites* (New York: General Learning Press, 1971). It should be emphasized that when, for example, Seligman speaks of open versus closed selection processes, he refers to an empirically related but conceptually different phenomenon to the one which is studied in this chapter.

within the single party, weighted by the parliamentary strength of that party within the party system.

Another hypothesis underlying these formulations is that the larger the personal investment an individual has made in order to get elected, the less probable is it that he will surrender voluntarily what he has achieved. When the position of legislator tends to be an easily obtained, additional status attribute, it is not a great loss to give it up. In contrast, when an institutionalized political career develops, the professional may suffer a major loss of status if he has to terminate the career. He not only will be deprived of his office but also will lose many material and psychological rewards conferred on that office.[41] If the parties did not provide "cushions," as they often do, giving up the legislative career would often mean becoming unemployed. In other words, once elected, the incumbents in the modern party will be strongly motivated not to give up their positions voluntarily.

Apart from these factors, we will also have to consider the possibility that the closing of the legislative elite is not simply a product of changes in the renewal processes in some or all of the parties but is also the result of more fundamental societal processes which happen to be mediated through the party system. It is this type of reasoning that, apparently, lies behind recent attempts to study the general phenomenon of political institutionalization. From its probably most daring formulation, Parkinson's Law, to the cautious discussion by Nelson Polsby, the hypothesis is that societies, organizations, or legislatures, go through a development which is essentially unidirectional: more institutionalized patterns follow less institutionalized patterns; and the process of institutionalization is, at least partially, interpreted as an aging process.[42] In the case of a legislature, such as the Danish one, it is difficult to formulate hypotheses at the level of the legislature itself which will allow us to explain the emergence of a boundary between the legislature and its environment in terms of renewal. If we do not want to formulate functional explanations, we may easily end up with mere restatements of the emergent phenomenon, or with hypotheses that essentially belong to the sphere of the party system.

Three different, although connected, lines of thought will be pursued here. I am not going to test specific propositions, either at the level of the party or at the level of the system of representation, but wish merely to give some illustrative examples of plausible hypotheses.

---

[41] Chong Lim Kim, "Toward a Theory of Individual and Systematic Effects of Political Status Loss," *The Journal of Developing Areas* 5 (1971): 193–206. Cf. also Seligman, *Recruiting Political Elites.*

[42] Huntington, *Political Order*, esp. pp. 13–14.

First, the fundamental changes in the legislature and in its role in the political system may have had a general effect upon the renewal process. The most conspicuous difference between the legislature of the mid-nineteenth century and that of today is that the legislature now is in session much longer and that it deals with more issues and more complex ones than before. To cope with the growing amount and complexity of its workload, it has developed an internal division of labor, which in turn tends to strengthen the specialization of the legislators: from generalists they have been turned into specialists who have to make high personal investments in terms of energy and time in order to avoid being considered failures by their colleagues. To become a respected member of the legislature the newcomer not only must learn his position in relation to his elder colleagues but also must learn his trade. He must become a competent specialist in those issue areas to which he is assigned. In the long run Danish legislators will tend to become either *lawmakers* or *spectators*, to use the concepts invented by James D. Barber.[43]

This trend toward specialization is parallel to the one already described as going on in the party organizations, and it is to be expected that it will have the same kind of effects upon the renewal of the legislature, although these effects will depend not on the age of the party but on the age of the legislature.

Second, we have to take into consideration a much more complex hypothesis about the relationship between the age of the system of representation and its degree of openness. Although this hypothesis is explicated here in terms of the Danish context, it is probably relevant for other political systems as well.

In Denmark the introduction of a legislature happened at a time when only a small segment of the population was politically mobilized. Among the predominantly upper-class politicians who carried through the constitutional reform there existed a certain fear of the possibility of a development which would bring the masses, "unenlightened, egoistic, and rude," as one of the leading politicians described them,[44] too abruptly into politics. According to a widespread opinion, the intelligentsia had and deserved a natural advantage because of its ability to analyze and decide political issues in a broad perspective, disengaged

[43] James D. Barber, *The Lawmakers* (New Haven: Yale University Press, 1965). The categories of *advertisers* and *reluctants* in Barber's scheme do not seem very relevant for an understanding of recruitment to and behavior in a modern *national* legislature.

[44] D. G. Monrad, quoted in Povl Bagge, *Studier over D. G. Monrads statstanker* (Copenhagen: Lewin & Munksgaard, 1936), p. 158.

from and above economic interests. To become a legislator was to some extent considered a duty for the intelligentsia and the well-to-do citizens, and the material and other rewards were, in accordance with this view, not set very high. The legislature was intended to be and in fact became a collective governing body of upper-class individuals, whose general social status was so high that the legislative position could be only a marginal means of raising it.[45] Only intense political ambitions would lead a candidate to make a heavy investment in a political career. The scope of such a career was in any case limited because the highest offices, those in the cabinet, were regularly filled with "outsiders" from the upper house or the civil service.[46]

This situation changed in two different ways. First, the mobilization of new groups into politics meant that the level of social eligibility was lowered considerably: the pool of individuals who could and would participate effectively in legislative politics and who, by doing so, in addition could advance socially, or at least would not have to sacrifice, became much larger.

Furthermore, the effects of lowering this threshold of social eligibility probably were reinforced, on the one hand by a status-downgrading of the intelligentsia and civil servants during the late nineteenth century,[47] and on the other hand by an upgrading of the position of the legislator in the status hierarchy. There is no firm evidence, but it would seem reasonable to expect that the breakthrough of the principle of government responsibility in 1901, the improvements in the economic conditions of legislators in this century, the downgrading and later abolition of the upper house, and the growth in the public sector would have had the effect of giving the M.F. a somewhat higher status in society.[48] This change, to the extent that it has taken place, has tended to enlarge the pool of candidates who are status-inferior and to decrease the number of those for whom the legislative position would give only psychological satisfaction. When the pool of individuals from which politicians are drawn becomes absolutely and relatively larger, we should expect this to affect the renewal processes not only in the lower-class based parties but also in all parties.

[45] For documentation of this description, see Pedersen, *Political Development and Elite Transformation.*

[46] From 1849 to 1865, approximately 80 percent of the cabinet members were *not* recruited through the Folketing. The corresponding number for the period after the Second World War is approximately 20 percent.

[47] Povl Bagge, "Akademikerne i dansk politik i det 19. århundrede," in *Historisk Tidsskrift,* 12, IV, 3 (Copenhagen, 1970), pp. 423–474, esp. pp. 454–459.

[48] About the relative social status of members of the Folketing, see Pedersen, "Lawyers in Politics."

These are speculations. Neither for Denmark nor for other countries do we know enough about the relative and changing positions in the status hierarchy of politicians, nor do we know enough about how and to what extent the distribution of discrete, static, and progressive political ambitions is affected by the relative social conditions of the aspiring individuals.[49] My primary reasons for sketching this argument are that it illustrates how the legislative renewal processes are embedded in more general processes of social and political change, and that it also illustrates the working of a general factor which can be thought of as relevant for all of the parties, irrespective of their age, size, and organizational structure.

Finally, a more simple argument ought to be considered in connection with the descriptive findings of the previous section. In the case of indicators III and IV it already has been mentioned that the pre-activity variable is debatable on grounds of validity: we should expect more pre-legislative activity among the legislators when the opportunity for such activities rises due to the development of a specialized political infra-structure. This argument, so far as it is not merely an over-simplification of some of the party-specific hypotheses already stated, can be understood only in the framework of a very general hypothesis about the existence of a "mirroring" tendency in the system of representation. In its generalized form this hypothesis would account for the rising age at departure and probably also for the rising age at first election. Through these variables it would be linked to various other variables used in this chapter for descriptive purposes.

I do not intend to discuss whether such a mirroring tendency is at work.[50] But I want to stress first that, if it does exist, its effects will be mixed up with the effects of other factors, and, second, that this factor then will belong to the class of general factors as here defined.

VI

A MODEL OF PERSONAL CIRCULATION AND SOME FINDINGS

IN the preceding pages, I have sketched a few hypotheses that might be relevant for an explanation of the closing of legislatures in general, and the Danish Folketing in particular. To test them rigorously requires access to data that are not available and that will never be available. The problem is that, though we have access to a small amount of data about *objective* career patterns, we do not know anything about

---

[49] The distinction between discrete, static, and progressive ambitions is due to Schlesinger, *Ambition and Politics*, chap. 1.

[50] But see the discussion in Eulau, *Micro-Macro Political Analysis*, chap. 3, esp. pp. 100–101.

past *subjective* careers. We know that the observed recruitment patterns of the past are traces of a process in which deliberate decisions about joining, sustaining, and leaving the legislative career have incessantly been taken by individuals whose ambitions may have been discrete, static, or progressive; these decisions, furthermore, have been taken under varying conditions with regard to competition among politically active individuals. These vital processes have left only traces, the interpretation of which is difficult. We may form hypotheses of the type just mentioned, but they have to be rather complex, involving not only operationalizable variables but also hypothetical variables, the function of which is to provide the inferential linkage.

It is, however, possible to take a first step in the direction of formulating a theoretical statement about the dynamics of the personal circulation on the basis of the scanty evidence at hand. The timing of the closing of the Folketing, as it was described earlier in this chapter, presents us immediately with a hypothesis: that the changes in the pattern of personal circulation are primarily dependent upon changes in the party system. The non-linear patterns envisaged in most of the time series and the tendency for the greatest shifts to be located in the formative period of the party system in the last quarter of the nineteenth century suggest that the general tendency in the data might be the product of factors that are primarily related to the renewal processes in the individual parties.

This hypothesis is difficult to test directly. By means of an indirect approach, however, we can get a fair estimate of its validity. The test takes as its point of departure the observation made in the previous section that the variations in the personal circulation of the legislature can be interpreted as a function of two sets of variables, those which affect the personal circulation of a single party and affect parties differently, and those which can be interpreted as neutral in relation to the parties because they affect the entire system of representation.

To estimate the relative weight of these two sets of factors, we can start by asking under what conditions we would feel inclined to hypothesize that general and not party-specific factors were of overriding importance for the variation in personal circulation. The answer is as follows:

Let us assume that parties A, B, . . . F have participated in the elections and have won seats throughout the period under inspection. Further let us assume that we have j observations taken for each party on the personal circulation variables. Thus we have f time series, which can be classed together in a fxj matrix. Furthermore we have a series of j observations, which describes the variations over time for the total

94

legislature, P_1, P_2, . . . P_j. Finally, let us assume that this series is indicating progressive, regressive or linear growth:

$$P_1 < P_2 < \ . \ . \ . \ < P_j \qquad (1)$$

If we next ask under what conditions with regard to the f party series (1) would be true, we have to admit that an infinite number of patterns can be thought of as relevant conditional connectives. One of these, however, does stand out as particularly relevant, both because it is easy to interpret and because it is useful as a technical aid for the comparison of the empirical findings:

$$\left[\begin{bmatrix} a_1 < a_2 < \ . \ . \ . \ < a_j \\ b_1 < b_2 < \ . \ . \ . \ < b_j \\ \cdot \qquad \cdot \qquad \qquad \cdot \\ \cdot \qquad \cdot \qquad \qquad \cdot \\ f_1 < f_2 < \ . \ . \ . \ < f_j \end{bmatrix} \wedge \left[\frac{da}{dt} = \frac{db}{dt} = \ . \ . \ . \ \frac{df}{dt} \right] \wedge \right. \qquad (2)$$

$$\left. [a_i = b_i = \ . \ . \ . \ f_i] \quad \right] \Rightarrow [P_1 < P_2 < \ . \ . \ . \ < P_j]$$

The verbal interpretation of this conditional connective is quite straightforward: *if* each of the time series for the parties is subject to incessant increase, *and if* the rate of increase is identical, *and if* the values are identical at least at one point in time, *then* the series for the total legislature will be subject to incessant increase, i.e., the situation depicted in (1) will be true. An even more simple interpretation in terms of graphic representation is that the *f* curves for the *f* parties are graphically identical, and also identical with the curve for the legislature i.e., the *f*+*l* curves in the diagram will overlap each other entirely and accordingly look like one curve.

Two comments are essential for the understanding of this model, which in its above formulation will be named the *model of the closing legislature*. First, it is easily seen that it can be generalized to situations with discontinued growth; situations with progressive, constant, or regressive decrease; and situations with constant values in the variables over time. This, of course, means that the model is equally relevant for understanding the closing and the opening of elites. This generalized model will be named the *model of uniform party change*. Second, the compound statement (2) is a conditional, but not a biconditional connective; i.e., (1) can be true also in those cases, where one, two, or all three components in the conjunction are false. Although I will abstain from doing so, it is equally easy to give a verbal and a graphical interpretation in each of these cases.

What the conditional connective (2) gives us is an expression of the situation in which variations in the personal circulation of the legislature, *in casu* its tendency toward closing, are entirely independent of variations in personal circulation in the individual parties; i.e., only factors which affect the system of representation as such are operating. We can take this situation as a pure type and use it as a technical aid for the analysis of the closing of the Danish legislature, because we can interpret deviations from this model as signifying that other factors are operating, and this means factors that have different effects upon the parties.

By means of this model and some measures of deviation from the situation described by the model we are now able to estimate the relative importance of the various types of factors in an explanation of the changing patterns of personal circulation.

For this purpose data sets pertaining to the individual election periods were combined into five subsets, each related to a fairly long period in the history of the system of representation (see Table 2–3).[51]

Next, only information about the renewal of the four "old" parties in the Danish party system has been considered, those parties which together have commanded from 80 to 100 percent of the total number of seats; which have existed uninterrupted for a sufficiently long period; and each of which has been large enough to make it possible for us to speak in quantitative terms about patterns of recruitment and derecruitment.[52]

For these parties and for each period, mean values of the individual indicator variables have been computed and ordered in 14 matrices: this set of matrices is the basis for the further analysis.

In accordance with the structure of the model, it should be asked: to what extent do the signs of the growth rates correspond with the predictions made by the model of the closing legislature? An answer

[51] The election periods from 1849 to 1852 and 1968 and later were excluded due to their atypical character, being the first and the last in the series.

[52] The classification of members according to party is a very difficult task to cope with in the nineteenth century. I have decided to classify non-socialist members in two main groups, Liberals and Conservatives, i.e., abstain from differentiation between the many and ever-changing factions. For further documentation and discussion, see Pedersen, *Political Development and Elite Transformation*. Due to these difficulties it was decided to skip indicator IV in the analysis because it is too hazardous to try to estimate the total number of seats belonging to the various factions.

TABLE 2–3. A SHORT LEGEND OF THE PERIODIZATION USED IN THE ANALYSIS

Period	Characterization of Party System	No. of Newcomers	No. of Leavers
1852–1870	Parliamentary factions tend to crystallize in a "left" and a "right" in the Folketing. No significant organizational activity in the country.	346	317
1870–1901	Constitutional conflict creates polarization in the Folketing. Party organizations develop in the country in the 1880s. Social Democrats gain representation 1884.	247	237
1901–1920	Modern party system comes into existence when Radical Liberal Party is founded 1905, and when Liberals and Conservatives are reorganized some years later. National interest organizations emerge.	239	205
1920–1945	Parties develop youth—and other auxiliary organizations. The introduction of P.R. 1920 tends to change the representational role.	189	204
1945–1968	The era of the mature party system. Towards the end of the period a reshuffle of the party system in the Folketing, when new small parties emerge.	292	277

is given in Table 2–4 (a) from which it can be seen that the fit with the model is far from perfect; however, for some of the variables, we find that the variations in the parties over time correspond fairly well with the predictions. The figures indicate that the increasing permeability and security of tenure, which were described in a previous section, are to some extent a result of parallel processes of closing in the parties. As the fit with the closing model is far from perfect for the legislature as a whole, it seems useful to ask: to what extent do the signs of the growth rates for the parties correspond with that found for the legislature? From Table 2–4 (a) it is seen that the fit with this model of uniform change in the parties is slightly better.

Until now only the signs of the growth rates have been compared. When we next look at the magnitudes of these growth rates, by analyzing the normalized average growth rates in the parties, shown in Table 2–4 (b), we begin to get a more differentiated picture. In the Social Democratic Party the pre-election career has actually become somewhat less demanding over time: candidates have had to run fewer

TABLE 2-4. COMPARISON OF EMPIRICAL DATA WITH THE MODEL OF THE CLOSING LEGISLATURE AND THE MODEL OF UNIFORM PARTY CHANGE

Indicator		Permeability					VI	Volatility			Continuity			Security of Tenure		
		I	II	III	IV	V		VII	VIII	IX	X	XI	XII	XIII	XIV	XV
Comparison of predicted and observed directions of change [a]	Fit with closing model / Fit with mdel of uniform change { standardized mean	69	62	69	62	69	—	67	58	42	58	58	45	75	100	67
	standardized mean	69	62	69	77	69	—	67	92	58	58	75	45	75	83	67
	simple mean	69	62	69	77	69	—	67	92	75	58	75	73	75	100	83
Index of relative growth [b]	Social Democrats	÷4	÷5	3	3	3	—	14	2	÷5	2	÷3	0	3	32	17
	Radical Liberals	39	13	3	÷5	3	—	31	13	0	3	÷10	÷9	8	88	37
	Liberals	13	3	10	5	2	—	15	4	1	÷1	0	÷3	4	32	15
	Conservatives	9	3	17	12	1	—	17	10	6	2	1	11	4	32	24
Coefficients of variability [c]	1852–1870	7	0	14	14	2	—	21	22	18	6	0	13	2	42	10
	1870–1901	20	1	56	28	8	—	13	10	6	5	5	6	1	11	16
	1901–1920	17	2	29	19	2	—	34	21	15	8	12	32	4	47	68
	1920–1945	23	8	17	10	3	—	16	8	5	6	9	20	2	32	43
	1945–1968	31	18	19	11	3	—	10	6	3	7	8	27	3	23	16

[a] The numbers in the table are the relative numbers of correctly predicted signs of slopes (growth rates), added up over parties and period. For indicators i through v the number of predictions was 13; for the remaining it was 12, and in the case of indicator XII only 11. The two models of uniform party change are based on the simple mean, and the mean standardized for difference in the size of parties.

[b] The index of relative growth is computed as the average growth rate for the party while represented, taken as a percentage of the grand mean for the indicator under inspection.

[c] The coefficient of variability is the standard deviation around the standardized mean, taken as a percentage of that mean.

times and in fewer constituencies in order to win elections. With regard to other variables the average growth rates in the largest party tend to be smaller than in the other parties, indicating that the pattern of personal circulation in the Social Democratic Party has been relatively stable over time. In contrast, the youngest and the smallest of the parties, the Radical Liberals did until 1968 tend to show a marked trend toward closing. Its candidates, on an average, had to run several times in order to get elected—in the period after the Second World War no less than four times. On the other hand, they did not have as extensive a record in previous political activity as, for example, the Social Democrats. Their legislative careers tended to become longer and more stable than that of representatives in the other parties. Finally, the security of tenure of the Radical group tended to grow over time: at the end of the period under inspection the typical member of the group ended his career voluntarily at a relatively old age. These two parties represent the extremes. The two other parties, the Liberals and the Conservatives, whose history can be traced farther back in time, have had a remarkably stable pattern of personal circulation in this century; they tended to close with regard to permeability, volatility, and security of tenure in the nineteenth century, especially between the first two periods, but, since then, the changes in the patterns have been relatively insignificant.

We have now seen that the fit with the model of the closing legislature is fairly good on most counts, but the fit with the model of uniform changes in the parties is somewhat better. On the other hand, the four parties do differ with regard to their patterns of personal circulation over time. The most significant finding in this respect is that the parties differ with regard to two aspects of permeability, the pattern of pre-election nomination careers, and the pattern of pre-election activity in organizations and local politics. The two parties that differ most with regard to permeability, volatility, and security of tenure are those which are the youngest of the four and which in the twentieth century have differed most in size and in direction of growth. Finally, in accordance with the structure of the model it should be asked: what is the amount of deviation from the model of uniform change, and has the amount of deviation changed over time, becoming larger or smaller? By calculating the standardized mean of the variables for each period and by computing the coefficient of variability with regard to this mean, as shown in Table 2–4 (c), we may obtain a deviation measure that is roughly comparable over the variables as well as over time.

The picture emerging is in accordance with the findings already reported in the sense that it confirms that party-specific factors are partly

99

responsible for the change over time for the personal circulation in the legislature as a whole. However, some new information is added. The first additional finding is that the slightly changing age structure of the legislature is due to a slight and uniform change of the age structures of all of the parties. Second, while the parties have tended to differ more and more with regard to the pre-election nomination career of their members, for the remaining variables we find a slight tendency toward convergence during this century, indicating that the parties have differed widely back in time, especially at the time when the Social Democrats and the Radical Liberals entered the scene, but that they have tended to become more alike with regard to such properties as pre-election political activity, volatility, and security of tenure.

VII
CONCLUSIONS

THIS test of various models has demonstrated that the changing patterns of personal circulation in the Danish Folketing cannot be accounted for entirely at the level of the legislature itself. Although there is a certain parallelism in development, each party has its own pattern of personal circulation, and these patterns apparently are related to size, to changes in size, and to other specific and changing properties of the parties.

This is neither a precise nor definitive conclusion. It only leads to the next set of questions, namely to what extent the hypotheses put forward in section V are relevant for an understanding of the phenomenon of personal circulation. The design used in this chapter has stressed the properties of the legislature, how the legislature has changed over time with regard to its renewal processes. To understand the relationship between changes in the party system and changes in personal circulation in the parties will require analysis at the level of the parties and at the level of the individual legislator, as well as empirical research involving both successful and unsuccessful candidates. This task is beyond the scope of this chapter, but the findings here suggest that the concepts of permeability, volatility, continuity, and security of tenure, however useful they are for descriptive purposes, are of limited value, because they are defined at the level of the legislature.

It would be extremely useful for an understanding of political recruitment and derecruitment patterns to pursue these questions about the causes of the closing of the legislature. We, nevertheless, should not forget that the findings implicitly have raised other, equally if not more important, questions pertaining to the consequences of this emergent phenomenon, questions which have not been dealt with satisfactorily as yet in the literature, even though they were raised by Pareto some years ago.

We have seen that the general trend in the personal circulation variables, both at the level of the legislature and at the level of most of the parties, is one of growing institutionalization—as the tendency of closing has been named by at least some students of legislative behavior and political development. Although, as mentioned earlier, there is no agreement about how to define the concept of political institutionalization, it is always treated as a positive, a valuable phenomenon, as a process "by which organizations and procedures acquire value and stability," to quote a leading proponent of this view.[53]

This study of the renewal process in the Danish Folketing, a legislature which presumably does not differ fundamentally from other European parliaments, has indicated that the legislature has tended to become more and more institutionalized in the sense that it has become more differentiated from its environment. The tendency toward closing reminds one very much of Polsby's similar finding for the United States House of Representatives.

This development is paradoxical because these boundaries have emerged at the same time when the formal rights to participate in the elections and the nominations have been extended to more and more citizens, and when political activity in the electorate has widened and become more extensive. Furthermore, the trend toward institutionalization is paralleled by a socio-economic transformation of the Danish parliament from being dominated by a narrow-based, traditional upper class toward becoming more "representative," even if it is still far from being a true mirror of the electorate.[54] When the elite was relatively open, its membership constituted a closed social circle; as the dominance of the social elite was broken, its membership at the same time tended to become more of a closed circle in another sense. If "the very fact of having been elected or selected—having been elevated through some mechanism of choice from one position into another—makes the 'chosen' fundamentally different from their choosers," [55] it is, nevertheless, true that one type of difference has been substituted for another. For those whose ideal is to minimize the distance between elector and elected in every respect it cannot be very comforting to find that socioeconomic equalization apparently goes hand in hand with institutionalization.

[53] Huntington, *Political Order*, p. 12. See also Polsby, "Institutionalization," p. 144.

[54] See Pedersen, *Political Development and Elite Transformation*.

[55] Eulau, *Micro-Macro Political Analysis*, p. 101.

101

3

Measurement of Attitude Changes among the Members of the French Chamber of Deputies, 1882–1884

ANTOINE PROST AND CHRISTIAN ROSENZVEIG

CHANGES in political attitudes are a well-known phenomenon. It has often been said that in France a deputy begins his political career at the extreme left, to end on the right. A traditional joke, which has to be told with the particular intonation of the South to get its specific flavor, sums up the people's feeling in this case. A father advises his son at the eve of an election: "Mon petit, quand tu choisis un député, prends-le bien rouge, parce qu'ensuite ils déteignent!" This could be translated: "Sonny, when choosing a deputy, do take the most red because he will lose his color!"

It is easy to understand how this view arose. The French political system in the nineteenth century was too centralized to allow candidates to become popular leaders by assuming local responsibilities and by proving themselves competent administrators as mayors of important cities. On the contrary, in an age when collective leisure was not organized and when political meetings provided entertainment, it was more natural and more usual to attempt to keep the constituents' favor or to gain their votes by a sparkling speech during the campaign or through the support of a regularly read local newspaper. Most French deputies entered the Chamber without any personal experience of public responsibilities. Their political attitudes often depended upon theories that might be generous, even revolutionary, but were also unrealistic. In the course of time elected deputies began to move toward more pragmatic positions, moderate or conservative. Such a process may well have constituted the basis for the observation that deputies slide toward the right.

This individual movement toward the right was balanced by a collective movement of the whole Chamber toward the left. From 1871 to 1914, each newly elected Chamber seems more left-oriented than the preceding one. Moderate Republicans like Dufaure and J. Simon were overtaken by progressives like J. Ferry, then Gambetta; at the beginning of the twentieth century, Radicals such as Combes came to office, and the legislative elections of 1910 and 1914 pushed ahead the members of Jaures's Socialist party. When the First World War began, a Socialist deputy, Viviani, was the president of the cabinet. From Dufaure to Viviani, undoubtedly, French politics was slipping toward the left.

This collective movement depended upon the behavior of the electoral body. Radical deputies superseded moderate Republicans, and later, Socialists superseded Radicals because they won over public opinion. But how did public opinion choose between several Republican candidates? By what process was the individual deputy who had slid too far to the right eliminated? Here lies the decisive difficulty that prevents us from gaining a true comprehension of French political behavior during the Third Republic. Probably some deputies realized they were no longer answering the wishes of public opinion and sought a more secure position; many of them became senators, for the electoral body that chose the senators was composed of delegates of community councils, especially of rural mayors, whose political feelings were quite moderate. Other deputies ended their careers because they were defeated in elections by newcomers who were more oriented toward the left. In both cases individual movements toward the right were accompanied by a movement of the legislative body as a whole toward the left; but it is impossible, in the present condition of our historical knowledge, to obtain a more precise view of these phenomena, however fundamental their importance is for an effective comprehension of French politics.

These are the kinds of questions with which this research is concerned. This chapter is only a preliminary attempt to define a method for measuring the attitude changes of individual deputies. Of course, the solution of the general problem that has been stated here first depends on our ability to measure individual slidings precisely.

I

PRELIMINARY CONSIDERATIONS ABOUT THE METHOD
AND THE SUBJECT

To measure individual changes of attitude it is necessary to compare the successive positions, over a period of time, of each deputy in the political spectrum of the whole Chamber. To do this, we must obtain sensitive and reliable indicators of political attitudes. Such indicators could be found in various kinds of data.[1] The best, the most objective,

---

[1] For example, the electoral proclamations of deputies. These have been discussed in Antoine Prost, *Vocabulaire des proclamations électorales de 1881, 1885, et 1889* (Paris: Presses Universitaires de France, 1974). Methods derived from statistical lexicography can be quite efficient in analyzing such data.

and the most practicable undoubtedly are the deputies' public votes. Our task is to analyze roll calls with methods that will measure precisely what the political attitude of each deputy was.

Most methods of roll-call analysis are useless for this purpose. Many deal principally with the problem of cohesion within the parties; by such devices as Guttman scales or cluster analysis they try to assign to each deputy his own place among other deputies of the same party. Each individual is assigned as many positions as there are issues analyzed, since there is a specific attitude scale for each issue.[2] This kind of roll-call study does not fit our purpose for the following reasons.

It is impossible to accept a roll-call study in the frame of actual partisan divisions without first proving that parties are relevant divisions of the whole Chamber. The French Chamber of Deputies during the first period of the Republic, however, appears like a mere collection of individuals. Only later did the political parties come into the political world, for example, the Radical Party in 1901 and the Socialist Section Française de l'Internationale Ouvrière in 1905. Although parliamentary groups existed in the 1880s, their cohesion was weak, and they constituted no more than an administrative facility, without any personal obligation or duty, or any coherent structure. Parties are not a sound basis for a study of the roll calls of this period.

Even if the party division of the whole Chamber were in accordance with political reality, as was the case during the Fourth Republic, a roll-call study based on parties would be inadequate to measure individual attitude change. Our question is the slidings of deputies, their "glissements," from one portion of the Chamber to another. It is difficult to base such an analysis upon party affiliations since this behavior involved the crossing of party lines.

Studying political differences on various issues one after another would give us far too diverse a view of individual attitudes to allow a general and synthetic assessment of each deputy's position within the whole Chamber. A deputy could vote with the center on one question and with the left on another. Positions were not held consistently with regard to the budget, the colonial wars, or the issue of clericalism. But we need a general estimate. Dividing the Chamber by attitudes on issues would make it as impossible to answer our question as would

[2] Among the outstanding roll-call studies of this kind, the one to which we are the most indebted is Duncan MacRae, Jr., *Parliament, Parties and Society in France, 1946–1958* (London: Macmillan & Co., 1967). But the Fourth Republic, with which Duncan MacRae dealt, was different from the Third, which we are considering here. Parties existed during the Fourth, and their influence was strengthened by the electoral system.

accepting the division of the Chamber into closed parliamentary groups.

These remarks define what the adequate method is not. They, furthermore, suggest the possibility of an alternative method that would take into account the attitudes of all deputies on each issue and would also give a more complete view of the whole Chamber. Such a method might be described as follows.

To avoid bias in selection we included in the study, for each of the three years under consideration, *every* roll-call vote or "scrutin public"[3] from the beginning of the autumn parliamentary session, up to the number of sixty.[4] In other words, we took the first sixty roll calls for each session. The number of roll calls that could be analyzed was limited by material conditions such as the computer's capacity and the budget of the research. Our procedure was designed to ensure that the analysis would not be biased by the weight of a single issue put to the vote many times. Fortunately, the autumn parliamentary session was devoted to the budget, which was discussed ministry by ministry. This gave the deputies an opportunity for a general review of the main political problems. As a result, each of our three samples of sixty roll calls for the years 1882, 1883, and 1884 included several votes upon each important issue of the period.[5]

[3] Each deputy's vote in a "scrutin public" is published at the end of that day's parliamentary debates by the *Journal officiel*. For each "scrutin public" the *Journal officiel* publishes four alphabetical lists of the deputies who, respectively, voted yea, voted nay, abstained, or were absent.

[4] The roll calls analyzed here are those made during the following periods: from November 11 to December 22, 1882; from October 25 to December 15, 1883; and from November 10 to December 16, 1884. These are relatively short periods: about two months. But it is not the usual parliamentary rhythm. This rapid pace is characteristic only of budget discussions. For other parts of the legislative session it is necessary to go through no less than four or five months of discussions to find sixty roll calls.

[5] Some question may be raised about how far it is legitimate to draw inferences from a comparison of the first sixty votes of each year with the first sixty votes of each of the other years. It could be argued that a deputy might vote more closely with Clemenceau in the first sixty roll calls of 1882 than in the first sixty roll calls of 1883, not because he had moved toward the center, but simply because the issues voted on were different. It is certainly possible that, if the votes selected for each year dealt with different subjects and did not reflect the principal political questions of the day, the results of the analysis might be biased. This danger, however, is largely obviated in this project because, in the 1880s, the discussion of the budget by the deputies, which is reflected in the early roll calls, amounted to a kind of general survey of political issues. The situation then was quite different from that in, for example, the legislature from 1936 to 1940, when the budgetary discussion had little political significance, and different issues were discussed separately over a much longer period. An additional safeguard is that the nature of the investigation has permitted the authors to check on this point. Factor analysis produces not only the kinds of configurations of deputies that are illustrated in Figures 3–1, 3–2, and 3–3 but also similar configurations of roll calls. From the

105

Each deputy was considered as an individual without regard to his party affiliation, and all the deputies were included in the study, except those leaving the Chamber before the end or entering it after the beginning of the period. It was necessary to compare the attitude of each deputy to that of all his colleagues in order to have a precise estimate of his own position, and it would have been useless or even dangerous to have in mind party affiliations during the comparison. Political labels are the output of the research, not the input.

The application of these two principles leads to the analysis of a tremendous number of individual votes, nearly 30,000 each year. Without mathematical devices especially adapted to such material it would be virtually impossible to produce any result. The specific method used here is that of Professor Benzécri's analysis of correspondences.[6] It is a kind of factor analysis in principal components. Its distinguishing feature is that it starts from a matrix of data, and not from a matrix of correlations, so that the factors extracted are meaningful both for the rows and for the columns. The very name of "correspondences" identifies this feature: the two sets, that of the rows and that of the columns, correspond to one another according to the same factors, and the factors extracted from the matrix take an algebraic value at the same time for each deputy and for each roll-call vote. The two sets have the same center of gravity and the same variance. Thus, if many deputies regularly voted the same way, each factor would take the same value for these deputies and for these votes, so that, as a result, the deputies would be represented at the same place on a factor axis. It is essential to note this feature of the analysis of correspondences, because it allows us to infer the meaning of the votes directly from the deputies who cast them, or conversely, to infer the deputies' political color directly from the meaning of the votes they cast.

A second special feature of the analysis of correspondences also should be pointed out because, in the present study, it may be misleading. As in every factor analysis, the factors are extracted succes-

---

latter, which have been used, though it is not necessary to present them here, it is easy to find out on what issue or issues the leftist or rightist sliding of a given deputy depended. A more elaborate version of the program of factor analysis has given us the mathematical contribution of each roll call to each of the first factors and has enabled us to ascertain exactly to what extent the political configuration was determined by a particular vote on a particular issue.

[6] Jean-Paul Benzécri, *L'Analyse de Données:* tome 1, *La Taxonomie;* tome 2, *L'Analyse de Correspondances* (Paris: Dunod, 1973). Professor Benzécri presented a shorter, general survey of the method in "Statistical Analysis as a Tool to Make Patterns Emerge from Data," in Satoshi Watanabe, ed., *Proceedings of the 1968 Honolulu Conference on Pattern Recognition* (New York: Academic Press, Inc., 1969), pp. 35–74.

sively, and their importance is descending. The first factor sums up the greatest possible part of the total variance of the matrix, the second, the greatest possible part of the remaining variance, and so on. Factor axes are mathematical results that express the latent pattern of the data without any previous hypothesis. They are not significant by themselves, any more than a regression line would be. But the way in which the data are distributed along the factor axes is meaningful and gives a meaning to the axes themselves. Hence it is possible to designate the first factor axis of 1882 as the "left-right" axis and the second as the "moderate-extremist" axis. But one should not forget that these axes are the result of a mathematical construction whose interpretation is the researcher's responsibility.

Here lies a critical point. In a previous study,[7] we tried to explain the political configuration of the Chamber from 1881 to 1885, according to the roll calls. The first two factor axes determined a plane upon which it was possible to represent the position of each deputy and of each roll call. The deputies' places were determined by their votes, and a precise study of the meaning of the votes helped to explain the whole configuration of the Chamber. The main finding of the earlier study was to show an inversion of the first two factors in the middle of the period. The meaning of the first factor was not the same in 1882 and 1883: in 1882 it was a "left-right" dimension, in 1883 a "moderate-extremist" one. In other words, the 1882 Chamber was structured principally by the opposition between the left and the right; the 1883 Chamber had a different major dimension: the struggle for or against Ferry's cabinet.

That article was devoted to the question of the hierarchy of the first two factors and was an attempt to determine the meaning of the first factor in each of the two configurations. This chapter deals with another question. Although an inversion of the first two factors occurred between 1882 and 1883, these two factors actually remained highly correlated with one another throughout the entire period. The issues discussed in the Chamber were different, and the factor analysis produced different parliamentary configurations, but these were still closely related. The 1883 configuration is not the same as that of 1882, but a strong coefficient of correlation between them exists, greater than .92 for the first two factors. Such a high coefficient means that the relative place of individual deputies in a changing configuration remains nearly

[7] Antoine Prost and Christian Rosenzveig, "La Chambre des députés (1881–1885). Analyse factorielle des scrutins," *Revue française de science politique* 21 (1971): 5–50. This chapter is based on roll calls used in that article, but they have now been differently coded.

107

the same. It is an "anamorphosis." We are now interested in dealing with the permanent pattern within the successive distorted figures, in order to find out how permanent it was and how much the position of each deputy changed.

For this purpose, we can neglect the inversion of the factors and consider only the same dimensions of the Chamber. That is why, in all the figures in this chapter, the meaning of the axes remains the same: the horizontal axis indicates the "left-right" dimension, and the vertical axis, the "moderate-extremist" dimension, irrespective of correspondence with the mathematical "first" or "second" factor.

The treatment of roll-call data by this kind of factor analysis opens up a new way of weighting the yeas, the nays, and the abstentions. The results of the analysis of correspondences are better if the various items of the input are of equal weight. For instance, the application of this analysis to a matrix, each row of which amounts to the same total sum gives better results than could be obtained from a matrix of which every row has a different weight. Hence it is desirable to code roll-call data in a way that will minimize the difference of weight between the deputies. In our earlier research we divided each roll-call vote into its two major alternatives, and we had two columns for each vote: the yeas and the nays. A yea vote was coded 1 in the first column, and 0 in the second, and vice versa, so that each roll call gave one point to each deputy. An abstention had to be coded 0.5 in both columns to make the same total as a yea or a nay vote.

Such a way of coding the abstentions departs from the usual method, which was not practical for that study. The regulations of the French Chamber of Deputies prescribed a roll-call vote for every financial decision, even the less important ones. For instance, to transfer a credit from one line of the budget to another required a "scrutin public" in which most deputies were not interested. This rule resulted in some routine roll-call votes where there were many yeas and an important proportion of abstentions, but no nays. In such circumstances, the reason for the abstentions was probably mere indifference, though in some cases an abstention might have represented a kind of half-hearted no. Since we consider *all* the roll calls until we have sixty each fall session, it is impossible to exclude these awkward votes. Putting the abstentions together with the yeas or nays would mean risking the introduction of a bias. These were the reasons for the adoption of the method used in the earlier study.

Though this way of coding the abstentions was logical, it led to new difficulties. Factor analysis of data thus coded gave a configuration where the most frequently abstaining deputies were on the edges, and sometimes far from the core of the scatter diagram, depending upon the number of votes they did not cast. In order to have a tighter diagram, it seemed better to adopt a new way of coding the abstentions by having three positions for each roll-call vote and then three columns representing, respectively, the yeas, the nays, and the abstentions. Such a device makes the data heavier, for the data matrix has 180 columns instead of 120, for 481 rows; but it makes the result clearer. The political configurations below (see Figures 3–1, 3–2, and 3–3) were obtained in this way, and they differ substantially from those we published earlier.

In order to pursue this analysis, it is necessary to compare successive configurations of the whole Chamber. Fortunately, it is possible to link each configuration to the next by a regression equation of a linear form.[8] Each factor of one configuration could be calculated from the first two factors of the preceding or following year. If F_1 and F_2 are the first and the second factors given by the analysis of the set of roll calls of one year, for instance $F_1(83)$, the first factor of the 1883 roll call analysis, it is possible to find the regression equations that link it to the first two factors of 1882 as follows: [9]

$$F_1(83) = .3463\ F_1(82) + 1.1333\ F_2(82), \text{ with a correlation} = .9206$$
and
$$F_2(83) = .7656\ F_1(82) - .3754\ F_2(82), \text{ with a correlation} = .9364.$$

The calculation of the above equations makes it possible to elaborate a hypothetical 1883 configuration, the one which would have been observed if the correlation between the two years had been perfect (see Figure 3–4). The two configurations, the 1883 real one and that deduced from the data for 1882, have the same scale and the same orientation, and consequently can be compared.

An example may make this calculation clearer. Let three deputies, A, B, and C, have as coordinates upon the first factor axis in 1882, a1, b1, and c1, these numbers being algebraic numbers, and $\alpha1$, $\beta1$, and $\gamma1$ as coordinates upon the second factor axis. It is possible to represent

---

[8] A more sophisticated regression equation has been calculated. It gives each of the first five factors in relation to the five of the next configuration. It is a formidable calculation, to obtain only a slightly better correlation.

[9] The regression coefficients between $F_1(83)$ and $F_2(82)$, on the one hand, and between $F_2(83)$ and $F_1(82)$, on the other hand, indicate clearly that the two factors have been inverted. To obtain directly superimposable diagrams, we had to take into account this inversion by rotating the axes by 90 degrees. This is the reason for the apparent difference between the diagrams published here and those published in the *Revue française de science politique*.

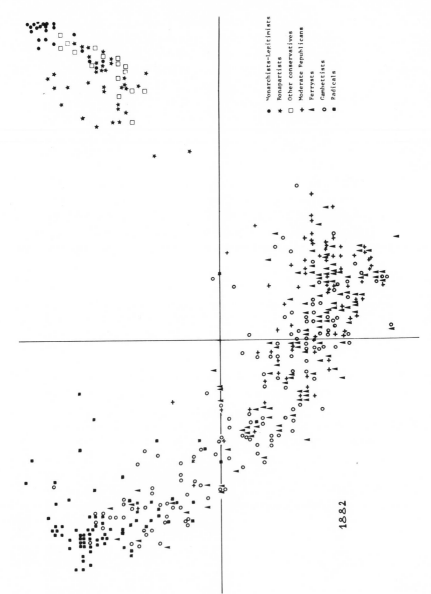

Legend (within figure):

- ● Monarchists-Legitimists
- ★ Bonapartists
- □ Other conservatives
- + Moderate Republicans
- ◄ Ferrysts
- ○ Gambettists
- ■ Radicals

1882

Figure 3–1.

Configuration of the French Chamber of Deputies Nov.–Dec. 1882

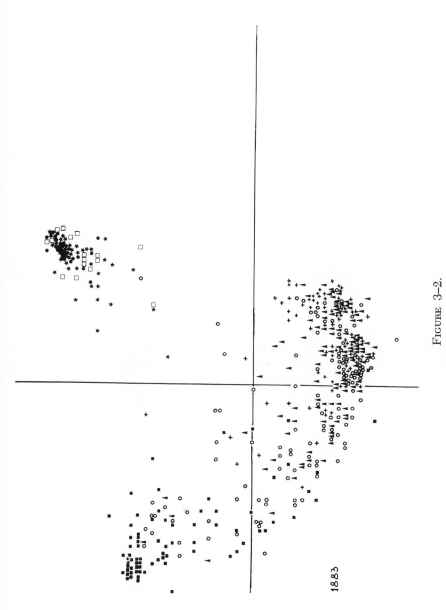

1883

Figure 3–2.

Configuration of the French Chamber of Deputies Nov.–Dec. 1883

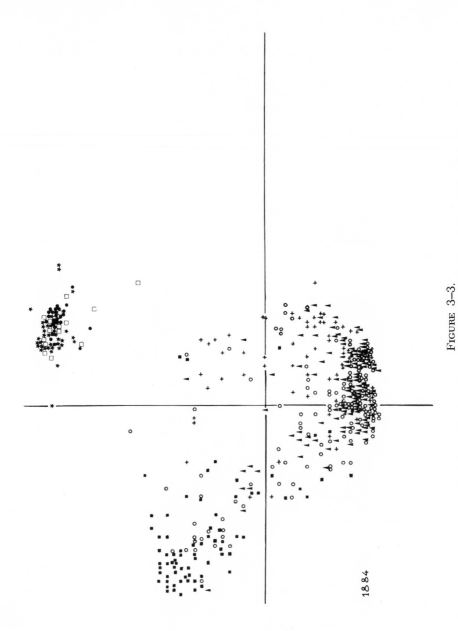

1884

FIGURE 3-3.

Configuration of the French Chamber of Deputies Nov.–Dec. 1884

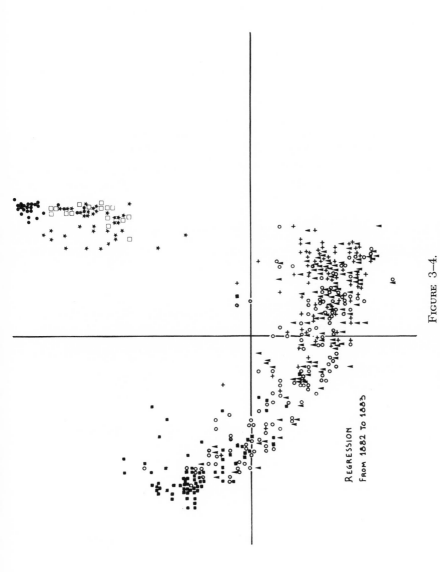

REGRESSION
FROM 1882 TO 1883

FIGURE 3–4.

Configuration of the French Chamber of Deputies Regression from 1882 to 1883

the position of these three deputies in 1882 by three points, A1, B1, and C1, in the plane defined by the two factor axes. Let us draw this figure, Figure 3–5, which is similar in logical structure to Figures 3–1, 3–2, and 3–3.

Given the regression equations and some other statistical data like the norm of each factor, we calculate the 1883 coordinates of A, B, and C, regressed from their 1882 coordinates, the relative position of these three points supposedly remaining the same. Let a1′, b1′, and c1′ be the new coordinates upon the left-right axis, and $\alpha 1'$, $\beta 1'$, $\gamma 1'$, upon the moderate-extremist axis. We can draw a new figure, Figure 3–6, which is similar to Figure 3–4.

The calculation of the new regressed coordinates has been made under conditions that allow us to compare them with the coordinates given by the factor analysis of the 1883 data. Let A2, B2, and C2 be the three points representing the real 1883 position of our three deputies. Without any further elaboration, it is possible to add them to Figure 3–6: we get Figure 3–7 easily.

Looking at Figure 3–7, one could observe that our three deputies moved in opposite directions and that their slidings were not equally extensive. It is possible to represent these movements. The coordinates of A in 1883, as given by the factor analysis of the 1883 data, are a2 and $\alpha 2$. According to the regression from his 1882 coordinates, A would have had a1′ and $\alpha 1'$ as coordinates in 1883, if he had remained exactly at the same place. The differences a2−a1′ and $\alpha 2−\alpha 1'$ are easy

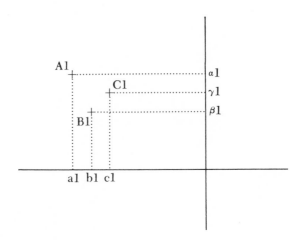

FIGURE 3–5.

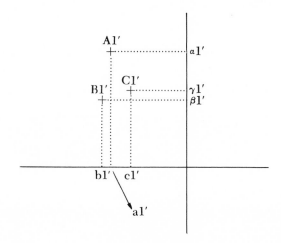

FIGURE 3–6.

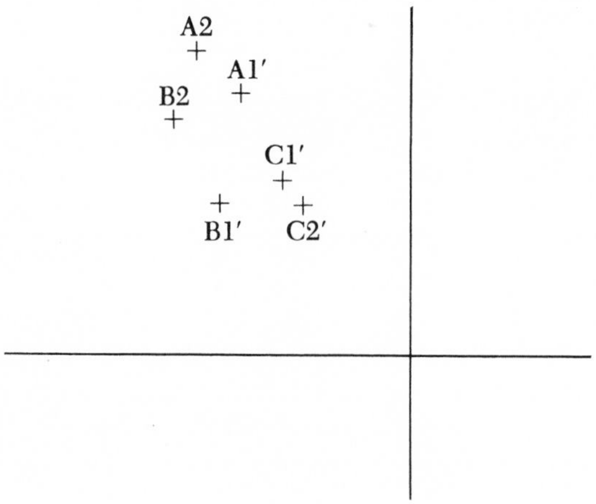

A2
+
          A1′
          +
B2
+
            C1′
            +
      +   +
    B1′   C2′

FIGURE 3–7.

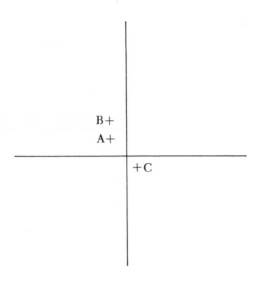

FIGURE 3–8.

to calculate: the results are new coordinates, for instance $x = a2 - a1'$, and $y = \alpha2 - \alpha1'$, which it is possible to represent with a new figure, like Figure 3–8. This figure is a representation of the individual movements of A, B, and C, from 1882 to 1883. Figures 3–9, 3–10, and 3–11 have been elaborated by a method like that one.

Of course, the regression from 1882 to 1883 gives a diagram rather different from the original one (cf. Figure 3–4 and Figure 3–1). But the relative position of the points inside the diagram has been entirely preserved. Hence, each deputy in the diagram of regression from 1882 to 1883 occupies the very place he would have had in 1883 if he had maintained exactly the same political attitude. By simply superimposing one of these diagrams upon the other, it is possible to find out how far and in what direction each deputy moved. An arrow drawn from the 1882 regressed position to the 1883 observed one indicates each deputy's sliding. The set of all the individual arrows gives an adequate representation of the changes that occurred within the whole Chamber. It should be pointed out, however, that the changes that are expressed by such a device are only relative changes. This information does not reveal whether the Chamber as a whole moved further to the left or to the right. By definition, its center of gravity remains the same, and the total of individual movements is zero, so that each movement in one direction is exactly canceled by movements in the opposite direction. By this method it is impossible for all arrows to be pointed in the same direction. Arrow diagrams are constructed so that they represent only the relative movements of the deputies compared to one another, the Chamber as a whole supposedly being entirely stable.

A further elaboration of the method allows us to compare not only two successive configurations but three or more. We already have the regression from 1882 to 1883. We can calculate a regression, mathematically similar, though chronologically inverted, from 1884 to 1883.[10] Upon the 1883 configuration, which is used as a common framework, we can superimpose the two regressed configurations: that from 1882 and that from 1884, so that the change of attitude of each deputy during these three successive years eventually emerges. By means of some additional and more sophisticated work,[11] it would be possible to push the comparison beyond this three-year period. But this first attempt, limited to three successive configurations, requires some attention if one wants to generalize the method.

II

MEASUREMENT AND DIRECTION OF THE
DEPUTIES' CHANGE OF ATTITUDE

ONE of the main findings is the evidence that political labels were meaningless in this period of French history. There was only one relevant parting line in the Chamber, that which divided the Anti-Republican right from the Republican majority. Within the right wing, Bona-

[10] The diagram resulting from this regression has not been published here. The regression equations from 1884 to 1883 are as follows:

$F_1(83) = .9481 \, F_1(84) - .2234 \, F_2(84)$, with a correlation $= .9439$
$F_1(83) = .1186 \, F_1(84) + 1.2877 \, F_2(84)$, with a correlation $= .9112$

One must keep in mind that the corresponding configuration has to be rotated, as the 1883 configuration has been, in order to be superimposed upon the others.

[11] To make a comparison between 1881 and 1883, it is necessary first to construct the 1882 configuration regressed from 1881, and then to construct the 1883 configuration regressed from that configuration of 1882 already constructed by regression. Let C_{83} be the original 1883 configuration, and C_{82} the original 1882 configuration. $C_{83}(C_{82})$ will be the configuration regressed from 1882 to 1883. The present paper deals with the three configurations: C_{83}; $C_{83}(C_{82})$; and $C_{83}(C_{84})$. One could add: $C_{83}(C_{82}(C_{81}))$ and so on. . . Of course, the correlation between C_{83} $(C_{82}(C_{81}))$ and C_{83} is not as good as between C_{83} and $C_{83}(C_{82})$, so that the research worker would have to decide whether the work was worth doing. In the present case, the question did not arise, for the fall session of 1881 was very difficult to compare with the next ones because of the senatorial election of January 1882 which introduced many deputies into the Senate, and caused the election of many new deputies.

117

partists and Monarchists were distinct, but there was no clear frontier that separated them. Within the Republican party, the Radicals were generally to the left of the Gambettists, and the latter to the left of Ferry's supporters. But this was only a general disposition to which there were many individual exceptions.

Hence, it is not surprising that the analysis of individual attitude change within each party does not lead to any clear conclusion, but merely identifies those deputies who changed most. Figures 3–9, 3–10, and 3–11 show the individual sliding of each deputy, one party after the other.

Each deputy is supposed to have been placed at the origin of the diagram so that all the deputies are supposedly starting from the same place, i.e., the crossing of the two axes. For each deputy, the difference between his coordinates of 1884 and 1882, as calculated in the manner described, allows us to represent his 1884 position by a point in Figures 3–9, 3–10 and 3–11. As the meaning of the axes remains the same, Figures 3–9, 3–10 and 3–11 are easily readable. A deputy represented by a point near the right end of the horizontal axis has slid very far toward the right. When he is represented by a point near the lower part of the vertical axis, he has moved toward the moderate center, and so on. Figures 3–9, 3–10 and 3–11 clearly show that the right-wing deputies slid less far than the Republicans: their change of attitude was very limited. The deputies who moved the farthest were to be found among the Radicals, and the direction of their movement is quite clear: some of them slid toward the center, but most strengthened their leftward orientation. The Gambettists moved considerably and in both directions, but we have to keep in mind that their starting zone was very large. Ferry's majority seems more stable, except that some deputies abandoned it and slid toward the radical left.[12]

But was there a great change of attitude during these years? The question does matter. What is measurement, if it is not an attempt to distinguish between the quantitatively large and small? Comparing things to one another is not enough: we need a unit of measurement, in the case of the present study, a distance unit. Mathematically, it is easy to base a distance unit on statistical information. Unfortunately, the meaning of such a unit would be uncertain. It is better to employ

[12] The diagrams of Figures 3–9, 3–10, and 3–11 do not include deputies who were absent from the Chamber for more than 15 roll calls a year. The absent deputies are coded zero in all three columns coresponding to a roll call, so that their total weight is weakened. Positions given to an item by the analysis of correspondences are somewhat imprecise when the item represented has a light weight.

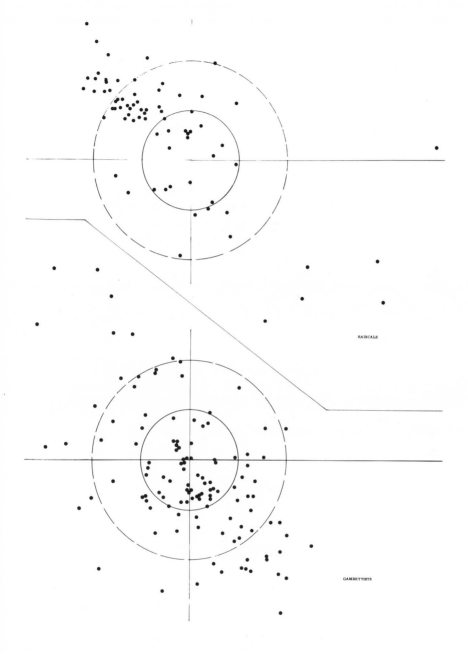

RADICALS

GAMBETTISTS

FIGURE 3–9.

Difference of Position 1882/1884 Radicals and Gambettists

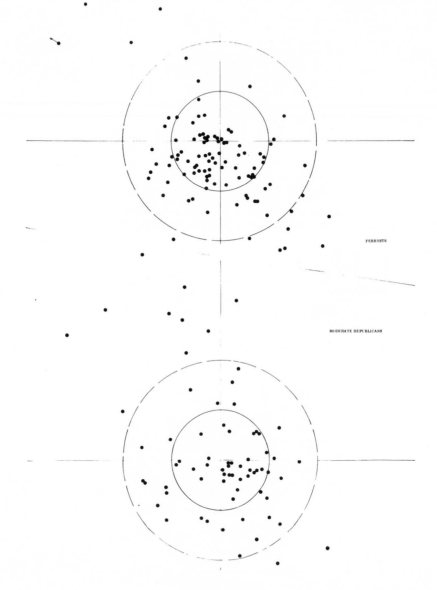

FERRYSTS

MODERATE REPUBLICANS

FIGURE 3–10.

Difference of Position 1882/1884 Ferryists and Moderate Republicans

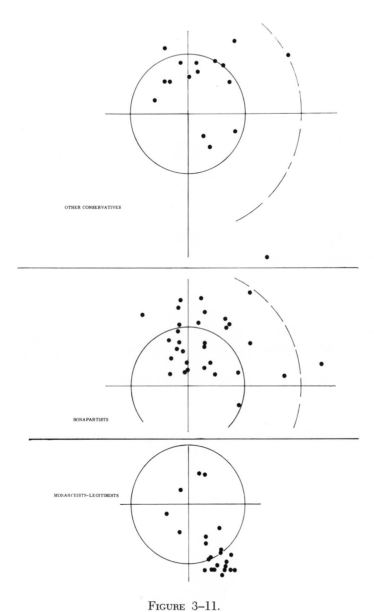

OTHER CONSERVATIVES

BONAPARTISTS

MONARCHISTS-LEGITIMISTS

FIGURE 3–11.

Difference of Position 1882/1884 Bonapartists, Monarchist-Legitimists, and
Other Conservatives

a distance unit that is also politically meaningful. It would have been possible to adopt the distance that separated pre-eminent deputies of the right and of the left, like Freppel and Lokroy, or De Mun and Clemenceau, but we finally decided to choose as our unit the distance between outstanding leaders of the Republican camp: one from the radical wing, Clemenceau, the other from the cabinet's majority, more precisely the head of the majority, Ferry, because the main finding of this paper is the opening of a gap between the two wings of the Republican camp.

Using the 1882 Ferry-Clemenceau distance as a unit, it is possible to measure the distance that each deputy covered between 1882 and 1884 and to build a histogram (see Figure 3–12). Its meaning can be described as follows. In the first column, we have 13.4 percent of the total number of the deputies: the movement of these deputies is less than

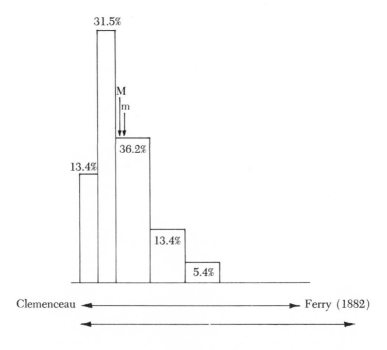

FIGURE 3–12.
Histogram of the Deputies' Absolute Movement 1882–1884

one-twelfth of the 1882 Ferry-Clemenceau distance. The second column contains 31.5 percent of the deputies: their movement is more than one-twelfth and less than one-sixth of the 1882 Ferry-Clemenceau distance, and so on.

This figure makes it possible to measure the importance of the attitude changes within the Chamber. Most of the deputies did not change very much. The mean change and the median one are nearly one-sixth of the 1882 Clemenceau-Ferry distance. Half of the deputies did not slide so far. Among those who slid farther, only 18.8 percent moved more than one-third of the initial Clemenceau-Ferry distance. Very few covered more than half that distance, but this is already an important change of attitude. As a conclusion, we can say that a large majority of the deputies remained in nearly the same position and that a minority slid more or less far from their initial places—some of them very far indeed.

It would be possible to use the information in Figures 3–9, 3–10, and 3–11 to elaborate various kinds of indices of attitude change for each parliamentary group. One could draw a movement histogram for each group and calculate an average change of attitude for each of them, as sophisticated statisticians sometimes do. From our point of view, such indices would be meaningless, the factor configuration being not a concrete thing, but only a mathematical representation of political relations. The reality of the configurations lies only in the relations they represent. Indices based upon the configurations probably would be misleading and confusing: a mathematical index is not a concrete one.

These measurements can, however, legitimately be used for more limited purposes. It is particularly illuminating to concentrate on the deputies who moved farthest, and to examine their original and their subsequent positions in the whole configuration.

Figure 3–13 shows what parts of the political spectrum were the more unstable. The framework of this figure is the same as that of Figure 3–4, but each deputy has been represented by a different symbol according to the importance of his movement as it is revealed in Figures 3–9, 3–10, and 3–11. Those who remained inside the inner circle in Figures 3–9, 3–10, and 3–11 and belonged to the first two classes in Figure 3–12 are said to be moving "less than the average." Those sliding beyond the outer circle in Figures 3–9, 3–10, and 3–11, and who constituted parts of the last two classes in Figure 3–12, are said to be moving "more than the average" and those between the two circles (or included in the mean class), "near the average."

What is rather surprising in Figure 3–12 is that many deputies of the

123

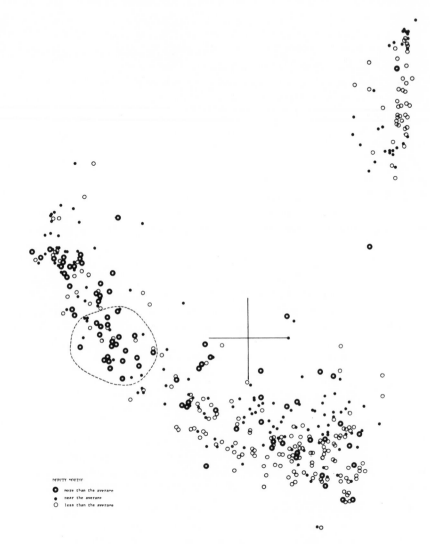

FIGURE 3–13.

Localization of the Deputies according to the Importance of their
Attitude Change 1882/1884

left wing slid quite far. From this point of view, the behavior of the two opposite wings of the Chamber seems very different. Since the beginning of the period, the right wing had been separated from the Republican camp by a large gap that nobody ever crossed in either direction. Consequently, this wing had no need to increase the distance that separated it from the center: its opposition was clearly marked from the start. The left wing had to choose its camp about 1883: was it better to support Ferry's government against the clerical right or to oppose it on account of the colonial issue or the municipal bill? To such a dilemma many deputies, especially Radical deputies, responded by a process of radicalization that drove them far from their initial position, however extreme it had been.

Different is the case of some deputies near Ferry, although they too went far enough. One might conjecture that they were disappointed supporters but, to establish this, further evidence would be needed and we would have to analyze each case.

It is impossible to do this at the present stage of research. We will, instead, center the analysis on the farthest-moving deputies. Those who have been identified as moving more than the average are too many (83) to be considered individually. But we can limit the analysis to those who moved the farthest of all.

Figure 3–14 shows the 31 deputies whose absolute movement was the greatest. Their slidings are represented by arrows, starting from their 1882 positions, which are marked by different symbols according to their official, but irrelevant, political labels. The extremity of the arrow marks a deputy's final position in 1884, and his place in 1883 is indicated by the angle in the line drawn from the 1882 to the 1884 position. In this figure, three prominent deputies have been identified: Clemenceau, the Radical leader; Ferry, the prime minister; and Ribot, one of the outstanding Moderate Republicans. The movement of these three political leaders furnishes a basis of comparison that clearly indicates the importance and the direction of the slidings of the farthest-moving deputies.

Clearly these slidings were extensive, and represented fundamental changes in political attitudes. A deputy like No. 219, who is Wilson, the son-in-law of the President of the Republic, literally slid from one wing of the Republican camp to the other. Probably his case was an extreme one; but all the deputies represented here had long slides. In these cases the change of attitude was not a mere adjustment caused by a new position on limited and minor issues; it was a major reorientation. Let us consider, for instance, some Radical deputies. No. 547, a deputy from a colonial constituency, and No. 500, a Radical represen-

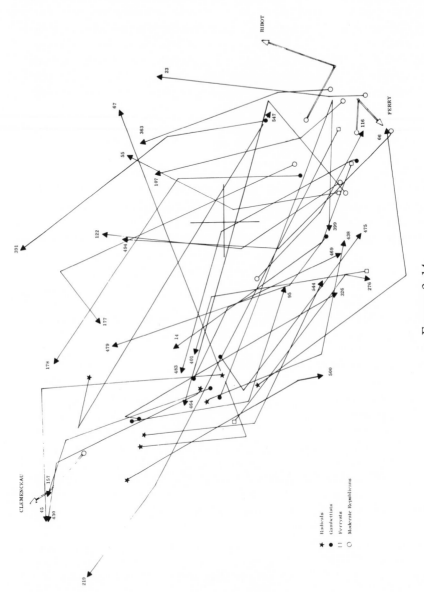

RIBOT

FERRY

CLEMENCEAU

★ Radicals
● Gambettists
□ Ferrysts
○ Moderate Republicans

FIGURE 3-14.

Movement of the Farthest Sliding Deputies

tative of the Var, a "red" department of the South, always cast their votes with Ferry against Clemenceau when a colonial issue was put to the vote, and there are twelve roll calls in our 1884 set dealing with this problem. On the religious issue, No. 500 always voted with Clemenceau, but No. 547 sometimes abandoned him to side with Ferry. An opposite evolution was that of Goblet, a member from the Somme (No. 483), who had been in Ferry's neighborhood in 1882; in 1884 Goblet, though hesitating about the colonial issue, often agreed with Clemenceau on religious votes.

What were the reasons for these important changes? It is difficult to answer the question within the frame of the present research. For a fuller explanation it would be necessary to draw on biographical materials. Figure 3–14, however, does suggest some possible reasons. Some of the farthest-moving deputies were from the same constituencies; and when this happened their evolutions were similar. Two Radical deputies sliding toward the center because of their support of Ferry's colonial policy, No. 66 (Rouvier) and No. 67, came from the Bouches du Rhone, which greatly benefited from the Tonkinese expedition. Conversely, two Moderate deputies sliding toward the left, Nos. 177 and 178, were the representatives of the Haute-Garonne. This cannot be explained simply by the fact that these deputies represented densely populated departments. Nothing of the sort happened in the Rhone or the Nord, quite populous too. It seems more likely that the deputies' changes of attitude were related to opinion in their constituencies, and it is possible that a further study of local politics would account for most of the phenomena observed here.

Although the relation between the change of attitude and local public opinion in the constituencies is probably important, legislative behavior also must be examined in terms of considerations relating specifically to the parliamentary structure. One might suggest the following scheme.

The parliamentary political configuration in this period was not permanent; it was a temporary result of individual positions on various issues and a combination of these positions. Political cleavages were determined by the emergence of dividing issues. The configuration of the Chamber was related to the set of questions discussed.

Two basic preliminary points about this configuration must be made. First, the major issue, which was responsible for the major gap within the Chamber, was the double question of the Republic and clericalism. Hence, the main opposition was that between the right wing and the Republicans. Second, the political configuration changed in 1883: some new features appeared then that were to be strengthened in 1884. The

127

Republicans divided on the colonial issue and the municipal issue. This new division allowed the Radicals to cast their votes with the right wing, sometimes against Ferry's cabinet.

Such was the general pattern of parliamentary evolution from 1881 to 1885. Its effects upon the changes of opinions are obvious. The position of the rightist deputies remained the same, and their changes of attitude were limited. The extreme left, on the contrary, was moving away from Ferry's supporters. The radical wing was becoming more and more radical in its opposition. Most of the leftist deputies slid increasingly toward the left. Clemenceau's movement, represented in Figure 3–14, is quite typical of that evolution. Thus, a gap progressively appeared between the left wing and the center of the Chamber so that the situation of those deputies who found themselves in the middle of the Republican camp became critical. They had to choose between the two edges of an opening gap: between the radicalizing left and the group more and more committed to Ferry's support.

This hypothesis may be tested by a closer examination of these particular deputies. The zone in which the gap would probably open is circumscribed by a dotted line in Figure 3–13. Figure 3–15 shows the sliding of the deputies starting from this zone with the same conventional representation as Figure 3–14. Here is striking evidence supporting our hypothesis. From 1882 to 1884, a kind of split occurred. Deputies very near to one another in 1882 slid in opposite directions. Their political labels did not matter at all. Two Gambettists, like Nos. 4 and 157, had cast almost all their votes the same way in 1882; by 1884 one had joined the Radicals and the other the Center. Two Radicals from Paris, Nos. 432 and 438, quite close in 1882, slid to opposite sides. A Radical like Rouvier (No. 66) provisionally ended his trajectory close to Ferry; and a Gambettist like No. 45, close to Clemenceau. As a result, the whole space of the Republican left was covered by these few deputies starting from a narrow zone.

This phenomenon deserves attention. It is a fine example of what could be the logic of a situation. These deputies slid neither because of their own instability nor because of the pressure of their constituents' opinion. They had to move because their initial positions became too uncomfortable. The opposition of Clemenceau's Radicals and of Ferry's supporters compelled them to choose—a choice that they probably would rather have avoided. Unfortunately, in a changing parliamentary configuration even deputies with unchanged opinions must change their political positions.

Figure 3–14 shows that the change of attitude was in some cases a decisive reconversion that may be difficult to explain without taking

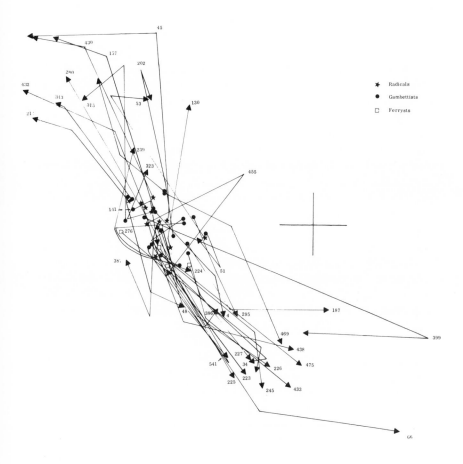

FIGURE 3–15.

Opposite Movements inside the Middle of the Left

into account changes in local public opinion. Figure 3–15 illustrates the logic of a particular parliamentary situation of which some of the farthest-moving deputies were the victims. But, in both cases, the political label did not matter. The parties were not only unrelated to divisions in the Chamber, as has been shown by the first four diagrams, but also they had no significance for the possible movement of any individual deputy. Knowing the political label of a deputy, as it appeared in his electoral proclamation, means knowing nothing. For this early period of the Third Republic, the "party"—the word is fairly inadequate—to which a deputy belonged tells the historian or the political scientist neither the real position of the deputy in the whole political spectrum nor the direction which he was likely to take. This does not mean that legislative behavior was irrational or unpredictable, but simply that the reasons for it are not accurately described by and cannot be deduced from party labels.

Further evidence for this conclusion is to be found in Figures 3–16 and 3–17 which represent the slidings of the so-called Gambettists. In order to be clear, for the arrow diagrams are often indistinct, we have preferred to draw two different diagrams, one for the Gambettists sliding toward the left and the other for those sliding toward the center. The Gambettists whose slidings were the most limited have not been represented.

Here, too, it is striking to see how wide the scope of the attitude change is. Gambettists sliding toward the center started from all parts of the 1882 Republican camp, most of them from the middle of it, a few from the Radical neighborhood, still fewer from Ferry's vicinity, but these last slid far enough to join the Moderates. A different picture appears in Figure 3–17, which shows those who slid toward the left. It is clear that the middle of the Republican camp was more often a starting zone for those moving toward the center than for those moving toward the left. Conversely, those Gambettists who slid toward the left started from a more radical or from a more moderate left. Consequently, the superimposition of these two diagrams would give the impression that the true reality of Gambettism lies in that perpetual motion in which individual movements in opposite directions counterbalanced each other.

The direction of the movements of most individuals was relatively constant through successive years. The diagrams show, for each deputy, his three successive positions: for the arrow is not a straight line from 1882 to 1884 but a broken line, and the break marks the 1883 position. It is striking that very few deputies reversed their movement in 1883. The most frequent pattern was that of deputies who continued to slide

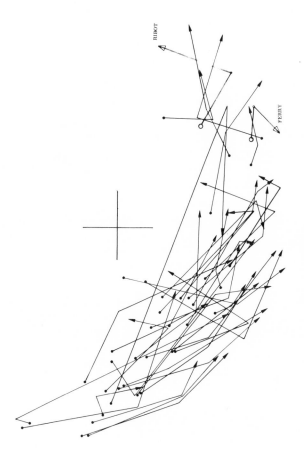

RUBOT

FERRY

CLEMENCEAU

FIGURE 3–16.
Gambettists Sliding toward the Center

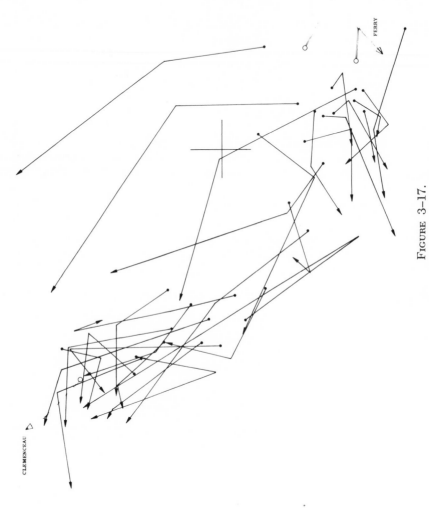

FIGURE 3-17.

Gambettists Sliding toward the Left

in nearly the same direction from 1883 to 1884. This fact indicates a regularity in the change of political attitude that is worth noticing, and makes it possible to say that the behavior we observe is not a mere optical illusion but is what really happened in that Chamber.

III
PROVISIONAL CONCLUSIONS

SEVERAL conclusions may be suggested. Some relate to method and others to our substantive findings about the behavior of members of the Chamber of Deputies.

METHOD

From a set of roll calls it is feasible to outline the political configuration of the whole Chamber, assigning to each deputy his precise position.

The political configurations obtained for each successive set of roll calls are closely correlated to one another (correlation coefficient $> .92$).

By means of the regression equations, it is possible to transform the original configuration directly extracted from one set of roll calls into a derived configuration so that (1) this new regressed configuration has the same center of gravity, the same variance, and the same shape as the original configuration extracted from another set of roll calls, and (2) within the new regressed configuration each single point preserves the same position in relation to all the others as in the original configuration.

The superimposition of the configuration extracted from one set of roll calls upon the regressed configuration derived from another set of roll calls is legitimate and practicable. This superimposition makes it possible to read directly the difference of position of each point in the two sets or, in other words, the change of political attitude of each individual deputy during successive periods. Arrow diagrams can make these movements clear, and are useful for expressing this part of legislative behavior. They are mathematically irreproachable and simple enough. The whole process involves not sophisticated mathematics but simply a large number of calculations.

LEGISLATIVE BEHAVIOR

There is no relevant partition of the French Chamber of Deputies for this period except that of Republicans and Anti-Republicans. Political labels like radicalism do not indicate with a sufficient degree of certainty either a deputy's position in the whole Chamber or the prob-

133

able direction of his evolution. Political labels are useful within limits because they make the parliamentary spectrum seemingly ordered and because it is easier to deal with a few groups than with the whole set of individual deputies. But one must always keep in mind that political labels are misleading. For this period of French history—and one could ask when it ended—the studies of legislative behavior ought to be based on an analysis of individuals rather than of parties or groups. This finding could open up a new political history which might be more difficult but would also be more accurate.

The attitude change of the majority of the deputies was very limited from 1882 to 1884. However, a few deputies slid far from their initial positions and apparently fundamentally revised their political attitudes. At this stage of the analysis there appear to be two possible explanations for such a radical change: (1) an important change of political attitudes and opinions within the deputies' constituencies, and (2) the opening of a gap within the Chamber, with some deputies being forced to choose between two sides which were becoming increasingly opposed to each other.

The political stability of the Chamber is an illusion that results from the diversity of individual changes of attitude, each of them being canceled out by others. The representation of legislative behavior suggested by the arrow diagrams is that of a great number of individual changes of attitude, more or less important, intermingled with one another. As in a stable gas the physical reality is the Brownian motion, so, in a Chamber, stable when considered as a whole, the underlying political reality is a combination of individual movements in various directions. Hence, it is possible to understand how the observer of French political life could have had the impression of a great stability and of a true evolution at the same time. The levels of analysis are not identical.

The next stage of this study would be to give special consideration to those deputies who left the Chamber either because they were promoted into the Senate or because they were defeated in an election. It would be interesting to see if these deputies retained their original positions or if they moved toward the center or toward the right. Furthermore, it would be interesting to carry forward the analysis into later Chambers so as to obtain more complete individual histories. For instance, we know the subsequent evolution of two of the farthest-moving deputies represented in Figure 3–14: Goblet (No. 483) and Germain (No. 178). Goblet was the Minister of Education who succeeded in passing the 1886 educational bill establishing the complete "laïcity" of the primary schools and forbidding the congreganists to teach in public primary schools. This bill was evidently supported by the more left-oriented deputies. It is interesting to observe, in the arrow diagram, Goblet's slide toward the left before he became a minister in the next legislature. Germain was a Moderate deputy in 1881 in a constituency previously held by a Conservative. In 1889, this obscure politician was a successful Radical candidate in the same district. Such an evolution may seem surprising, but the arrow diagrams show that it had been foreshadowed by Germain's earlier changes of attitude. It would be interesting to pursue this inquiry.

4

Radicals and Whigs in the
British Liberal Party, 1906–1914

GEOFFREY HOSKING AND ANTHONY KING

In the first decades of the twentieth century the Liberal Party lost its position as one of the two major parties in the British parliamentary system, and was replaced by the Labour Party as the main opponent of the Conservatives. This chapter is concerned with a small but possibly important aspect of the Liberal Party's decline, namely the nature of the divisions within the party in the House of Commons during the Liberals' last period of indisputable strength, between their election victory of 1906 and the outbreak of the First World War. The thesis of the chapter is that these divisions did not in any way portend the split in the party that eventually took place in and after 1916.

I

THE story of the decline of the Liberal Party can, in broad terms, be told very quickly.[1] In January 1906 the Liberals won a larger overall majority in the House of Commons than has been won by any party in this century except for Labour in 1945; indeed the Liberals' 1906 majority over the Conservatives alone was even greater than Labour's was to be forty years later. The Liberals went on to win two general elections in 1910 (although after 1910 they could govern only if the Irish Nationalists did not oppose them). In 1916, however, in the middle of the First World War, the first signs of a split in the party appeared: Lloyd George, a Liberal Cabinet Minister, was largely responsible for deposing the Liberal Prime Minister, Asquith, and for establishing a coalition administration with the Conservatives. The split was widened by differences that arose among Liberals in the

The authors of this chapter wish to acknowledge the invaluable help, especially in the methodological sphere, of David St Maur Mills, of the University of Essex, and of Michael Leavitt and Peter Smith, of the University of Wisconsin. They are, of course, not responsible for our errors and misconceptions.

[1] There is no general work on the subject which covers the whole period; but see Trevor Wilson, *The Downfall of the Liberal Party 1914–1935* (London: William Collins Sons & Co., 1966); P. F. Clarke, *Lancashire and the New Liberalism* (Cambridge: Cambridge University Press, 1971); and Henry Pelling, *Popular Politics and Society in Late Victorian Britain* (London: Macmillan & Co., 1968), chap. 6.

House of Commons over the conduct of the war, and in the general election of 1918, immediately after the war, the Liberals went to the polls a divided party: Lloyd George's followers secured 133 seats, Asquith's only 28. The Labour Party, which before the war had never won more than 42 seats, now won 63 and became the official Opposition. The split between Lloyd George and Asquith was later bridged after a fashion, and in 1923 there was a momentary Liberal revival. But, even reunited, the Liberals never again held as many seats in the House as Labour, and after 1924 the party's decline was precipitous. Table 4-1 tells the story.[2]

This decline is a remarkable phenomenon. In a two-party system, with a single-member simple-plurality electoral system, it is very rare for one of the two major parties to be displaced altogether.[3] An examination of this exceptional case might tell us a good deal about the way in which two-party systems function; yet political scientists have shown little interest in the Liberals' fall. Historians, by contrast, have taken an active interest in the subject; but no single, sustained treatment of it exists, and one has to extract historians' views from a variety of monographs, essays, and books concerned mainly with other subjects. Nonetheless, two broad schools of thought can fairly easily be discerned. It is a simplification, but not a caricature, to label these two schools the "inevitablist" and the "accidentalist." [4]

TABLE 4-1. INDICATORS OF THE LIBERAL PARTY'S DECLINE, 1906-1935

		1906	1910 Jan.	1910 Dec.	1918	1922	1923	1924	1929	1935
Seats	Liberals	400	275	272	28	54	159	40	59	21
	Labour	30	40	42	63	142	191	151	288	154
% share of total vote	Liberals	49.0	43.2	43.9	12.1	17.5	29.6	17.6	23.4	6.4
	Labour	5.9	7.6	7.1	22.2	29.5	30.5	33.0	37.1	40.3

[2] The Table is drawn from David Butler and Jennie Freeman, *British Political Facts 1900-1968*, 3rd ed. (London: Macmillan & Co., 1969), pp. 141-142. The results of the 1931 general election have been excluded; in that election the Liberals were split three ways and it would have been hard to give meaningful summary figures for them.

[3] See Maurice Duverger, *Political Parties* (London: Methuen & Co., 1954), pp. 207-228.

[4] These are not entirely satisfactory terms, but perhaps they will do for the purposes of our argument. The point is that there does seem to be a division, in general terms, between those who hold that the Liberals' decline was inevitable, even had there been no war, and those who argue that it would not have happened at all but for the war. It is historiographically a little dubious to treat the war as an "accident." More correctly it might be regarded as "exogenous" to the British

The inevitablist school, consisting mainly of Labour-inclined historians, holds that the Liberal Party had its electoral base in the bourgeoisie, and that, mainly for this reason, it had an ideology that appealed to the bourgeoisie and could not be adapted to meet the demands of the increasingly assertive working class. Once the working class had obtained the franchise, this school argues, and once an independent Labour Party had been formed specifically to represent its interests, then the fate of the Liberal Party was sealed. The Liberals could, and did, espouse moderate social reforms; but, given their dependence on middle-class electoral support and given the high proportion of middle-class M.P.s among their parliamentary following, they could not move far enough toward meeting working-class demands for "fundamental changes in the economic and social system." [5] This school holds, furthermore, that the working classes were demanding not merely major social and economic change but also direct working-class representation in Parliament. This the Liberals were reluctant to grant them, partly because they did not see a clear necessity for it, and partly because prospective working-class candidates could not contribute enough money toward the very high election expenses that constituency associations had to bear.

In so far as a coherent inevitablist case can be discerned, then, it is mainly electoral in its thrust, and rests on fundamental changes taking place in Britain's social and economic life at the beginning of the century. In its conscious opposition to the accidentalist case it is perhaps most clearly expressed by Henry Pelling:

> The decline of Liberalism was not due to a sordid intrigue between Lloyd George and a few Conservative leaders and press lords, as many widely read historians of the present day would have us believe. Nor was it due, solely or predominantly, as Dr Wilson has suggested, to the impact of the war upon Liberal values and upon the unity of the parliamentary Liberal Party. Rather it was the result of long-term social and economic changes which were simultaneously uniting Britain geographically and dividing her inhabitants in terms of class; enabling the population to achieve the full dimensions of

---

political system. However, the terms "exogenist" and "endogenist" seemed to us impossibly recondite, so perhaps we may be excused a certain terminological looseness. Of the writers cited in note 1 above, it is fair to label Wilson and Clarke "accidentalists" and Pelling an "inevitablist." For a statement of the inevitablist position in addition to Pelling's, see the introduction to Alan Bullock and Maurice Shock, eds., *The Liberal Tradition from Fox to Keynes* (London: A. & C. Black, 1956).

[5] Bullock and Shock, *The Liberal Tradition*, p. xlviii.

political democracy but condemning it to years of bitter strife owing to the forced contraction of the staple industries which had prospered so remarkably in the later Victorian era—an era politically as well as socially distinct from that of the inter-war period.[6]

By this view the 1916 split in the Liberal leadership did no more than hasten the decline of a party that was doomed to near extinction anyway.

The accidentalist school disagrees. It notes, first, that Liberal dependence on middle-class electoral support was declining; second, that the Liberals were continuing to shed their traditionalist laissez-faire wing; third, that the Liberal Governments of Campbell-Bannerman and Asquith were "making the running" in the field of social reform;[7] fourth, that, for a party allegedly doomed to extinction, the Liberals had done remarkably well in the general elections immediately prior to 1914; and, fifth, that in the years between the general election of December 1910 and the outbreak of the First World War, when the Labour Party should have been doing particularly well in by-elections, it was in fact doing particularly badly, gaining no seats, losing four, and invariably finishing at the bottom of the poll. The accidentalists admit that the Liberals were adopting few working-class candidates, but claim that they *were* adopting convinced social reformers and that, if their failure to adopt workers was alienating the working-class portion of the electorate, then there were no unambiguous signs of it. P. F. Clarke, in a recent development of the accidentalist thesis, confronts Pelling directly:

> The first quarter of the twentieth century saw two sorts of change in British politics. The first sort centered upon the emergencies of class politics in a stable form; the second sort upon the effective replacement of the Liberal party by the Labour party. But the first . . . does not in any simple way explain the second. For one thing, the chronology is wrong. By 1910, the change to class politics was substantially complete. That from Liberalism to Labour had not really begun. Nor were there signs that it must begin. It was not a light thing to overturn one party and make another to put in its place. At the beginning of the second decade of the twentieth century it looked as though both Labour and Liberalism would be subsumed in progressivism.[8]

[6] Pelling, *Popular Politics,* pp. 119–120.
[7] Wilson, *Downfall,* p. 17.
[8] Clarke, *Lancashire,* p. 406.

139

Conceivably, on such a view, the progressive current in British politics might have brought into being a broad-based party rather like the American Democrats: largely middle-class, even upper-class, in leadership, but substantially working-class in electoral support. It follows from such a view that the Liberals declined, not because of class changes that had taken place in British society before the war, but because of a split in the party that was occasioned by wartime issues and would not have occurred but for the war. The pre-1914 developments, writes Clarke, "were not only cumulative but cumulatively favourable to progressivism." It was the war that made the difference.

It is not our intention in this chapter to adjudicate between these two views of the Liberals' fall. The debate between them (if such it can be called) has not been very lucidly conducted. The findings of electoral-behavior research, crucial to the inevitablist case, have not been brought to bear on the question, and, perhaps even more important, neither side has stated its propositions precisely enough to enable one to test them. Partly because no single author has produced a sustained treatment of the subject, the two sides to the argument have often been, so to speak, ships passing in the night.

The point to which we address ourselves is a limited, but perhaps important one that certainly has a bearing on the argument, although neither side has yet tackled it explicitly. That is the question whether the pre-1914 divisions in the parliamentary Liberal Party in any way foreshadowed the split that began in 1916. It is an essential part of the accidentalist case that the 1916–1919 split was occasioned by the war, would not have occurred but for the war, and, more than that, opened in the party a fissure which was specific to the war and could not have been predicted from anything that had taken place before the war. By the same token, it would strengthen the inevitablists' case (though they nowhere explicitly say so) if it could be shown that the war merely widened a breach that already existed apart from the war and which, had it not been widened by the war, would have been widened by something else. It would strengthen the inevitablists' case even further if it could be shown that this breach grew out of a division to which they *do* characteristically call attention—namely, the division between, on the one hand, the traditionalist, bourgeois Liberals and, on the other, the Liberals who, though not themselves of working-class origin, were nonetheless active in the cause of radical social reform.

The question we asked ourselves, in short, was whether there was anything about the nature of the divisions within the Liberal Party before 1914 that would have led one to expect the party to split eventually, whether or not the war had occurred. Was there a geological fault in the party that was bound to result in an earthquake sooner or later? Or was the war a bomb dropped suddenly on an otherwise peaceful, if variegated landscape?

II

WE shall turn to our evidence bearing on these questions shortly; but, before we do, it is worth taking note of how politicians and journalists at the time viewed the structure of the divisions in the party, and also of how they have been viewed by historians since. Contemporaries were conscious that, as they often put it, the Liberals were a "composite" party.[9] One of the Liberal whips, Murray, referred in a letter to Churchill in 1907 to "the miscellaneous elements who go to form our majority." [10] But even the whips, as far as one can make out, did not spend much time trying to make sense of these miscellaneous elements, and certainly there was no agreed view about the nature and bases of the party's divisions. One has to draw what inferences one can from a variety of more or less casual references in newspapers, periodicals, and private letters.

A sample of such references, drawn from periodicals, will convey a sense of contemporaries' thinking about the subject:

> One's first observation about the new Parliament is its freshness. . . Take even the new Labour Party, whose advent every right-thinking Liberal who is sure of his principles should welcome. . . Then there will be the new moderate group, shading off into something like pure Liberalism. Then will come a powerful contingent of Radicalism. It is impossible to assess precisely the quality of the new advanced Socialistic or semi-Socialistic Party.[11]

> . . . nothing threatens the Government, and the first session will certainly be fruitful. The relations with the Labour Party have been cordial, and though the power of this section is great, it is exercised with discretion and is not offensive to any but a very small Whig section of the Liberal Party. Perhaps this section is not altogether happy. But I do not think it at all numerous, and it contains men able and sympathetic enough to accept the general Radical tendencies of politics.[12]

> . . . the present majority will not be easily managed, and the Left wing will tend to break away towards the Labour group on the other

---

[9] H. W. Massingham, *The Speaker,* 20 January 1906, p. 390.

[10] Alexander Murray, Master of Elibank, to W. S. Churchill, 5 May 1907, Elibank Papers, National Library of Scotland.

[11] H. W. Massingham, *The Speaker,* 20 January 1906, p. 390.

[12] H. W. Massingham, *The Speaker,* 14 April 1906, p. 34.

141

side of the House. There are two ways . . . of averting such a tendency. [One] is to keep the Radical and social side of the Government's work firmly to the front.[13]

[THE unity of the Liberal Party as the 1906 Parliament enters its second year] is something of a surprise when the profound divergence of opinion is recognised between the extreme right and the extreme left of the party of reform. At the one end are representatives but little, if at all, distinguishable from the Conservative Free Trader, and in many respects more Tory than the Tories. At the other end are advanced Radicals who accept all the old extreme positions in respect of armaments or democratic government which were the shibboleths of the fifties and sixties in England; and convinced Collectivists who on socialistic legislation are prepared to push forward more rapidly than many of the Labour Party.[14]

These comments are typical and, if one were to rely on them alone, one probably would be led to the conclusion that pre-1914 Liberal M.P.s could be arrayed along a single ideological dimension, with Radicals or Collectivists on the left wing of the party and Whigs or Moderates on the right. The implication, stated fairly explicitly, is that, were the Liberal Party to split, the Radicals would move off toward the Labour Party, the Whigs toward the Conservatives.

Yet even the quotations above make one wonder about such a simple ordering. There is the looseness of the vocabulary: "moderate," "pure Liberalism," "pure Radicalism," "advanced Socialistic or semi-Socialistic Party," "Radical and social," "advanced Radicals," "convinced Collectivists." Elsewhere such terms as "economists," "Imperialists," and "individualists" were used. Moreover, the terms Radical and Whig are never really defined, even implicitly; the single dimension is never given an issue content. Perhaps most important, as soon as one writer, the last of those quoted above, starts to look at the party's divisions in detail, he begins unself-consciously to postulate more than one dimension. On the one hand, he speaks in single-dimension terms of "extreme right" and "extreme left." On the other, it seems that the extreme left position is occupied, not by one group defined in issue terms, but by two: the old-fashioned "advanced Radicals" and the

---

[13] H. W. Massingham, *The Speaker*, 1 December 1906, p. 257.

[14] C. F. G. Masterman, *Independent Review*, January 1907, p. 32. It is interesting to see Masterman using the concepts of "left" and "right;" these concepts did not come into general use in Britain until the 1920s. See Samuel Brittan, *Left or Right: The Bogus Dilemma* (London: Martin Secker & Warburg, 1968), esp. chap. 1.

newer "convinced Collectivists." One is entitled, at the very least, to suspect that even where the two groups acted in concert they may have assigned quite different priorities to different kinds of issues, the Radicals being preoccupied with, for example, the reduction of armaments, the Collectivists with, for example, the enactment of a minimum wage for miners.

Historians have not been any more anxious than those active in politics at the time to make sense of the Liberals' divisions. As in the case of the views of contemporaries, one has to infer historians' views largely from casual references. The classic remark is Dangerfield's: "[The Liberal Party] was an irrational mixture of Whig aristocrats, industrialists, dissenters, reformers, trade unionists, quacks and Mr Lloyd George." [15] Dangerfield thus confuses the issue-based, ideological divisions in the party with the social or religious sources of those divisions. Rowland is somewhat clearer:

> The Liberal Party, like any Radical party at any time, was a mixture of factions. Potential reformers who wished to see their ideas actually implemented or who were personally ambitious had been left with no real alternative but to sail into power on the Liberal side. . . The term Liberal, then as now, was vague enough to allow unlimited latitude and respectable enough to attract support from all levels of society. High Churchmen and Nonconformists, fiery Radicals and cautious reformers, Imperialists and Little Englanders, staid suburbians and the apostles of anarchy, were able to pull together in the same boat without too many questions asked about individual destinations. [16]

Rowland thus implies that the differences in the party were multidimensional, and he identifies the bases of three dimensions: religion ("High Churchmen and Nonconformists"), social reform ("fiery Radicals and cautious reformers"), and foreign policy ("Imperialists and Little Englanders"). But he does not say what the relationship among these various dimensions was. For example, could one infer from the fact that someone took the Nonconformist side on religious questions that he was probably also a social reformer and/or an advocate of reduced spending on the army and navy? Or not? This is the sort of question that, so far, historians have not attempted to answer. [17]

[15] George Dangerfield, *The Strange Death of Liberal England* (London: Constable & Co., 1936), p. 15.

[16] Peter Rowland, *The Last Liberal Governments: The Promised Land, 1905–1910* (London: Barrie & Rockliff: The Cresset Press, 1968), pp. 31–32.

[17] Most historians have done little more than allude to the subject, but it is

III

UNFORTUNATELY, anyone who does seek to answer such questions has only very limited evidence to rely on. The public record, as we shall see, yields little, and contemporary observers of politics did not record the sorts of facts—abstentions on votes in the House of Commons, for instance—that they normally would today. Indeed, reading the press and the private correspondence of politicians before 1914, one is struck by the lack of interest in collecting systematic evidence and by a general lack of attention to systematic variations in political phenomena. Whatever else they may have done, the social sciences have made journalists more alert than they once were to questions other than those of the "who said what to whom" variety. Journalism may be impressionistic today; it was far more so sixty years ago.

Two types of evidence bearing on the structure of issue divisions within the party suggest themselves. The first has to do with the pressure groups in the House of Commons formed by Liberal Members. These groups were formed partly to discuss issues and prepare policy positions, but mainly to bring pressure to bear on the Cabinet—pressure to introduce particular pieces of legislation, pressure to make particular kinds of appointments, pressure to increase or decrease certain kinds of expenditure. Such pressure was exerted by means of deputations to ministers and signed petitions ("memorials"), by means of the publicity that a group's activities might attract, and ultimately by means of votes against the Government in the division lobbies.

The composition of these groups—who belonged to them, who attended their meetings regularly, who joined deputations, how far the membership of the various groups overlapped—could tell us a great deal about the structure of Liberal opinion in the House. Predictably, however, detailed data are not available (nor are they ever likely to be), and all one can do is note the existence of the various groups and who their leading members appear to have been. The impression one gets is of a high degree of fragmentation, with groups forming and reforming and tending to concentrate on a specific issue or cause or on promoting the interests of a particular part of the country. Among the backbench groups between 1906 and 1914, some of them formally organized and permanent, some of them not, were: the Scottish Members, the Welsh Party, the London Liberal M.P.s, the agricultural M.P.s, the Land Values Group, the anti-Lords Campaign, the arms reduction movement, and the Liberal foreign affairs group.

---

probably fair to say that most of them, like Rowland, incline towards a multidimensional view.

Only one group in the House was organized on the assumption that there could be identified a single, Radical point of view. This was the Advanced Radical Committee which Sir Charles Dilke, the *doyen* of Liberal social reformers, had gathered together on his return to the House of Commons in 1892. "We have always regarded it as essential," Dilke wrote in 1906, "that we should have no 'party', no Chairman, and no whips." The Committee's purposes were to keep Governments up to the mark and to make the best use of private Members' time: "It was always understood that the whole of the Section were favourable to the Miners Eight Hours' Bill, and were favourable to very drastic action with regard to the House of Lords and to payment of members. Most of them were supporters of adult suffrage and Home Rulers. All of them took part in the balloting for Labour measures." [18] Some sixty M.P.s attended the first meeting of the Committee in the 1906 Parliament, and the group continued to meet regularly until Dilke's death in 1911 and for a short time afterward. But it counted for little. Dilke himself was a slightly pathetic figure, his political career having been destroyed by a spectacular divorce case in the 1880s. Most Liberal backbenchers devoted themselves to specific causes. Perhaps most important, the group was never united. Dilke hinted at some sources of division in the passage quoted above. Josiah Wedgwood, a member of the group, remarked years afterward: "We agreed on nothing . . . save that we loved and respected Dilke, who had been a great man before we were born." [19] The Liberals thus really lacked a focus for generalized left-wing views of the sort provided by the Tribune Group in the modern British Labour Party or by the Democratic Study Group in the U.S. House of Representatives.

No firm conclusions, however, can be drawn from the experience of these backbench groups for the reason already given: we simply do not know enough in detail about their membership. It is from a second type of evidence—the record of actual votes (divisions) on the floor of the House of Commons—that we might expect to learn rather more. And it is to this type of evidence that we now turn.

We cannot of course expect too much from this source, because by 1906 the great era of the independent Member was already over and most divisions in the House of Commons were party divisions, in the sense that nearly all of the Members of at least one of the major parties went into the same division lobby. Lowell calculated that, in 1899, in

[18] Memorandum, 31 January 1906, Dilke Papers, British Museum Add. MSS. 43,919, ff. 16–17.
[19] Josiah Wedgwood, *Memoirs of a Fighting Life* (London: Hutchinson & Co., 1940), p. 62.

145

only 2.3 percent of all divisions did neither party cast a "party vote" (defined as 90 percent or more of a party voting in the same lobby); in the same year Liberal M.P.s cast party votes 76 percent of the time.[20] In 1903 the Liberals cast party votes in 88 percent of all divisions, and in 90 percent of the divisions in which the whips were on—this despite the fact that the party was still in some state of disarray following the Boer War.[21] Beer's "coefficient of cohesion" for the Liberals, after their return to power, was 96.8 percent in a sample of whipped divisions in 1906, and 94.9 percent two years later.[22] It goes without saying that the state of affairs reflected in these figures greatly reduces the usefulness of House of Commons votes for our purposes: one cannot infer differing opinions from identical behaviors. It is for this reason that political scientists studying Britain have made little use of legislative roll-call analysis in their research.[23]

But, although party cohesion was fairly complete from 1906 to 1914, it was not absolutely complete: there were a number of occasions on which Liberal backbench M.P.s voted against their own Government. We did not attempt to make a complete catalog of all such occasions: it would have been a labor of months to do so and, given the high level of party cohesion, the rewards of our labor would almost certainly have been meager. Instead, we tried to identify the main instances of backbench rebellion from the writings of historians, from the contemporary press (the Liberal *Daily News* was read for the entire period), and from the politicians' own papers.

Altogether 28 divisions presented themselves in which more than a handful of Liberal Members defected from their party. A brief description of these 28 divisions is given in the Appendix. The number of divisions in which rebellions occurred in each year, and the number of M.P.s rebelling in each division is set out in Table 4–2.

Two points must be made straight away about the number of divisions and the number of rebels, and about how the divisions were spread across the nine parliamentary sessions. The first is that the totals we are dealing with are very small; Aydelotte, for example, in his

[20] A. Lawrence Lowell, *The Government of England*, 2 vols. (New York: Macmillan Co., 1908), 2: 79, 81.

[21] Hugh Berrington, "Partisanship and Dissidence in the Nineteenth-Century House of Commons," *Parliamentary Affairs* 21 (1968): 342.

[22] Samuel H. Beer, *British Politics in the Collectivist Age* (New York: Alfred A. Knopf, 1965), p. 257. Beer's coefficient of cohesion is computed by multiplying by two the difference between 50 and the percentage of party members voting on one side (see p. 122, n. 4). Beer himself, curiously, claims to be *dividing* the difference by 50, but the figures he arrives at cannot be produced that way.

[23] But cf., among students of modern British politics, Peter G. Richards, *The Politics of Conscience* (London: Allen & Unwin, 1970).

TABLE 4–2. DIVISIONS IN WHICH LIBERAL M.P.s REBELLED AND NUMBER OF REBELS IN EACH [a]

1906	1907	1908	1909	1910	1911	1912	1913	1914
4	6	5	6	1	2	3	0	1
(1)	(5)	(11)	(16)	(22)	(23)	(25)		(28)
46	13	58	14	24	37	65		16
(2)	(6)	(12)	(17)		(24)	(26)		
18	21	71	22		9	4		
(3)	(7)	(13)	(18)			(27)		
35	39	8	23			29		
(4)	(8)	(14)	(19)					
50	47	18	19					
	(9)	(15)	(20)					
	18	6	40					
	(10)		(21)					
	48		26					

[a] The numbers in parenthesis correspond to the numbers assigned to the divisions in Appendix.

analysis of the House of Commons from 1841 to 1847, dealt with 815 M.P.s in 114 divisions, and the numbers handled in roll-call analyses of the U.S. Congress are often larger still.[24] The fact that, in contrast to most other roll-call analysts, we are in possession of such a minute quantity of data means that the range of analytic techniques available to us is correspondingly limited. The number of techniques that we felt had to be ruled out on these and other grounds was disconcertingly large: Kruskal-Goodman multi-dimensional scalogram analysis, cluster-bloc analysis, Guttman-Lingoes smallest space analysis. Indeed we did in the end use one technique—factor analysis—whose weight the data, being so light, ought perhaps not to have had to bear.

The second point to be made about Table 4–2 aggravates the first. In the 1906 Parliament the Liberals had an overall majority of 130 seats. In the 1910 and 1911 Parliaments, however, as a result of the two general elections in 1910, the Liberals did not have an overall majority at all; they could govern only if the Irish Nationalists did not oppose them and if either the Irish Nationalists or the Labour Party voted with them. This meant that, whereas between 1906 and 1909 Liberal Members could vote against their Government with impunity, confident that they did not run any serious risk of bringing it down, from 1910 onward

[24] William O. Aydelotte, "Voting Patterns in the British House of Commons in the 1840s," in Don Karl Rowney and James Q. Graham, Jr., eds., *Quantitative History* (Homewood, Ill.: Dorsey Press, 1969), p. 419. Professor Aydelotte informs us that he is now in fact working with 186 divisions.

Liberals could rebel only if they were absolutely sure that they would not be joined by the Conservatives or by the Irish Nationalists. Since there was always a danger, however remote, that the Government might be defeated in this way, the number of rebellions fell off sharply. This in itself would not have mattered too much from our point of view (though it makes a small body of data even smaller) had it not been for the additional fact that there was a high rate of turnover among Liberal M.P.s between the 1906 and the 1910 and 1911 Parliaments; for example, of the 400 Liberals returned in 1906, fully 205 were no longer in the House by 1911. In consequence, because of the extraordinarily large volume of missing data, we had to exclude the 7 divisions that took place in and after 1910 from some of our analyses.

There is, however, one connection in which we can usefully look at all 28 of our divisions as well as at a subset of them. Contemporary observers were, as we have seen, not very clear about how the "left" wing of the party was to be characterized, but they were fairly clear about the "right." They believed they could identify on the Liberal back benches a Whig group, which was unhappy about the newer, more radical tendencies in Liberalism, and which could be expected under pressure to break away toward the Conservatives. Although they did not say so explicitly, contemporaries seem to have assumed that the members of this group would be consistently right-wing in their behavior and would seldom if ever side with the Radicals.

The picture that emerges from our data is a good deal more blurred. In most of the 28 divisions—in 19, to be precise—the Liberal rebels either went on their own into the division lobby or were joined only by Labour Members or Irish Nationalists. In the other 9 divisions the Liberal rebels found themselves voting with a fairly substantial number of Conservatives. In 3 of these 9 cases, however, it is clear from the preceding debate and from contemporary press comment that, although some Liberals voted the same way as some (indeed most) Conservatives, they did so for very different reasons; their being in the same lobby was, in effect, a coincidence. That leaves us with 6 divisions in which the Liberal rebels not only supported the Conservatives in the lobby but actually intended to.[25] It is in these 6 divisions that a Whig group, if it existed, should have been in evidence.

The total number of Liberals rebelling in these divisions was 48, and one is struck immediately by how few of them rebelled in a "Whiggish" direction more than once. Of the 48, only 14 rebelled on two or more

---

[25] The six divisions in which Liberal M.P.s consciously went into the lobbies in support of a Conservative position were Nos. 5, 9, 13, 15, 17, and 26 (see Appendix). The "coincidence" divisions were Nos. 2, 6, and 24.

occasions, only 6 rebelled as many as three times, and only 1 rebelled on four occasions; no one rebelled on all of the possible occasions. Moreover, on only one occasion were all 6 of the most consistent rebels in the same lobby at the same time, and on only one other occasion were 4 of them in the lobby together. If a Whig group did exist, it was either very tiny or else made its presence felt somewhere other than in the division lobbies. And the picture is further blurred by another fact about the 48: namely, that no fewer than 16 of them, i.e., one-third of the total, rebelled at least once in a Radical direction. In fact, 2 of these "right-wing" rebels (although admittedly they rebelled in this direction only once) were among the 84 Liberal M.P.s who, over the whole period from 1906 to 1914, had the highest Radical-rebellion scores (see below). In other words, the Whig group was not only tiny and incohesive in voting terms but also it was not ideologically stable: if someone on occasion voted with the Whigs and Conservatives, one could not infer that he would not on some other occasion vote with the Radicals or even with Labour.

There is another connection in which it makes sense to look at the divisions throughout the period—despite the decline in the number of rebellions after 1909 and despite the high turnover among Liberal Members. Of the 500 M.P.s who sat as Liberals between 1906 and 1914, no fewer than 276—55.2 percent of the total—voted against the Government at least once. Of these 276, only 32 (i.e., the 48 who rebelled in a Whig direction minus the 16 who at least once also rebelled in a Radical direction) can be classified as "right-wing" rebels. The remainder, 244 M.P.s altogether, either had a mixed record, in the sense that they sometimes voted one way, sometimes the other, or else were exclusively Radical rebels. It is possible to assign to each of these 244 M.P.s a Radical-rebellion score, computed simply by dividing the number of occasions on which they did rebel by the number of occasions on which they could have rebelled (i.e., were currently in the House of Commons). A sense of the extent of the propensity to rebel on the Liberal benches is conveyed by Table 4–3. The Table is the more striking when we remember that it includes all Liberal M.P.s and therefore includes a large number of ministers who could rebel only if they first resigned from the Government.

Using the varimax factor rotation procedure, we discovered two factors that appeared both to explain more variance and to be more obviously meaningful than any of the others. They are set out in Table 4–4.

Factor I is clearly made up of issues connected with social class and social conflict; Factor II, despite two outsiders, seems to be concerned

149

TABLE 4–3. RADICAL-REBELLION SCORES OF ALL LIBERAL M.P.s,
1906–1914

	0.000	0.045–0.238	0.250–0.381	0.400–0.688	0.706–1.000
Number of M.P.s	176	157	44	34	9
% of all Liberal M.P.s	41.9	37.4	10.5	8.1	2.1

with foreign and defense policy. So far, so good: given the accepted wisdom about the Liberal Party at this time, we might expect two dimensions of this sort to emerge. But it *is* interesting that, in fact, more than one factor does turn up in this analysis: this would not be the case if there had been a single Radical bloc whose members voted more or less regularly with one another over the whole range of issues. Evidently, that kind of bloc did not exist.

Up to this point in the analysis we have been using the term "Radical" in the conventional sense, as though it denoted a definite group of Members holding the same or similar opinions. We have spoken of "rebelling in a Radical direction" as though it were clear that that phrase meant something, and that it meant only one thing. But of course it is one aim of this chapter to consider whether or not the divisions within the Liberal Party were unidimensional in the way that this vocabulary implies. We already have cast some doubt on the notion that there was a single, issue-defined Whig bloc. It is time to ask the same sorts of questions about the Radicals.

Because of the missing-data problem, we have to exclude from our analysis the 7 post-1909 rebellions. For simplicity's sake (and also because the numbers involved are very small), we are also excluding

TABLE 4–4. DIVISION OF ISSUES INTO FACTORS
(VARIMAX ROTATED FACTOR MATRIX)

Factor II		Factor II	
Trade Disputes	.742	Dreadnoughts	.704
House of Lords 1	.640	House of Lords 2	.625
Cromer Grant	.636	South Africa	.572
Right to Work	.598	Arms Reduction 1	.520
Smallholdings 2	.518	Russia Cowes	.519
(Secular Education)	.456	Unearned Income	.515
		(Russia Reval)	.485
Eigenvalue 4.11		Eigenvalue 1.33	
% of total variance 17.5		% of total variance 16.5	

5 divisions in the 1906 Parliament in which the Liberal rebels supported the Conservative Party and in which the majority of those rebelling never on any occasion voted with the Radicals (however that term is construed).[26] We are left, therefore, from our original 28 divisions, with 16 from which to try to draw conclusions about the structure of "Radical" opinion.

This is, to repeat, a very small body of data on which to rely, especially when we realize that the maximum number of M.P.s rebelling in any of these divisions was only 71 and the minimum a mere 4 (see Table 4–2). Further the total number of Members rebelling in all 16 divisions was only 216. Nonetheless, it seemed worth while to submit the data to a factor analysis, not because we thought that the answers that emerged should necessarily be taken at their face value, but because we hoped that they would give us some clues about whether such a thing as a single Radical or left wing in the party really existed.

Perhaps, then, there were two Radical blocs, one concerned with issues of social class, the other with foreign and defense policy. To find out whether this was so, we looked at the scores of each individual M.P. on each factor: these were expressed in terms of standard deviations from the mean. If there *were* two fairly tightly knit voting blocs, then this fact would make itself apparent, on each factor, in a bunching of scores around two standard deviations from the mean in one direction. If, on the other hand, there were no such blocs, and votes were distributed more or less randomly over the dimension, then one would find no such bunching. Now, with 403 Liberals in Parliament from 1906 to 1909, one would expect, on a random distribution of votes, to find 2.27 percent of them, or roughly 9 M.P.s, two or more standard deviations from the mean in any one direction. For Factor II the actual figure was 12, which is not significantly greater than random. For Factor I, the figure was 21, which does suggest something of a bunching at one end. If, however, to check further, one takes 1.7 standard deviations as the threshold (beyond which level a normal distribution would give 4.46 percent, or roughly 18 M.P.s, at one end), then the discrepancy weakens: Factor I gives a figure of 27 M.P.s, and Factor II exactly 18.

Furthermore, looking at the individual roll calls within each factor, one finds that those M.P.s with a high dissident score on the factor concerned usually contributed less than half of the rebel vote (see Table 4–5).

[26] The excluded divisions are Nos. 5, 9, 13, 15, and 17.

TABLE 4–5. CONTRIBUTIONS OF M.P.s WITH A HIGH DISSIDENT SCORE TOWARDS THE TOTAL REBEL VOTE ON KEY ISSUES WITHIN THE FACTORS

	M.P.s More Than 2 Standard Deviations from the Factor Mean	M.P.s More Than 1.7 Standard Deviations from the Factor Mean
Factor I		
Secular Education	10 out of 46	12 out of 46
Trade Disputes	19 out of 50	25 out of 50
House of Lords 1	19 out of 39	23 out of 39
Cromer Grant	16 out of 47	19 out of 47
Smallholdings 2	15 out of 48	18 out of 48
Right to Work	17 out of 71	20 out of 71
Factor II		
Arms Reduction 1	10 out of 58	15 out of 58
Russia Reval	5 out of 18	9 out of 18
Russia Cowes	6 out of 19	9 out of 19
Dreadnoughts	11 out of 40	14 out of 40
South Africa	7 out of 26	9 out of 26

Evidently, on individual votes within the factors, the regular rebels were usually joined (and indeed outnumbered) by more casual dissidents.

It is fairly clear from these figures that the Radicals were not voting as a single bloc, or even as two blocs, and that rebel votes were to a large extent cast by men who were dissidents only on odd occasions. This suggests that there were actually not all that many *persistent* rebels either. And indeed, returning to our Radical-rebellion scores, but compiling them now for the 16 divisions from 1906 to 1909 analyzed above, we find that only 17 M.P.s had scores of more than 0.4. Furthermore, only 9 of these dissented regularly on both the major sets of issues captured by the factors (to the extent of casting three or more votes against the Government on each).[27]

The inferences to be drawn from these figures are not absolutely clear. For one thing, we must bear in mind the limitations of our data: they are not only small in quantity but also they may conceal other forms of rebellion, such as abstentions in divisions, speeches against the

[27] The seventeen (in descending order of Radical-rebellion scores from 1906 to 1909) were A. Ponsonby, A. H. Scott, W. Byles, G. J. Cooper, H. C. Lea, H. C. F. Luttrell, V. H. Rutherford, W. Brace, J. Ward, J. Williams, W. R. Cremer, P. Alden, C. Fenwick, J. Johnson, R. C. Lehmann, J. Rowlands, W. C. Steadman. In addition, a certain W. Lawson secured a score of 0.5 by casting one out of two votes against the government; we felt, however, that he could scarcely count as a persistent rebel! The nine whose dissident votes were widely spread over both factors were P. Alden, W. Byles, G. J. Cooper, H. C. Lea, R. C. Lehmann, H. C. F. Luttrell, V. H. Rutherford, A. H. Scott, J .Ward.

Government in the House, and so on. All the same, considering that we have examined the 16 most contentious divisions in Parliament from 1906 to 1909 it seems to us that the total of 17 persistent rebels (and a score of 0.4 does not really indicate a very high degree of rebellion) is quite remarkably low. They amount, in fact, to less than 5 percent of the Liberal Party in the 1906 Parliament.

Two more general conclusions suggest themselves. First, it seems that, at least in the 1906 Parliament, dissident Liberal M.P.s can, in general terms, be arrayed along two policy dimensions, one concerned with social issues, the other with foreign affairs and defense. But, second, in neither field is there evidence of a large or cohesive dissident bloc; still less is there evidence that such a bloc was consistently voting against the Government in both fields. Indeed, so far as it is possible to identify a genuinely Radical group, consisting of M.P.s who felt strongly about a wide range of issues, that group was small to the point of being scarcely visible.

Even at that, one might ask whether the large number of casual dissidents in the Liberal Party was not a sign of some sort of disease in the party organism. This point can best be answered by reference to Beer's coefficient of cohesion, noted above.[28] Beer gives the Liberals figures of 93.2 percent for all (including unwhipped) divisions in 1906 and 95 percent for 1908, and quotes them as examples of *growing* party discipline. Certainly, they indicate greater cohesion than the Liberals had ever previously achieved, even if in retrospect their voting record looks untidy. On Beer's evidence, indeed, it is the Conservatives who were more "diseased": they have figures of 89.8 percent for 1906 and 88.4 percent for 1908.

It seems proper to conclude that, to judge by the voting record, the Liberal Party between 1906 and 1914 was not subject to any major split, nor was it even seriously threatened by the prospect of one.

IV

If this is true, then the post-1916 split in the party can scarcely be related to any pre-1914 split. This assertion would be strengthened still further if we could relate our pre-1914 data to a body of data concerning the subsequent split. Such data are hard to come by. The party affiliations of candidates in the 1918 election are peculiarly hard to ascertain (precisely because of the Liberal split);[29] and, so far as we

[28] Beer, *British Politics*, p. 257.
[29] See Wilson, *Downfall*, Part 2. One of Wilson's major contributions, it should be noted, is to caution us against assuming that the split in the party as it emerged in 1918 was a direct consequence of the Maurice debate, or that the

know, no one has attempted the large task of tracing the subsequent political careers of all those who had served as Liberal M.P.s before 1914. But there is one piece of evidence that at least gives one some purchase on the problem—namely, the vote at the end of the Maurice debate in the House of Commons on 9 May 1918. The details of the debate do not concern us here. Suffice it to say that Asquith, by now deposed as Prime Minister, moved that a select committee be set up to inquire into certain allegations made by a former Director of Military Operations at the War Office, and that his motion was opposed on behalf of the Government by Lloyd George. Lloyd George chose to treat the motion as a motion of censure on the Government's general conduct of the war. It was the first and last such motion to be pressed to a division during Lloyd George's premiership. In the division the Liberal Party was badly split, 100 Liberals voting with Asquith against the Government, 71 supporting Lloyd George.

Most historians have seen the Maurice division as the beginning of the end of a united Liberal Party, and we thought it would be interesting to examine the division list in the light of our findings about the earlier period. The results of this exercise indicated that even the divisions that did exist in the party before 1914 were not related to the split that occurred subsequently.

We first looked at a group that might be labelled (if one were hard-pressed) the "arch-Whigs," i.e., those Liberal Members who in the six divisions referred to earlier voted against the Government on two or more occasions (see above, pp. 148–149). There were 14 of these and all of them who voted in the Maurice division voted with Lloyd George and his Conservative allies and against Asquith; however, only 4 out of the 14 did vote in the Maurice division, so wider inferences are impossible to draw. The behavior of the "Radicals," as we might by now have expected, could not in any way be predicted from their overall voting records. Of the 40 M.P.s who had a Radical-rebellion score in the 22 Radical divisions of 0.4 or more, 15 voted in the Maurice division; 8 voted with Asquith, 7 against him. Of the 84 Members with Radical-rebellion scores of 0.25 or more, 28 took part in the division, 17 with Asquith, 11 against him. These figures are roughly proportional to the voting in the party generally. Whatever the "Radicals" were agreed upon, in other words, it was not this.

The only slight suggestion of a connection between pre-1914 divisions and the Maurice debate—and the suggestion is very slight—comes if

granting of "coupons" at that election to followers of Lloyd George and the withholding of them to followers of Asquith can neatly be related to the Maurice division. So the Maurice division list is used here *faute de mieux*.

we look, not at the pre-war Radical rebellions in general, but only at those relating specifically to foreign policy and defense. We have already seen that this issue was one unambiguous factor in our analysis (Factor II); and altogether 8 of the 22 pre-war Radical rebellions were on foreign affairs and defense matters.[30] It seemed worth considering these 8 divisions separately, with a view to finding out whether perhaps M.P.s who were critical of the pre-war Government's posture toward (especially) Germany and Russia might also have been disposed, for whatever reasons, to be critical of Lloyd George's handling of the war (or possibly simply of his handling of the Maurice affair). And some suggestion of this does emerge from the figures. Altogether 46 Liberal Members voted in the Maurice division who had on one or more occasions opposed the Government in foreign affairs before the war. Of the 46, 32 voted with Asquith, only 14 against him. Moreover, the great majority of those M.P.s who had voted most frequently against the pre-war Government now voted with Asquith and against Lloyd George. Too much should not be made of this finding, however: the numbers involved are too small to account for more than a small fraction of what was happening in the Maurice division.

This chapter, as we said at the outset, has been concerned with a small aspect of a large problem. Our findings have largely been negative. We looked for signs of a single, major rift in the pre-1914 Liberal Party, and failed to find them. We did not even find evidence of a number of different issue-defined rifts any one of which might, by itself, have led to the eventual break-up of the party. It seemed that in only very few cases could an M.P.'s vote in one division be predicted from his votes in other divisions. Consistent anti-Government voting across a number of different policy fields was relatively uncommon. Even within single policy fields, consistent anti-Government voting was not at all common; for example, of the 46 M.P.s mentioned above who voted in the Maurice division, having previously opposed the pre-war Government on foreign affairs, only 13 had rebelled in 3 or more of the 8 divisions. Thus, the pattern we found, admittedly on the basis of our very limited evidence, was essentially of an absence of pattern. To revert to the metaphor we used earlier, there was no geological fault in the Liberal Party before 1914; the landscape was too scattered with ditches and hedgerows to be interpretable in such terms.

However negative our findings, they do have some bearing on the debate between accidentalists and inevitablists. For they do support one of the main accidentalist contentions—namely, that the split in the

[30] The eight divisions were (see Appendix) Nos. 6, 11, 14, 19, 20, 23, 27, and 28.

Liberal Party, when it occurred, was occasioned by the war and would not have taken place without the war. Now, admittedly the inevitablist case rests mainly, not on a consideration of the internal state of the Liberal Party, but on socio-economic factors and their alleged electoral consequences. Nevertheless, if our conclusions are correct, then one possible buttress of the inevitablist case is clearly removed.

Appendix

Brief Description of Divisions

1 *Secular Education*   28 May 1906   *46 rebels*
Amendment to achieve complete secularization of education in public elementary schools.

2 *Education Bill*   27 June 1906   *18 rebels*
Objection to clause in Education Bill that would permit denominational teaching in public elementary schools if ballot among parents indicated such a demand.

3 *India*   20 July 1906   *35 rebels*
Expression of disapproval by certain M.P.s of British misrule in India.

4 *Trade Disputes*   3 August 1906   *50 rebels*
Objection to possible interpretation of the qualification that picketing must be done "peaceably and in a reasonable manner."

5 *Small Landholders (Scotland)*   30 April 1907   *13 rebels*
Amendment to base land reform on purchase, rather than rental, of land from its present owners.

6 *Territorial Army*   5 June 1907   *21 rebels*
Objection to clause that implied the possible introduction of conscription.

7 *House of Lords 1*   26 June 1907   *39 rebels*
Amendment to abolish House of Lords entirely.

8 *Cromer Grant*   1 August 1907   *47 rebels*
Objection to the payment of a £50,000 grant to Lord Cromer for outstanding service to his country.

9 *Smallholdings 1*   13 August 1907   *18 rebels*
Amendment to enable Councils to sell as well as lease land acquired for Smallholdings and Allotments.

10 *Smallholdings 2*   13 August 1907   *48 rebels*
Amendment to safeguard County Councils from land speculators.

11 *Arms reduction*   2 March 1908   *58 rebels*
Amendment to render innocuous a resolution to reduce arms expenditure.

12 *Right to Work*   13 March 1908   *71 rebels*
Amendment to render innocuous a bill proposing to shoulder the Government with the responsibility of providing jobs for the unemployed.

157

13 *Licensing Bill*   4 May 1908   *8 rebels*
A bill to regulate the sale of liquor.

14 *Russia Reval*   4 June 1908   *18 rebels*
Objection to the King's proposed journey to Reval to meet the Tsar.

15 *Miners' (8 hours) Bill*   6 July 1908   *6 rebels*
Objection to a second reading of the bill—on the grounds that the proposals would devastate the national economy.

16 *House of Lords 2*   22 February 1909   *14 rebels*
Motion to curtail the powers of the House of Lords.

17 *Finance Bill*   22 June 1909   *22 rebels*
Amendment to exclude agricultural land from the domain of the proposed land taxation.

18 *Unearned Increment*   12 July 1909   *23 rebels*
Amendment to remove proposed tax-exemption for increments in land values from inheritors.

19 *Russia Cowes*   22 July 1909   *19 rebels*
Objection to proposed visit of Tsar to Cowes (Isle of Wight).

20 *Dreadnoughts*   26 July 1909   *40 rebels*
Motion to reduce naval expenditure.

21 *South Africa*   19 August 1909   *26 rebels*
Objection to implied racial discrimination in proposed South African Constitution.

22 *Civil List Bill*   26 July 1910   *24 rebels*
Motion to transfer from the royal to the public accounts the revenues from the Duchies of Cornwall and Lancaster.

23 *Arms Reduction 2*   13 March 1911   *37 rebels*
Proposal to reduce arms expenditure.

24 *National Insurance Bill*   19 July 1911   *9 rebels*
Objection to inclusion of employers' share of National Insurance contributions in the back payments of employees who had fallen behind through illness.

25 *Miners' Wage*   26 March 1912   *65 rebels*
Motion to compel employers to pay the current average miners' wage as a future minimum wage.

26 *Ulster Exclusion*   18 June 1912   *4 rebels*
Amendment to exclude four counties of Ulster from the domain of the proposed Irish Parliament.

27 *Arms Reduction 3*   25 July 1912   *29 rebels*
Motion to reduce arms expenditure.

28 *Naval Estimates*   23 March 1914   *16 rebels*
Motion to reduce naval expenditure.

5

Legislative Voting Analysis in Disciplined Multi-Party Systems: The Swedish Case

AAGE R. CLAUSEN AND SÖREN HOLMBERG

THIS chapter is addressed to researchers, primarily historians and political scientists, who are presently using or may be persuaded to use the voting records of legislative assemblies in their political and historical investigations. *Our central concern is to examine the utility of a policy dimension analysis in a disciplined multi-party system.* This concern springs, first, from an awareness that the different forms of dimensional analysis, such as cluster, factor, and Guttman scale analysis, have usually been applied only to legislatures in which inter-person, intra-party variation in voting behavior has been substantial; and, second, from our observation that dimensional analyses are frequently rejected for the study of disciplined multi-party systems where intra-party variation tends to be very low. The thrust of the following discussion is that a policy dimensional analysis is appropriate to multi-party legislative assemblies in which there are at least three parties, regardless of the level of party discipline, provided that party policy positions are known. We shall also be stressing the point that a dimensional analysis is a useful, if not an indispensable, preliminary to further investigations of legislative voting behavior. Although the latter point is taken for granted by many legislative researchers, apparently the message has not gotten across to others.

This discussion of dimensional analysis in a disciplined multi-party system is conducted in the context of a study of roll-call voting in the 1967 session of the Swedish Riksdag. Two methods of analysis will be employed and the results compared. The first of these methods con-

We wish to express our appreciation to the various organizations that have contributed to the work described here. They are the Institute of Political Science, University of Göteborg, Sweden; the Swedish National Bank Anniversary Fund; the National Science Foundation, for its support of the facilities of the Computing Center, University of Wisconsin; Ograduerade Forskares Fond, University of Göteborg; Polimetrics Laboratory, Department of Political Science, Ohio State University.

Also we wish to thank those individuals who have contributed to this work; Bo Särlvik and Olof Petersson of the University of Göteborg; Warren E. Miller of the University of Michigan; Ann Rappoport, and the office staff of the Department of Political Science, Ohio State University.

sists of a cluster analysis of roll-call voting in which the unit of analysis is the individual; this method or a variant on it (factor or Guttman scale analysis) is common in studies of legislative voting where the level of party discipline is moderate to low. The second method of dimensional analysis uses the party as the unit of analysis, and consists of an investigation of party conflict patterns leading to a definition of policy dimensions. The rationales for these two methods will be explained later in the chapter.

In comparing the results of the two methods of dimensional analysis, we will focus upon the dimensional structure that each reveals in the data. Initially, this comparison is made simply in terms of the dimensional "locations" of the individual roll calls, i.e., do the same roll calls fit with the same dimensions in the two analyses? Subsequently, the focus shifts to a comparison of the substantive interpretations of the voting patterns reflected in the dimensional structures suggested by the two methods of dimensional analysis.

Part of the argument for the dimensional approach is that it sets the stage for further analyses of legislative behavior. Our contention is that the differentiation of voting behavior achieved by defining policy dimensions, and subsequently using the measures of the policy dimensions as the dependent variables (rather than the individual roll calls taken separately or all in a heap), leads to different, and we believe more meaningful, results than are obtained without the prior dimensional differentiation.

In support of this argument, we conducted a study of party cohesion showing the different conclusions derived from using different measures of the dependent variable. In addition, the measure of the dominant voting dimension in the 1967 Riksdag was used to calculate distances between parties along a common major dimension. We went one step further than this, however, to compare these party distance measures with distance measures derived from data on the behaviors and attitudes of members of the electorate. To our knowledge, this comparison between party distances among the electorate and party distances among an elected elite has been attempted only rarely. Party distance measures have more commonly been made for the electorate alone, partly because access to elites is often limited.[1] However, such studies

[1] For examples and discussion of party distance studies consult Philip E. Converse, "The Problem of Party Distances in Models of Voting Change," in M. Kent Jennings and Harmon Zeigler, eds., *The Electoral Process* (Englewood Cliffs, New Jersey: Prentice-Hall, 1966), pp. 175–207; Philip E. Converse and Henry Valen, "Dimensions of Cleavage and Perceived Party Distances in Norwegian Voting," *Scandinavian Political Studies* 6 (1971): 107–152; Mogens N. Pedersen, Erik Dam-

can be made for elites as well, particularly when they are members of legislatures for whom a public record of policy positions is available. Such information can be obtained for legislators in a great many countries.

I

UNIT OF ANALYSIS: THE PARTY OR THE INDIVIDUAL?

THE dimensional analysis of legislative voting is often equated with the study of roll-call voting in which the individual is the unit of analysis. Therefore, in legislatures where a high level of party cohesion prevails, the dimensional analysis may appear inappropriate because the level of inter-person variation is so low. Thus, policy dimension analysis may be rejected for the study of legislative voting in disciplined multi-party systems on the ground that the party cohesion is too high.

This rejection of the dimensional analysis may be premature for two reasons. In the first place, although the general level of party cohesion may be high, there may still be certain types of legislative questions, involving a small number of roll calls, on which the party cohesion is not so high. Such roll calls may provide revealing insights into the politics of the polity precisely because they reflect the conditions under which political cleavages cut across party lines.

The second reason why a rejection of a dimensional analysis may be premature in the instance of a disciplined multi-party system is that it ignores the possibility of treating the party rather than the individual legislator as the unit of analysis. Yet this is a very live option since dimensional analyses may be conducted on any units for which a response to a common stimulus has been recorded.

The objection may arise, with respect to the use of the party as the unit of analysis, that the number of parties in most assemblies is too small to hold much promise for a dimensional analysis. If the number of parties is small, the number of different party orderings is severely limited. This would appear, at first glance, to be a serious objection because it is probably safe to say that few assemblies include more than ten parties and that the median size is certainly no greater than five or six.

It is granted out of hand that, if there are only two parties in a disciplined party system, a dimensional analysis is foredoomed because there is only one possible ordering of two parties. However, when the number of parties increases to three, the number of possible orderings

gaard, and P. Nannestad Olsen, "Party Distances in the Danish Folketing, 1945–1968," *Scandinavian Political Studies* 6 (1971): 87–106.

(dimensions) increases to three. Thus, there are three distinct ways of ordering three parties: *A B C, A C B,* and *B A C.* Note that there are three additional orderings of the three parties, *C B A, B C A, C A B,* but these are mirror images of the first three orderings and do not constitute orderings different from the first three designated.

The number of different party orderings literally soars as the number of parties increases. When there are four parties, there are twelve possible orderings, five parties can be ordered and reordered in sixty different ways; and six parties can yield three hundred and sixty orderings. In short, the opportunities for dimensional analysis, using the party as the unit of analysis, are substantial even when the number of parties is very small.

One of the questions that may arise is how there can be so many orderings of the parties in the condition where the parties have only two response alternatives. It is not hard to see, for example, that it is possible to have sixty different orderings of five parties if each of the parties can take a unique position on *each* roll call. The law of permutations applies here; it states that there are 5! ways of ordering five elements. Given that half of these permutations are mirror images of the other half, this means that there are sixty non-redundant ways of ordering five parties.

However, the sixty orderings of the five parties are not possible on individual roll calls where only two positions are scored, e.g., yea and nay. In the dichotomous response condition, the party orderings can not be ascertained without observing differences in party alignments over a number of roll calls. When a number of roll calls *are* included in an analysis, it is possible to ascertain the prevalent party orderings; these are the party orderings that are compatible with the most common party alignments on individual roll calls. This is the direct equivalent of determining which orderings of individual legislators are most prevalent when Guttman, factor, or cluster analysis is performed; the only difference is the unit of analysis.

As an example of what we mean by party alignments on individual roll calls that are consistent with party orderings, consider the hypothetical case of five parties ordered on a Left-Right dimension:

Left———A   B   C   D   E———Right

Consistent
alignments: A/BCDE   AB/CDE   ABC/DE   ABCD/E

As indicated, there are four different kinds of party alignments, in a dichotomous choice situation, that are consistent with this one ordering of the five parties.

162

The same is true for any other ordering of five parties. Accordingly, an investigation of the party alignments across a number of roll calls can be designed so as to identify the party orderings that account for the greatest portion of the variance in voting behavior, to use the terminology of factor analysis. In short, it is feasible to conduct dimensional analyses, using the parties as the units of analysis, whenever there are three or more parties in the legislature.

The availability of options, such as the choice between individuals and parties as the units of analysis, has the advantage of flexibility but carries with it the burden of making a choice between the two modes of analysis. Of course, no choice is involved when there are no data on individual behavior and only the party positions are known. However, when, as in the Swedish case, the opportunity exists for studying voting dimensions using either the individual or the party as the unit of analysis, a choice must be made. Furthermore, this is a choice that should be made in terms of a consideration of the roles of the individuals and the parties in the legislative process.

It could be argued that, since the parties are the essential actors in a disciplined multi-party system, the most interesting and truly significant analysis is that which addresses itself to the *patterns of party conflict*. However, this is not an argument against policy dimension analysis. It is the view, rather, that policy dimensions are most clearly and validly defined by reference to the policy positions of the parties, with an equal weighting of each party. (Subsequently, individuals may be ordered on the policy dimensions.) Thus, in the Swedish Riksdag the Communist party may be very important in defining a policy dimension because of its ideological position relative to the other parties. But, because it constitutes only 4 percent of the membership of the Riksdag under study, its influence on the definition of policy dimensions gets lost in the shuffle of a dimensional analysis when the latter is performed using the individual legislator as the unit of analysis.

A second perspective on the choice of the units of analysis, individual versus party, is that the individual is the significant actor. Parties as such do not act, and the behavior of parties is a composite, however complex in form, of individual behaviors. This view is represented by the individual-level analysis where the focus of the study is upon the behavior of the individual legislators, and party is but one among many predictors of individual voting acts.

Leaving aside any effort to resolve the methodological issue that has been raised, we do find that this issue has sensitized us to the several options that one has in conducting a policy dimension analysis in a disciplined multi-party parliament where some measure of intra-party variation exists. Included among the possible options are the following; for each of these options we consider the weight accorded to party: (1) a dimensional analysis based upon the correlations between roll calls using the individual legislator as the unit of analysis; relative to the impact of party, this option provides a differential weighting of the party input according to the relative sizes of the parties; (2) a dimensional analysis of voting using the party as the unit of analysis, defining the majority position within the party as the party position, and weighting the parties according to size; the impact of party is weighted somewhat more than in option (1) in that a party position carries the full weight of its membership; and (3) a dimensional analysis using party as the unit of analysis, defining the majority position within the party as the party position, and giving an equal weighting to each of the parties; this treats parties as equals and is based on the view that ideological or policy positions deserve equal consideration irrespective of the force of numbers behind them.

The options used in our analysis of Swedish Riksdag voting were (1) and (3). Option (1) uses the individual as the unit of analysis, letting party emerge as a major factor in the dimensional ordering of legislators, to the extent such is in fact the case. In option (3), the dimensional analysis is directly and initially concerned with party orderings, and each party is treated equally regardless of size. These two options represent the polar alternatives among a range of methods giving varying weights to the relative impact of the individual and the party in defining the voting dimensions.

The differences and similarities in the results of the dimensional analysis using the two methods will be given shortly. Before doing so, we want to establish the context of the analysis in terms of the general properties of the Swedish party system and the general pattern of voting in the Swedish Riksdag.

II
LEGISLATIVE VOTING AND THE SWEDISH PARTY SYSTEM

THE prevalent view of the Swedish party system, with its five traditional parties, is that of a two-bloc system consisting of the Communists and Social Democrats on the one hand, and the Center, People's and Conservative (renamed and now translated, inaccurately, into English as the Moderate Party) parties, on the other. The two blocs are usually referred to as the Socialist and Bourgeois blocs, respectively. This view of the party system has dominated both public and scholarly discussions at least since the Agrarian (now the Center) party left a coalition with the Social Democrats in 1957. The party system is subject to

164

greater differentiation, however, than this view would suggest. When the parties are viewed in relation to a Left-Right dimension, the usual practice is to locate the Communists and the Conservatives as the polar parties, with the Social Democrats, the Center, and the People's party ordered between, reading from left to right. This unidimensional view of the Swedish party system is shown here:

Communist	Social Democrat	Center	People's	Conservative
Left				Right

Support for this ordering of the Swedish parties has been generated in an analysis of electoral behavior conducted by Bo Särlvik. Thus Särlvik has found that voting preferences change in accordance with this party ordering, i.e., when voters shift their preferences from one election to the next, most of the shifts occur between the adjacent parties. In addition, Särlvik has shown that this ordering of the parties is consistent with the voters' cognitions of the party system.[2] In the following analysis we examine how far this party ordering applies to voting behavior in the lower house of the Swedish Riksdag. There are three aspects to this analysis. The first concerns the generality of the party ordering across voting divisions, the second is a determination of the policy content of the roll calls associated with the Left-Right dimension, and the third is an effort to measure party distances in legislative voting that can be compared to party distance measures based on electoral data. Earlier studies of voting in the Riksdag have indicated the relevance of this Left-Right ordering of the parties to legislative behavior, although they were not expressly designed to provide a test of its applicability and generality.[3]

Complementing the view of the prevalent ordering of the five parties in Swedish politics, as the one most likely to dominate legislative voting, is the indisputable fact that a high degree of party cohesion is a feature of voting behavior in the Riksdag. In the 1967 session, the level of party cohesion was measured for each of the five parties on the set of roll calls ($N = 308$) on which a majority of each party cast either a yea or nay vote; the total number of roll calls taken during the session was 386. (Electronic voting is used.) The cohesion level, using the Rice

---

[2] Bo Särlvik, "Partibyten som mått på avstånd och dimensioner i partisystemet," ["Party changes as measures of distances and dimensions in the party system"] *Sociologisk forskning*, No. 1 (1968) and "Voting Behavior in Shifting Electoral Winds: An Overview of the Swedish Elections, 1964–1968," *Scandinavian Political Studies* 5 (1970): 241–283.

[3] Nils Stjernquist and Bo Bjurulf, "Party Cohesion and Party Cooperation in the Swedish Parliament in 1964 and 1966," *Scandinavian Political Studies* 5 (1970): 129–164.

cohesion index, for each party was: Communist, 93; Social Democrats, 95; Center, 91; People's, 88; and Conservative, 91. When one considers that a cohesion level of 90 is achieved when 95 percent of a party's members vote in the same direction, it is clear that the cohesion level was high indeed! [4]

Despite what appeared to be less than promising conditions for a dimensional analysis of individual voting behavior, this form of analysis was undertaken and is described briefly in the next section. This will be followed by a description of the analysis of party orderings, using the party as the unit of analysis. In each case the results will be presented. These results then will be compared in terms of dimensional structure and content.

III
INDIVIDUAL-LEVEL ANALYSIS

THREE items of information about the Swedish Riksdag relate to the individual-level analysis. First, there was a very large number of roll calls, 386. Second, as shown, the party cohesion was high. Third, the Left-Right ordering was expected to dominate the legislative landscape.

The large number of roll calls made a cluster or factor analysis cumbersome, if not impossible, given computer program capabilities. However, the selection of a random sample of roll calls would not have been useful because of the inadequate representation of the smaller number of roll calls on which intra-party variation was substantial. The sampling procedure, of course, could have been adjusted to take this problem into account, but not without more trouble than the procedure of analysis that we used on the full set of roll calls. In devising our procedure of analysis we made use of our knowledge and expectations of the data to conduct a cluster form of dimensional analysis using different shortcuts to define the roll-call clusters.

Our expectation of the dominance of the Left-Right ordering suggested the feasibility of first identifying a cluster of roll calls characterized by a high degree of correlation with each other *and* with the Left-Right ordering of the parties. These roll calls were those whose correlations with the Left-Right ordering were no less than .95 (gamma).[5] The intercorrelations of all roll calls meeting this criterion would far exceed the usual .8 or .7 levels used in forming clusters.

---

[4] Description and applications of the cohesion index are found in Stuart A. Rice, *Quantitative Methods in Politics* (New York: Alfred A. Knopf, 1928).

[5] Leo A. Goodman and William H. Kruskal, "Measures of Association for Cross-classifications," *Journal of the American Statistical Association* 49 (1954): 749–754.

Other clusters of roll calls were defined by using our knowledge of the high level of party cohesion. Thus, it was anticipated that there would be a number of roll calls, characterized by highly cohesive non-Left-Right party alignments, and that particular alignments would reoccur.[6] Roll calls exhibiting identical party alignments and high party cohesion would necessarily also be highly intercorrelated, as required by the clustering criteria to be specified presently.

The remaining roll calls were of two types. The first type included roll calls on which there was a significant abstention vote (either more than 60 members in the 233-member body, or one-half of at least one party's members). These roll calls were analyzed separately. The interpretation of the meaning of abstentions, in the dimensional context, is difficult, and has not been attempted in this chapter.

Roll calls of the second type, those included neither in the Left-Right cluster nor in the cohesive party alignment clusters, were subjected to the customary form of cluster analysis. Only yea and nay votes were considered, and clusters were formed such that no intra-cluster pairing of roll calls involved a gamma of less than .6; furthermore, the average correlation had to exceed or equal .7.

When all of the sorting and clustering of roll calls was completed, here is what emerged. The initial identification of Left-Right roll calls accounted for 47 percent of all roll calls. The high cohesion-party alignment analysis revealed two additional party alignments that occurred sufficiently often to warrant our attention. In one of these, the middle parties (Center and People's) were in opposition to the parties of the Left (Communist and Social Democrat) and the party of the far Right, the Conservative. This alignment characterized 8 percent of the roll calls. The other alignment, with the Social Democrats in league with the Conservatives against the remaining parties, occurred on 2 percent of the roll calls.

Among the "unclassified" roll calls, those fitting neither the Left-Right ordering, given the stringent criteria used, nor qualifying as high cohesion party alignments, five clusters were formed ranging in size from four to thirty roll calls. Each of these clusters could have emerged as a measure of a separate dimension but this was highly unlikely given the method of analysis. Indeed, it was anticipated from the beginning, when the procedure of analysis was devised, that some of the scales formed on the several clusters of roll calls would be so highly correlated that a dimensional differentiation would be difficult to defend.

---

[6] High party cohesion roll calls are those for which the party vote correlation was .95, using the lambda one-way coefficient of association predicting vote position from party membership. The lambda coefficient is presented in Goodman and Kruskal, "Measures of Association," pp. 740–745.

It was imperative, therefore, to continue the dimensional analysis by computing correlations between cluster-scales and reviewing the resultant matrix of correlations in search of a dimensional structure (see Table 5–1).

The general structure brought out by our arrangement of the correlation matrix is reflected in three subsets of scales. There is a Left-Right subset of two scales, consisting of the large Left-Right scale and one scale from the set of "unclassified" roll calls. In addition to the Left-Right dimension there are four scales which measure some variant of the party ordering in which the "middle" parties (People's and Center) coalesce in opposition to a Conservative-Social Democratic coalition, with the Communist party shifting from one coalition to the other on different roll calls. The third subset of scales is truly "residual" in nature. They are not correlated highly with each other or with scales in the other two subsets; in addition they are small in size (four and five roll calls).

Essentially, the dimensional structure is one in which the principal distinction is between the Left-Right dimension, which accounts for 50 percent of all roll calls (or 63 percent of non-abstention roll calls), and the non-Left-Right dimensions. At this time we are unwilling to conclude that each of the non-Left-Right scales is a measure of a distinct dimension.

With this dimensional structure in mind, as one which is extracted by using the individual as the unit of analysis, we turn to the structure of voting that is found using the party as the unit of analysis. A comparison of the results of the two methods follows.

TABLE 5–1. INTER-CORRELATIONS (GAMMA): CLUSTER-SCALES AND PARTY

	L–R	Uc–2	C&P	SD&Con	Uc–1	Uc–3	Uc–4	Uc–5	Party
Left-Right scale (L–R)		.86	.54	.51	.63	.71	.15	.21	.95
Unclassified scale -2 (Uc–2)			.41	.29	.48	.46	.09	.02	.92
Center and People's (C&P)				.89	.78	.77	.25	.55	.51
Social Democrats & Conservatives (SD&Con)					.74	.77	.40	.61	.40
Unclassified scale–1 (Uc–1)						.67	.16	.45	.54
Unclassified scale-3 (Uc–3)							.32	.39	.67
Unclassified scale-4 (Uc–4)								.54	.06
Unclassified scale-5 (Uc–5)									.09
Party (Left-Right)									–

IV

PARTY-LEVEL ANALYSIS

THE party-level analysis exercises the option of weighting the parties equally and considering the majority vote within the party as the party position. Again, abstention votes were set aside; also excluded were roll calls on which the majority of all five parties were in agreement and roll calls on which one of the parties divided evenly.[7] This narrowed the analysis to 299 out of the total of 386 roll calls taken during the 1967 session.

Given five parties and two behavioral options, yea or nay, there is a maximum of fifteen party alignments that can occur. There are five different ways in which one party can vote against the other four and ten ways that two parties can align against the other three. Note that the maximum number of party alignments on individual roll calls is much lower than the number (60) of possible orderings of the five parties. This results from the fact that the orderings of the parties *within* the coalitions formed on individual roll calls is not articulated because only two voting positions are available to the legislators. However, as noted previously, it is possible for party alignments over a number of roll calls to be consistent with any one of sixty orderings of the five parties. The party-level analysis moves toward the definition of the most common ordering of the five parties, as reflected in the total set of party alignments observed on the 299 roll calls.

The most common party alignment, on individual roll calls, is one which pits the two parties of the Left (Social Democratic and Communist) against the Bourgeois parties of the Center and Right (see Table 5–2). Forty-two percent of the roll calls evoke this most basic and pervasive cleavage in Swedish politics! The next most common (18 percent) party division is the Conservative party of the far Right voting against the rest. Both of these party alignments are consistent with the Left-Right dimensional ordering of the five parties.

The Center and People's party coalition against the parties of the Left and Right is the third ranking party alignment, accounting for 13 percent of the roll calls.

Although our analysis is not directly comparable to one performed by Stjernquist and Bjurulf, the three dominant party alignments in the

[7] The abstention roll calls have been analyzed using the party as the unit of analysis. See Sören Holmberg, "Party Cohesion and Left-Right Voting in the Swedish Riksdag, 1967," mimeographed (Institute of Political Science, University of Göteborg), pp. 21–29.

TABLE 5–2. FREQUENCY OF PARTY ALIGNMENTS (N = 299)

Party Alignment	Number of Roll Calls
One vs. Four	
Conservative vs. others	55
Communist vs. others	13
People's vs. others	12
Social Democratic vs. others	10
Center vs. others	8
Two vs. Three	
Communist & Social Democratic vs. others	128
Center & People's vs. others	35
People's & Conservative vs. others	16
Center & Conservative vs. others	9
Social Democratic & Conservative vs. others	9
Social Democratic & Center vs. others	1
Communist & Center vs. others	1
Communist & People's vs. others	1
Communist & Conservative vs. others	1
Social Democratic & People's vs. others	0

1967 Riksdag also appear to have prevailed in the 1964 and 1966 sessions of the Riksdag studied by these two researchers.[8]

The percentage of roll calls associated with the remainder of the fifteen possible alignments of the five parties drops first to a plateau of three to five percent per alignment, and secondly to the floor, where appear four party alignments occurring once each; finally, there is one alignment that never occurs.

Having identified the frequencies of the fifteen possible party alignments on individual roll calls we moved to the next step, that of determining which of the sixty possible orderings of the five parties is most common. In other words, which single ordering of the five parties is consistent with the party alignments on the largest number of roll calls?

One hypothesis advanced in this paper is that there exists one dominant unidimensional ordering of the political parties in Sweden, the Left-Right dimension, which has been defined in terms of electoral behavior. The expectation is that this same dimension will occupy a dominant position in the determination of legislative voting behavior as well.

Indeed, we found that the dominant ordering of the legislative parties is the Left-Right ordering of: Communist, Social Democrat, Center, People's, Conservative. This ordering is consistent with the party

[8] Stjernquist and Bjurulf, "Party Cohesion and Party Cooperation," p. 151.

TABLE 5-3. NUMBER OF ROLL CALLS WITH PARTY ALIGNMENT CONSISTENT WITH TEN ORDERINGS OF THE FIVE PARTIES (N=299)

Ordering	Number of Roll Calls
1. Communist, Social Democratic, Center, People's, Conservative	212
2. Social Democratic, Communist, Center, People's, Conservative	209
3. Communist, Social Democratic, People's, Center, Conservative	205
4. Social Democratic, Communist, People's, Center, Conservative	202
5. Communist, Social Democratic, Conservative, Center, People's	188
6. Social Democratic, Communist, Conservative, Center, People's	185
7. Communist, Social Democratic, Conservative, People's, Center	184
8. Social Democratic, Communist, Conservative, People's, Center	181
9. Communist, Social Democratic, Center, Conservative, People's	169
10. Social Democratic, Communist, Center, Conservative, People's	166

alignments on 212, or 71 percent, of the 299 roll calls (Table 5-3). The form and frequency of the consistent party alignments are as follows: Communist vs. others, 13; Communist and Social Democrat vs. others, 128; Communist, Social Democrat, and Center vs. others, 16; and others vs. Conservative, 55.

Note carefully that the criterion of consistent party alignments used here requires that the parties within the majority coalition and the parties within the minority coalition must be adjacent on the Left-Right dimension. Attention to this point became important to us in comparing the results of our analysis of the Swedish Riksdag with results reported on the Danish Folketing by Erik Damgaard.[9] Damgaard found that 90 percent of the conflict votes in the period from 1953 to 1970 were consistent with a single unidimensional ordering of the Danish parliamentary parties. This carried the implication that voting was even more simply structured in the Folketing than in the Riksdag; in the latter case "only" 71 percent of the roll calls were lined up with the Left-Right dimension. However, it appears that Damgaard included voting divisions in which adjacent middle parties opposed the parties on the two extremes, thus enlarging the number of roll calls that can appear compatible with a single ordering of the parties. Whatever the merits of the two approaches—a question that cannot easily be resolved in a brief discussion—the result is that the general dimensional structure of voting in the two parliaments appears to be about the same.

Although the hypothesized Left-Right ordering of the parties is the most common one in the Swedish Riksdag, it is apparent that other

[9] Erik Damgaard, "A Coalitional Approach to Legislative Politics: The Case of Denmark" (Paper prepared for the Annual Meeting of the Midwest Political Science Association, Chicago, April 27–29, 1972).

orderings are strong competitors. The three strongest competitors involve relatively minor reorderings within either the two Left or the two middle parties. The Conservative party holds its position on the far Right in these competing orderings, also the two Left parties occupy the Left flank, while the two middle parties remain in the Center. It is clear, moreover, that whichever particular unidimensional ordering of the parties prevails, it must be compatible with the two-bloc model of Swedish politics: the Bourgeois versus the Left.

A brief historical observation should be made concerning the ten most common orderings of parties in the Riksdag. Only two of these orderings, 1 and 3, have any standing in public and scholarly conceptions of the Swedish party system. Both of these orderings have the Communist party on the far Left, with the Social Democrats next in order, and have the Conservative party on the far Right. The only difference between the two orderings is whether the People's party or the Center party should hold the leftmost position, while both parties remain in the middle.

The People's party worked rather closely with the Social Democrats in the beginning of the twentieth century; they formed a coalition government from 1917 to 1920. However, the Center party, formerly the Farmer party, has cooperated with the Social Democrats on a unilateral basis more recently. Thus, the "red-green" (Left-Farmer) coalition occurred both during the 1930s and more recently in the 1950s. Consistent with this historical development, it has been proposed that the Center party has slowly moved to the Left, past the People's party, since the 1920s. This proposition is discussed by Särlvik in his analysis of the voters' cognitions of the party system.[10]

V
COMPARISON: INDIVIDUAL-LEVEL AND PARTY-LEVEL ANALYSIS

1. DIMENSIONAL LOCATION OF ROLL CALLS

The primacy of the Left-Right dimensional ordering of the parties is apparent in both the individual- and party-level analysis. In the party analysis, 212 of the non-abstention roll calls are characterized by a party alignment consistent with the dominant Left-Right ordering. In the individual-level analysis, 189 of these 212 roll calls, or 89 percent, are identified with the Left-Right dimension. Thus, there is a high

[10] Särlvik, "Voting Behavior in Shifting Electoral Winds," p. 269; and idem, "Sweden: The Social Bases of the Parties in a Developmental Perspective," in Richard Rose, ed., *Electoral Behavior: A Comparative Handbook* (New York: The Free Press, 1974), pp. 371–434.

degree of similarity in the major outlines of the dimensional structure of voting as revealed by the two approaches.

One main point of difference is that there are 7 roll calls which emerge on the Left-Right dimension in the party-level analysis but are absent when the individual is the unit of analysis. These roll calls are ones in which the small Communist party is in opposition to the other four parties. This is a good example of the power of the small party to make its weight felt in defining policy dimensions when parties are equally weighted and the party is used as the unit of analysis.

In general, the difference between the results produced by the two methods is that the Left-Right dimension is more inclusive when the party-level analysis is performed. We attribute this to the fact that the criteria of "belongingness" are less stringent when there is a minimum requirement that the majorities of the five parties must be consistent with a particular party ordering, as in the party-level analysis. To produce the same result when the analysis is conducted at the individual level, the votes of something like 90 percent of all members must be consistent with a Left-Right ordering of individuals.

In sum, there is a high degree of convergence between the two methods of voting analysis in making the major distinction between Left-Right and "other" roll calls. The convergence is perhaps not surprising. It is often the case that two procedures lead to similar results. However, this example may be grossly misleading because, in this case, the parties were highly cohesive. From the slight indications we have had, it would appear that the results of the two methods may diverge substantially when the cohesion level is lower and the majority position of the party becomes a relatively poor indicator of the individual voting decisions. We would expect that a party-level analysis would provide less dimensional differentiation, in comparison with the individual-level analysis, as party cohesion drops.

2. DIMENSIONAL CONTENT ANALYSIS

With the focus upon the distinction between Left-Right and non-Left-Right roll calls, let us turn to a content analysis of the dimensional structures produced by the two methods of analysis, looking first at the content of the Left-Right dimension. Fourteen content categories were used in this analysis: housing, economic, business, social welfare, agriculture, crime and police, defense, foreign aid, education, localization, religion and moral, constitutional, radio and TV, and a "miscellany" category of minor and odd questions. The comparison of the content of the roll calls in the two definitions of the Left-Right dimension is shown in Table 5–4. Also shown is the content distribution of the roll

TABLE 5–4. ISSUE CONTENT OF VOTING DIMENSIONS: PARTY-LEVEL AND
INDIVIDUAL-LEVEL ANALYSIS COMPARED

Issue	Left-Right Party Level	Left-Right Individual Level	Party But Not Individual Level	Non-Left-Right Party Level
Business (Bus)	17%	19%	4%	6%
Housing (Hous)	12	13	4	2
Economic (Econ)	11	11	–	–
Social Welfare (SW)	8	7	13	28
Agriculture (Ag)	7	8	–	6
Crime-Police (CrPo)	6	5	9	6
Education (Ed)	6	6	4	4
Religion-Moral (ReMo)	5	4	13	1
Defense (Def)	4	5	–	6
Foreign Aid (FAid)	4	3	18	6
Constitutional (Const)	3	3	–	2
Radio-TV (R-TV)	2	3	–	–
Localization (Lcal)	2	3	–	10
Miscellany (Misc)	13	10	35	23
Total	100	100	100	100
Number of Roll Calls	(212)	(189)	(23)	(87)

calls included on the Left-Right dimension in the party-level analysis
but excluded from it in the individual-level analysis. Finally, we show
the content of the roll calls excluded from the Left-Right dimension in
the party-level analysis.

Given the high degree of congruence in the dimensional locations of
the roll calls, there has to be a high degree of similarity in the content
interpretation of the two dimensional structures. In both analyses,
three categories concerned with the government's role in the economic
system—business (regulation of), economic policy, and housing—con-
tribute approximately one-half of the roll calls found on the Left-Right
dimensions.

There is, however, a perceptible tendency in the party-level analysis
to include, not only more roll calls, but also roll calls that lessen the
homogeneity of the Left-Right dimension compared to the Left-Right
dimension defined by the individual-level analysis. Note that of the
roll calls included on the dimension in the party-level analysis, but
excluded in the individual-level analysis, few come from the categories
associated most closely with the Left-Right dimension. As a matter of
fact, these roll calls come from categories more closely associated with
the non-Left-Right dimensions.

The categories of content most closely associated with the non-Left-
Right dimensions are social welfare, localization (assistance to indus-

trially impoverished areas), foreign aid, and miscellany (Table 5-4). Notable for their relative absence from this dimension are the economic issues included in the Left-Right dimension.

Another perspective on the substantive differentiation of the Left-Right and non-Left-Right roll calls is obtained by looking at the percentage of the roll calls in each content category that fall on the Left-Right dimension (Table 5-5). This perspective affirms our interpretation of the Left-Right dimension and provides an empirical base for a few remarks on the status of various policy questions in Swedish politics.

Few observers of Swedish politics will be surprised to find that economic, housing, and business questions are heavily loaded on the Left-Right dimension. The same holds for the radio and TV question since it involved a conflict between opposing desires for government and private control over important media of communications.

The issue questions ranking lower in their association with the Left-Right dimension require more comment. The low ranking of the defense issue may come as a surprise to observers of Swedish politics. Although defense has not been a consistently salient issue, whenever it has arisen a Left-Right conflict has developed. This was the case during the 1920s and 1930s, and again in the late 1960s, particularly in the battle over defense expenditures in 1968. However, roll calls on this subject in the 1967 session were of a minor character and consisted of efforts by the middle parties to reduce expenditures by a small amount.

Foreign aid, on the other hand, is quite understandably low in its ranking as a Left-Right issue. The Communist party and the middle parties, especially the People's party, were fighting for a substantial increase in aid to developing countries in 1967 and in the election campaign of 1968. The Social Democrats and Conservatives resisted this, although they were not opposed to increased aid at a slower pace.

The low ranking of the social welfare domain is a particularly interesting phenomenon, given the traditional positions of Left and Right parties on this subject. This issue area was one of the major battlefields in Swedish politics during the period from 1920 to 1960; furthermore, it was a Left-Right issue. It is our view, although systematic evidence is lacking, that the social welfare questions have become less partisan during the 1960s. Thus none of the roll calls in 1967 dealt with any major social welfare issues. The area is ranked low with respect to the Left-Right dimension primarily because the two middle parties wanted to give more aid to some under-privileged groups, e.g., disabled persons, than did the other parties. However, further study of roll-call voting in more sessions of the Riksdag is needed before one can con-

TABLE 5–5. Percentage of Each Issue Category Falling on the Left-Right Dimension

	Econ[a]	R-TV	Hous	ReMo	Bus	Educ	Ag	Const	CrPo	Def	FAid	SW	Lcal
Percentage Left-Right	100	100	93	91	86	80	75	75	71	64	64	41	36
Number of Roll Calls	22	5	28	11	43	15	20	8	17	14	14	41	14

[a] For full titles see Table 5–4.

clude that the social welfare issue is no longer a Left-Right question.

The localization issue, possibly one which will assume increasing importance, and one which currently evokes many non-Left-Right responses, has undertones of decentralization, the thrust of which is to reduce the migration of people from agricultural to metropolitan areas. The middle parties, especially, the Center (formerly Farmer) party, voted for higher expenditures for this purpose.

In general, the division of policy content between the Left-Right and non-Left-Right roll calls corresponds to the pattern of voting in the United States Congress during the same period. In the Congress there is an economic policy dimension with a sharp partisan division, and a social welfare dimension that cuts across the two-party division.[11] Similarly, in the Swedish Riksdag we observe the dominant partisan alignment forming on economic questions while social welfare questions tend to evoke a different partisan alignment.

Not only do the social welfare questions produce other than Left-Right party alignments, they are also characterized by a lower level of party cohesion. The variation in levels of cohesion across dimensions and issue areas will be discussed in the next section on party cohesion and party distance.

VI

PARTY COHESION AND PARTY DISTANCE

As pointed out in our introductory remarks, the dimensional form of analysis can be a useful preliminary for other analyses. In general, measures of policy dimensions constitute the best means of describing the dependent variable, legislative voting behavior, and they may be used for a variety of explanatory models of roll-call voting. Perhaps the best illustration of the utility of the dimensional model is found in representation studies where the policy decisions of legislators are compared with the policy preferences of their constituents. This comparison would be impossible if discrete policy questions were used in the articulation of the representational linkage; only at the general policy concept level can the analysis succeed.

An illustration of a kind of inquiry that can be sharpened by the use of policy dimensions is the analysis of party distance and party cohesion. Rather than base measures of these properties of the party system on the squishy mass consisting of all the roll calls voted upon in a

[11] Aage R. Clausen and Richard B. Cheney, "A Comparative Analysis of Senate-House Voting on Economic and Welfare Policy," *American Political Science Review* 64 (1970): 138–152.

AAGE R. CLAUSEN & SÖREN HOLMBERG

given session or term, we can examine them in relation to particular policy dimensions.

1. COHESION

The first part of our study of party cohesion in Riksdag voting is concerned with the proposition that the Leftist parties are more cohesive than parties to the Right. This proposition is supported by MacRae's work on the French Assembly (1946–1958) in which he finds a monotonic relationship between party cohesion and a Left-Right ordering of French parties.[12] Pedersen finds that the Communists and Social Democrats are more cohesive than the Bourgeois parties in the Danish Folketing (1953–1965).[13] Stjernquist and Bjurulf report the same results for the Swedish Riksdag in the 1964 and 1966 sessions.[14] However, the waters are muddied as more evidence is added for other legislatures at other points in time. This proposition is contradicted by data on the Finnish Riksdag (1948–1951)[15] and on the Swedish Riksdag (1943–1944 and 1947–1948).[16] However, none of these studies utilizes the dimensional analysis as a basis for more differentiated, more precise, and thereby more meaningful measures of party cohesion. Indeed, there is a large number of studies of cohesion that use the shovel rather than the scalpel; at most, they sort roll calls into subjectively defined substantive categories.[17]

In the 1967 Riksdag, when *all* of the non-abstention roll calls form the basis for party cohesion measures, there is evidence that the two Left parties are more cohesive than the three Bourgeois parties (see cohesion scores given in section II above). However, the relationship between party cohesion and Left-Right positioning proves not to be monotonic when the individual parties are ordered.

A better understanding of the party cohesion phenomenon is provided by measuring cohesion separately for the Left-Right dimension

[12] Duncan MacRae, Jr., *Parliament, Parties and Society in France, 1946–1948* (New York: St. Martin's Press, 1967), pp. 55–57.

[13] Mogens N. Pedersen, "Consensus and Conflict in the Danish Folketing, 1945–1965," *Scandinavian Political Studies* 2 (1967): 143–166.

[14] Stjernquist and Bjurulf, "Party Cohesion and Party Cooperation."

[15] Pekka Nyholm, "Riksdagstruppernas sammanhållning under 1948–1951 års mandat-period," ["Party cohesion during the 1948–1951 session"] in Jan-Magnus Jannsson, ed., *Studier i Finländsk Politik* [*Studies in Finnish Politics*] (Stockholm: Läromdelsförlagen, 1968), pp. 211–243.

[16] Lars Sköld, "Partisammanhållningen i Riksdagen," [Party cohesion in the Riksdag"] *Tiden* 5 (1950): 278–285.

[17] A wide-ranging review of the cohesion literature is found in Ergun Ozbudun, "Party Cohesion in Western Democracies: A Causal Analysis," Sage Professional Paper, Comparative Politics Series: 01–006 (Beverly Hills, California: Sage Publications, 1970).

TABLE 5-6. PARTY COHESION ON LEFT-RIGHT AND NON-LEFT-RIGHT
ROLL CALLS

Party	Left-Right Roll Calls	Non-Left-Right Roll Calls
Communist	95.9	89.5
Social Democratic	96.0	93.3
Center	92.9	86.6
People's	92.0	81.3
Conservative	95.1	83.5
Number of Roll Calls	212	87

roll calls and the non-Left-Right votes (see Table 5-6). Two observa-
tions can be made. First, for each party the level of cohesion is clearly
higher on the Left-Right roll calls. Indeed, one may expect to find it
to be the general case, in disciplined multi-party systems, that the
dominant dimension evokes the highest level of party unity. An order-
ing of parties that appears in vote after vote is likely to be an ordering
that marks a major line of cleavage in the society and its politics. Con-
sequently, a high level of party discipline can be expected and, as a
result, a high level of party cohesion.

The second observation is that the level of party cohesion is higher
for the parties on both extremes of the Left-Right ordering. This obser-
vation is supported by interview data on the personal attitudes of mem-
bers of the Riksdag toward Left-Right policy questions: the members
of the "middle" parties show less agreement in their attitudes.[18] Ac-
tually, it makes good sense that parties occupying more extreme posi-
tions should be more cohesive, just as individuals taking more extreme
positions are more intense in their views. At least this social-psychologi-
cal component of the level of party cohesion deserves a hearing along
with more sociological explanations of the cohesion phenomenon.[19] At
any rate, it is clear that a monotonic relationship does not exist between
party cohesion and a Left-Right ordering of the Swedish parties.

Cohesion varies not only with party position and with dimension but
also varies across issue areas within dimensions, and in a meaningful
way. Significantly, the pattern is one in which the central issues on a
dimension evoke the most cohesive party divisions. On the Left-Right
roll calls in the party-level analysis, cohesion across all five parties

[18] Sören Holmberg, "Politiska Sakfrågor och den Representativa Demokratin,"
["Political issues and representative democracy"] mimeographed (Institute of
Political Science, University of Göteborg, 1971), pp. 14–19.
[19] Various explanations of party cohesion are offered in Ozbudun, "Party Co-
hesion in Western Democracies," pp. 343–353.

ranged from 100 to 94 for the economic, business, and housing issues. These three policy areas encompass about 40 percent of the roll calls on the Left-Right dimension. In contrast, roll calls on social welfare questions are not only less likely to evoke Left-Right division but, when they do, the party cohesion is also lower. The cohesion scores of the five parties on social welfare issues, within the Left-Right cluster, range from 96 to 90.

The different levels of cohesion on economic and social welfare roll calls, and the closer identification of the economic policies with the major Left-Right dimension, suggest that cohesion is higher on issues provoking class conflict. Although social welfare questions were once the focus of such conflict, this is no longer the case, since government responsibility for social welfare is well established in Sweden. In contrast, economic policies continue to evoke the traditional Left-Right cleavage.

In sum, it is our view that the study of party cohesion can be advanced substantially by giving more attention to the differences between dimensions of voting. This implies, as well, a more careful examination of the factors and conditions contributing to the level of cohesion observed in different parties.

2. PARTY DISTANCE

The measurement of party distance on the Left-Right dimension conducted in this study is of particular interest because it is based on data drawn from both the electorate and the elected. In the latter instance, the distances between the five Swedish parties are calculated on the basis of the voting behavior of the members of the Riksdag. The distance measures for the electorate are based on both policy attitudes and voting behavior. This combination of measures allows us to engage in a cross-validation of measures of party distance, using both different populations (elite and mass) and different measures on a single population (mass). The latter also gives us an insight into different properties of party distances, suggesting that distances between any pair of parties, measured with respect to the *same* dimension on the *same* population, can differ according to the aspect of the dimension being measured. This is saying something quite different from one of the points made in a study of Norwegian voters by Converse and Valen.[20] They demonstrated that perceptions of party distances depend upon the vantage point from which the individual views the parties, specifically his location in the social, economic, geographic, and political structure.

[20] Converse and Valen, "Dimensions of Cleavage," pp. 126–150.

Now there are perhaps many who will view the analysis of party distance being presented here as provocative at best, and downright inappropriate at worst, depending upon their apprehensions regarding the use of interval-level assumptions. Without entering into the details of this argument, which is far from being a one-sided affair, let us consider this temporary adjustment to the problem. Certainly, the interval-level assumption is appropriate to the numerical scores assigned individuals, and there is no doubt that the numbers may be manipulated at the interval level. What remains is for readers to reach their own conclusions regarding the value of the inferences that are drawn by the authors, who proceed as though the discrepancy between the "true" scores and the assigned ones, at the interval level, is not sufficient to invalidate those inferences.

Our measurements of party distance in the Riksdag are based on the scale scores assigned to individual legislators on the Left-Right dimension. The distances between the parties are simply the differences in the mean scores of the five party memberships. The data on party means and on the range of scores assigned to members within each party are presented in Table 5–7.

There are few surprises when the positions of the Swedish parties and their members are characterized in this way. The widest gap is between the Bourgeois and the Left parties. The Conservative party is on the far right as expected, and the Center parties are close to each other in what appears to be Right-Center. The one surprise, but one based on weak evidence, is that the Communist party is positioned to the right of the Social Democrats. The evidence is weak because there are only eight Communists; when such a small number of individuals is involved, individual idiosyncrasies can have a great effect. In another session, different results may occur.

An additional datum provided by this analysis, one which enriches the meaning of party distance as measured by the differences in means, as well as being of some comfort to those disturbed by the interval-level assumption, is the degree of overlap in the scale positions of individual members from different parties. Thus, the substantial dis-

TABLE 5–7. PARTY SCALE SCORES ON LEFT-RIGHT DIMENSION

Party	Mean	Range	N
Communist	1.19	1.04–1.43	8
Social Democratic	1.12	1.02–1.50	109
Center	2.32	2.22–2.43	34
People's	2.47	2.31–2.63	40
Conservative	2.87	2.65–2.99	34

TABLE 5–8. PARTY DISTANCES ON THREE MEASURES OF LEFT-RIGHT
DIMENSION: ONE ROLL CALL MEASURE AND TWO VOTER MEASURES

	Communist	Social Democratic	Center	People's	Conservative
Roll Call	96	100	33	24	00
Voter: Party Preferences	100	57	36	21	00
Voter: Left-Right Attitudes	100	78	27	20	00

tance between the Conservatives and the two parties of the Center is
indicated also by the absence of any overlap in the scale positions of
individual members from the two sets of parties. The Left and the
Bourgeois parties are, similarly, sharply distinguished. However, there
is substantial overlap in the scale positions of Communists and Social
Democrats and in the positions of Center and People's party members.

The distance between the parties on the Left-Right dimension in the
Riksdag is, as promised, compared with distances computed on the
electorate. The first comparison is with the distance between the par-
ties calculated by Bo Särlvik based on changes in voting preferences
among voters.[21] In Särlvik's analyses, the distance between parties in
the electorate is inversely related to the number of voters who switch
their preferences, from one election to the next, between the parties.[22]
The results derived from this measure of party distance are compared
with the legislative-based measures, both scales adjusted to a range of
0 to 100 (see Table 5–8).

The comparisons between these two measures of party distance,
legislative voting and voter party preferences, are particularly inter-
esting with respect to the dissimilarities that emerge, although we are
struck by the similarities as well. Briefly, with respect to the latter, note
the striking, almost unbelievable, similarity in the distances between
the Bourgeois parties in the two measures.

A fascinating aspect of the dissimilarity between the two measures
of party distance is the distance between the Social Democrats and the
Communists. This distance is very large when the measurement is
based on voter preferences while it is very small when based on policy
decisions made in the Riksdag voting. One possible explanation for
this difference between the two measures is "coalition thinking" in the

[21] Särlvik, "Partibyten som mått på avstånd."
[22] Ibid., p. 58. This measurement is based on the Coombs-Goodes method and is
comparable in its results with a distance measure using the Guttman-Lingoes
smallest space analysis.

parliamentary situation. Roll-call voting, by this view, is not merely an expression of policy positions but is also a product of strategic imperatives.[23] In the present case, there is a strong need for the Communists to support the Social Democrats and their policies even while preferring more radical alternatives, in order to avoid the removal of the Social Democratic party from power, or to keep it from having to form a coalition with a more moderate party supportive of even less "leftish" policies.

There is an alternative explanation for the different distances between the two Left parties produced by these two measures. In moving toward the second explanation, consider that the legislature-based measure is concerned with policy positions while the electorate-based measure is concerned with party preferences and thereby taps partisan affect. The content differences between the two measures may be the explanation for the differences between them. Fortunately, we can get a hold on this problem by bringing in a second measure of party distance in the electorate that is based on policy positions.

The second measure of party distance in the electorate is derived from the attitudes of voters on six questions of policy comparable to those raised in the roll calls on the Left-Right dimensions in the Riksdag. Thus, policy content is involved now in both measures of party distance. The distances between the parties according to the voter attitude measures are more similar to the party distances in the Riksdag than was the case for the voter party preference measure. Still, there remains a greater difference between the two Left parties among the voters than in the Riksdag. These observations lead us to the following conclusions.

The relative closeness of the Social Democratic and Communist parties in the Riksdag is due in part to the strategic imperatives of the parliamentary situation, but it is also due partly to the fact that, for mass and elite alike, policy differences between the two Left parties are not very sharp; or at least not as sharp as both parties would like to think. We propose that there is, however, a high level of negative *partisan* affect between the two parties. As indicated in the Converse-Valen study of the Norwegian electorate, the partisan antipathy may be asymmetric in that the antipathy which the Social Democrats (and other parties for that matter) feel toward the Communists may be much stronger than the negative affect in the Communists' orientation toward the Social Democrats (and other parties).[24] Whether the negative parti-

[23] For a discussion of these problems see Gunnar Sjöblom, *Party Strategies in a Multi-Party System* (Lund: Studentlitteratur, 1968).
[24] Converse and Valen, "Dimensions of Cleavage," pp. 132–133.

san affect is symmetric or asymmetric, it is our expectation that a measure of partisan preference among the members of the Riksdag would produce results paralleling those found in the study of the electorate. In short, the findings for party distances along the same dimension differ depending upon whether partisan affect or preference is used to measure these distances or whether policy attitudes are considered. Thus, the measurement of party distances is plagued not only by the problem of multidimensionality but also by the problem of multifaceted unidimensionality.

The purpose of this cohesion and party distance analysis has been, not to test a substantive hypothesis, but to demonstrate the potentialities of measures of voting dimensions, even for a highly disciplined party system. Furthermore, we have only scratched the surface, since we have restricted our analysis to the major distinction between the Left-Right and other dimensions, without exploring the facets of legislative voting exhibited in particular measures of non-Left-Right dimensions.

VI
CONCLUSION

THE analysis of roll-call voting described here is part of a study of political representation in Sweden from 1968 to 1969. For this, it was necessary to obtain behavioral measures for members of the Riksdag that could be used in conjunction with measures of members' attitudes, and, equally important, with measures of constituency attitudes. This imperative, in turn, suggested the need for measuring legislative behavior in terms of policy dimensions, for at that level of generality it was both feasible and useful to make comparisons between the policy positions of the representatives and the represented.

Initially, and to a degree that is difficult for the reader to appreciate after the fact, there were serious questions as to the potentials of a dimensional analysis of legislative voting behavior in Sweden, given the image of a highly disciplined, party-dominated legislature. Three related questions confronted us: (1) what could be learned that was not apparent from looking at party programs and the popular press; (2) was there enough inter-person, intra-party variation in behavior to warrant an individual-level analysis; and (3) in the absence of opportunities for individual-level analysis, or from the perspective that parties rather than individuals are the appropriate units of analysis, what were the opportunities for dimensional analysis using the party as the unit of analysis?

These questions led us to give substantial attention to the methodology of policy-dimension analysis in disciplined multi-party systems.

184

We have considered various approaches to this analysis, with particular attention to two options for analyzing legislative voting behavior. One option involves the use of the individual as the unit of analysis, and the second employs the party as the unit of analysis. Neither approach has been foreclosed by our investigations, nor has either been given preferred status. Of course, when the votes of individuals are not considered or not recorded, or when the parties are very cohesive in their voting, the only option is to use the party as the unit of analysis. In the latter condition, we have argued that a meaningful dimensional analysis can be performed with as few as three parties.

The principal finding of the dimensional analysis, using either the individual or the party as the unit of analysis, was the presence of a dominant Left-Right dimension. This was an expected finding, but not one that had been offered in previous studies with the same degree of explicitness. In addition to the Left-Right dimension, the analysis extracted a secondary set of dimensions. These were characterized by the opposition of the middle parties, on the Left-Right ordering, to the parties of the Left and Right extremes. With certain interesting exceptions, the same dimensional structure emerged regardless of whether the party or the individual was used as the unit of analysis.

Dominating the Left-Right dimension were questions of economic policy, whereas there was a higher concentration of social welfare, foreign, and decentralization policy items on the "other dimensions." This content differentiation of the voting dimensions is similar to that found in the United States Congress during the same period.

The utility of a dimensional analysis of legislative voting in a disciplined multi-party system was considered also with regard to two properties of party systems that are of general interest: cohesion within parties and distances between them. In the first instance, a cohesion analysis was conducted, taking advantage of the prior measurement of voting dimensions to enhance the precision and meaningfulness of the cohesion measurements. In the second instance, party distance measures were constructed on the Left-Right dimensions and related to party distance measures derived from the attitudes and party preferences of members of the electorate. The differentiation of legislative voting behavior in terms of policy dimensions made an important contribution to the analysis of both party cohesion and party distance.

The conclusion that may clearly be drawn from our experience is that the dimensional analysis of voting behavior in a disciplined multi-party system is not only feasible but also highly desirable. Neither the small number of parties nor the relative lack of inter-person, intra-party variation should be looked upon as final arguments against pursuing dimensional analysis.

185

6

The Making of the Mexican Constitution

PETER H. SMITH

THE Mexican Constitution of 1917 has gained a widespread reputation as one of the most "progressive" charters in the Western world. Article 27 established the means for land distribution, Article 123 spelled out workers' rights, other stipulations put strict limits on the power of the Church. According to most standard views, the Constitution represents the noblest ideals of the movement that overthrew Porfirio Díaz in 1910 and grew into one of the first mass-based revolutions of this century. But, notwithstanding frequent exegesis of the text, there has been little effort to explain the reasons for its social content.[1] Why such a radical document?

The traditional explanation, avidly promoted by the leaders of the country's political system, is that the convention delegates faithfully represented the popular will. In support of this contention, it commonly is held that the deputies were themselves men of humble social background, often from backward rural areas; that they were young, and therefore bent on innovation; and that, as active soldiers in the Revolution, they had gained intimate familiarity with the needs of the povertied masses. Traces of conflict at the assembly present an awkward problem for this quasi-official view, which tends to stress the unanimity and continuity of the revolutionary tradition (of which the

I would like to thank the ACLS–SSRC Joint Committee on Latin American Studies and the Graduate School of the University of Wisconsin for helping to support this research. Gerald Marwell gave invaluable advice on methodological matters, and David R. Olson provided expert assistance with the computer programming; all errors of fact, procedure, and interpretation are my own responsibility. A preliminary version of this paper was presented at the 86th Annual Meeting of the American Historical Association, New York, December 1971; a translation of that early draft has been published as "La política dentro de la Revolución: el Congreso Constituyente de 1916–1917," *Historia Mexicana* 22 (1973): 363–395.

[1] The most thorough treatment to date, descriptive in form and uncritical in tone, is E. V. Niemeyer, Jr., *Revolution at Querétaro: The Mexican Constitutional Congress of 1916–1917* (Austin: University of Texas Press, 1974). Other works include Gabriel Ferrer de Mendiolea, *Historia del Congreso Constituyente de 1916–1917* (México: Biblioteca del Instituto Nacional de Estudios Históricos de la Revolución Mexicana, 1957); Germán List Arzubide, *La gran rebelión de los Constituyentes de 1917* (México: Ediciones Conferencia, 1963); Daniel Moreno, *El Congreso Constituyente de 1916–1917* (México: Universidad Nacional Autónoma de México, 1967); and Charles C. Cumberland, *Mexican Revolution: The Constitutionalist Years* (Austin: University of Texas Press, 1972), chap. 9.

current one-party regime purports to be the sole and legitimate heir), but this inconvenience is dismissed with elegant simplicity: the more radical deputies at the convention were just a bit *more* humble, young, and empathetic than were their less ardent colleagues. Cast in this light, the Constitution stands as a major political symbol: made both by and for the people, it is the consummate expression of the Mexican national will.[2]

Despite the transparently self-serving quality of this interpretation, or perhaps because of it, there has not yet appeared a systematic, empirical study of the subject. In an effort to meet this challenge, I shall here focus on three fundamental problems. *First,* what was the social composition of the constitutional convention? To what extent was it a "popular" group? How did it represent the *campesinos*[3] and the workers? *Second,* what were the sources of discord, or did harmony prevail? Was there substantial disagreement over the desirability and direction of social change? *Third,* was there any relationship between social background and attitudinal alignment? Did the Constitution reflect the triumph of one "class" or social group over another? As I shall try to demonstrate, these questions bear significant implications for more than just the constitutional congress; they can illuminate some crucial aspects of the Mexican Revolution as a whole.

As an example of historical analysis, this inquiry also derives conceptual and methodological importance from several specific characteristics. By definition, a constitutional convention is not a "legislative body" in the strictest sense of that term. Its major concern is not passing laws; a constituent assembly concentrates on building institutions. The practical distinction between these two functions can become extremely vague, of course, but it still reflects a basic difference in purpose and orientation. Whereas legislative groups tend to work on immediate policy issues about which individual lawmakers commonly have precious little knowledge, constitutional conventions deal with general matters of governmental structure, about which most people have some ideas. Such conditions would seem bound to have an impact on patterns of cleavage and consensus.

[2] This interpretation is implicit throughout virtually all the studies mentioned in note 1. Explicit political manipulation of these themes can be found in *Mexicano: esta es tu constitución* (México: Cámara de Diputados, 1970), a document that was widely distributed to the public during the presidential campaign of 1970; see esp. pp. 7–17. Note also the statements by the official candidate, Luis Echeverría, in [Partido Revolucionario Institucional], *Luis Echeverría: praxis política* (México: Cultura y Ciencia Política, 1970), 1: 24–27; and 2–3, 22–25.

[3] John Womack, Jr., has suggested that the term "peasant" is inappropriate for the Mexican campesino or "country person." *Zapata and the Mexican Revolution* (New York: Alfred A. Knopf, 1969), p. x.

Further analytical complications grow out of the immediate Mexican context. The country was still in the throes of a violent and massive revolution. As will be shown below, the men who gathered at Querétaro were typically young and lacking in political experience. Unlike most congressmen or parliamentarians, who commonly reach office after working in or through some formal organization (such as a political party), these Mexicans had no strong institutional commitments. They were united only by allegiance to the triumphant faction of the Mexican Revolution. Yet they took differing sides on many key issues. A principal goal of this investigation is to find out how and why they did.

I

Composition of the Congress

One of the most elementary purposes of this convention was to establish a legal claim to political legitimacy. In 1916 there were still three major rivals struggling to control the Revolution: Pancho Villa in Chihuahua, Emiliano Zapata in Morelos, and, by far the strongest, Venustiano Carranza. Cautiously deferring to the revolutionary cry for "no re-election," Carranza held on to the title of "First Chief of the Constitutionalist Army" [4] so that he would be able to step directly into the presidency. Yet he still required additional leverage. A constitutional congress, by laying down the rules for presidential succession, would admirably meet this need.

Recognizing the convention's political functions, Carranza took no chances on its composition. His call to elections explicitly prohibited the nomination of anyone who had "served . . . governments or factions hostile to the Constitutionalist cause," and a further ruling restricted the vote to those who had proved, "with actual deeds, their adherence to the Consitutionalist cause." *Zapatistas, Villistas,* participants in the coalition government of Eulalio Gutiérrez, and any other anti-Carrancistas simply were excluded from contention. Nor did competitive parties appear. People ran for positions in the assembly as individuals or factional spokesmen, not as representatives of rival institutions. Probably as a result, the elections took place in October 1916 without exciting popular enthusiasm—"as if," one witness recalled, "we had found ourselves under the influence of the Porfirian terror." [5]

Some of the men who won seats at the constitutional congress were

---

[4] Carranza's movement was initially known as "Constitutionalist" because of his desire to uphold the prerevolutionary Constitution of 1857, not because of any plan to draw up a new charter.

[5] On the election see Niemeyer, *Revolution,* pp. 31–36; the quotation is on p. 35.

TABLE 6-1. HIGHEST NATIONAL OFFICES HELD BY DELEGATES TO CON-
STITUTIONAL CONVENTION [a]

Office	Before Convention	After Convention
Cabinet [b]	9	14
Subcabinet	2	4
Governor [c]	6	22
Senator	0	23
Deputy	13	59
Ambassador	0	2
Totals	30	124

[a] Offices ranked in loose order, from top to bottom. For a much more refined ranking system, referring to the contemporary political structure, see Frank R. Brandenburg, *The Making of Modern Mexico* (Englewood Cliffs, New Jersey: Prentice-Hall, 1964), pp. 158–159.

[b] Includes heads of important *departamentos* and some acting cabinet secretaries (*encargados del despacho*).

[c] Includes provisional and interim Governors.

already prominent, but most of them were not. As shown in Table 6-1, only 30 out of the total of 219 had held national political positions prior to the convention. Afterward, however, 124 would have some sort of post (101 of them for the first time).[6] Office-holding provides an exceedingly dubious index of "power" in modern Mexico, especially on the congressional level, but the data have two far-reaching implications. First, by reaping the benefits of victory, participants in the constitutional congress furnish a meaningful (non-random) sample of political leadership in the post-revolutionary period. Second, in possible anticipation of this fact, Carranza may have had yet another purpose in calling the convention: it would facilitate consolidation of a political team.

Because of their diverse and important roles, the social backgrounds of the delegates assume special significance. According to Table 6–2, which summarizes available biographical information on the 219 Deputies,[7] these were men of privilege. Albeit impressionistically, sur-

[6] These figures are based on linkages with the names of office-holders in virtually every significant national political position from 1900 through 1971, compiled for a study still in progress. The count is preliminary and subject to possible (but minor) modification.

[7] Most of the information on personal background has come from an "Autobiografía" file at the Asociación de Diputados Constituyentes in Mexico City, by far the most important single source; newspaper articles, particularly a series by Gabriel Ferrer de Mendiolea on "Constituyentes del 17" in *El Nacional*, 1957–1958 (for a guide to these and other relevant articles see Stanley R. Ross, ed., *Fuentes de la historia contemporánea de México: periódicos y revistas* [México:

TABLE 6-2. SELECTED SOCIAL CHARACTERISTICS OF DELEGATES TO CONSTITUTIONAL CONVENTION

"Social Class"

	N	%[b]
Lower	25	11.4
Middle	186	84.9
Upper	8	3.7

Professional Title [a]

	N	%
None	103	47.0
Licenciado	56	25.6
Doctor	24	11.0
Profesor	14	6.4
Ingeniero	21	9.6
Contador	1	0.5

Highest Education

	N	%[c]
Primary	4	2.9
Secondary	3	2.2
Commercial	5	3.6
Military	2	1.4
Normal	7	5.0
Preparatory	9	6.5
University	108	78.3
Unknown	81	–

Age

	N	%[c]
20–29	35	26.5
30–39	55	41.7
40–49	31	23.5
50 plus	11	8.3
Unknown	87	–

Military Status

	N	%
Civilian	153	69.9
General	21	9.6
Colonel	27	12.3
Lt. Col.	12	5.5
Major	5	2.3
Captain	1	0.5

[a] Titles, in respective order: lawyer, doctor, professor, engineer, accountant.
[b] Percentages may not add up to 100 because of rounding.
[c] Percentages for Highest Education and Age exclude "unknown" cases.

viving participants have categorized less than 12 percent of the Deputies as "lower class" in origin, placing almost 85 percent in a loosely defined "middle class." [8] *Over half* the delegates claimed professional titles of one sort or another, with lawyers as the largest group,[9] and nearly the same proportion appears to have had a university education.[10] In a society where most adults could neither read nor write,[11] this was hardly a "representative" group. It was disproportionately learned and, without being upper class, it was disproportionately well-to-do.[12]

El Colegio de México, 1951], 1: [881]–939); Francisco Naranjo, *Diccionario biográfico revolucionario* (México: Editorial Cosmos, [1935]; and the *Diccionario Porrúa de historia, biografía y geografía de México* (México: Porrúa, 1965; and supplement, 1966). Examination of two other standard sources—Juan López de Escalera, *Diccionario biográfico y de historia de México* (México: Editorial del Magisterio, 1964) and Miguel Angel Peral, *Diccionario biográfico mexicano,* 2 vols. plus Apéndice (México: Editorial P.A.C., 1944)—turned up very few extra data. Since the writing of this paper some additional information has appeared in Niemeyer, *Revolution,* appendix F, pp. [263]–267.

[8] Estimates of "social class" background are based almost entirely on the collective and remarkably concordant judgment of three historical participants whom I interviewed separately in 1970. One was custodian of the Asociación de Diputados Constituyentes and had been a personal aide to Venustiano Carranza; the other two, a lawyer and a professor, had been Deputies at the convention. I asked each respondent to categorize delegates according to socio-economic status; they all volunteered the upper-, middle-, and lower-class distinctions. For several Deputies I also used explicit comments on social origin in documentary sources.

[9] My data on professions and occupations differ widely from the figures in Enrique A. Enríquez, "En memoria de cuatro Constituyentes," *El Nacional,* September 29, 1958, but conform quite closely to the estimates by Jesús Romero Flores on pp. 8–9 of Asociación de Diputados Constituyentes, *Antología literaria: recopilación de discursos, artículos y poemas* (México: Partido Revolucionario Institucional, 1969); see also Niemeyer, *Revolution,* p. 39. Unless data show otherwise I have assumed that Deputies with professional titles were practicing those professions as their basic occupations. In all cases I have tried to identify the primary occupation just prior to the convention, but the coded data might refer to subsequent occupational activities in a few instances.

[10] Data on "highest level of education" refer to the highest level of school *attended* as distinct from *completed.* Where direct information is missing I have assumed that all Deputies with professional titles of Licenciado, Doctor, or Ingeniero went to a "university" or its equivalent and have coded them accordingly. This procedure might over-estimate the number of university graduates, since some people may have claimed titles without having degrees, but I believe that my figures are still quite reliable.

[11] For extensive data on the national population see México, Secretaría de Economía, Dirección General de Estadística, *Estadísticas sociales del Porfiriato, 1877–1910* (México: Talleres Gráficos de la Nación, 1956); and Arturo González Cosío, "Clases y estratos sociales," in *México: Cincuenta años de Revolución,* vol. 2, *La vida social* (México: Fondo de Cultura Económica, 1961), pp. 29–77.

[12] The designation of "class" is an extremely difficult and arbitrary process. It would be quite possible to argue that there were only two classes in Mexico's stratification system at this time and therefore, on the basis of my data, most Deputies belonged to the upper class.

191

TABLE 6–3. PROFESSIONAL TITLE AND MILITARY STATUS

| Professional | Military Status | | |
Title	Military	Civilian	Totals
No title	41	62	103
Title	25	91	116
Totals	66	153	219
	gamma=.41		

It was also a youthful group. Among those of known age, 26.5 percent were still in their twenties (as of January 1, 1917), and 41.7 percent were in their thirties. Nearly 70 percent had not yet reached the age of 40. One implication of this fact is obvious: many if not most of the Deputies started taking active part in politics after 1910. Some no doubt forged their ideals during the course of the Revolution itself, rather than during the later stages of the Díaz dictatorship.

About a third of the delegates were officers in the Constitutionalist Army.[13] Military distinction provided a channel of upward mobility for some, but not for a very large group. At least 29 of the 66 officers appear to have enjoyed university educations and, as Table 6–3 reveals, 25 used professional titles. Self-made soldiers comprised a small minority at this convention.

All in all, these findings sharply contradict standard notions about the "popular" social origins of the constitutional congress. The Carrancista delegates formed a select group: young and ambitious, to be sure, but of extremely high educational and occupational status in relation to the country as a whole. Only nine of the Deputies are known to have been laborers or union leaders, and merely two were campesinos. At Querétaro, the masses had few spokesmen of their own.

On the leadership level, one major force within the Mexican Revolution thus represented an essentially middle-class challenge to Porfirio Díaz's *científico* clique. Toward the end of his dictatorship, the Porfirian ruling groups held simultaneous keys to economic, political, and social influence; they made widespread use of nepotism to keep

[13] My total number of military officers is a bit higher than shown in the list of "Military Delegates" at the convention in Edwin Lieuwen, *Mexican Militarism: The Political Rise and Fall of the Revolutionary Army, 1910–1940* (Albuquerque: University of New Mexico Press, 1968), Appendix C, p. 155. His roster is somewhat confusing since it appears to match first names with the wrong surnames; for example, "Ascención Terrones B." mixes up the names of Ascención Tépal and Alberto Terrones Benítez. These errors might possibly originate in a misreading of the data in Anon., "El Congreso Constituyente de Querétaro," *Gráfico* (*Magazín del Gráfico*), February 7, 1932.

power within their own circles; and, in time, they grew extremely old.[14] It appears that young men of ambition—particularly those who, by background and education, fancied themselves to be potential leaders—resented these restrictions on their own advancement. Out of frustration many joined the Revolution, and a substantial number found their way into the constitutional convention.

In view of this situation, there was every reason to expect the convention to produce a moderate reformist constitution. Hoping this would be the case, Carranza presented the delegates with a bland proposal to revise the liberal Constitution of 1857 without making any strong provision for workers' rights or land distribution. To assure approval of his draft, Carranza gave the Deputies only 60 days in which to finish their task. And yet the Deputies rebelled! Laboring under intense pressure, they rewrote major portions of the First Chief's proposal and added the sections on labor and land. What can account for this behavior? To repeat my original question: Why such a radical document?

II

MODERATES AND JACOBINS

MEXICO's revolutionary constitution came from a socially privileged group, but not a harmonious one. Almost all qualified observers agree that the congress split into two camps: "rightists" or "moderates" in the minority, and "leftists" or "Jacobins" in the majority. Moderates are said to have been loyal to Carranza, supporting his proposed draft for a new charter. Jacobins allegedly drew their inspiration from General Álvaro Obregón, then Carranza's Minister of War and later on a President, and it was the Jacobins who set about rewriting the nation's Constitution.

Yet there is little agreement on the size, composition, or attitudinal leanings of the two factions.[15] In 1932, for example, an anonymous article in the *Magazín del Gráfico* identified 103 Deputies as belonging to the "left," 92 as belonging to the "right," and 17 as intermediate.[16] Six years later Juan de Dios Bojórquez, a delegate to the convention

[14] Probably the best existing discussion of the late Porfirian elite is in Francisco Bulnes, *El verdadero Díaz y la Revolución* (México: Editora Nacional, 1967), first published around 1920. I plan to treat the subject in some detail in my book-length study of political elites in twentieth-century Mexico (in progress).

[15] For a dispute on the size of the two groups see Juan de Dios Bojórquez [Djed Bórquez, pseud.], *Crónica del Constituyente* (México: Editorial Botas, 1938), pp. 158–159.

[16] "El Congreso Constituyente de Querétaro," *Gráfico* (*Magazín del Gráfico*), February 7, 1932.

Table 6-4. Classification Schemes for Constitutional Deputies

Rating in *Magazín* *del Gráfico* (1932)	Rating by Bojórquez (1938)		
	Leftist	Rightist	Totals
Leftist	92	16	108
Undefined	12	5	17
Rightist	35	57	92
Unlisted	2	0	2
Totals	141	78	219

Excluding the "unlisted" category, gamma = .75.

from Sonora, put 141 colleagues on the "left" and 78 on the "right" with none in the middle.[17] Table 6-4 compares the two classifications and reveals considerable difference between them. Only 68 percent of the delegates were in the same cells; a total of 51—23.3 percent—were "rightist" in one scheme and "leftist" in another. Aside from this discrepancy, which makes both schemes shaky as foundations for analysis, the classifications do not contain or express any explicit criteria. In and of themselves, such labels as "left" and "right" have no precise meaning. So there remains a double task: first, identifying the substantive sources of disagreement; second, placing individuals in their respective camps.

My principal instrument for this purpose involves the statistical analysis of roll calls and petitions at the constitutional congress. Official proceedings of the convention contain 24 complete roll-call votes on a wide variety of issues, apparently selected for publication because they brought about considerable discord. From "no" votes only, I have been able to reconstruct divisions on three additional roll calls which are adjacent to full votes on other issues (partial listings of affirmative or negative sides could not be used this way in other cases because of fluctuating attendance at the meetings). Finally, I have included five petitions, treating a signature as analogous to a "yes" vote on a roll call. In all there are 32 variables which provide the basis for analysis.[18] (See the Appendix for a list of roll calls and

[17] Bojórquez, *Crónica*, "Directorio," pp. [735]–744. One wonders if Bojórquez also composed the *Gráfico* list, allegedly consisting of "notes for an unpublished book," possibly his own. If so, he changed his mind about a lot of people!

[18] Roll calls and four petitions have been taken from *Diario de los debates del Congreso Constituyente*, 2 vols. (México: Imprenta de la Cámara de Diputados, 1922); and checked against a later edition, sponsored by the Comisión Nacional para la Celebración del Sesquicentenario de la Proclamación de la Independencia Nacional y del Cinquentenario de la Revolución Mexicana, also in 2 vols. (México: Instituto Nacional de Estudios Históricos de la Revolución Mexicana, 1960). The fifth petition appears in Bojórquez, *Crónica*. For full citations see the Appendix.

petitions and their respective Riker indices, which measure general "significance" as a function of both participation and conflict.)[19]

It is clear from the subject matter of the 24 recorded votes that the Deputies divided over a wide variety of questions. But which sets of issues were the most "important" ones? Which ones provoked the Moderate-Jacobin split?

For coping with these problems I have resorted to factor analysis, which makes it possible to identify underlying and mutually independent dimensions of conflict, and also to create a scale for rating every deputy on each dimension.[20] To reduce error variance I eventually decided to delete four uncontested roll calls, arbitrarily defined as those with less than 22 minority votes (10 percent of the entire deputy sample). Table 6–5 presents five different "raw" or unrotated factors and their statistical relationships (or "loadings") with the remaining 28 variables, which furnish clues about the latent content of each factor.[21] Factor I is highly suggestive: it has loadings of .60 or stronger with the vote on Article 3, the hotly debated matter of state vs. religious education (.73); the manifesto of January 31, 1917, in which self-designated "Jacobins" accused their opponents of reactionary obstructionism (.68); a vote on whether the Senate or the Supreme Court should resolve political crises within states (.65); two issues involving state or federal control of penitentiaries (.64 and .61); a decision on Congress's right to call special sessions without presidential approval (.63); an article authorizing a central bank (.61); and another which would have placed Mexico City under the direction of the national government (−.60). Except for the manifesto, which

[19] On computation of the Riker index see Lee F. Anderson et al., *Legislative Roll-Call Analysis* (Evanston, Illinois: Northwestern University Press, 1966), pp. 81–84.

[20] Consult Benjamin Fruchter, *Introduction to Factor Analysis* (Princeton, New Jersey: Van Nostrand, 1954); Anderson et al., *Roll-Call Analysis*, chap. 7; Duncan MacRae, Jr., *Issues and Parties in Legislative Voting: Methods of Statistical Analysis* (New York: Harper and Row, 1970), esp. chaps. 4–5; and Rudolph J. Rummel, *Applied Factor Analysis* (Evanston, Illinois: Northwestern University Press, 1970). For a demonstration of factor analysis in a comparable context see S. Sidney Ulmer, "Sub-group formation in the [United States] Constitutional Convention," *Midwest Journal of Political Science* 10 (1966): 288–303.

[21] Results have been obtained through FACTOR 2, a packaged program in the STATJOB series at the University of Wisconsin Computing Center. Roll calls were coded as follows: yes = +1, not voting = 0, no = −1. For petitions the coding was: signed = +1, did not sign = −1. This scheme produced a matrix of Pearson product-moment correlations, which was factored by the "principal components procedure" in a common factor analysis model. A preliminary run yielded eight factors with eigenvalues greater than 1, which together explained 60.4 percent of the total variance. In deciding to present the first five factors, I have relied on (a) general interpretability and (b) the so-called "scree test" (Rummel, *Applied Factor Analysis*, pp. 361–362).

TABLE 6–5. LOADINGS IN RAW FACTOR MATRIX

Roll Calls or Petitions	Factors				
	I	II	III	IV	V
1. Credentials: Ezquerro	.34	—.30	—.04	—.37	—.11
2. Credentials: Palavicini	———		deleted		———
3. Credentials: Martí	—.34	—.10	—.23	.01	—.35
4. Estados Unidos-República	(.60)[a]	—.18	.16	.04	—.09
5. Credentials: Vizcaíno	—.36	—.24	—.48	—.41	.05
6. Article 3	(.73)	.00	—.05	.01	.10
7. Jury Trials for Press #1	.47	.40	.07	.09	—.45
8. Right of Assembly	(.51)	—.26	—.31	—.02	—.06
9. State-Federal Jails #1	(.64)	.06	.11	.05	.09
10. Preventive Arrest	.30	(—.53)	—.06	—.19	.13
11. State-Federal Jails #2	(.61)	—.04	—.34	—.20	.03
12. Jury Trials for Press #2	.49	.34	—.09	—.18	(—.50)
13. Qualifications for Congress: Nationality	(.52)	—.21	.21	—.14	.29
14. Qualifications for Congress: Age	———		deleted		———
15. Qualifications for Congress: Residence	—.39	—.17	—.34	—.22	—.19
16. Qualifications for Congress: Military	———		deleted		———
17. Qualifications for Congress: Public Office	———		deleted		———
18. Fuero Militar	.10	—.33	.41	.11	—.13
19. Capital Punishment	—.29	(—.53)	—.10	.40	—.36
20. Punishment for Rape	—.18	—.49	—.16	(.64)	—.11
21. Federal District	(—.60)	—.04	.05	—.13	.00
22. Congressional Autonomy	(.63)	.18	.18	.14	.15
23. Senate-Supreme Court	(.65)	—.09	—.12	—.15	—.12
24. Central Bank, Anti-Trust	(.61)	—.27	—.01	.00	—.10
25. Congress-Elections	(—.56)	.04	.03	—.02	—.10
26. Moral Austerity Vote	.29	.26	(—.63)	.32	.16
27. Right to Worship	(—.51)	—.34	—.08	—.15	.24
28. Resignation by Ugarte	(.53)	.01	.11	.06	—.03
29. Article 123	—.11	—.01	.00	—.20	(—.51)
30. Moral Austerity Petition	.21	.26	(—.65)	.22	.10
31. Stamp Tax	.45	—.47	—.15	.11	.01
32. Manifesto of January 31	(.68)	—.22	.03	—.04	—.08
% of Factor Variance	49.9	16.3	13.7	10.1	9.9
% of Total Variance	23.6	7.7	6.5	4.8	4.7

[a] Parentheses indicate variable loadings $\geqq |.50|$.

referred to no specific issue, all these matters seem to have concerned the concentration and use of power by the central government.

Factor II has notable loadings with only two roll calls, one on arrest procedures (—.53) and the other on capital punishment (—.53). Factor III has strong relationships with a petition seeking to prohibit various vices and with a vote on that same issue (—.65 and —.63, respectively). Factor iv is linked primarily to a decision on capital punishment for rape (.64). Factor v bears some connection to the pro-labor petition on Article 123 (−.51) and to a vote on legal rights of the press (−.50).

For statistical and substantive reasons I believe that Factor i captures the Moderate-Jacobin conflict. According to Table 6–5, it explains a much higher percentage of variance than any of the other factors. It has high loadings with issues which one delegate, Juan de Dios Bojórquez, later described as crucial to the Moderate-Jacobin split (variables 6, 11, and 32).[22] Factor scores for individual deputies[23] reveal that well-known Moderates (Alfonso Cravioto, José Natividad Macías, Félix F. Palavicini, Luis Manuel Rojas, Gerzayn Ugarte) cluster together at the negative end of the scale, while famous Jacobins (Enrique Colunga, Heriberto Jara, Luis G. Monzón, Francisco J. Múgica) show up on the positive side.[24] When inactive deputies are excluded, scores for 179 remaining "participant" delegates[25] have a neat bimodal distribution, as illustrated by Figure 6–1, demonstrating the existence of two definite opposing camps. Furthermore a dichotomous categorization of delegates with scores above or below −.30, the point which separates the modal groups, yields a total of 68 Moderates and 111 Jacobins, a proportional ratio which is consistent with key roll-call tallies and eyewitness accounts.

In addition, scores on Factor i generally comply with other classifica-

[22] Bojórquez, *Crónica*, pp. 221–222 and [735].
[23] Factor scores for the 219 Deputies have been computed by applying a linear transformation to the standardized raw data; in FACTOR 2, scores have a mean of 0 and a variance of 1.
[24] As interpreted here, the Moderate-Jacobin distinction relates to only Factor i; by definition, scores on the other raw factors reflect totally different alignments. Ordinarily I would be reluctant to use any scale of this sort as a conclusive indicator of operative attitudes because, in most situations, legislators often vote according to "log-rolling" bargains; they can also change their minds from time to time. But because Deputies at this particular convention had little to gain from log-rolling—and little time to change their minds during the two months of intensive activity—I believe the factor-score scale is valid in this case.
[25] In order to qualify as "participants," Deputies had to vote on at least three of six selected roll calls—variable numbers 4, 6, 9, 11, 23, and 25, which had the highest loadings on the first and foremost factor in an unrotated matrix for a FACTOR 2 analysis of all roll calls (petitions excluded). Application of this same criterion to the six roll-call votes with highest loadings on the Centralization factor for roll calls plus petitions would have eliminated 18 more delegates, for which reason I have used the other set of votes, but the procedures are virtually interchangeable: a Q-coefficient for the two participant-nonparticipant dichotomies comes out to .95. On the average, the 179 Deputies included in the analysis voted "yes" or "no" on over 80 percent of all the roll-call votes. Delegates who took little part in the convention were usually alternates for regular Deputies or regular Deputies being replaced by alternates.

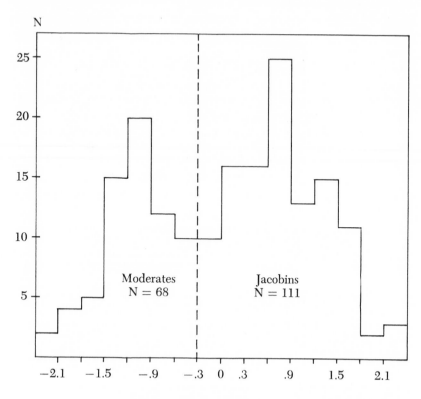

FIGURE 6–1.
Bimodal Distribution of Scores on Factor I

tion schemes. To substantiate this point Table 6–6 displays a matrix of gamma correlation coefficients, along with the percentages of deputies placed in like cells, for (a) a dichotomous Moderate-Jacobin categorization by factor scores, divided at −.30, (b) the rating in the *Magazín del Gráfico*, (c) the rating by Bojórquez, and (d) a classification based on interpersonal agreement scores with two reputed leaders of the opposing blocs, Félix Palavicini and Francisco Múgica.[26] The factor-score dichotomy has by far the highest set of coefficients with .93 for the *Gráfico* rating and .98 for the agreement-score clustering.

[26] To qualify for either major camp, a Deputy had to have a minimum agreement score of 67 percent with either Palavicini or Múgica on the six roll calls described in the previous note; otherwise he was put in an "independent" group. This method identified 57 members of a Palavicini bloc, 90 members of a Múgica bloc, and 32 independents.

198

TABLE 6-6. COMPARISON OF CLASSIFICATIONS FOR 179 PARTICIPANT
DEPUTIES

Gráfico (3)[a]	Bojórquez (2)	Agreement Scores (3)	Factor Scores (2)	
–	.83[b] (74.9)[c]	.86 (70.4)	.93 (82.1)	Gráfico
	–	.85 (69.8)	.84 (78.2)	Bojórquez
		–	.98 (79.9)	Agreement Scores
			–	Factor Scores

a Number of categories, excluding the "unlisted" category in the Gráfico rating.
b Gamma coefficients.
c Percent of Deputies in same categories.

For all these reasons, I interpret Factor I as the "Moderate-Jacobin" factor. Encouraged by the stability of the gamma coefficients in Table 6-6, I shall later employ individual deputy scores on this factor as an interval measure of voting behavior. So far, however, these procedures have merely served to identify the Moderates and Jacobins. We must still search out the substantive dimensions of their disagreement.

An orthogonal varimax rotation of the original five-factor matrix [27] sheds considerable light on this question. According to Table 6-7, the first rotated factor—like the unrotated Factor I—entails the concentration and use of governmental power. Variables 4, 6, 8, 11, 23, 24, and 32 have loadings of .50 or stronger in both matrices. Several of the other variables with noteworthy loadings on the first raw factor (9, 13, 21, and 25) have loadings of .40 or better on the rotated factor. Roll call 10, which shows up in the rotated matrix with a loading of .58, dealt with the role of municipal authorities in preventive arrest procedures. Variable 31, with a loading of .61, involved an attempt to abolish a kind of stamp tax which had long been regarded as an instrument of political repression. Except for the first vote on credentials, whose loading (.53) might simply represent a spurious relationship, all issues connected with this factor reflect an abiding concern with the use of centralized power. I regard the first rotated factor as a "Centralization" factor.

[27] See Rummel, Applied Factor Analysis, chap. 16.

TABLE 6–7. LOADINGS IN ROTATED FACTOR MATRIX
(ORTHOGONAL VARIMAX ROTATION)

Roll Calls or Petitions	Factors				
	I	II	III	IV	V
1. Credentials: Ezquerro	(.53)	.14	.06	—.17	—.15
2. Credentials: Palavicini	———		deleted		———
3. Credentials: Martí	—.15	.46	.13	.02	.23
4. Estados Unidos-República	(.51)[a]	—.34	.19	—.11	.06
5. Credentials: Vizcaíno	.08	(.68)	—.29	.14	—.14
6. Article 3	(.55)	—.41	.15	.19	—.12
7. Jury Trials for Press #1	.10	—.26	(.71)	.09	—.05
8. Right of Assembly	(.61)	—.02	.09	.22	.08
9. State-Federal Jails #1	.41	—.47	.17	.07	—.12
10. Preventive Arrest	(.58)	.05	—.25	—.13	.04
11. State-Federal Jails #2	(.60)	—.07	.14	.31	—.21
12. Jury Trials for Press #2	.25	—.04	(.72)	.10	—.21
13. Qualification for Congress: Nationality	.49	—.38	—.16	—.14	—.18
14. Qualifications for Congress: Age	———		deleted		———
15. Qualifications for Congress: Residence	—.06	(.61)	—.06	.04	.05
16. Qualifications for Congress: Military	———		deleted		———
17. Qualifications for Congress: Public Office	———		deleted		———
18. Fuero Militar	.15	—.17	.01	—.45	.26
19. Capital Punishment	—.01	.26	—.04	—.20	(.74)
20. Punishment for Rape	.01	.06	—.19	.09	(.81)
21. Federal District	—.40	.37	—.22	—.19	.00
22. Congressional Autonomy	.29	(—.60)	.17	.10	—.13
23. Senate-Supreme Court	(.61)	—.15	.27	.09	—.12
24. Central Bank, Anti-Trust	(.62)	—.21	.16	—.01	.09
25. Congress-Elections	—.44	.33	—.08	—.13	.07
26. Moral Austerity Vote	.11	—.12	.06	(.81)	.06
27. Right to Worship	—.14	.39	(—.52)	—.13	.05
28. Resignation by Ugarte	.36	—.36	.20	.01	—.03
29. Article 123	—.01	.36	.38	—.20	.03
30. Moral Austerity Petition	.09	.00	.09	(.76)	.01
31. Stamp Tax	(.61)	—.09	—.08	.06	.27
32. Manifesto of January 31	(.64)	—.27	.19	—.03	.01
% of Factor Variance	34.5	23.1	15.5	14.4	12.5
% of Total Variance	16.3	10.9	7.3	6.8	5.9

[a] Parentheses indicate variable loadings $\geq |.50|$.

The second rotated factor commands a good deal of interest. The strongest loading (.68) refers to a vote on the acceptability of Fernando Vizcaíno, a professional soldier who had served the reactionary regime of Victoriano Huerta and whose credentials as a revolutionary were therefore in doubt. The next highest loading (.61) concerns a vote on whether men should be allowed to run for Congress after residing in their constituent states for only six months. Another related vote (−.60) centered on Congress's ability to call special sessions without presidential permission. All these roll calls focused on questions of representativeness and congressional power, so I would label this dimension as the "Popular Control" factor. Because of the configuration of these votes, a negative score on this factor corresponds to a posture in favor of Popular Control.

Factor III has positive associations with roll calls about jury trials for the press (.71 and .72) and a negative loading with a vote on restrictions upon religious worship (−.52). Though some opponents of the Church-related bill were holding out for tighter restrictions, many seem to have been upholding the right to free worship. Somewhat uncertainly, I see this factor as involving "Civil Rights."

The remaining factors are relatively clear but unimportant. Like one of the unrotated factors, Factor IV is associated with two decisions (.81 and .76) on the matter of "Moral Austerity." Factor V, which also has two strong loadings (.74 and .81), deals with the issue of "Capital Punishment."

In an exploratory way, results from this analysis make it possible to qualify and comprehend cleavages at the Querétaro convention. To illustrate relationships between the rotated factors and the unrotated Moderate-Jacobin factor, Table 6–8 displays product-moment correlation coefficients for individual delegate scores. For all 219 Deputies and for the selected group of 179 "participants," the findings are virtually identical. The Moderate-Jacobin factor has a very close association with the rotated Centralization factor (r = .75 in both cases), a fairly close association with the issue of Popular Control (r = −.54 and −.56), and a mild association with the Civil Rights dimension

TABLE 6–8. RELATIONSHIP BETWEEN RAW FACTOR I AND FIVE ROTATED FACTORS

		Correlations with Moderate-Jacobin Raw Factor I [a]	
	Rotated Factors	All Deputies (N=219)	Participant Deputies (N=179)
I	Centralization	.75	.75
II	Popular Control	−.54	−.56
III	Civil Rights	.32	.35
IV	Moral Austerity	.16	.15
V	Criminal Punishment	−.13	−.14

[a] Product-moment correlations among individual factor scores.

(r=.32 and .35). The other relationships rapidly taper off, suggesting that Moral Austerity and Capital Punishment did not comprise important parts of the Moderate-Jacobin conflict.[28]

Employed in these various ways, factor-analytic techniques yield a basic proposition of this chapter: Moderates and Jacobins divided over the related questions of (1) whether to centralize political power; (2) if so, whether it should be concentrated in the executive or legislative branch of government; and (3) whether individuals should retain inalienable rights in the face of a strong state. Such ideas call for further exploration.

III
DILEMMA OF A REVOLUTION: POWER VS. FREEDOM

THE first and foremost factor in the varimax rotation, Centralization, involves a complex series of problems with historical roots stretching far back into the Mexican past. On a substantive level, the conflict took shape from varied roll calls in the constituent congress: disputes over the name of the country, control of the Church, congressional-executive relations, and matters of local autonomy. To show how the Moderates and Jacobins voted on all issues, Table 6–9 gives the respective percentages voting "yes" on each roll call (or signing petitions) and an "Index of Disagreement" based on the difference between the two percentages.

Jacobins wanted a strong central government. Over half of them voted to change the name of the country from "Estados Unidos Mexicanos" to "República Federal Mexicana," thus giving explicit recognition to the superiority of the national government, while only 5.2 percent of the Moderates cast affirmative votes (variable 4). An overwhelming proportion of Jacobins, 94.6 percent, favored strong state control of education with virtual elimination of religious teaching (variable 6). As nationalists, they would restrict political office to native-born Mexicans, while the more cosmopolitan Moderates tended to vote against this restriction (variable 13). Over 90 percent of the Jacobins supported the idea of a central bank that would give the government substantial influence over the economy; only a third of the Moderates agreed (variable 24). Thus the Jacobins loom as proponents of an "active" and interventionist State, while Moderates emerge as advocates of limited governmental interference in society.

[28] In stepwise regression models (from a program known as STEPREG2) for the participant Deputy group, scores on the first two rotated factors explain 86 percent of the variance in scores on the unrotated factor; scores on the first three rotated factors account for 96 percent of the variance.

TABLE 6–9. MODERATE AND JACOBIN POSITIONS ON ROLL CALLS AND
PETITIONS

Variable No.	Moderates		Jacobins		Index of Disagreement
	No. Voting	% Voting Yes	No. Voting	% Voting Yes	
1.	47	42.6	91	82.4	39.8
2.	46	2.2	81	6.2	4.0
3.	50	80.0	85	50.6	29.4
4.	58	5.2	95	55.8	50.6
5.	60	80.0	87	51.7	28.3
6.	55	12.7	92	94.6	81.9
7.	55	12.7	92	52.2	39.5
8.	53	58.5	91	96.7	38.2
9.	47	6.4	85	72.9	66.5
10.	48	22.9	70	60.0	37.1
11.	54	42.6	89	96.6	54.0
12.	57	24.6	86	76.7	52.1
13.	52	26.9	93	83.9	57.0
14.	62	100.0	95	98.9	1.1
15.	62	83.9	96	51.0	32.9
16.	62	95.2	94	89.4	5.8
17.	63	98.4	94	92.6	5.8
18.	67	64.2	98	72.5	8.3
19.	65	72.3	101	49.5	22.8
20.	63	42.9	100	26.0	16.9
21.	51	66.7	72	7.5	59.2
22.	53	1.9	88	63.7	61.8
23.	54	33.3	93	98.9	65.6
24.	51	33.3	99	90.9	57.6
25.	51	80.4	82	15.9	64.5
26.	50	22.0	85	47.1	25.1
27.	53	90.6	92	38.0	52.6
28.	–	1.5[a]	–	22.5[a]	21.0[b]
29.	–	42.4[a]	–	28.8[a]	13.6[b]
30.	–	29.4[a]	–	45.0[a]	15.6[b]
31.	–	2.9[a]	–	31.5[a]	28.6[b]
32.	–	5.9[a]	–	70.3[a]	64.4[b]

[a] Refers to those who signed petitions as percentage of entire bloc; figures for roll calls refer to percentages among those voting.
[b] Based on percentages signing petitions.

The conflict concerned not so much the direction of social change as the appropriate means to achieve it. Regarding Article 3, for instance, both sides agreed that the State should be much stronger than the Church. Speaking for the Jacobins, Francisco Múgica (who had a raw factor score of +.74) argued that parochial schooling was "only a preparatory means for usurping the functions of the State" and thus a threat to "the natural development of Mexican society";

therefore it had to be abolished. Moderates saw the measure as an infringement on "freedom of education" that, in turn, could spark a popular revolt. As Luis Manuel Rojas (−1.84) warned, "a serious error by the constitutional congress could ignite a conflagration throughout the country . . ." Alfonso Cravioto (−1.30) echoed the point: "when suppressed, liberties explode. [By approving Article 3] we would furnish a pretext for a powerful revolution that would be not reactionary but liberal, to overthrow us justifiably and restore the Constitution of 1857." [29]

At least on this issue, Moderates considered governmental over-activism to be not only dangerous but also ineffective. As José Natividad Macías (−1.51) maintained, Article 3 would not eradicate religious superstition. "Popular customs do not change from night to day . . . for this *the triumph of the Revolution is not enough.*" Mexico needed a system of education which, in the course of time, would lead to mass enlightenment. Government could not achieve this goal.[30]

A further aspect of this dispute involved the propriety of State action in the socio-economic sphere. Jacobins regarded strong con-stitutional articles on labor, land, and the central bank as necessary instruments of social justice. Often voicing laissez-faire assumptions, Moderates declared that such intervention would obstruct the natural interplay of market forces and limit the right of free choice. For example Fernando Lizardi (−1.09) thought the eight-hour clause in Article 123 would be "like giving a pair of pistols to a Sacred Christ," since it would presumably prohibit a man from choosing to work extra hours. Retorted the Jacobin Luis Fernández Martínez (+1.06): "Very well, gentlemen; if Christ had had a pistol when they took him to the Calvary, Christ would not have been killed." [31]

Another part of the conflict dealt with legal precedent. Moderates tended to stress the importance of law. After one Deputy deduced that restoration of land to communal *ejidos* in Article 27 would under-mine a large number of existing real estate titles, Múgica burst out with a typical Jacobin challenge: "Are we going to leave [the ejido question] this way just because the law allows it? Will we consent to it? Then curse the Revolution, curse it a thousand times, if we agree to this . . . If justice conflicts with the law, then I say down with the law!" [32]

[29] *Diario* (1922 edition), 1: 436, 440, 454.
[30] Ibid., 1: 467; my italics.
[31] Ibid., 1: 678, 706.
[32] Ibid., 2: 809.

At bottom, the Centralization issue evoked different ideas about the relationship between socio-economic change and political change. Moderates seem to have felt that political development—which they construed as the establishment of democracy—must be the *result* of social improvement. As Carranza declared, "Social progress is the base on which political progress should be established." [33] Jacobins, on the other hand, generally believed that political action should be the *cause* of social improvement.

Despite the absence of a mathematical relationship, the dispute over Centralization bore a substantive connection to the matter of Popular Control, as I have called rotated Factor II. While Jacobins sought to strengthen central power, they felt that the people—mainly through Congress—should retain control over the use of that power. On the votes defining Popular Control, they were suspicious of Vizcaíno's past and hence of his ability to represent the Revolution (variable 5). After leading the fight against the admission of foreign-born citizens into the national Congress (variable 13), Jacobins generally maintained that elected representatives should be natives of the states they served or at least should have lived there for quite a long time (variable 15). Jacobins also tended to believe that Congress should have the right to call special sessions without the approval of the President (variable 22).

The six-month residence proposal brought the Popular Control issue into sharp relief. Defining the predominantly Jacobin view, Modesto González Galindo (who had a raw factor score of +.74) argued that such a weak requirement would allow the central government to put political favorites in office, just as in the Díaz era. The resulting "administrative centralism" would lead to the hegemony of "professional politicians" who, in turn, would pay no heed to the people. Taking up the point, Cayetano Andrade (+.84) declared that a two-year residence requirement would "greatly favor federalism and eliminate the so-called intellectual 'elites' . . . I want rule by true politics, not politics for a privileged few, but politics for all who have ability, so that future Congresses shall be an exact reflection of the Republic, in which citizens of all the states should be in perfect harmony." [34]

Some roll calls with strong relationships to rotated Factor I, or to both the first and second factors, brought additional expressions of Jacobin concern over centralized power. As shown in Table 6-9, they

[33] Ibid., 1: 269.
[34] Ibid., 2: 174, 179.

believed that the states, rather than the central government, should be responsible for maintaining jails (variables 9 and 11). In contrast to Moderates, they felt that "preventive arrest" should not take place without the permission of municipal authorities (variable 10). They refused to place Mexico City under the control of the federal government (variable 21). They thought that Congress should have the power to call special sessions without approval of the President (variable 22), and that the Senate—rather than the Supreme Court—should resolve political conflicts within states (variable 23).

These issues raised the basic problem of maintaining law and order. Carranza spoke at length on the matter in his speech at the convention, asserting the necessity for strong presidential authority. Government should respect legal procedure, said the First Chief, but it must also "be inexorable with those who disrupt order and the enemies of society . . ." For this purpose, he reasoned, power should be centralized. Only a President could take decisive steps in times of crisis.[35]

Perhaps in distrust of Carranza, or in distasteful recollection of the Díaz regime, Jacobins feared that centralized power could lead to dictatorship. They proved to be jealous guardians of civil liberties, strongly upholding a free press and the right of assembly (see variables 7, 8, and 12 in Table 6-9; and note how 7 and 12 relate to the rotated Factor III, which I have labeled Civil Rights). Giving clear articulation to this view a committee under Múgica took a firm stand in its report on the penitentiary question. "We declare ourselves to be against all centralization [which can bring on] absolutism . . . Such a great reduction in the sovereignty of states would permit the arbitrary use of central power, principally in regard to political crimes."[36]

In summary, it appears that the Jacobins wanted to build up the power of the government *as a socio-economic institution* in order to compete with rival institutions, particularly the Church and private banks. Yet they also sought to limit the *political* power of the central government and especially of the President. If centralization occurred, they wanted Congress, not the Executive, to have ultimate control of power. Jacobins faced a fundamental dilemma: they would have to centralize political authority in order to bring about social and economic transformation, but they would have to disperse political authority in order to prevent the rise of tyranny.

[35] Ibid., 1: 268.
[36] Ibid., 1: 644.

What Moderates seem to have feared is anarchy. Their voting records and their remarks in the *Diario de los debates* imply a belief that immediate and excessive socio-economic intervention by the state would disrupt societal relationships in a community already torn by years of civil war. Disregard for legal precedent would spread uncertainty and apprehension. Writing land reforms into the Constitution would stir unnecessary passion. Too much concern for civil liberties would open the door to partisan politics and counterrevolutionary intrigue. Restrictions on the President would paralyze the government.

There is no evidence that Moderates and Jacobins disagreed about the socio-economic goals of the Revolution. After the Jacobins asserted their control of the convention, at least, Moderates played an active part in formulating constitutional provisions for socio-economic change. Of the 23 Deputies who helped draft Article 27, on property rights and agrarian reform, 10 came from the Moderate group; 13 out of the 23 men who drafted Article 123 were Moderates; [37] and of the 61 delegates signing the proposal for labor reform, 29 were Moderates. According to the *Diario* both these articles—perhaps the most innovative measures in the entire Constitution—passed unanimously and with little debate.[38] The data are both indirect and inconclusive. But existing indications, such as they are, plainly suggest that the dispute between Moderates and Jacobins concerned means and not ends.

Nor were the lines of conflict particularly rigid. Neither group seems to have had a fully articulated "ideology." In testimony to the difficulty of resolving the dilemma of power and freedom, there was frequent disagreement within the two camps. And as shown by Figure 6-2, voting patterns displayed substantial flexibility. On a scale from 50 to 100, the average relative cohesion score on all roll calls for the

[37] Membership on *ad hoc* committees has been taken from Pastor Rouaix, *Génesis de los artículos 27 y 123 de la Constitución Política de 1917* (Puebla: Gobierno del Estado de Puebla, 1945), pp. 85–87 and 124–125. These lists may be incomplete and might exaggerate the Moderate contribution to the committees (Rouaix himself was a Moderate, with a raw factor score of −1.11). For an overtly partisan exposition of the Moderate viewpoint see Félix F. Palavicini, *Historia de la Constitución de 1917*, 2 vols. (México: n.p., 1938).

[38] One observer claims that the first 15 votes on the roll call on Article 27 were negative, and implies that the official record was falsified in order to show complete consensus. Andrés Molina Enríquez, *Esbozo de la historia de los primeros diez años de la revolución agraria de México (de 1910 a 1920)*, 2nd ed. (México: Museo Nacional de Arqueología, Historia y Etnografía, 1936), 5: 179. Unfortunately I have not been able to locate manuscript minutes of the convention, so I have no means of verifying the published data in the *Diario;* there is no particular reason to believe that Molina Enríquez was right, but I cannot prove him to have been wrong. Niemeyer does not shed any light on this question: *Revolution*, p. 164.

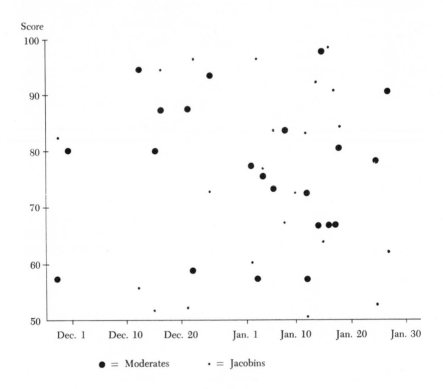

FIGURE 6-2.

Relative Cohesion Scores for Moderates and Jacobins over Time
(Contested Roll Calls Only)

Moderates was 79.2; for the Jacobins, it was 76.7. Over time, as well
as on specific issues, the figures demonstrate considerable fluidity in
alignments at the constituent congress. According to these measures,
neither faction grew in solidarity throughout the course of the
convention.[39]

The data also suggest that individual leaders may have exerted fairly
little control over the assembly. Personalist blocs normally have great
cohesiveness. Figure 6-2 implies that neither Carranza nor Obregón—
or their putative lieutenants, Palavicini and Múgica—could keep strict

[39] The absolute values of all variable loadings on raw Factor I, plotted over time,
reveal a similar absence of structure.

discipline within their groups. Without necessarily rejecting the personalist hypothesis,[40] we might now look for other explanations.

IV

THE SOCIAL BASIS OF CONFLICT

THE attitudinal differences at the convention, together with the information on the social background of the delegates, combine to raise a crucial question: Was there any relationship between social origin and political views? Did Moderates tend to come from one sort of background and Jacobins from another? Was this a struggle between socially definable groups?

One efficient means of exploring this problem is through a statistical procedure known as Automatic Interaction Detector (A.I.D.), with voting scores as the dependent variable and social background attributes as class-coded independent variables. Basically, A.I.D. makes repeated use of analysis-of-variance techniques to find the optimal combination of independent variables for predicting the dependent variable. Taking the entire sample in question, this computer program examines the explanatory power of every dichotomous permutation of every independent variable and proceeds to divide the population into two subgroups, let us call them A and B, according to that permutation of the independent variable V_1 that explains the highest proportion of variance in the dependent variable. It then selects the most powerful permutation of another variable V_2—or another permutation of V_1—for dividing subgroup A, then does the same for subgroup B, and so on in successive iterations until "final" groupings appear.[41] Applied to data on the constitutional convention, this routine makes it possible to delineate multivariate social characteristics of the voting blocs.[42]

With interval-scale scores on the Moderate-Jacobin factor (unrotated Factor i) as the dependent variable—the more positive the score the more Jacobin the stance, the more negative the score the more Moderate the stance [43]—I have employed eight independent variables for

[40] See Moreno, *Congreso*, pp. 36–37.

[41] John A. Sonquist and James N. Morgan, *The Detection of Interaction Effects: A Report on a Computer Program for the Selection of Optimal Combinations of Explanatory Variables* (Ann Arbor, Michigan: Institute for Social Research, 1964).

[42] For an application and discussion of this technique, see Peter H. Smith, *Argentina and the Failure of Democracy: Conflict among Political Elites, 1904–1955* (Madison, Wisconsin: University of Wisconsin Press, 1974), esp. chaps. 4–5 and appendix B.

[43] Scores are for the 179 "participant" delegates only, taken from the factor analysis involving all 219 Deputies.

the A.I.D. analysis, thus providing empirical tests for several hypotheses, most derived from standard literature on the convention: [44]

Age as of January 1, 1917, the supposition being that younger Deputies would tend to be disproportionately Jacobin. I have set up five categories or "classes": age 20–29, 30–39, 40–49, 50 or over, and age unknown.[45]

Social Class as reported by informants (see note 8), the hypothesis being that Jacobins would tend to come from relatively low socio-economic origins. Three categories: lower class, middle class, and upper class.

Highest Level of Education, to test the notion that men of higher learning would fall in the Moderate camp. Three categories: university training (without necessarily having received a degree), less than university education, and unknown.

Occupation, with the idea that men in low-status or manual work would be Jacobins and that white-collar types would tend to be Moderates. Seven categories: laborers, campesinos, clerks and bureaucrats, businessmen and industrialists, professionals, other, and unknown.

Professional Title, to examine the same basic hypothesis as Occupation, the expectation being that non-professionals would line up as Jacobins and professionals as Moderates. Six categories: none, Licenciado (lawyer), Doctor, Profesor, Ingeniero (engineer), and Contador (accountant).

Military Status, the supposition being that military men would be Jacobin and the civilians Moderate. Two categories: military, civilian.

Birthplace, with the anticipation that men of rural background would be disproportionately Jacobin. Four categories: born in the Distrito Federal (Mexico City), born in a state capital, born outside a state capital, and unknown.

Region, to see if delegates from the north, especially Sonora, home of a famous presidential dynasty, formed a Jacobin group. Five categories, in accordance with official census usage: Pacific North, North, Center, Gulf, and South Pacific.[46]

[44] For example see Niemeyer, *Revolution,* pp. 60–62 and 215–224; List Arzubide, *La rebelión,* pp. 19–20; Rouaix, *Génesis,* pp. 48–49 and 211–212; Palavicini, *Historia,* 1: 144; and John J. Johnson, *Political Change in Latin America: The Emergence of the Middle Sectors* (Stanford: Stanford University Press, 1958), pp. 133–134.

[45] It is necessary to categorize independent variables for the A.I.D. process, although the dependent variable should have an interval (or dichotomous) scale. I have included "missing data" as a category in the analysis because complete information on all variables is available for only 71 of the 179 "participant" Deputies.

[46] The Pacific North includes the states and territories of Baja California, Nayarit, Sinaloa, and Sonora; the North contains Chihuahua, Coahuila, Durango,

TABLE 6-10. RELATIVE POWER OF VARIABLES FOR PREDICTING VOTING

Rank Order of Variables	BSS/TSS[a]	No. of Classes
1. Region	.09	5
2. Social Class	.05	3
3. Birthplace	.03	4[b]
4. Age	.03	5[b]
5. Military Status	.02	2
6. Professional Title	.02	6
7. Occupation	<.01	7[b]
8. Education	<.01	3[b]

[a] Between Sum of Squares/Total Sum of Squares.
[b] Includes "unknown" category.

The first important discovery from the A.I.D. analysis finds expression in Table 6-10, which ranks the independent variables according to their predictive power. It turns out that Region explains the highest proportion of variance in factor scores for the 179 participant deputies. At the same time, none of the variables has an awesome quantity of strength; even the optimal permutation of Region accounts for only 9 percent of the variance. The problem demands a multivariate solution.

For the sake of clarity and elegance, multivariate analysis requires a parsimonious model. For all its rich implications, an A.I.D. program involving all eight independent variables pretty much defies interpretation (see Figure 6-5).[47] I have attempted to deal with this problem by trying a series of A.I.D. runs with different combinations of variables, searching for a model with relatively high explanatory power and relatively few variables.[48] Table 6-11 sets forth the results.

Model 3—with Region, Military Status, and Age—meets these cri-

Nuevo León, San Luis Potosí, Tamaulipas, and Zacatecas; the Center has Aguascalientes, the Distrito Federal, Guanajuato, Hidalgo, Jalisco, México, Michoacán, Morelos, Puebla, Querétaro, and Tlaxcala; the Gulf spans Campeche, Quintana Roo, Tabasco, Veracruz, and Yucatán; the South Pacific includes Chiapas, Colima, Guerrero, and Oaxaca. State affiliations actually refer to membership in state delegations at the convention; for the vast majority of Deputies for whom data are available, delegates came from the same states that they represented.

[47] One difficulty with A.I.D. derives from the reliance on average scores, which become notoriously unstable in small groups.

[48] All A.I.D. runs had no weighting variable, and employed the following options: split eligibility criterion for candidate groups=.05; split reducibility criterion for dividing groups=.01; maximum allowable number of final groups=20; minimum number of observations for a group to be considered for splitting=30. All independent variables were submitted as free (rather than monotonic) variables. See Sonquist and Morgan, *Detection*, pp. 22-23, 27-28, and esp. pp. 114-121.

TABLE 6-11. EXPLANATORY POWER OF SELECTED A.I.D. MODELS

Model	Independent Variables	R²
1.	Region, Education, Military Status	.21
2.	Region, Professional Title, Military Status	.24
3.	Region, Military Status, Age	.27
4.	Region, Professional Title, Military Status, Age	.27
5.	Region, Professional Title, Age, Military Status, Education, Occupation	.33
6.	Region, Professional Title, Age, Military Status, Education, Occupation, Birthplace	.34
7.	Region, Professional Title, Age, Military Status, Education, Occupation, Birthplace, Social Class	.34

teria best. Although it does not have the highest total R^2, it explains more variance per variable than any of the other models. It also employs variables with reasonably strict definitions (unlike "Social Class") and reasonably complete data (of the three, only Age has missing information).

With this particular model, A.I.D. produced the breakdown of voting blocs which appears in Figure 6-3. From top to bottom, each cell in the diagram contains: (1) the social attributes of the group according to the operative independent variable, (2) the number of deputies in the group, and (3) the average factor score for members of the group. As shown in the figure, the program began with a total sample of 179 Deputies having a mean factor score of +.07. The first split came on Region, 35 delegates from the Pacific North and Gulf having a mean factor score of +.70, the 144 delegates from other areas having a mean score of −.09. The Pacific North plus Gulf group then broke on Age, those of known years having an average score of +1.03 and men of unknown years having an average of +.13 (this difference has no apparent substantive significance, but may reveal that biographical dictionaries and other such sources have tended to favor extreme Jacobins). The "other" group divided on Region again, separating the North (−.52) from the Center plus South Pacific (+.04). The program went on to make a total of seven splits.

The diagram reveals a fairly clear typology. The most decisive categorization is by Region. The Pacific North and Gulf emerge as Jacobin areas [49] with delegates having a mean factor score of +.70. The Center and South Pacific occupy middle ground with an average of +.04. The

[49] The same regional breakdown emerged as the most powerful explanatory variable in an A.I.D. run involving the 71 Deputies for whom I have complete data.

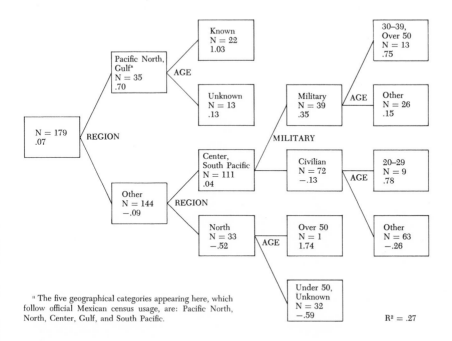

Figure 6–3.

Voting and Social Background (Model 3)

North comes out as a Moderate stronghold, with an average score of −.52 (or −.59, not counting one senior Deputy with a highly Jacobin score of +1.74).

Within the Center and South Pacific, whose delegates comprised three-fifths of the entire sample, there is a tendency for military men to be more Jacobin than civilians (+.35 against −.13). Army officers show no clear breakdown by age but the civilians do, with Deputies in their twenties taking a more Jacobin stance than their elders (+.78 against −.26). Thus Military Status and Age bear the expected relationships to voting, but only after Region has had its effect.

To give another picture of the relationship between geography and voting, and also to move beyond the arbitrary census categories, the map in Figure 6–4 indicates the geographical location of constituencies with delegations having the 15 most extreme average factor scores on

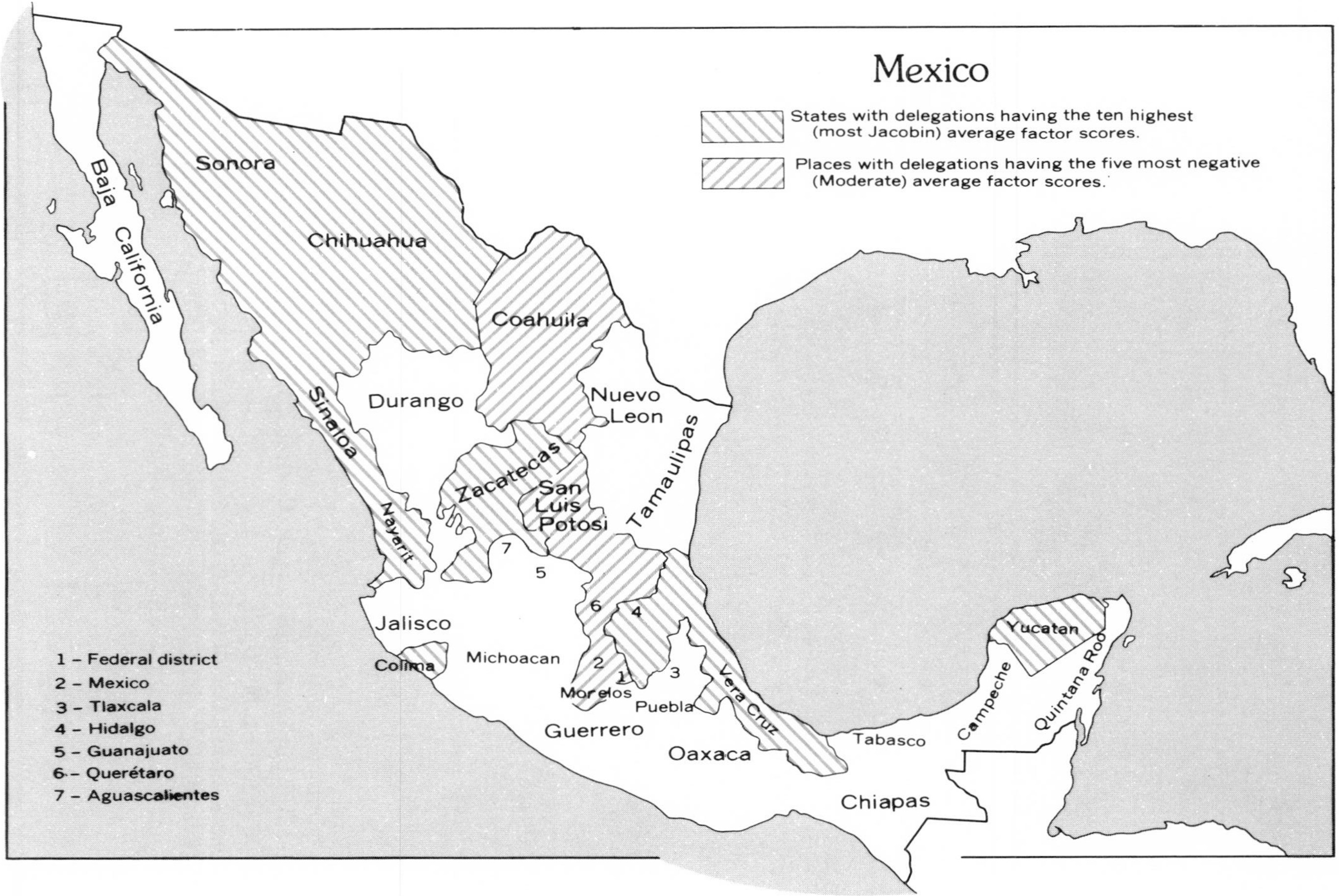
Mexico
States with delegations having the ten highest (most Jacobin) average factor scores.
Places with delegations having the five most negative (Moderate) average factor scores.
Baja California
Sonora
Chihuahua
Coahuila
Durango
Sinaloa
Nuevo Leon
Tamaulipas
Zacatecas
San Luis Potosi
Nayarit
Jalisco
Colima
Michoacan
Morelos
Puebla
Guerrero
Oaxaca
Vera Cruz
Tabasco
Chiapas
Campeche
Yucatan
Quintana Roo
1 – Federal district
2 – Mexico
3 – Tlaxcala
4 – Hidalgo
5 – Guanajuato
6 – Querétaro
7 – Aguascalientes

FIGURE 6–4.

Centralization, 10 from the Jacobin camp and 5 from the Moderate side.

Establishing the importance of regionalism is one thing; explaining it is quite another. I do not know of any commonly recognized historical affinity between the Pacific North and Gulf, or any obvious reason why they should produce predominantly Jacobin delegations. Despite the anti-clerical implications of the vote on Article 3, which has a high loading on Factor I, there is no demonstrable relationship between Church strength and voting; a product-moment correlation between average factor scores per state delegation and the ratios of priests to population for states in 1910 comes out to $-.02$. Nor does there exist any strong association between standard indicators of social "development," literacy and urbanization, and voting tendencies of state delegations.[50] Interpretation must necessarily be tentative, but I would suggest four reasons for the regional alignment on Centralization. In no particular order:

First is distance. States in the north—Sonora, Chihuahua, Sinaloa—and Yucatán in the Gulf were located far from the center of national power in Mexico City. Often neglected by federal authorities, sometimes threatened by foreign countries, they developed a kind of political independence that seems logically consistent with the Jacobin view. Separatist tendencies in Yucatán, though not expressed at the constitutional convention, furnish classic evidence of this tradition.

Second is political autonomy. Hidalgo, Tlaxcala, and Veracruz were fairly close to Mexico City, but seem to have built up relatively strong and stable statewide political systems. The last governors of all three states during the Porfirian regime—Pedro Ladislao Rodríguez, Próspero Cahuantzi, and Teodoro Dehesa—enjoyed long tenure in office, and were even capable of resisting Díaz on occasion. Delegates from such areas tended to be Jacobin.

Third is partisan control. Carranza had his personal base in the north, particularly in his home state of Coahuila,[51] and he exerted

---

[50] I have computed zero-order product-moment correlations between the average factor scores for state delegations and state-by-state figures on urbanization, literacy, and "poverty level" for 1910, 1921, and the rate of change in each between 1910 and 1921; none of these variables explains more than 6 percent of the variance in average factor scores. Data on urbanization, literacy, and "poverty level" (the arithmetic mean of figures on illiteracy, percent adults in rural areas, and percent speaking an Indian language only) have been adapted from James W. Wilkie, *The Mexican Revolution: Federal Expenditure and Social Change in Mexico since 1910* (Berkeley and Los Angeles: University of California Press, 1967), Tables 9-1, 9-4, and 9-10. For some critical remarks about this poverty index see Thomas E. Skidmore and Peter H. Smith, "Notes on Quantitative History: Federal Expenditure and Social Change in Mexico since 1910," *Latin American Research Review* 5, no. 1 (Spring 1970): 71–85.

[51] Perhaps inadvertently, Bojórquez revealed the importance of this situation by

military authority around the Federal District and northward at the time of the convention. These areas were mainly Moderate (from the map, it almost looks as though Moderate strongholds followed a military supply route!). It also appears that Carranza's predominance possessed a transient quality: the state of Veracruz, where he maintained his headquarters and Constitutionalist government from 1914 to early 1916, produced one of the most Jacobin delegations at the entire Congress.

Fourth is the strength of organized labor, with which Carranza broke in 1916. Veracruz and Yucatán passed strong statewide labor laws prior to the convention, and some other Jacobin areas, such as Sonora and Chihuahua, had vigorous workingmen's movements. As Ramón Ruiz has pointed out,[52] employment in these regions received a devastating blow from the international financial crisis of 1907, since most of their industries produced goods for the export market. Delegates from these places may have feared that Carranza, as President, would try to roll back labor's local gains, so they stood up for state autonomy; to protect their position, perhaps, they eventually decided to force his hand by framing Article 123.[53]

Where regional forces do not exert much influence, in the Center and South Pacific, voting patterns need additional interpretation. It is possible that Army officers leaned toward Jacobin views out of distrust for civilian "politicians," who presumably could not understand the Revolution because they had not fought for it. Furthermore the loosely knit structure of the Constitutionalist Army, in which individual generals often had their own domains, probably led to a preference for decentralized power: it was the only kind that they had ever held.

Among civilians from these areas, the tendency for young Deputies to vote Jacobin may have resulted from their generational experience. By definition, virtually all the delegates in their twenties reached their majority just as the Revolution was beginning. They had seen the decay of the Porfirian system and they had opposed the reactionary regime of Victoriano Huerta; in their eyes, excessive presidential power was bound to mean corruption. They also entered the political scene just as workers and campesinos were mounting demands on revolutionary leadership and, perhaps out of youthful idealism, they came to espouse the cause of social justice and the restriction of corporate privilege with

maintaining that Jorge Von Versen would have voted consistently with the Jacobin majority "if he had not been from Coahuila." *Crónica*, p. 376.

[52] In his comments at the A.H.A. session, December 1971.

[53] Alfonso López Aparicio, *El movimiento obrero en México: antecedentes, desarrollo y tendencias* (México: Editorial Jus, 1952), esp. pp. 154–159 and 163–171. Note that Article 123 left responsibility for specific labor legislation in the hands of the state governments.

special fervor. To a limited extent, experience may have produced a Jacobin generation.

Thus Region, Military Status, and Age had noticeable influence on the Moderate-Jacobin split. Together, as interpreted here, these variables combine to suggest that the process of *socialization* had more effect on political attitudes than did social *origin*. None of the proxy "status" variables—Social Class, Education, Professional Title, or Occupation—explains much variance in factor scores, either alone or in conjunction with other variables (see Tables 6–10 and 6–11). Jacobins and Moderates were made, not born.

Nevertheless, it would be inappropriate to over-emphasize the impact of socialization. The Region variable accounts for only 9 percent of the variance in voting scores; the selective A.I.D. run, with three independent variables, explains only 27 percent of the variance; and in a model employing all eight of the independent variables, social background attributes explain just 34 percent of the total variance. Here might be our most impressive finding: *much of the voting had nothing to do with the social characteristics used for this analysis.* Either some other social variable is needed to resolve the problem, or voting blocs were not congruent with social blocs.

Negative as it may be, this discovery points up the relative absence of structure in the constitutional convention. A young and inexperienced group of delegates, not bound by parties or other formal affiliations, subject to conflicting cross-pressures and struggling to define a revolutionary purpose, was bound to undergo a fair amount of confusion. Erratic behavior would have to be construed as normal. Considered in this light, the socialization variables explain a respectable percentage of the variance in voting.

The unstructured character of this assembly gives rise to yet another consideration: personal ambition. As already shown in Table 6–1, over half the total of 219 delegates held national office after the convention, presumably because they wanted to. In part, the Moderate-Jacobin split may have reflected a conflict over patronage. Moderates might have supported central authority in the expectation that Carranza, as President, would reward them in appropriate ways. Jacobins might have opposed central authority in the fear that Carranza would use his executive influence to strip them of their local power bases, prevent them from gaining office, and exclude them from all major forms of patronage. This hypothesis cannot be tested here, nor would it be an easy one to test,[54] but it still merits close attention.

[54] The kind of data behind Table 6–1 is inadequate for this purpose because it is unclear whether Carranza controlled the distribution of all national offices in 1917–1920, whether he tried to use them to co-opt real or potential opponents,

V

CONCLUSIONS

THIS analysis has yielded a number of significant findings about Mexico's constitutional congress of 1916–1917:

1. The convention was dominated by a socially privileged group, of high educational and occupational status, rather than a cross-section of Mexican society. The presumed beneficiaries of the Constitution, especially laborers and campesinos, had very few representatives of their own.

2. In contrast to the aged and exclusive Porfirian elite, the Carrancista clique—many of whose members came to hold national office—was young, ambitious, and "middle-class."

3. The split between two groups at the convention commonly known as the Moderates and the Jacobins concerned three issues, in order of importance: centralization of government authority, maintenance of popular control, and protection of civil rights.

4. The Jacobins sought to create a strong central government in order to challenge the power of the Church and other socio-economic institutions, but they also wanted to limit presidential political power. Moderates wanted to uphold law and order.

5. There is no evidence that Moderate-Jacobin conflict concerned the desirability or direction of social change. The dispute focused largely on the role of the State as an instrument of socio-economic transformation and on the political implications of centralized power.

6. The difference between Moderates and Jacobins had a perceptible social basis, principally regarding geographical region. In particular, delegations from the Pacific North and the Gulf tended to be Jacobin; those from the North were mainly Moderate.

7. Within the Center and South Pacific—that is, controlling for the effect of Region—military delegates tended to be Jacobin. And within the civilian group, young men also tended to vote Jacobin.

8. Other standard hypotheses—most notably, that Moderates were exceptionally well-educated professional men—do not stand up to empirical analysis. The process of socialization, and perhaps political aspirations, had more to do with voting than did social origin.

9. Even so, most of the Moderate-Jacobin conflict did not bear any apparent relationship to any social background variables.

The relative weakness in behavioral patterns probably stemmed from the nature and the context of this assembly. Because of the essential familiarity and generality of issue content, constitutional conventions

---

and how many positions actually represent defeat or reprisal for individuals aspiring to higher office.

may have a basic tendency to be unstructured.[55] Moreover this particular group was mostly new to politics, had no binding institutional or reference-group affiliations, met under urgent conditions, and had little time to create acceptable codes for interaction.

Finally, these various findings offer the basis for some provocative speculation about the development and outcome of the Mexican Revolution. In yielding power to Carranza's Constitutionalist movement, the Revolution found its ultimate leadership in a highly educated middle-class elite that had little if any direct interest in labor unions or land distribution. But it was an elite that recognized the need for social change, at least at the Querétaro convention, and one whose members showed considerable independence of judgment. Such qualities may well have emerged in response to pressures from below. By 1916 popular demands for labor and land reform were too great to ignore. Years of fighting had also destroyed institutions in whole or in part, broken many social bonds, and, in so doing, liberated men from their social backgrounds. Free from the past, a Deputy could vote according to his conscience—or his view of political reality—rather than according to his sense of status.[56] Violent upheaval may have comprised a necessary precondition for the making of Mexico's revolutionary Constitution.

[55] To test this hypothesis it would be necessary and highly desirable to undertake a comparative study of constitutional conventions.

[56] This phenomenon might partially explain why my personal informants remembered the composition of the Congress as being so "middle class" and thus, in a sense, as being "classless."

Appendix

Roll Calls and Petitions at Constitutional Convention

Roll Calls Variable No.	Decision on Whether:	Riker Coefficient of Significance
1.	To accept Carlos M. Ezquerro as a delegate despite his previous service in the administration of Eulalio Gutiérrez; passed 111–50 (107–48). 1: 118–19. 28 November 1916.[1]	.45
2.	To reject credentials of Félix F. Palavicini because of alleged electoral irregularities; defeated 142–6 (137–6). 1: 153–154. 28 November 1916.[2]	.15
3.	To admit Ruben Martí as a delgate despite his Cuban birth; passed 101–57 (97–56). 1: 244. 30 November 1916.	.51
4.	To change name of country from "Estados Unidos Mexicanos" to "República Federal Mexicana"; defeated 108–57 (108–56). 1: 420. 12 December 1916.	.57
5.	To accept Fernando Vizcaíno, a professional soldier, despite his service to Victoriano Huerta; passed 105–59. 1: 497. 15 December 1916.	.57
6.	To approve committee version of Article 3, replacing Carranza's proposal for "freedom of education" by virtual prohibition on religious teaching; passed 99–58 (99–57). 1: 534–535. 16 December 1916.	.55
7.	To guarantee jury trials in all cases brought against the press; defeated 101–61 (99–61). 1: 595. 21 December 1916.	.59
8.	To approve committee draft of Article 9, affirming basic right of assembly and association; passed 127–26. 1: 619–620. 22 December 1916.	.33

Roll Calls Variable No.	Decision on Whether:	Riker Coefficient of Significance
9.	To adopt committee report stipulating that states should maintain their own jails, in contrast to Carranza's proposal for federal penal colonies; defeated 70–69 (70–67). 1: 667. 25 December 1916.	.56
10.	To stipulate that "preventive detention" could take place only with approval of municipal authorities; defeated 68–56 (67–56). 2: 29. 2 January 1917.	.44
11.	To pass amendment endowing state governments with prime responsibility for penal institutions; passed 155–37 [sic?] (116–36). 2: 56. 3 January 1917.	.40
12.	To guarantee trial by jury in cases involving the press; passed 84–70 (84–69). 2: 81. 4 January 1917.	.63
13.	To require national Deputies to be Mexican citizens "by birth"; passed 98–55 (98–58). 2: 158. 6 January 1917.	.57
14.	To set the minimum age for Deputies at 25; passed 169–2 (168–2). [Names appear for only negative votes in Diario; list of affirmative voters constructed from roll calls for adjacent votes.] 2: 184. 8 January 1917.[2]	.23
15.	To stipulate that Deputies be six-month residents—not necessarily native-born —of the states they represent in Congress; passed 110–61. 2: 184. 8 January 1917.	.64
16.	To prohibit men on active military duty from serving in Chamber of Deputies; passed 158–13 (156–13). [Only negative votes in Diario.] 2: 184. 8 January 1917.[2]	.30
17.	To oblige high public officials desirous of running for the Chamber of Depu-	.27

Roll Calls Variable No.	Decision on Whether:	Riker Coefficient of Significance
	ties to resign from office 90 days prior to election; passed 163–8 (161–8). [Only negative votes in *Diario*.] 2: 184. 8 January 1917.[2]	
18.	To preserve the *fuero militar*, a special military tribunal; passed 122–61 (122–58). 2: 220. 10 January 1917.	.65
19.	To approve capital punishment for specific crimes, without reference to rape; passed 110–71. 2: 257. 12 January 1917.	.73
20.	To extend capital punishment to men convicted of rape; defeated 119–58. 2: 257. 12 January 1917.	.63
21.	To put government of Mexico City under control of the national government; defeated 90–44. 2: 298. 14 January 1917.	.38
22.	To broaden congressional authority for calling special legislative sessions; defeated 94–50 (93–59). 2: 341–342. 15 January 1917.	.55
23.	To authorize Senate—instead of Supreme Court—to restore constitutional order within states undergoing political crisis; passed 112–42 (111–42). 2: 360. 16 January 1917.	.43
24.	To approve Article 28, authorizing government to establish a central bank and excluding producers' cooperatives from anti-trust regulation; passed 120–52 (118–50). 2: 402–403. 17 January 1917.	.53
25.	To have Congress select a new President, in case of incapacitation, rather than calling popular elections; defeated 83–59 (82–58). 2: 463–464. 18 January 1917.	.48
26.	To prohibit various vices: liquor, un-	.48

Roll Calls Variable No.	Decision on Whether:	Riker Coefficient of Significance
	prescribed drugs, gambling, bullfights, cockfights; defeated 98–54 (97–54). 2: 696. 25 January 1917.	
27.	To prohibit religious ceremonies outside of temples; passed 93–63 (93–69). 2: 753–754. 27 January 1917.	.60
Petitions		
28.	To demand that Gerzayn Ugarte resign from convention because of alleged incompatibility with his role as Carranza's private secretary; 27 signatures. 2: 83–84. 4 January 1917.	–
29.	To propose amendment on labor, later Article 123; 68 signatures. 2: 261–265. 13 January 1917.	–
30.	To propose amendment prohibiting vices (see variable 26); 74 signatures. 2: 678–680. 22 January 1917.	–
31.	To propose abolishing *Ley del Timbre,* a kind of stamp tax; 40 signatures. 2: 771–772. 17 January 1917.	–
32.	To condemn tactics of "obstructionist" minority; 91 signatures. Taken from Juan de Dios Bojórquez [Djed Bórquez, pseud.], *Crónica del Constituyente* (México: Editorial Botas, 1938), pp. 555–562. 31 January 1917.	–

[1] First numbers show outcome as announced by recording secretary; in cases of discrepancy, numbers in parentheses show outcome as coded in computer data set (which does not include several individuals who attended preliminary sessions but did not vote in regular proceedings). Most differences are minor and are due to clerical errors in the *Diario.* Volume and page citations refer to the *Diario de los debates del Congreso Constituyente,* 2 vols. (México: Imprenta de la Cámara de Diputados, 1922). Calendar dates give the day of roll-call votes; dates for petitions refer to the day of signing, not the day of publication.

[2] Deleted from factor analysis.

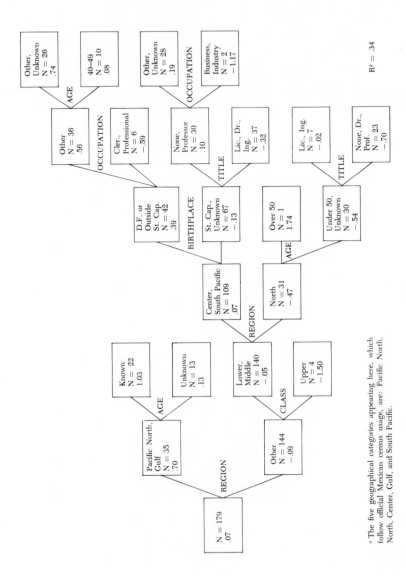

R^2 .34

FIGURE 6–5.

Voting and Social Background (All Variables)

[a] The five geographical categories appearing here, which follow official Mexican census usage, are: Pacific North, North, Center, Gulf, and South Pacific.

7
Constituency Influence on the British House of Commons, 1841–1847

WILLIAM O. AYDELOTTE

How far and in what way constituencies exercise influence over those who represent them in a legislature is a crucial problem in the study of representative government. Yet our knowledge on this subject is still inadequate. It may seem obvious that legislators must follow the wishes of the individuals who elect them, and who can reject them at the next election. Representative government is sometimes described as a system designed to ensure that this will happen: that the decisions or actions of the representatives will, so far as possible, meet the expectations and demands of the electorate. This objective is achieved presumably through the mechanism of elections by which the public gives its representatives a mandate to follow certain lines of policy or expresses its approval or disapproval of the policies that have been followed. Occasional indications have been found, however, that matters may not be quite so simple and that this model, plausible though it is, does not entirely correspond to the facts. A good deal of evidence that challenges it has been brought to light recently, particularly in systematic studies of American politics that have been conducted over the last couple of decades. Some scholars contend that the model is no longer acceptable, and have suggested new ways of looking at the evidence and new lines of research to explore.[1] Others, however, have tended to maintain the earlier view in a more sophisticated form, and, in recent monographs, have presented arguments pointing to a substantial amount of constituency influence over legislatures.[2]

With regard to Britain in the mid-nineteenth century, there has been much testimony to the growing strength of popular opinion after the

[1] John C. Wahlke, "Policy Demands and System Support: The Role of the Represented," in Gerhard Loewenberg, ed., *Modern Parliaments: Change or Decline?* (Chicago and New York: Aldine-Atherton, 1971), pp. 141–171; David Easton, *A Systems Analysis of Political Life* (New York: John Wiley & Sons, 1965); Raymond A. Bauer, Ithiel de Sola Pool, and Lewis Anthony Dexter, *American Business and Foreign Policy: The Politics of Foreign Trade* (New York: Atherton Press, 1963), chaps. 29–33 (these chapters are largely by Dexter).

[2] John W. Kingdon, *Congressmen's Voting Decisions* (New York: Harper & Row, 1973); Morris P. Fiorina, *Representatives, Roll Calls, and Constituencies* (Lexington, Mass.: D. C. Heath and Company, 1974); Frank J. Sorauf, *Party and Representation: Legislative Politics in Pennsylvania* (New York: Atherton Press, 1963).

reform legislation of 1832. This legislation, it is said, even if it did not change the character of the membership of the House of Commons, at least created a situation that must have restricted the liberty of action of men sitting in it. Public opinion, more than ever before, exercised ultimate control over the extent and direction of aristocratic rule, and no politician on either side of the House could ignore it with impunity.[3] Yet discussions of this question have often been in general terms and it might be useful to attempt to find out how far assertions about the power of the constituencies in the mid-nineteenth century can be supported by a systematic marshalling of some of the evidence that is still available.

One important aspect of this subject, on which there has been brisk disagreement, is the extent of control or manipulation of the electorate from above by bribery or by influence. The mid-nineteenth century has been described as an age when it was considered normal that a man's tenants should vote as he directed and the practice of influence, according to one historian, forms the larger part of the electoral history of the period from 1832 to 1885. This view has been strongly pressed by D. C. Moore in his research based on early Victorian poll books in which he analyzed constituencies according to estates rather than as undifferentiated masses, a choice that proved to make all the difference.[4] On the other hand, Richard W. Davis and R. J. Olney, in their studies of electoral politics in Buckinghamshire and Lincolnshire in this period, have found evidence indicating that the extent of electoral influence has been exaggerated and that there existed a substantial amount of local independence.[5] I can make no contribution to this argument since my research has been on legislative history rather than on electoral history, although the problems I have encountered have made me

[3] Norman Gash, *Politics in the Age of Peel: A Study in the Technique of Parliamentary Representation, 1830–1850* (London: Longmans, Green and Co., 1953), pp. xiii, 28–29.

[4] Gash, *Politics in the Age of Peel*, chaps. 7–9; G. S. R. Kitson Clark, "The Electorate and the Repeal of the Corn Laws," *Transactions of the Royal Historical Society*, 5th ser. 1 (London: Royal Historical Society, 1951), pp. 111–115, 118–119; H. J. Hanham, *The Reformed Electoral System in Great Britain, 1832–1914* (London: The Historical Association, 1968); D. C. Moore, "Social Structure, Political Structure, and Public Opinion in Mid-Victorian England," in Robert Robson, ed., *Ideas and Institutions of Victorian Britain: Essays in Honour of George Kitson Clark* (London: G. Bell & Sons, 1967), pp. 20–57.

[5] Richard W. Davis, *Political Change and Continuity, 1760–1885: A Buckinghamshire Study* (Newton Abbot, Devon: David and Charles, 1972): R. J. Olney, *Lincolnshire Politics, 1832–1885* (London and New York: Oxford University Press, 1973). I am indebted to Professor Davis for some extremely illuminating comments upon an earlier draft of this paper. He is not, of course, responsible for any of my contentions.

acutely aware of the importance of local history and of how much a study of local conditions may be able to contribute to an explanation of what went on in Parliament.

In this chapter I will deal with a different issue: not who controlled decisions in the constituencies; but whether and in what way constituencies influenced the decisions and behavior of their representatives in Parliament. I can make only a small contribution to this large subject, but I have some materials on the Parliament which sat from 1841 to 1847 that may at least advance the discussion of it and indicate certain problems with which students of parliamentary history will have to cope. I wish to raise two questions: first, whether the kind of constituency a Member of Parliament represented was related to his political slant; and, second, how this relationship, if it existed, was produced.

A start might be made by examining the relation of constituency to party affiliation: how far constituencies of different types tended to return men of different parties to Parliament.

The party affiliations of these M.P.s can be identified fairly unequivocally with the aid of successive editions of Dod's *Parliamentary Companion* checked by certain other sources including, in some cases, reports of local elections in the London *Times*. To make the analysis less cumbersome, only two main party groups will be shown in the tables: the Conservatives; and the nexus of parties or factions, loosely allied, which can as a short cut be referred to as the "Liberals," though it included men who called themselves Whigs, Liberals, Reformers, Radical Reformers, or Repealers. The use of a two-way party division is an oversimplification and assumes a more rigorous system of party organization than actually existed in the mid-nineteenth century. It will be possible, however, to take care of some of these refinements, some of these divisions within parties, presently in the discussion of the relation of constituency to attitudes on issues.

Constituencies are harder to classify. If we want to learn whether constituencies tried to impose their wishes upon Parliament, it would be useful to ascertain what these wishes were. Yet, though we know something about opinion trends in a few constituencies that have been intensively studied, our knowledge on this subject for the electorate as a whole is inadequate. Historians, in any case, do not have the kind of information about popular opinion that is taken for granted in much modern survey research which is based on interviews with samples of the electorate or, in other words, obtained from confrontations with live respondents, but is not available in research that deals with the dead. An effort might be made to infer the opinions of constituents

227

from demographic information about the communities they lived in, and this is occasionally done in studies of present-day conditions,[6] but there are standard objections to this: it has been found that the political choices of constituencies do not invariably correspond to their environmental circumstances, that individuals in an electorate do not in all cases vote in the way we might predict from our knowledge of their social and economic backgrounds, and that people don't always want what is good for them.[7]

For the classification of constituencies, demographic information, though not of high quality, is what we have to work with, and it is worth seeing what can be made of it and what relation it has to the behavior of Members of Parliament. Unfortunately, such information, on a constituency basis, is hard to get for the mid-nineteenth century. The statistics are incomplete and different kinds were collected for different geographical units. As Henry Pelling has discussed in some detail,[8] it is often extremely difficult to arrange these materials in such a way that they can be used for political history.

Even so, there are a few guidelines that permit at least approximate classifications. Constituencies in Great Britain in the mid-nineteenth century were identified as counties (or divisions of counties), boroughs (or comparable categories for Scotland and Ireland), and universities. The university seats are so few, 6 out of a total of 658, that they do not constitute a problem; in the analysis I have, for convenience, grouped them with county seats. Whether a constituency was a county or a borough might be regarded as a rough guide to whether it was rural or urban in character. This is still not good enough, however, since many borough constituencies, particularly in England, were tiny and of such a kind that it would be misleading to think of them as urban communities.[9] This problem can be met to a limited extent by classifying borough constituencies by size of electorate, which has been done here, and by treating boroughs of different sizes separately in the analysis, taking advantage of the findings to determine what are the most suitable cut-off points. This classification is imprecise and there are undoubtedly refinements that elude it. A fairly big borough, for example, might still be largely rural in character. On the other hand, even

[6] V. O. Key, Jr., *Public Opinion and American Democracy* (New York: Alfred A. Knopf, 1961), p. 483.

[7] Henry Pelling, *Popular Politics and Society in Late Victorian Britain* (London: Macmillan & Co., 1968), chap. 1; Philip E. Converse, "The Nature of Belief Systems in Mass Publics," in David E. Apter, ed., *Ideology and Discontent* (New York: The Free Press, 1964), pp. 206–261.

[8] Henry Pelling, *Social Geography of British Elections, 1885–1910* (London: Macmillan & Co., 1967).

[9] Gash, *Politics in the Age of Peel*, pp. 68–69.

with these crude measurements it has proved possible to get surprisingly good correlations.

Table 7–1 shows, for the 815 men who sat in the Parliament of 1841–1847, the relation between constituency and party. It makes use of a set of ten detailed constituency categories, those that have proved most useful for displaying the character of the evidence, and, at the bottom, includes a summary that brings out the trends more sharply. It turns out that constituency had a clear and decided relation to party although it was not always the same attributes of a constituency that determined this relationship. In Ireland what mattered was the location of the constituency, not its type. Both county and borough Members tended strongly to be Conservatives if they came from Ulster whereas, if they came from Southern Ireland, they tended strongly to belong to one of the parties on the left. The twenty-nine Repealers who sat in this Parliament all came, of course, from Southern Ireland. The line of division between parties in Ireland seems to be regional: presumably national or religious in character rather than social or economic.

In the rest of the United Kingdom, on the other hand, party was

TABLE 7–1. TYPE OF CONSTITUENCY AND PARTY
(THE 815 MEN WHO SAT IN THE PARLIAMENT OF 1841–1847)

	Conservatives %	Liberals %	N
England and Wales:			
County and University	87	13	197
Small Borough (108 to 789 electors)	60	40	195
Middle-sized Borough (790 to 1,759 electors)	53	47	122
Large Borough (1,774 to 30,122 electors)	30	70	99
Scotland:			
County	69	31	39
Borough	8	92	26
Ulster:			
County	91	9	23
Borough	80	20	15
Southern Ireland:			
County and University	25	75	59
Borough	22.5	77.5	40
Total	58	42	815
Summary:			
England and Wales, County and University; all Ulster; Scotland, County	87	13	235
England and Wales, small and middle-sized Borough (108 to 1,759 electors)	59	41	356
England and Wales, large Borough (1,774+ electors); Scotland, Borough; all Southern Ireland	25	75	124

229

related to type rather than to location of constituency. Members for counties in England, Wales, and Scotland tended strongly to the right, and borough Members in Scotland strongly to the left. All university Members were Conservatives. The 416 men who sat for boroughs in England and Wales were divided almost equally between the two party groups: 51% were Conservatives and 49% were Liberals. If, however, size of electorate is controlled, as has been done in the table, a trend appears that was concealed in the more general figures: Members from the smallest boroughs, presumably those most rural in character, were 60% Conservative, those from the middle-sized boroughs were about equally divided between the parties, while only 30% of those from the largest boroughs were Conservatives. Regional differences in England, Wales, and Scotland were trifling. County Members in Scotland were slightly less Conservative than county Members in England, and Wales, but the percentage difference is not impressive and the figures involved are small. The line of division in England, Wales, and Scotland was rural-urban rather than regional.

There was, then, a clear relation between the party affiliation of a Member of Parliament and certain readily identifiable attributes of the constituency he represented. The correlations, though far from complete, are strong. Of the independent variables examined, constituency has proved to be the one most closely related to party; the relation is much closer, for example, than that between party and personal background.

It may be useful to push this inquiry a stage further and to consider whether constituencies were related, not only to the party affiliations of Members of Parliament, but also to their attitudes on issues. It will put the argument in a broader context if, in examining the relation of constituencies to disagreements within parties, we also consider how far these disagreements did or did not constitute deviations from the party line. The subject of breaks from the party line, their nature and possible causes, has attracted a certain amount of attention from students of legislative behavior.[10] The term "party line," however, has been used in different senses. I will take as a definition of it not the side on which the majority of the party voted but, following Hugh Berrington's excellent suggestion, the side on which the majority of the

[10] A. Lawrence Lowell, "The Influence of Party upon Legislation in England and America," *Annual Report of the American Historical Association for the Year 1901* (Washington, 1902), pp. 321–542; Julius Turner, *Party and Constituency: Pressures on Congress*, rev. ed. by Edward V. Schneier, Jr. (Baltimore: Johns Hopkins Press, 1970); Hugh Berrington, "Partisanship and Dissidence in the Nineteenth-Century House of Commons," *Parliamentary Affairs* 21 (1968): 338–374.

party leaders voted, defining "leaders" as those who had held Cabinet or immediately sub-Cabinet posts before the dissolution of this Parliament in 1847. It is useful to consider as well, following another fruitful suggestion of Berrington's, not only the extent but also the direction of rebellions from the party line: whether they were, to use his terms, "extremist" or toward the ideological extremes of Parliament, far left for the Liberals, far right for the Conservatives; or whether, on the other hand, they were "cross-bench" in the sense of being toward the ideological center of Parliament or the point of the break between the two party groups, so that the rebels in each case tended to cross the House and to vote with the opposite side.

In contrast to the crudeness of the categories in which constituencies must be described, it has proved possible to develop good measures of the positions Members of Parliament publicly assumed on the issues of the day. These measures have taken the form of cumulative scales of the Guttman type, based on the votes in the division lists. The attempt to construct such scales for this Parliament has been remarkably successful and has revealed, by means of a multi-dimensional analysis, a high degree of consistency in voting.[11] At present I am working with twenty-four scales, though some of these are related and classify respondents in a similar fashion, so that the number of distinct dimensions is considerably less. The scales vary in character, and were set up to serve different purposes. Some are topical, in the sense of being restricted to items on a single subject, while others are derived empirically and include all items, often on a variety of topics, that, after testing, turned out to fit together in a scale. For this analysis only one scale will be used, an empirical one that has proved helpful in earlier work. I have come to refer to it as the "Big Scale" although actually several of the other empirical scales have turned out to be almost as large. It includes 120 or nearly 65% of the 186 items analyzed, and contains divisions on issues such as political reform, the income tax, the Corn Laws, customs, religion, Ireland, and the special privileges of the landowners. It appears to be a general dimension that subsumes a number of major questions which were, apparently, closely connected in the minds of contemporaries. It has been possible to classify by this scale 777 or 95% of the 815 men who sat in this Parliament.

For several reasons the Big Scale is a particularly useful tool for examining the differences of opinion within parties. It is a more refined instrument of measurement than a single division would be since it pro-

[11] William O. Aydelotte, "Voting Patterns in the British House of Commons in the 1840s," *Comparative Studies in Society and History* 2 (1963): 134–163.

vides, instead of a dichotomous classification, degrees or gradations. In this investigation it has been set up as a five-step continuum. The scale is useful also for testing the relation of constituency to attitude since it presents, not responses on a single issue, but a more general description of attitudes based on a man's positions on a number of questions. There is some evidence that electorates, even when ill-informed about detailed questions, may still make choices in broader terms between alternative general lines of policy.[12] If this is the case, a man's position on a scale, which is based on his votes on many questions and gives a general indication of his political orientation, might be more useful than his votes on individual issues as a means of detecting a relation between his constituency and his behavior. It should be added, however, that the question of whether an electorate is likely to respond in terms of a broad ideological spectrum is controversial. Some argue that constituents may feel strongly about a couple of issues and bring pressure to bear on them, while ignoring most of the other questions before the legislature. If this is the case, the use of dimensions might make the correlations lower rather than higher. I have tried to protect myself against this possible pitfall by also testing for the relation of constituency to attitudes on individual issues, using for this purpose the scales restricted to single topics such as, for example, political reform, the Corn Laws, or religious questions. The outcomes of these additional tests confirm the results reported here, though they do not provide such a full and detailed picture.

Another feature of the Big Scale is that, if collapsed into two parts, it fits the party break almost exactly. The Big Scale contains five scale-types. Almost all the Liberals in this Parliament fit into the first three, 311 of the 318 classifiable, or 98%. On the other hand, almost all the Conservatives fit into the last two scale-types, 457 of the 459 classifiable, or 99.6%. For the whole Parliament, party predicts whether a man is in the upper or lower part of the scale, in scale-types 1, 2, and 3, or in scale-types 4 and 5, in 768 of the 777 classifiable cases, about 99%; there are only 9 mavericks. Yet the Big Scale, though it is closely related to party, also provides a means for examining intra-party disagreements, since party predicts only the general range of a man's position on the scale, whether he was in the upper or lower part, but does not predict the exact scale-type to which he was assigned. On the contrary, the scale reveals extensive differences of opinion within each party and constitutes a convenient standard for measuring them.

[12] Warren E. Miller and Donald E. Stokes, "Constituency Influence in Congress," *American Political Science Review* 57 (1963): 47–48.

The fact that the Big Scale fits party so neatly in the sense described makes possible an initial simplification of the analysis. It seems hardly necessary, in these tests, to control for party. Instead, it is possible simply to take scale-types 1, 2, and 3 as the Liberals and scale-types 4 and 5 as the Conservatives, and this has been done in the tables that show scale positions. As a result the figures in these tables—all except Tables 7-1, 7-5, and 7-8—are slightly inaccurate. The seven Liberals who were assigned to the lower part of the scale are represented as Conservatives, and the two Conservatives who were assigned to the upper part of the scale are represented as Liberals. The distortion resulting from this procedure is so small in terms of percentage difference that it is not worth bothering about. To control for party and to insert the mavericks in separate columns with the fragments of one percent that belonged to them, though this would have been formally correct, would not have repaid the trouble and would have been merely a nuisance. Furthermore, the purpose of the tables where this matter comes up is to show the relation of constituency to policy output and it could be argued that for this it is more illuminating to rate a man by how he voted than by what he called himself. If the difference between the two were large, we might discuss the matter a little, but the difference is insignificant.

Constituency was clearly related not only to party but also to breaks within parties. Within the Liberal Party, as appears in Table 7-2, Members for counties in England and Wales tended strongly to the right, while Members for boroughs in England and Wales inclined increasingly toward the left as their constituencies increased in size.

The party line among the Liberals, shown in Table 7-4, appears to be in the ideological center of the party, scale-type 2, which includes 61 percent of the leaders, though it must be admitted that a party line that excludes nearly two-fifths of the leaders is not well marked. It is clear enough from Table 7-4, however, that the backbenchers showed a pattern of voting quite different from that of the leaders and were more inclined to the extreme left, scale-type 1, which contained 36 percent of the backbenchers as compared to 12 percent of the leaders. This fits with Berrington's finding, for the Parliaments he examined, that rebellions in the Liberal Party tended to be of the extremist rather than of the cross-bench variety. The relation of constituency to these deviations can be observed in the summary at the bottom of Table 7-2. Members for the first group of constituencies were decidedly to the right of the party; for the second group of constituencies the distribution between the three scale-types was almost

TABLE 7–2. TYPE OF CONSTITUENCY AND BREAKS WITHIN LIBERAL PARTY;
SCALE-TYPES 1–3

(INCLUDES ONLY THE LIBERALS CLASSIFIABLE BY BIG SCALE)

| | Scale-Type in Big Scale | | | |
| | 1 | 2 | 3 | N |
	%	%	%	
England and Wales:				
County and University	5	25	70	20
Small Borough (108 to 789 electors)	23	51	27	71
Middle-sized Borough (790 to 1,759 electors)	39	51	10	51
Large Borough (1,774 to 30,122 electors)	44	39	17	66
Scotland:				
County	18	64	18	11
Borough	48	43	9	23
Ulster:				
County	0	0	100	1
Borough	33	33	33	3
Southern Ireland:				
County and University	27	57	16	37
Borough	37	57	7	30
Total	32	48	20	313
Summary:				
England and Wales, County and University; all Ulster; Scotland, County	11	37	51	35
England and Wales, small and middle-sized Borough (108 to 1,759 electors)	30	51	20	122
England and Wales, large Borough (1,774+ electors); Scotland, Borough; all Southern Ireland	39	47	13	156

the same as that for the party as a whole; while Members for the third group were more inclined to the left.

There is also, as Table 7–3 shows, a relation between constituency and the break in the Conservative Party, though the relation is of a different kind. In Ireland, when the Conservatives alone are considered, the difference is no longer regional but turns out to be demographic. In both Ulster and Southern Ireland county Members inclined strongly to the right of the party and borough Members to the left. Another difference between Table 7–3 and the first two tables relates to representatives from the boroughs in England and Wales. In the first two tables the size of these boroughs mattered greatly: the small ones tended to the right and the larger ones to the left. For the Conservatives, however, the size of the borough made almost no difference between the two wings of the party. This phenomenon may be due to the fact that, at the time of the Corn Law crisis in 1846, a cer-

TABLE 7–3. TYPE OF CONSTITUENCY AND BREAKS WITHIN CONSERVATIVE
PARTY; SCALE-TYPES 4–5
(INCLUDES ONLY THE CONSERVATIVES CLASSIFIABLE BY BIG SCALE)

	Scale-Type in Big Scale		
	4	5	N
	%	%	
England and Wales:			
County and University	21	79	91
Small Borough (108 to 789 electors)	54	46	116
Middle-sized Borough (790 to 1,759 electors)	46	54	63
Large Borough (1,774 to 30,122 electors)	57	43	28
Scotland:			
County	50	50	26
Borough	50	50	2
Ulster:			
County	33	67	21
Borough	75	25	12
Southern Ireland:			
County and University	18	82	17
Borough	67	33	9
Total	39	61	464
Summary:			
County and University	25	75	234
Borough	54	46	230

TABLE 7–4. THE PARTY LINE IN EACH OF THE TWO PRINCIPAL PARTY
GROUPS
(INCLUDES ONLY THE LIBERALS AND CONSERVATIVES CLASSIFIABLE BY
BIG SCALE)

	Liberals				Conservatives		
					Scale-Types in Big Scale		
	Scale-Types in Big Scale			N			N
	1	2	3		4	5	
	%	%	%		%	%	
Leaders	12	61	27	51	77	23	57
Backbenchers	36	45	19	262	34	66	407
Total	32	48	20	313	39	61	464

Note: "Leaders" are defined as those who had held Cabinet or immediately
sub-Cabinet office before the dissolution in 1847; "Backbenchers" are all the others.

tain amount of electoral influence in the small boroughs was exerted to support Peel's government. These features of the evidence make it possible to summarize the table in two categories, county and university Members as opposed to borough Members. This is not, of course, a straight rural-urban division since Members for the small boroughs, which were clearly rural in character, are classed with Members for the larger boroughs in the group that was more inclined to support the more liberal wing of the party, represented by scale-type 4. This summary shows a fairly strong trend. The county and university Conservatives tended heavily to the right: 75 percent of them were in scale-type 5. The borough Conservatives were divided about equally between scale-types 4 and 5, 54 percent to 46 percent.

The party line for the Conservatives is more clearly indicated than that for the Liberals, since 77 percent of the Conservative leaders were in the left wing of the party, scale-type 4. In this case, however, the leaders did not carry the majority of the party with them. Of the 407 backbenchers, only 34 percent were in scale-type 4, and 66 percent were in scale-type 5. The pattern is just the opposite from that described, for the later nineteenth century, by Berrington who found that Conservative rebellions, in the Parliaments he studied, tended to be of the cross-bench variety. In the 1840s, however, rebellions by his definition were extremist in both parties, not only among the Liberals but also and even more decidedly among the Conservatives. In 1846 it was the leaders of the Conservative Party who displayed a cross-bench behavior: the repeal of the Corn Laws was carried with the aid of the opposition and against the wishes of the majority of the government's former supporters. The close relation of constituency to the deviations from party line in the Conservative Party emerges clearly from the summary at the bottom of Table 7–3.

The answer to the first question raised at the outset, whether constituency was connected with political slant, is clearly in the affirmative. The evidence shows that the demographic attributes of constituencies were related both to party and also to differences on issues within each party. In mid-nineteenth century Britain constituencies of the same type appear to have had extremely similar political preferences. The "focus" of representation, in the sense in which Heinz Eulau uses the term,[13] appears to have been, for most of these M.P.s, more local than national.

The findings I have presented in earlier papers about the policy

[13] Heinz Eulau, "Legislative Roles," in John C. Wahlke, Heinz Eulau, William Buchanan, and Leroy C. Ferguson, *The Legislative System: Explorations in Legislative Behavior* (New York: John Wiley & Sons, 1962), pp. 268–272.

objectives of parties in this period and the kinds of issues around which conflict crystallized [14] help to make these relationships intelligible. What is known about the lines of controversy in Parliament—the dispute between the establishment and the new order, between landed wealth and commercial or industrial wealth, between rural interests and urban interests—fits not too badly with the evidence about the constituencies for which men on different sides of this controversy sat. Members of Parliament tended to take lines on these subjects that were, so far as we can tell, appropriate for the needs of their own constituencies. This is not to say that they granted all demands made upon them. On the contrary, Parliament in this period often resisted popular pressure. What does seem to be true is that differences in policy between Members of Parliament reflected the circumstances of the different kinds of constituencies that they represented.

It might appear that the second question raised at the outset, whether constituencies exercised an influence over Parliament, has also been answered. The strength of the correlations between parliamentary behavior and constituency suggests that Members of Parliament must have taken account not only of the needs of their constituents but also, it seems reasonable to suppose, of their wishes. The fact that different types of constituencies clearly preferred politicians of different parties and with different views appears to make this inference inescapable. Although a correlation does not prove the existence of a cause-and-effect relationship, the findings are certainly consistent with the hypothesis that constituencies exercised a considerable influence over their representatives. Before going this far, however, it may be useful to consider the means by which this influence may have been exerted. The issue now is not whether M.P.s voted their constituencies, which they obviously often did, but whether they were *constrained* to do this. It is hard to get evidence on such a subject, but there is a little information that may throw light on it.

One fact that makes the hypothesis of constituency influence over Parliament in this period somewhat less plausible is the relative infrequency of election contests. In the general election of 1841, 51 percent of the seats were uncontested and, in the general election of 1847, 56 percent.[15] It was true in principle that a Member of Parliament could be unseated at the next election. Yet when so many of the seats

---

[14] Aydelotte, "Voting Patterns in the British House of Commons in the 1840s," pp. 145–150; idem, "Parties and Issues in Early Victorian England," *Journal of Briitsh History* 5 (1966): 95–114.

[15] William O. Aydelotte, *Quantification in History* (Reading, Mass.: Addison-Wesley Publishing Co., 1971), p. 108.

were uncontested the danger of being rejected was, one might suppose, reduced considerably. The low incidence of contests may raise some question about how firm or emphatic the control of constituencies over Parliament in the mid-nineteenth century could have been.

For purposes of the present inquiry, however, perhaps this special feature of the evidence can be turned to advantage. The fact that, in the general election of 1841, about half the seats were contested and about half were not may provide an opportunity for—what is usually hard to obtain—a controlled observation by which it may be possible to find out how far a contest made a man more likely to vote his constituency. Plausible hypotheses could be, and have been, set up in either direction. A man who contested his seat might feel himself more bound to his constituents, more under a mandate to follow their wishes, than one who did not. Or, it could be argued, a Member who did not have to fight a contest may have been more acceptable to the constituency as a whole and, hence, more likely to be a good spokesman of its wishes. If the first hypothesis were valid, we should expect the occurrence of a contest to heighten the relationship between constituency and behavior whereas, in the second case, the occurrence of a contest would lessen this relationship. To test these points it is necessary to find out whether Members who contested their seats, as compared to those who did not, were more conservative in the constituencies that have been shown to have been of a conservative persuasion, more liberal in the liberal constituencies, and so on. Table 7–5 gives this information for the three summary categories that have already proved useful. The more detailed figures, which I have not shown, tell approximately the same story. There was, as appears from these summaries, a considerable difference in the incidence of contests in different types of constituencies: they were infrequent in counties, and most frequent in the large boroughs of England and Wales. The question here, however, is whether, in the *same type* of constituency, Conservatives or Liberals were more likely to have contested their seats. The difference between them in this respect, as the figures in Table 7–5 show, was minimal: whether a contest occurred or not apparently did not affect the relation between a Member's party and his constituency. The table does not give figures on the smaller group of M.P.s who were elected at by-elections, but I have run a test on these too and the results were also negative.

The relation of contests to breaks within parties is shown in Tables 7–6 and 7–7, for the same categories of constituencies that were used to summarize the findings in Tables 7–2 and 7–3. Among the Liberals, in Table 7–6, those who contested their seats in each of the three classes

TABLE 7–5. ELECTION CONTEST IN 1841: CONSTITUENCY AND PARTY
(INCLUDES ONLY THE 658 MEN ELECTED IN GENERAL ELECTION OF 1841)

		Conservatives %	Liberals %	N
England and Wales, County and University; all	Contest	81.5	18.5	54
Ulster; Scotland, County	No Contest	85	15	168
England and Wales, small and middle-sized Borough (108 to 1,759	Contest	53	47	154
electors)	No Contest	58	42	98
England and Wales, large Borough (1,774+ electors); Scotland, Borough; all	Contest	28	72	113
Southern Ireland	No Contest	17	83	71
Total		56	44	658

TABLE 7–6. ELECTION CONTEST IN 1841: CONSTITUENCY AND BREAKS
WITHIN LIBERAL PARTY; SCALE-TYPES 1–3
(INCLUDES ONLY THE LIBERALS CLASSIFIABLE BY BIG SCALE)

		Scale-Type in Big Scale			
		1 %	2 %	3 %	N
England and Wales, County and University; all	Contest	11	56	33	9
Ulster; Scotland, County	No Contest	6	39	56	18
England and Wales, small and middle-sized Borough (108 to 1,759	Contest	34	49	17	65
electors)	No Contest	23	46	31	39
England and Wales, large Borough (1,774+ electors); Scotland, Borough; all	Contest	41	45	14	78
Southern Ireland	No Contest	32	56	12	57
Total		31	48	20	266

WILLIAM O. AYDELOTTE

TABLE 7–7. ELECTION CONTEST IN 1841: CONSTITUENCY AND BREAKS
WITHIN CONSERVATIVE PARTY; SCALE-TYPES 4–5
(INCLUDES ONLY THE CONSERVATIVES CLASSIFIABLE BY BIG SCALE)

| | | Scale-Type in Big Scale | | |
		4 %	5 %	N
County and University	Contest	15	85	46
	No Contest	31	69	144
Borough	Contest	58	42	110
	No Contest	54	46	68
Total		42	58	368

of constituencies were somewhat to the left of those who did not, but
the percentage differences are not impressive. Among the Conserva-
tives, shown in Table 7–7, county Members who had to fight contests
were somewhat more conservative than county Members who did not,
though the difference is not large. For Conservative borough Members
the occurrence of a contest made almost no difference.

Although there are a few details that might merit further considera-
tion, the general result of these tests is negative. Contests show little
statistical relation, when constituency is controlled, either to party or to
breaks within parties, and they apparently had no effect, for Parliament
as a whole, on the relations between constituency and behavior. Both
the hypotheses just stated must be rejected. The results do, however,
make it difficult to argue that contests were an important element in
the exercise of control by constituencies.

It may be possible to get a better lead on the exertion of pressure by
constituencies upon their representatives and to make a more decisive
test by examining the evidence on re-elections to the next Parliament,
the one that sat from 1847 to 1852. The object of this test is to show
how far constituencies of different types sought to exert pressure upon
Parliament by re-electing those members who supported their interests
and rejecting those who did not. The question is whether men whose
parties or attitudes were more in accordance with the apparent demo-
graphic circumstances of their constituencies were more likely to be
re-elected.

Because of the limits of my information, the tests described here can
be only crude, and their results must be regarded as tentative. My
figures on "re-election" include all those who sat in the Parliament of

240

1847–1852 at any time in its five-year course. While the great majority of these were elected at the general election of 1847, some were not, and I do not have the means of distinguishing between these two groups. The figures do not show, for those elected to the following Parliament, whether they were elected for the same constituency or a different one. Cases of the latter type produce a distortion, the extent of which I do not have the means of estimating, in the results reported here. I do not have information on the men who stood for re-election in 1847 and were defeated, or on those who voluntarily withdrew from what may have seemed a hopeless contest. Nor do I have data on the new Members, those elected in 1847 who had not sat before. When I was collecting these materials some time ago, I did not anticipate that I was going to make tests of this kind; if I had, I would have arranged things differently. These are, however, the only figures that I have, or that anyone else has, and it may be worth seeing what can be learned from them.[16]

To give a more sharply defined picture, the tests have been limited to the incumbents, those still sitting at the time of the dissolution in 1847: 656 men instead of 658 because of the disfranchisement of Sudbury with its two seats in 1844. Of these, 457 or 70 percent sat in the Parliament of 1847–1852 and 199 or 30 percent did not. (Of the 159 men who sat in the Parliament of 1841–1847 but left it before the dissolution only 10, 6 percent, served in the next Parliament.) In Tables 7–8, 7–9, and 7–10 "re-election," in the sense in which I am using the term, has been treated as a *dependent* variable because of the form of the question, and the percentages have been figured accordingly. The issue here is whether belonging to a particular party or voting in a particular way improved or weakened the chances of Members from different types of constituencies of sitting in the next Parliament.

These figures, so far as they constitute a reliable guide, do not indicate that constituencies attempted to reinforce their apparent preferences by the sanction of acceptance or rejection. If this had been the case we would expect, for example, that, among county Members, Conservatives would be more likely to be re-elected and that, among borough Members, Liberals would be. No trends of this kind appeared. The summary figures—the detailed figures tell a similar story—are given in Table 7–8. In the first category of constituencies, which includes the counties in England and Wales, 77 percent of the sitting

[16] Since writing this chapter I have undertaken a further investigation and have assembled information that permits making tests while controlling for these variables. The results, which in general support the contentions made here, provide some useful additional points on which I hope to report in a later paper.

WILLIAM O. AYDELOTTE

Conservatives and 78 percent of the sitting Liberals were elected to the next Parliament. In the third category of constituencies, which includes the big boroughs in England and Wales, 66 percent of the sitting Conservatives and 65 percent of the sitting Liberals reappeared. Different kinds of constituencies still showed strong party preferences, but this had nothing to do with chances of further parliamentary service. In each of the three classes of constituencies in the table, Conservatives and Liberals were almost equally likely to be re-elected. This was also the case for Parliament as a whole, as appears from the figures at the bottom of Table 7–8. Of the Conservatives sitting in Parliament at the time of the 1847 dissolution, 69 percent sat in the following Parliament; of the comparable group of Liberals, 70 percent did.

If party did not affect re-election, it is conceivable that attitudes on issues might, particularly after this stormy Parliament in which one of the major parties had broken apart over an issue, the repeal of the Corn Laws, which had been the subject of intense public controversy. Even here, however, there was little difference. In the summary fig-

TABLE 7–8. ELECTION OF INCUMBENTS TO PARLIAMENT OF 1847–1852: CONSTITUENCY AND PARTY
(INCLUDES ONLY THE 656 MEN SITTING AT TIME OF DISSOLUTION IN 1847)

	Re-elected	Conservatives %	Liberals %	Total %
England and Wales, County and University; all Ulster; Scotland, County	Yes	77	78	77
		N=183	N=36	N=219
	No	23	22	23
England and Wales, small and middle-sized Borough (108 to 1,759 electors)	Yes	60	75	66
		N=149	N=104	N=253
	No	40	25	34
England and Wales, large Borough (1,774+ electors); Scotland, Borough; all Southern Ireland	Yes	66	65	65
		N=41	N=143	N=184
	No	34	35	35
Whole Parliament	Yes	69	70	70
		N=373	N=283	N=656
	No	31	30	30

242

ures on the 266 scalable Liberals in Table 7–9 it is difficult to find, in any of the three classes of constituency, any decided relation between scale-type and re-election. The percentage differences are unimpressive, particularly in view of the small frequencies involved in some cases. Among the 372 scalable Conservatives, shown in Table 7–10, those in scale-type 4, roughly the Peelites, and those in scale-type 5, roughly the Protectionists, were almost equally likely to be re-elected: the difference was slight for county Members and almost non-existent for borough Members. Policy output was apparently not a factor in determining public approbation or disapprobation in either party in any of the three classes of constituencies. The same can be said for Parliament as a whole, regardless of type of constituency, as appears from the figures at the bottom of Tables 7–9 and 7–10. The five groups of individuals assigned to the five scale-types had approximately equal chances of serving in the next Parliament. The range is from 64 percent to 75 percent.

I attempted to improve these results by refining the constituency variable. Since constituencies are so closely related to behavior in Parliament, it seemed reasonable to expect that the use of categories

TABLE 7–9. ELECTION OF INCUMBENTS TO PARLIAMENT OF 1847–1852: CONSTITUENCY AND BREAKS WITHIN LIBERAL PARTY; SCALE-TYPES 1–3 (INCLUDES ONLY THE LIBERALS CLASSIFIABLE BY BIG SCALE)

| | | Scale-Type in Big Scale | | | |
	Re-elected	1 %	2 %	3 %	Total %
England and Wales, County and University; all Ulster; Scotland, County	Yes	75	90	71	77
		N=4	N=10	N=17	N=31
	No	25	10	29	23
England and Wales, small and middle-sized Borough (108 to 1,759 electors)	Yes	71	76	83	76
		N=31	N=51	N=18	N=100
	No	29	24	17	24
England and Wales, large Borough (1,774+ electors); Scotland, Borough; all Southern Ireland	Yes	71	57	72	64
		N=52	N=65	N=18	N=135
	No	29	43	28	36
	Yes	71	67	75	70
Whole Parliament		N=87	N=126	N=53	N=266
	No	29	33	25	30

TABLE 7–10. ELECTION OF INCUMBENTS TO PARLIAMENT OF 1847–1852:
CONSTITUENCY AND BREAKS WITHIN CONSERVATIVE PARTY;
SCALE-TYPES 4–5
(INCLUDES ONLY THE CONSERVATIVES CLASSIFIABLE BY BIG SCALE)

	Re-elected	Scale-Type in Big Scale		
		4 %	5 %	Total %
County and University	Yes	74	79	78
		N=31	N=156	N=187
	No	26	21	22
Borough	Yes	60	58	59
		N=86	N=99	N=185
	No	40	42	41
Total	Yes	64	71	69
		N=117	N=255	N=372
	No	36	29	31

providing a more exact description of them would result in better fig-
ures. Certain additional attributes of Early Victorian constituencies
can be precisely measured. For each we have information on the size
of the population and the size of the electorate, and from this it is pos-
sible to get good measures of the extent of enfranchisement (the ratio
of population to electorate) and of the extent of malapportionment,
how far a constituency was over-represented or under-represented
(the ratio of electorate to seats). Early Victorian constituencies differed
greatly in both respects. For every constituency these ratios have been
calculated and put on tape, and the appropriate tests have been run.
The outcome of these tests, however, was almost entirely negative,
and the complicated tables summarizing them have not been included
in this chapter. It turned out that, if the type of constituency was
controlled, the extent of enfranchisement or malapportionment had
almost no impact on the party or votes of the constituency's representa-
tive. Apparently, behavior was not affected by political arrangements
of this kind.

In summary, the results give a double picture. On the one hand,
there was a relation, strongly marked despite the crudeness of the mea-
surements, between the party and votes of Members of Parliament and
the demographic attributes of the constituencies they represented. It
is not plausible to maintain that there was no link between constituency
and behavior. On the other hand, it is still not clear what mechanism

produced this relationship. This evidence, so far as it goes, does not support the hypothesis that the link was due to pressure from the constituencies. It cannot be shown that those who contested their seats had a special mandate, as compared to those who did not, or that constituents enforced their wishes upon their representatives by rejecting, at the next general election, those who did not behave in the desired fashion. Furthermore, the degrees of enfranchisement or malapportionment, if the demographic variable is controlled, turn out to have no relation to party or attitude, which makes it difficult to attribute the behavior of Members to electoral arrangements that permitted or did not permit the expression of a larger public opinion. The behavior of Members can be "explained" in a statistical sense, so far as it can be explained at all—the correlations are, of course, only partial—by the demographic variables, whereas the political variables appear not to matter much one way or the other.

It must be remembered that not all M.P.s voted their constituencies. There were enough exceptions to this pattern to make some tests possible. The tests, however, indicate that it did not signify, for re-election, whether Members voted their constituencies or not. Indeed the evidence points to a still wider generalization. For Parliament as a whole, there was not any kind of behavior that made M.P.s for any type of constituency more likely to be re-elected. In all kinds of constituencies, sitting Members of all political stripes stood equal chances. In general, behavior was apparently unrelated to likelihood of further parliamentary service.

These findings are only part of the story. The tests are crude, and I have reservations about them which I have stated. They may be too coarse a net to catch some of the things that mattered most. Also these results are for the whole of Parliament, and there may be important exceptions to this general pattern. We already know of a number of such exceptions, of cases in which Members of Parliament seem to have deferred to the wishes of their constituencies. Some of the Conservatives who were converted to free trade in the crisis of 1845-1846 left Parliament voluntarily, apparently because their new opinions were unacceptable to their constituents or to the local wielders of influence. Davis and Olney have identified cases in which stands on controversial issues were apparently motivated by electoral considerations. There are instances in which it appears that efforts to please constituents ensured re-election or that failure to please them ensured defeat. In any case, the findings of this paper are subject to correction from the work of local historians. It will be difficult to speak with much con-

245

fidence about the influence of constituencies on Parliament until we know a great deal more about local conditions.

On the other hand gross figures, even if they miss details, may reveal important general trends. What is interesting in this case is that, despite individual exceptions that are known or that may be found, the general picture for Parliament as a whole was so consistent and that, in all the different kinds of circumstances that have been examined, behavior appears to have been uniformly unrelated to opportunities for further parliamentary activity.

Perhaps the most striking feature of the evidence is the continuity of service, the fact that 70 percent of those sitting at the dissolution sat in the next Parliament. This trend was so strong that it engulfed the other variables considered here: it was affected neither by party nor by voting record nor by the relation of either of these to type of constituency. All the groups defined by these various criteria were approximately equally likely to reappear in Parliament later. Not even type of constituency was closely related to re-election. This appears from the figures in the right-hand column of Table 7–8. Re-election was slightly more likely for county Members, but not much. In the three groups of constituencies used for this table the proportions of sitting Members re-elected were 77 percent, 66 percent, and 65 percent. If this was the case, however, if re-election was the normal pattern regardless of the other matters considered here, questions naturally arise about the practical importance of general elections and about how far they can have served as an instrument of control by the constituencies over Parliament.

8

Cue-Taking by Congressmen:
A Model and a Computer Simulation

DONALD R. MATTHEWS AND JAMES A. STIMSON

"RESEARCH on legislative behavior," Wahlke and Eulau wrote ten years ago, "has been more sensitive to problems of technique than to problems of conceptual clarification. Yet, the most sophisticated technical developments are meaningless unless research findings are presented in a theoretically, or at least conceptually, viable framework which will give more than *ad hoc* significance to the great variety of factors that constitute the legislative process." [1]

A decade later Robert Peabody began his systematic review of recent research on Congress with a nearly identical observation. "Research on Congress," he wrote, "has reached an important middle stage in its development. Over the last two decades and especially since 1960 a proliferation of empirical studies has yielded much new data, richer insights, and a better understanding of the internal workings of Congress, executive-legislative relations, and the representative process. Despite these significant advances, political scientists have not yet produced a conceptually clear and comprehensive theory of Congressional behavior." [2]

This chapter is an extensive revision and updating of our "The Decision-Making Approach to the Study of Legislative Behavior," a paper presented at the Sixty-Fifth Annual Meeting of the American Political Science Association, New York, September 1969.

The financial support of the Ford Foundation and the State University of New York Foundation and the hospitality of the Brookings Institution have greatly facilitated our research on decision making by members of the U.S. House of Representatives. None of these institutions, however, should be held accountable for the contents of this paper.

[1] John C. Wahlke and Heinz Eulau, eds., *Legislative Behavior: A Reader in Theory and Research* (Glencoe, Illinois: Free Press, 1959), p. 355.

[2] Ralph K. Huitt and Robert L. Peabody, *Congress: Two Decades of Analysis* (New York: Harper & Row, 1969), p. 3. For additional comments along the same lines see Gerhard Loewenberg, "Toward a Paradigm for Legislative Research" (Paper presented at the Conference on Comparative Legislative Behavior Research, University of Iowa, 1969), p. 2; Heinz Eulau and Katherine Hinckley, "Legislative Institutions and Processes," in James A. Robinson, ed., *Political Science Annual* (Indianapolis: Bobbs-Merrill Co., 1966); Samuel C. Patterson, "Notes on Legislative Behavior Research," mimeographed (University of Iowa: Laboratory for Political Research, 1965); Norman Meller, " 'Legislative Behavior Research' Revisited: A Review of Five Years' Publications," *Western Political Quarterly* 18 (1965): 792–793.

Despite these complaints about lack of theory, the study of legislative behavior has not been devoid of "approaches," "conceptualizations," "models," and "theories of the middle range." Indeed, one problem has been the sheer number and variety of intellectual constructs used by researchers in the field. In such a balkanized theoretical context "theories" go untested by research and research has little cumulative impact.[3]

But the plethora of concepts and theories used by students of legislative behavior is not the only problem. A far more serious defect is that the theories employed over the last decade or so have not been highly comprehensive—that is, they have not been applicable to enough different types of legislatures, legislative subsystems, situations, or contexts. Nor do these theories have much explanatory or predictive power. Finally, most of the theorizing that does exist focuses our attention on demand-input variables rather than toward outputs, the ultimate dependent variable of political research.[4]

In this paper, we shall present a theory of legislative behavior which seems to avoid most of these difficulties. Then we shall report on our effort to test this theory by means of a computer simulation of the roll-call voting behavior of members of the U. S. House of Representatives.

I

THE DECISION-MAKING ORIENTATION

LEGISLATURES make authoritative decisions on public policy. If we are to explain these policies, we must first describe and explain the process by which they are made. This explanation can proceed at either the institutional-aggregate level, in the classic tradition of *Congress Makes A Law* [5] and other descriptive case studies of legislative decision making, or the focus can be on how the individual legislator makes choices.

---

[3] We shall use the word "theory" very loosely to indicate any general statements about regularities of behavior or relationships between variables. Most of the statements fall short of meeting the requirements of scientific theory—hence the use of quotation marks here. For the sake of visual clarity we shall dispense with quotation marks henceforth, but the reader should be warned that, strictly speaking, they ought to be employed throughout the paper.

[4] See John C. Wahlke, "Public Policy and Representative Government: The Role of the Represented," mimeographed (University of Iowa: Laboratory for Political Research, 1967). For a more extended critique of the major theoretical orientations see Donald R. Matthews and James A. Stimson, "The Decision-Making Approach to the Study of Legislative Behavior," (Paper presented at the Sixty-Fifth Annual Meeting of the American Political Science Association, New York, September 1969), pp. 1–6.

[5] Stephen K. Bailey, *Congress Makes A Law* (New York: Columbia University Press, 1950).

248

While this second approach has been rarely attempted,[6] we believe that it has great merit as an orientation to legislative research.

Decision making—the conscious and unconscious selection of courses of action or inaction—by individual legislators covers a broad range of behavior in a wide variety of settings, in committees and subcommittees, on the floor, in legislative offices, back home in "the district" and so on. And the job-related decisions of the individual legislator vary in their importance to the actor and to others, both in and outside the legislature. Ultimately, we hope to be able to describe and explain most of these decisions but as a beginning we are concentrating our research on the member's roll-call voting decisions only.

Our study focuses on the *process* of decision followed by individual members when called upon to cast a yea or nay vote on the floor. Students of legislative voting have rarely attempted to explain this process. Rather they have been content to settle for statistical correlaions between indicators of presumed "causes" (rather summarily chosen from the U. S. Census) and voting patterns (often elegantly measured) without regard to intervening variables and processes. Thus demographic and political attributes of congressional districts have been statistically associated with the voting records of congressmen *ad nauseam;* the predictive power of party labels for congressional voting also has been demonstrated over and over again. But *how* these independent variables are translated into votes remains largely a mystery. It is this very process which we are seeking to describe and explain.

The advantages of focusing on roll-call decision making are mostly self-evident:

1. Roll-call votes are public, are available for the past as well as the present, and usually have an extensive printed record which accompanies them.

2. Roll calls are numerous in most American legislatures. In the contemporary House of Representatives the 435 members cast 65,000 to 100,000 votes each year. Since the individual vote is the unit of analysis the "small N" problem which plagues most legislative research is eliminated.

3. While roll-call votes, in the House of Representatives at least, may

[6] The study of individual legislator decisions is now less rare than when these words were first written in 1972. See particularly the now influential work of Aage R. Clausen, *How Congressmen Decide: A Policy Focus* (New York: St. Martin's Press, 1973) and John W. Kingdon, *Congressmen's Voting Decisions* (New York: Harper & Row, 1973). Cleo H. Cherryholmes and Michael J. Shapiro, *Representatives and Roll-Calls* (Indianapolis: Bobbs-Merrill Co., 1969) was among the earliest efforts to examine individual decision making in Congress.

be less important in shaping public policy than decisions made by subsets of members earlier in the legislative process, these preliminary decisions must be ratified by the membership at large before they become authoritative. How and why this occurs has never been fully explained. The aggregation of individual roll-call votes *is* the policy output of the legislature—the ultimate dependent variable of legislative research.

4. By focusing on the final stages of the legislative process we are then able to work backwards in time toward antecedent "causes." This strategy is comparable to that followed by the authors of *The American Voter* [7] who, by focusing on the processes immediately preceding the voter's decision, were able to revolutionize the study of electoral behavior. We hope that by focusing our research on legislative decision making at the output end of "the funnel of causality" we may achieve a breakthrough in the study of legislative behavior as well.

Every conceptual or theoretical orientation has drawbacks—the one we have adopted in our research on the House of Representatives is no exception.

For one thing, if one tries to describe, explain, and predict all roll calls by all members, as we are attempting to do, there is an inevitable sacrifice of depth for breadth of understanding. Bailey, for example, in analyzing the behavior of the dozen or so leading figures in the enactment of the Employment Act was able to go into their personal histories, values, and political situations in a reasonably exhaustive way. Our research is not confined to leading figures or a single atypical bill, and hence is of far more general value. But our research lacks the rich and often revealing detail of the case study. There is much to be said for and against both approaches.

Second, the decision-making approach may not be too helpful in studying legislatures that rarely make recorded decisions and/or that are dominated by political executives. Legislators still have to make decisions in these institutions, of course, but these may be difficult to get at and relatively trivial once described. For American congressmen, however, the casting of roll-call votes is scarcely a trivial activity.

II
The Context of Congressional Decision Making

"I have to vote on 150 different kinds of things every year—foreign aid, science, space, technical problems, and the Merchant Marine, and

[7] Angus Campbell, Philip Converse, Warren Miller, and Donald Stokes, *The American Voter* (New York: John Wiley & Sons, 1960).

TABLE 8-1. NUMBER OF ROLL-CALL VOTES HELD IN U.S. HOUSE OF REPRESENTATIVES, 1958-1974

Year	Congress and Session	Number of Roll Calls
1974	93rd, 2nd	537[a]
1973	93rd, 1st	541[a]
1972	92nd, 2nd	329[a]
1971	92nd, 1st	320[a]
1970	91st, 2nd	266
1969	91st, 1st	177
1968	90th, 2nd	233
1967	90th, 1st	245
1966	89th, 2nd	193
1965	89th, 1st	201
1964	88th, 2nd	113
1963	88th, 1st	119
1962	87th, 2nd	124
1961	87th, 1st	116
1960	86th, 2nd	93
1959	86th, 1st	87
1958	85th, 2nd	93

Source: *Congressional Quarterly Almanac* (Washington, D.C.: Congressional Quarterly, Inc., 1959–1975).

[a] Including recorded teller votes.

Lord knows what else. I can't possibly become an expert in all of these fields." Thus does a member of Congress describe the formidable decision-making task facing him and his colleagues.[8]

The *number* of roll-call votes cast each year is large and growing larger (see Table 8–1). When non-recorded floor votes are added—to say nothing of the many decisions congressmen must make in committee, in their offices, etc.—it is clear that members are required to make an incredible number of decisions.

The subject matter of these decisions is as varied as twentieth-century America is complex. In a single day in 1969 the House discussed the financing of airport facilities, the disposal of surplus lead, the sale and advertising of cigarettes, congressional ethics, the use of Defense Department facilities for the production of movies, aid to the arts, the treatment of laboratory animals, the creation of a national wildlife refuge, textile imports, the payment of postal employees, chemical and

[8] A portion of our research consists of 100 tape-recorded interviews with a random sample of rank-and-file members of the U.S. House of Representatives conducted during the spring of 1969. All quotations from members used in this chapter are drawn from these interviews.

biological warfare research, patents and copyrights, and more.[9] The *scope* of decisions that congressmen make is staggering.

Perhaps the number and scope of decisions asked of congressmen would be manageable if Congress wrote policy in the round. But Congress, for the most part, does not operate that way. Most legislative proposals are *complex, specific,* and *technical;* they order specific actions in specific cases in an attempt to cover every contingency. They attempt "fine tuning" around an already existing body of legislation that is itself specific and technical, containing amid the many nuances of precise legislative prescription the unclear and often inconsistent outlines of a general policy.

This mode of decision making requires technical knowledge and time. Time devoted to developing technical competence in one or a few policy areas is subtracted from that available to consider everything else. Members say that it takes years of service to understand fully proposed legislation in a handful of areas; the time available for the evaluation of proposals outside their areas of special interest is reckoned in hours or minutes each week, and not very many at that. Some members confess a little sheepishly that they spend *no time at all* in legislative study outside the areas of their special interest and activity!

If members had the time to make independent analyses of all legislation, would they have the necessary information at hand? The answer is yes and no. Information of a sort exists in superabundance in the congressional environment. Facts and figures on anything and everything are available in committee reports, from the Legislative Research Service, from lobbyists, from staff studies, and from the mass media. There may even be too many facts and figures, because the processing of such information into a yea or nay vote is extremely time-consuming, and, as we have noted, the time available for this activity is very limited. But information of another sort is not so readily available. Answers to such questions as, "Is this legislation consistent with my voting record?" or "How do my constituents feel about it?" or "How will they be affected?" or "What will be the effect of this legislation in general?" are not easy to obtain. Thus the congressman who seeks to undertake an independent analysis of a piece of legislation risks drowning in a deep well of facts while at the same time failing to find answers to the questions about which he is most concerned.

Despite all those difficulties congressmen seek to cast their votes as rationally as possible. All we mean to say here is that, when faced with

---

[9] *Congressional Record* (daily edition), 91 Cong., 1 sess., 8 June 1969, pp. H4937–H5004.

the necessity of casting a yea or nay vote, congressmen attempt to cast the vote so as to enhance the chances of achieving their goals. Different congressmen pursue quite different goals—re-election, power and prestige in the House, the approval of the editorial writers of the *New York Times*, a good shot at a seat in the U.S. Senate, the framing of policy in the national interest, etc.—but congressmen do have goals and try to use their votes on the floor of the House to enhance the probabilities of attaining them. A few "bad" votes may not significantly alter the congressman's chances for successful goal attainment, but the innate prudence of ambitious men dictates strenuous efforts to avoid mistakes and to calculate the consequences of their actions and votes as much as possible.

Moreover, previous research on legislative roll-call voting suggests that the voting records of most congressmen display properties that are consistent with rational behavior, or more precisely, are sharply in conflict with what could be expected if congressmen regularly voted in extremely irrational ways.[10] The members seem to be following relatively predictable decision strategies in casting their yeas and nays. The potential payoffs to congressmen for casting roll-call votes in a fairly rational way are so great, and the potential risks of following any other course so large, that members try hard to be reasonable.

The context of congressional decision making thus can be summarized as follows: there are too many decisions to be made across too wide a span of subjects; the issues they involve are too complex for quick decision; and there is too little time for anything else. Even so, the congressman must cast his vote in a reasonably rational way or face the high probability of defeat or failure to achieve his personal and political objectives.

How, then, given this perplexing situation do congressmen make up their minds: Whatever the number and complexity of bills, they can not avoid making decisions, however much they might like to. As one member puts it: ". . . It's not uncommon for me to go to the floor with the bells ringing, votes being taken, and it's on a bill or issue that I have never heard of before. I haven't the remotest idea of the issues involved. You've got to make up your mind; you can't vote 'maybe' and

---

[10] See especially D. R. Brimhall and A. S. Otis, "Consistency of Voting by Our Congressmen," *Journal of Applied Psychology* 32 (1948): 1–74; Duncan MacRae, Jr., *Dimensions of Congressional Voting* (Berkeley: University of California Press, 1958); H. Douglas Price, "Are Southern Democrats Different?" in Nelson W. Polsby, Robert A. Dentler, and Paul A. Smith, eds., *Politics and Social Life* (Boston: Houghton Mifflin Co., 1963), pp. 740–756; Aage R. Clausen, "Measurement Identity in the Longitudinal Analysis of Legislative Voting," *American Political Science Review* 61 (1967): 1020–1035.

you can't vote 'present'—you don't want to. So you have to make a decision on the best basis you can."

III
Low-Information Strategies of Decision

Making a decision "on the best basis you can" implies finding short-cuts that will produce a reasonable decision with a good deal less input of information, time, and wisdom than a complete and independent assessment would require. There are several such strategies; none has gone unobserved.

One way that decisions can be simplified, presumably, is for the member simply to "*vote his district.*" The laborious job of analyzing measures can be dispensed with in favor of seeing how the wind is blowing back home and voting accordingly. "Vote your district" may be an article of faith among congressmen as much because it helps simplify their decision-making problems as because it contributes to their political survival.

But a second look at this low-information strategy of decision shows it to be far more difficult to employ than it seems at first glance. In order to "test the wind," there has to be some wind blowing; constituents must have opinions and communicate them in some fashion. But members agree that their constituents seldom tell them what they want. When they do, it is often on items of high emotion and little import. "I think the only time they become really concerned," comments one member, "is when we have emotional issues. . . . But then there is an area, maybe 90 percent of the bills, that they don't take any interest in at all." Other members say that their constituents sometimes are vocal on important matters, but only if they are personally affected: "Unless it's a matter that your constituents are affected by directly, and unless they know about it, and keep informed on it, you don't know. You've got to form your own opinion on it. . . . Like I know people are concerned about stream pollution, but they aren't going to get all fired up about it unless their own stream is polluted and they're getting bad water."

If constituents do not communicate, can members guess what their opinions would be if they did have them and expressed them? Certainly Southern members can anticipate the feelings of their constituents on a civil rights bill, although the recent enfranchisement of many southern blacks has made gauging the effective division of sentiment on this issue more difficult than it used to be. Perhaps every congressional district has a few issues on which preponderant opinion is easily anticipated, even though not overtly expressed. But we are impressed by the fact that virtually all members claim to have a district that is complex in social makeup and contradictory in political sentiments; most say that their district is one of the most heterogeneous in the country! While congressmen often try to "vote their district," it is not a strategy that makes their decisions much easier, except on a small number of votes.

Another way that members can minimize the cost of decision is simply to follow their own *precedents,* to vote the same way they did the last time a similar measure was before them. The usefulness of this *stare decisis* voting strategy depends on the nature of the measure in question as well as the seniority of the member. Nothing is ever exactly the same one year as it was before. Even if the bill is almost identical, there may be important changes in the political environment or a different parliamentary situation that can cause a member to reverse an earlier decision. "Needless to say, the longer you're here," a Republican comments, "the more you are likely to be bound by your own voting record. . . . The longer you're here, the more the pattern of your own votes determines the next one. You've been voting to protest the debt increases. Suddenly with the Republican in the White House —he asks for a debt increase; what do you do? . . . It's that kind of thing that makes voting interesting. You're never quite sure how you're going to vote yourself."

It is hard to assess how often congressmen vote purely on the basis of personal precedent. We can say, however, that those with more seniority do it more often, simply because they have the opportunity more often, and that members do it more often on legislation that reoccurs at relatively short and regular intervals, such as foreign aid or appropriations bills.

Incrementalism is another means of reducing the costs of decision making.[11] By following this path the member avoids the necessity of making overall judgments of a program and its place in his complicated hierarchy of priorities. Instead he has to evaluate only relatively minor changes in it, thereby reducing the arduousness of his task from virtually impossible to merely difficult.

To some extent incrementalism characterizes most legislation. Congress normally modifies policy around the edges rather than deciding on wholly new programs. But to say that a piece of legislation is a policy increment is not to say that it is easy to evaluate in anything but

[11] See David Braybrooke and Charles E. Lindblom, *A Strategy of Decision* (New York: Free Press, 1963).

a relative sense. Probably only in the appropriations area does the incremental nature of legislation make for quick and easy decision, although other factors work to complicate the appropriations bill in spite of its incremental nature.[12]

The application of a coherent structure of beliefs about government and politics, in short, an *ideology*, is another way to simplify the making of decisions.[13] It allows the member to group large numbers of bills into sets, all of which can be handled similarly. When employing such a strategy, the member need only decide whether a bill is "liberal," "conservative," or whatever, and vote accordingly.

Although ideology undoubtedly accounts for many voting decisions in Congress, its scope is sharply circumscribed. To begin with, this voting strategy requires that bills be susceptible to ideological classification. While there is wide disagreement among members about the number that can be thus handled, it is a distinct minority of all roll-call votes. A more severe limitation is the fact that ideology can be the sole basis of decision only if a member is prepared to vote for (or against) all liberal or conservative legislation without any evaluation of the probabilities that the bill will have the desired effects or without any consideration of its costs and side effects. Otherwise the tasks of analysis and evaluation are still necessary. "I think that we've got to read the fine print," comments a liberal member. "What is going to be the practical impact of this, I would put more stress on that. It can sound great, but if it isn't going to work. . ." Another makes the point in even stronger language: "I don't think I would ever decide on ideology in that sense. I would want to read it. If you're thinking of a bill entitled, 'A Bill to Help Poor People,' which I normally would want to help; would I vote for it just on that? The answer is, 'Hell no.' It could be a screwy way of helping poor people." Conservatives expressed similar sentiments: "In fact you seldom find any given piece of legislation with which you can agree in its entirety. And there are so many of them that are just borderline in your own ideology, and you just get to the point of where you have to weigh what, in your judgment, is bad and what's good. . . . And somewhere you have to weigh that evaluation and come up with a judgment."

There are some members of Congress, both liberals and conservatives, who are said to vote purely on an ideological basis. But they are

---

[12] See Aaron Wildavsky, *The Politics of the Budgetary Process* (Boston: Little, Brown and Co., 1964).

[13] See Anthony Downs, *An Economic Theory of Democracy* (New York: Harper & Row, 1957), for a discussion of the relationship between ideology and the costs of decision.

a small minority and they risk the disrespect of their colleagues. "I am impressed by Congressmen who you can't put into boxes," one Democratic member said. "I know that 'X' is always going to find out what the liberal position is and vote it that way. And I know 'Y' is always going to find out what the conservative position is and vote it that way. I like the ones who think about these things and jump around."

Thus there is a considerable constraint on the effect of ideology *as a simplifying device* in congressional decisions. But this is not to say that it is an unimportant determinant of decision making; later we shall discuss other ways in which its effect bears upon the decision process.

Specialization is another means of coping with the number, scope, and complexity of congressional decisions. The vast majority of members of the House narrow the focus of their attention to a relatively few issue areas and develop a degree of expertise in these subjects while largely ignoring everything else.

The member's areas of specialization are often determined by constituency considerations. ". . . So you have to select those areas in which you can do the most good for your constituency," one member explained. "After all, that's what you're down here for." Once they have built up enough seniority, members ordinarily obtain seats on one of the committees dealing with legislation in the area of their special concern. But sometimes a committee assignment will lead to the development of a legislative interest rather than vice versa: "I didn't particularly want to get on the Post Office and Civil Service Committee. I came here and jumped twelve places in three years and sort of became 'Senior Statesman' of the committee accidentally, and you hate to give this up." And the member's personal background or training often affects his choice of specialty as well. A member of the Appropriations Committee says: "I had the pleasure and privilege of starting out in the state legislature on the Appropriations Committee, and so the experience gained there in attempting to meet the money needs of the state was kind of brought with me here, and it was just a natural." One effect of the almost universal practice of specialization is to reduce the number of issues upon which members even attempt an individual assessment of the merits of legislative proposals. But at least in a few fields of particular interest to him the average member is able to make decisions on a high-information basis. The cost of this strategy, however, is to reduce further the time and energy available to make independent analyses of legislation outside the member's specialty. Specialization then makes some voting decisions easier at the same time that it makes most voting decisions more difficult.

257

IV

CUE-TAKING: THE "NORMAL" DECISION PROCESS

IF the low-information decision strategies discussed above are insufficient to make possible the casting of hundreds of reasonable roll-call votes each year, what do congressmen do?

First, the congressman, in the areas of his specialty, makes decisions pretty much as the textbooks say congressmen do on all issues. He is relatively well informed in these areas; the larger share of the time he has to devote to legislation is spent here. A personal and independent assessment of the merits of legislative proposals is conceivably possible. But even in areas of his specialty the member will usually be forced by the sheer complexity of mid-twentieth century problems to resort to low-information strategies of decision—such as "voting his district," following his past record, or the use of incrementalism or ideology as decision-making aids.

The "normal" or "typical" roll-call vote, however, falls *outside* the area of specialty of the member. When the congressman is confronted with the necessity of casting a roll-call vote on a complex issue about which he knows very little, he searches for cues provided by trusted colleagues who because of their formal position in the legislature or policy specialization have more information than he does and with whom he would probably agree if he had the time and information to make an independent decision. Cue-givers need not be individuals. When overwhelming majorities of groups which the member respects and trusts—the members of his party or state delegation, for example— vote the same way, the member is likely to accept their collective judgment as his own.

Nothing is unusual about what we have said of cue-taking as a low-information strategy of decision. Its existence has been noted before. What is different in our approach is that we look upon it as *the normal process of congressional decision making*, to which the other processes are exceptions.

We think, for instance, that when a liberal-conservative split occurs on a typical roll-call vote the best explanation for the votes of individual members is not that they studied the bill and accepted or rejected it on the grounds of its fit with their ideologies, but rather that they took cues from the experts whose ideology they usually support, liberals following liberal experts and conservatives following conservative experts. Or to cite another example: when the pattern of roll-call votes on an issue seems to follow the interests of the members' constituents, this does not ordinarily mean that the members ascertain the opinions and interests of their constituents directly and independently; rather, non-specialist members probably chose to follow the specialists whose district interests were similar to their own. The end result is similar in both examples, but the process of decision is quite different. The costs of decision are considerably less for cue-taking members than for those who independently sought to apply ideology or constituency opinions to the problem.

Why take cues from other members? Expertise certainly is not limited to the Congress. But there are a number of reasons why members usually seek out other members, rather than looking to outside cue-givers. First of all, the congressional expert is also a professional politician, and thus can be assumed to have weighed political factors in reaching his decision. Members value such political judgment highly, and no one is in as good a position to make such judgments as another member.

Members come to have long experience in dealing with their colleagues over a host of issues. They are thus in a good position to evaluate the judgment of the expert on many other matters to see if it is good (i.e., similar to their own). Thus the judgment comes from a source of known performance. The cue-taker need not evaluate the information source as well as the information itself, as is generally the case with "outside" information.

The congressional cue-giver is available at the time the decision must be cast on the floor of the House. That advantage is all-important in the many cases where the member comes to the floor with no information at all. Then, only a colleague can supply such information. The importance of this factor should not be underrated, because this situation is common.

The congressional cue-giver is forced to be trustworthy. At the first sign of unreliability, the member's influence is likely to be permanently impaired. Members *do* trust their colleagues, and it is partly the result of the continuing sanctions they have over them. One comments: "I go to a person on the committee who I trust, and whose views are more or less synonymous with mine. . . . That's my best source of information, since they have to live with me. As a colleague, I am able to hold them accountable better than anybody else." The withholding of trust is a powerful sanction. Cue-giving and cue-taking together constitute a reciprocal process, and one that continues over a long period of time. The actors in the game understand that deception on one occasion will likely lead to a position of legislative isolation in the future, where others' advice is no longer given and theirs is no longer sought.

259

To say that cue-taking is the "normal" process of decision for House members is merely the beginning of a better understanding of decision making by the House of Representatives. The conditions under which "abnormal" decision strategies are followed must be further specified. Why rank and file member "A" follows specialist "B" rather than specialist "C," how cues are transmitted, why members choose to specialize in one area rather than another, and many more unanswered questions arise. We have some tentative answers to them, but they are beyond the scope of this chapter.[14]

V

DEVELOPING AN OPERATIONAL MODEL:
SOME PRELIMINARY CONSIDERATIONS

IF members of Congress make decisions by taking cues, and if their cue-taking strategies are relatively simple, then cue-taking should be both measurable and predictable. There were about half a million recorded individual voting decisions from 1961 to 1969, each one a test of and a challenge to a general theory of congressional voting behavior. This awesome task invites a computer simulation. The flashing lights and razzle-dazzle technology we did not need; speed was all we required.

THEORY AND OPERATIONAL MODEL

We began with a set of assumptions about the roll-call voting behavior of congressmen which we wished to test. By now, most of them should be familiar:

1. The normal situation of the member of Congress with regard to most of the roll-call voting decisions he makes is one of low information.

2. The cost of raising his information base to a level adequate for fully independent decisions consistent with his multiple goals is prohibitive, given the number, scope, and technical complexity of the decisions he is expected to make.

3. Cues—pro or con evaluations of legislative issues—are available from a variety of sources (with a corresponding variety of influence bases) in the House at the time of decision.

4. Such cues are an exceedingly economical means for the member

[14] Many of these matters are treated at length in Donald R. Matthews and James A. Stimson, *Yeas and Nays: Normal Decision-Making in the U.S. House of Representatives* (New York: Wiley-Interscience, 1975).

260

to estimate what his position would be if he had the time and information necessary for an independent decision.

5. Members vote by taking cues, and develop over time decision strategies in the form of regularized hierarchies of cue-givers.

6. These strategies are influenced by such factors as ideology and constituency (and others) and are, in fact, the normal process by which such causal influences are mediated into the ultimate decision.

7. Such decision strategies are relatively constant across issues (roles of cue-givers in the hierarchy are constant—role incumbents may vary by issue area) and over time.

A computer simulation can be only a partial test of these hypotheses. First, while the predictive accuracy of the simulation either lends credence to or tends to undermine them, they stand or fall *as a set*. They are not individually "tested." Second, much of the operationalization of the theory requires specific stipulations that are not themselevs dictated by the theory. Thus, the simulation is far more specific than the theory—it must be to make specific predictions—and it is only one of many possible operational models. We would like to ascribe all virtues to the theory and all vices (bad predictions) to the operational model; no doubt the model itself is responsible for some good predictions and the theory not without vice. The gap between theory and operation is always with us.

SIMULATION

Computer simulation has been widely attempted and the number of definitions of it lags not far behind the number of its applications. We will not join the debate about what a computer simulation either "is" or "should be," but only stipulate here how we use the word. The word "simulation" is a convenient label for our operational model; we have no other motive for using it.

There are two essential elements to our notion of simulation. One is that the simulator makes specific testable predictions of events that are unknown (but not necessarily in the future). That attribute is shared with many forms of scientific endeavor. In this case the predictions are of the form, "Member(i) voted yea/nay on roll call(j)." If the member actually voted, the prediction is then either right or wrong; otherwise it is ignored.[15] The event to be predicted, while "known" to the com-

---

[15] Note the implicit assumption that non-voting is irrelevant to cue-taking and therefore unpredictable. Genuine abstention we believe is rare in the United States Congress; most non-voting is due to member absences, not refusal to take positions.

261

puter (i.e., contained in core storage), is unknown to the simulator (which does, however, know how everyone else voted).

The other element of simulation—the less common one—is that the *process* followed by the simulator is analogous to that of the actor being simulated. The simulation itself can test only accuracy of prediction, but we make the twin assertion that the process the simulator follows— its program—is itself a *description* of the process of congressional decision making.[16] Human cognitive and evaluative processes are ordinarily exceedingly complex, and attempts to simulate them with a simple-minded computer an insult to reality. But we have hypothesized an exceedingly simple behavior, forced by the multiple constraints on decision making, susceptible to *approximation* by computer. The computer (properly, its program) is still far more simple-minded than the congressional decision maker, but not so much so that it can not engage in behavior analogous to the congressman. "Simulation" then, as we use it, means prediction of unknown events by a process analogue.

PREDICTION: HOW ACCURATE IS ACCURATE?

Predicting past events, like shooting ducks in a pond, is not much of a sport without· some restrictions. Without concern for parsimony or theoretical justification only predictive perfection limits the number and variety of refinements that may be added to a computer model. In our model, for example, if we allowed every member to serve as a cue-giver for every other, our predictions would be highly accurate, but without theoretical interest. Thus we have limited our cue-givers to nine, all institutionally defined. This is one of the more important respects in which the simulation is far more specific and restricted than the theory from which it is derived.[17] It is a price to be paid to eliminate spurious accuracy; some probably still remains.[18]

We measure accuracy in percentages of accurate predictions, from zero to one hundred. But the real baseline is not zero. Any number of simple prediction rules can make drastic improvements in accuracy if zero is the baseline. A coin toss should be accurate half the time. Predicting that all members vote yea on every roll call or that everyone

---

[16] That the assertion of the descriptive accuracy of the simulation was untestable was the major reason for the congressional interviewing program.

[17] The most important cue sources that are missing from the simulations, to judge from the interviews, are rank-and-file committee members. They could not have been included without building in, at the same time, a high probability of many spuriously accurate predictions. Their influence, however, is felt, in the various intermediary cue-givers, where they are in an early and crucial part of the nuclei of majority sentiments.

[18] We are indebted to W. Phillips Shively and Duncan MacRae, Jr., for detailed and insightful critiques of our early work that were particularly helpful on the question of spurious accuracy.

votes on the winning side would substantially improve on that. These simple and theoretically useless prediction rules do not themselves establish a baseline—sophisticated models can make predictive errors on votes that come easily to simple spurious ones—but they do establish a context of expectations. Failing perfection, the judgment of the accuracy of the simulations ultimately becomes a question of parsimony—how good is the batting average compared to how many inputs?

INFORMATION GATHERING ON THE FLOOR

We assume in the simulations that the position of every salient cue-giver is known to each member. How can we assume that cues are known at the same time that we deny the availability of other important information?

First, the positions of other members on a bill or resolution can be learned easily by a member at any stage in the slow-moving legislative process—the answer is as close as the nearest telephone. Members can and do find out "how the good guys are going" without taking any initiative at all. Members "lobby" one another incessantly. Gossiping about colleagues is at least as common in the halls of Congress as in hotel corridors during academic conventions and serves a more laudable end. In the normal round of his day-to-day existence, the congressman picks up cues without investing time and energy in the process.

Even when a member remains entirely uninformed about the positions of his cue-givers until the time to vote has arrived, the ritual of the roll-call vote permits him to find cues while the vote is in progress.

The milling about on the floor of the House during a roll call is one of the strangest sights in American politics. Hundreds of men (and a few women) taking up and breaking off conversations, coming and going, moving from side to side, from front to back—all seemingly oblivious to the official business of the House. What's happening is communication and information gathering—visible but unfortunately inaudible from the gallery. Its best parallel may be the floor of a stock exchange, hundreds of individually rational acts creating the impression of collective madness.

The calling of the yeas and nays, under either traditional [19] or electronic [20] procedures, provides the last useful opportunity for the undecided member to search for the cue of his choice. The traditional

[19] For a good description of the traditional roll-call vote see Lewis A. Froman, Jr., *The Congressional Process: Strategies, Rules, and Procedures* (Boston: Little, Brown and Co., 1967), pp. 62–89.

[20] See *Congress and the Nation* (Washington: Congressional Quarterly, Inc., 1973) 3: 387 for a description of electronic voting procedures.

roll call gave him thirty to forty-five minutes to listen to the twice-repeated alphabetical call of the roll. The electronic system gives him fifteen minutes to watch his colleagues record their positions on a wall scoreboard. Under either system the safest assertion we make is that the cue-taker, if he has not already done so, easily can find the cue of his choice on the floor of the House at the time of the vote.

VI

Nine Cue-Givers Operationally Defined

THE nine cue-givers in our roll-call simulations were chosen *a priori*. The reader searching for surprising new revelations about the sources of decision cues will be disappointed. None are new to informed congressional observers, nor to congressmen themselves, who produced essentially the same list in open-ended interviews.[21]

The essential idiocy of computers requires highly specific operational definitions of cue-givers. Computers are very good at counting and calculating, very bad at pattern recognition. Where individuals of mediocre intelligence can observe phenomena and see obvious patterns, computers see only what they are *specifically* instructed to look for. Specific often means arbitrary, and many of the parameters that make up the operational definitions of cue-givers are arbitrary. The guiding rule in all these operational decisions has been that they be *intuitively reasonable in the context of low-information decision making on the House floor*.[22]

The nine cue-givers and their operational definitions are:

The President: The president is the only one of our cue-givers not present on the Floor at the time of the vote. His position is nonetheless well known; it appears repeatedly in debate, is discussed on the Floor, and is available from the nearest doorkeeper. Data on presidential positions are from the *Congressional Quarterly Almanac*.[23]

---

[21] The chief sources of voting cues mentioned in the interviews, but not considered in the simulation design, are rank-and-file committee members and the Republican socio-legislative groups whose influence we did not appreciate. They have, however, been noted in the literature. See Charles L. Clapp, *The Congressman: His Work As He Sees It* (Washington: The Brookings Institution, 1963), chap. 1.

[22] Specifically excluded is empirical determination of parameters, allowing the computer to optimize prediction by systematic variation. While empirical determination makes sense in some contexts, here the number of predictions and their complexity encourage us to pay the price of a loss of predictive accuracy (probably a small one) in order to have an intuitively justifiable operational model.

[23] Compiled and copyrighted by Congressional Quarterly, Inc., Washington, D. C. The annual volumes from 1957 through 1969 have been utilized.

264

Like all others, the presidential cue has three states, yea, nay, or not available.

State Party Delegation: This cue is defined as "available" to a member whenever three-fourths or more of his colleagues from his state and party vote together on a roll call. The three-fourths figure is used as a cut-off on the assumption that in units as small as the "SPD's" (the lower limit is two voting members), the mathematics of the situation can create a false impression of majority sentiment where diversity is really the case. Consider for example the four-man SPD. The member whose behavior is being observed or predicted is, of course, excluded, leaving two possible states for the other three, unanimity or a two-to-one split. A cut-off of two-thirds would define a voting cue even in the case of maximum diversity, which seems unreasonable. Again for intuitive reasons, we followed the *Congressional Quarterly* practice of breaking up some of the largest states into smaller "perceived delegations" (e.g., New York City and Upstate New York) to assess the effects of this cue. We have not noted any net change in predictive accuracy from this practice.

Party Leadership: A cue is considered available from the party leadership whenever the floor leader and whip of the member's *own party* vote together.[24] This cue can be "given" unintentionally; the two leaders may easily and frequently vote together by chance on non-party matters. The theory of cue-taking predicts that the intentions of cue-givers may be irrelevant to the member searching for a cue, and hence these chance agreements are not excluded.

Committee Chairman: This cue is simply the vote of the chairman of the committee reporting the bill or resolution under consideration. In case of votes on rules the substantive committee chairman's position is used, *unless the rule itself is subject to controversy.* Closed rules (barring amendments) and rules waiving points of order (where the legislation violates House Rules, e.g., legislating in an appropriations bill) are in the latter category.

Ranking Minority Member: The position of the ranking minority member of the reporting committee is operationalized in the same fashion as that of the chairman. Note that the ranking member and chairman cues are each available to members of both parties.

Conservative Coalition: The conservative coalition cue is defined

[24] The Speaker of the House cannot be used as an operational cue-giver because he does not vote. However well his position may be known to members of his party, it cannot feasibly be determined for the operational model.

when a majority of Southern Democrats votes with a majority of Midwest Republicans against a majority of non-Southern Democrats. Because all three conditions are required concurrently, and therefore presumably visibly, only 50 percent majorities are required. Our version of the conservative coalition differs slightly from the well-known *Congressional Quarterly* definition, and indeed is only one of several that we have employed.[25]

Democratic Study Group: Since the D.S.G. does not take formal public positions on votes, we look to the leadership element (as best we can determine it) for unanimity as a cue. Again, as we pointed out with regard to party leaders, it is possible for the seven leaders we use to agree without intention of cue-giving.

Party Majority: The member's party colleagues may act as a collective cue-giver if majority sentiment is clearly perceptible (two-thirds or more voting together). With this and all other cues the member's own vote is excluded from consideration when the existence and direction of cues are determined.[26]

House Majority: This cue is defined when two-thirds or more of the whole membership of the House vote together. Very high levels of response to this cue are assumed to represent bandwagon tendencies.

VII
THE SIMULATION MODEL

WE turn now to a non-technical description of the simulation model. The model we will describe (program name: LEARN) is the most recent of three approaches to simulating roll-call votes we have developed. All three are consistent with the theory of cue-taking, differing in approaches to operationalization.[27]

[25] For an earlier definition and discussion, see Matthews and Stimson, "Decision-Making by U.S. Representatives: A Preliminary Model," in S. Sidney Ulmer, ed., *Political Decision-Making* (New York: Van Nostrand, 1970).

[26] The nuisance exceptions are party leaders (four members) and D.S.G. leaders (seven members) who are likely to take cues from themselves on those votes where their respective cues are available. Their nuisance value is that they would be easy to predict in any case—without circularity. The circularity could have been eliminated with special routines for these eleven members, but the difference in percentage (total) accuracy would have been so small (probably no more than one-hundredth of a percent) as not to justify the special attention. The possibility of circularity exists for committee chairmen and ranking minority members, but is considerably less likely to have any effect—certainly no appreciable effect—than party and D.S.G. leaders. The reason is that the chairman's own position could only serve as a cue to him if: (1) his committee reported the bill, *and* (2) the chairman (role) was his highest cue-giver, very infrequently the case. Similar logic applies to ranking minority members.

[27] Matthews and Stimson, "Decision-Making," describes the first model, SIMULATE, and contains a proposal for the second, INDCUE. INDCUE and

We postulate that cue-taking is learned behavior, that members develop "cue response hierarchies" over time as they react to cue-givers on one roll call after another. These hierarchies, rough rank orderings of cue-givers the individual member carries around in his head, answer the questions: "Whom will I turn to first (second, third, etc.) for a cue?" Because they are learned behavior, the response hierarchies are changeable over time, particularly for new members. Taking one roll call at a time in chronological order the program carries out three "functions" for each member. The three functions are measurement (observation of past cue-taking behavior), evaluation (the determination of response hierarchies), and prediction of the member's vote.[28] We take them up one at a time.

For member "i" and roll call "j" the *measurement* segment of the program observes the member's cue-taking patterns on the 50 roll calls previous to "j"—or all roll calls if fewer than 50 have occurred at that point in the session.[29] The effective memory of 50 votes is large enough to avoid assigning undue weight to a short series of strange votes, small enough to allow for genuine change of response hierarchies if it does occur.

The product of the measurement segment is, for each cue-giver, two running tallies, VWC (number of times member *voted with cue-giver*) and CAMV (number of items the *cue* was *available* and the *member* was *voting*) such that the ratio "VWC/CAMV" represents the proportion of agreement of member "i" with the cue-giver in question (number of agreements over number of opportunities). The maximum size of both numerator and denominator is 50, the proportion ranging between zero and one. The 18 tallies (VWC and CAMV for each of the 9 cue-givers for member "i") are the input to the evaluation segment.

For member "i" and roll call "j" the *evaluation* segment of the program determines and rank orders "cue-scores." The cue-scores are determined by the formula:

$$\text{Cue-Score}(k) = (\text{VWC}(k)/\text{CAMV}(k)) - .5;$$
where k is a numeric code for one of the nine cue-givers.

---

a third program CUETEST were measurement programs, whose output was input for SIMULATE, which did the actual simulation. The LEARN program described above combines the measurement and prediction aspects of the simulation.

[28] The actual sequence of the three functions in LEARN is different than we present them here, but for purely technical reasons. The logic is identical.

[29] On the first roll call of the session the measurement segment is bypassed and arbitrary information (every member votes with his party majority) passed on to the prediction segment. That produces 100 percent accuracy on votes for Speaker in the first session of a Congress, mixed results on the first vote of the second session.

The score is thus a simple proportion of agreement with cue-giver (k) minus the expected agreement by chance (.5).[30] Cue-scores may then vary between −.500 (always voted against cue-giver) and +.500 (always voted with cue-giver). Scores in the middle range indicate that the member probably ignored the cue-giver, voting with him (or it) about as often as we would expect by chance.

For the purpose of determining cue response hierarchies, the program rank orders the nine scores by their *absolute values*, presumed to measure intensity of response, whether positive or negative. The evaluation segment thus produces for each member on each roll call two sorts of information that will be employed in the prediction segment, the rank order of cue-givers and the direction of response to each, positive or negative.

The *prediction* segment of the LEARN program differs only in focus from measurement and evaluation; it performs one of the same tasks, ascertaining positions of cue-givers, except that it does it on the current roll call, "j"; and instead of comparing member "i's" vote to the positions of cue-givers, it uses them and "i's" predispositions (cue-scores) to predict "i's" vote. It first seeks out the position of "i's" highest ranked cue-giver. If a cue is available from that source, it determines its direction (yea or nay) and predicts the cue-taker's response from his predisposition (positive or negative cue-score) to that cue-giver.[31] If no cue is available from the first cue-giver, it seeks out the second, and so on, until it finds an available cue for prediction. What may seem to be a complex cognitive process in reality is not, because the usual case is

[30] Note that .500 is only an approximation of expected chance agreement, perfectly accurate only in the limiting case of a 50–50 split. Assuming a 65–35 percentage split to be closer to average, the proportion of chance agreements between two members is: the probability that the cue-giver is in the majority (.65) times the probability that the cue-taker is in the majority (.65) plus the probability that the cue-giver is in the minority (.35) times the probability that the cue-taker is in the minority (.35) or: $(.65 \times .65 = .4225) + (.35 \times .35 = .1225) = .545$. We use .500 for its intuitive appeal, both because adjusting the parameter for the average size of the majority on the last 50 votes after each roll call is burdensome and adds complexity to a model already too complex, and because we fear it might spuriously inflate the importance of negative cue-taking to use a higher figure. The model already contains a tie-breaking device that (unintentionally) resolves ties between positive and negative cue-scores in favor of the negative, with some strange results in votes taken early in the session.

[31] This is a simpler procedure for prediction than in the earlier models. They treated cue-scores as measures of intensity of predisposition, and combined cue responses (from up to three cue-givers) until "information sufficiency" was reached. Intellectually appealing, the intensity and information sufficiency notions produced predictions of about the same overall accuracy as the present "one-cue" model, and were abandoned in the interest of parsimony. The interview materials give the impression that members differ in this regard.

268

that the member votes with (or against) his highest ranked cue-giver, and need not look at the others.

After predicting the vote, the simulator scans its memory for the actual vote, compares prediction and vote, and keeps a running tally of accuracy, by member and by roll call. It then moves on to member "i+1," and when all members have been simulated on roll-call "j" it moves on to "j+1" and repeats the process.

This model is dynamic; it allows for change in cue response patterns over time.[32] It is *not* cybernetic—there is no success/failure feedback loop that modifies future behavior—for we do not believe the real-world congressman operates that way in his cue-taking behavior.

The computer model is a simplification of reality; indeed it is a simplification of the theory of cue-taking. The question is of degree. We have asserted earlier that the actual decision-making process by cue-taking is quite simple, because of the heavy constraints faced by members in their decision making. Thus we believe the degree of simplification in the model is not great. It surely errs on the side of simplicity, but not far.

Our greatest misgiving about the simulations was that communication between cue-givers and cue-takers had to be *inferred* from the observed regularities of voting patterns. Communication was so central to the theory of cue-taking that independent evidence of its existence was required. Extensive interviews with House members produced that independent evidence—all the members of the random sample to whom we talked said that cue-taking was a common mode of decision making in the House. We now have confidence in the simulations as rough *descriptions* of the decision process. Their other test is predictive accuracy.

VIII
PREDICTIVE ACCURACY OF THE MODEL

ALTHOUGH our simulations produced mind-boggling mounds of output that we are still in the process of trying to comprehend, the predictive accuracy of the model can be simply reported. In the course of making predictions on the 400,000 individual votes cast in the House from 1965 through 1969, LEARN was right 88.1 percent of the time. Earlier versions of the model were almost as accurate for other years.

While far from perfection, this level of predictive accuracy seems to

[32] Inspection of the massive simulation printouts leads us to believe that the response patterns rarely change within a session and not frequently between sessions, except in the obvious cases where role incumbents change (e.g., Nixon replaces Johnson as President).

DONALD R. MATTHEWS & JAMES A. STIMSON

TABLE 8–2. PREDICTIVE ACCURACY OF LEARN (AND EARLIER PROGRAMS)
BY YEAR

Year	Number of Roll Calls	Predictive Accuracy
1958[a]	93	85.7%
1960[a]	93	86.0%
1962[a]	124	89.3%
1964[a]	113	87.7%
1965	201	89.2%
1966	193	89.5%
1967	245	88.6%
1968	233	86.5%
1969	177	86.7%

Average Yearly Accuracy: 88.1%
Weighted Average[b] Accuracy: 88.1%

[a] Accuracy figures for these years are based on the early SIMULATE program. They are included for reference, but not included in the averages.

[b] The weighting factor is the number of roll-call votes per year. Weighted average accuracy including the early years is 87.9%.

provide substantial support to the theory of cue-taking. Predictions were made on *all* issues on which roll calls were held whether they were significant or trivial; partisan, bipartisan, or nonpartisan; closely contested battles or lopsided reaffirmations of the House's collective belief in motherhood and apple pie. The votes of *all* members of the House were predicted accurately almost nine times out of ten, knowing only the positions of nine cue-givers and the cue-taking propensities of members. In making each prediction, the computer knew nothing of the member's policy attitudes, his previous votes on comparable issues, his ideology or role orientations, or the characteristics of his constituency.

Little yearly variation is evident. The range of variation for the five years simulated by LEARN is 3.0 percentage points, from the 89.5 percent of 1966 to the 86.5 percent of 1968 (see Table 8–2). Given the large number of predictions underlying each yearly accuracy figure (approximately 80,000), even the most trivial percentage differences from year to year are *statistically* significant. We are more impressed, however, by the year to year similarity.

The small differences that do appear conform to common sense expectations. Three of the four most inaccurate years (1958, 1960, 1969, weighted average = 86.3 percent) were years with Republican presidents and Democratic congressional majorities. The shifting from alliance to warfare and back again between majority party cue-givers and

270

minority presidents must considerably confuse cue-taking patterns.[33] The fourth relatively inaccurate year, 1968, like other presidential election years in the period (weighted average for 1960, 1964, and 1968 is 86.7 percent) seems to reflect the disturbing influence of presidential politics on the affairs of the House.

The 89th Congress (1965–66), noted for its unusual burst of legislative activity, is the single Congress most accurately simulated (weighted average: 89.3 percent). We speculate that the improved accuracy of these years is due to the fact that party cues were stronger during the 89th than before or since.

These figures hide some variation in accuracy between roll calls and between members.[34] We are in the process of cataloguing and analyzing the causes of such variation. That analysis is both too extensive and too preliminary to report here. We think it important to note now, however, what does *not* appear to be related to accuracy of prediction for roll calls—their *content*. Our preliminary analysis of patterns of error and accuracy by roll call has failed to turn up any issue domain, either specific or general, that is consistently predicted more or less accurately than others. Furthermore, the predictive accuracy of our model is *not* significantly affected by the fact that we simulate all roll calls, including a number of unanimous or near unanimous ones. If these "hurrah votes" are dropped from the analysis, the model's overall predictive accuracy is reduced by only a percentage point or two. Indeed, the model does an especially good job of predicting the votes of individual members when the division within the House is nearly 50–50!

IX

CONCLUSIONS

LET us conclude by examining briefly the picture of the House of Representatives as an institution implicit in our preliminary, individual level findings.

The House of Representatives, when viewed within the context of our theory, becomes a complex system of legislative specialists who serve as input mechanisms for most of the new ideas and information entering into congressional decisions. These specialists process these ideas and facts, make choices between alternative policies, and then retail them out to the general membership in the form of cues. Cue-

[33] See David B. Truman, *The Congressional Party* (New York: John Wiley & Sons, 1959), chap. 8, for a discussion of party voting structure under conditions of divided party control of the presidency and Congress.

[34] See Matthews and Stimson, *Yeas and Nays*, for a more detailed analysis.

271

givers and cue-takers vary from issue to issue, with *all* members taking cues much of the time and some members providing cues when matters on which they have some expertise are before the House.

This structure of cue-giving and cue-taking is closely articulated with the formal committee system but is not identical with it. Most "experts" on a subject belong to the committee that regularly deals with it, but not all of them do. Then, too, other structures in the House compete with the standing committees as centers of effective cue-giving—the party leadership, state delegations, and informal groups like the Democratic Study Group or the Wednesday Club, for example. Often the cues emerging from these other structures can be traced back to the committee specialists through overlapping memberships—for example, state party delegations are extremely potent cue-giving agencies, yet committee-based experts frequently dominate their voting positions. The structure of cue-giving and cue-taking in the House, nonetheless, is a considerably more pervasive and complex phenomenon than the formal committee system.

We have asserted that cue-taking produces a decision for the member that is "similar" to what he would have arrived at had he undertaken individual analysis and evaluation. If the result were always the *same* by *either* process, the net effect would be zero. If the result differed only by infrequent random fluctuations, the net effect would approach zero. But there is reason to think that the resulting decision is not always the same, and that the deviations, although perhaps infrequent, are not random. Cue-givers in most policy areas are a biased sample of the House membership; in almost all policy areas they tend both to be more senior than the average member, and to be from congressional districts particularly affected by the policies in which the cue-givers specialize. Service on at least the better integrated House committees is likely to socialize the specialist into an overall committee point of view that may diverge from the views of the House as a whole. These biases in the development of experts result in House decisions that diverge systematically from the probable collective decisions which would be arrived at if each member had made up his mind independently. The directions of this bias are the familiar correlates of seniority on the one hand, and the committee outlooks on the other. The policies that result from cue-taking are thus more conservative and more sensitive to the wants and needs of the immediate parties-at-interest than would be the case with fully independent decision making. While this is scarcely news, the decision-making perspective does add explanatory depth to this familiar picture of House outputs.

272

Coping with complexity has been the crowning achievement of Congress. Specialization and decision making by cue-taking have been the means by which Congress has survived in the mid-twentieth century. National legislatures which have been unwilling or unable to adopt this expedient have withered into relative impotence, abdicating their policy-making role to bureaucracies and political executives. Paradoxically, biased policy outputs may be the price of institutional survival for modern day legislatures.

The same may be said for the achievement of legislative competence and more or less rational collective decisions. Few institutions provide more power to the exceptionally competent member than does the House of Representatives. A Wilbur Mills on taxation or an H. R. Gross on governmental economy probably knows more about his area of public policy than any other member; within that realm his power is awesome. The collective decisions of the House are disproportionately influenced by its most expert members. The costs of this happy state are a loss of representativeness and responsiveness in policy making—a high price indeed. But the benefits are high, too: technically competent decisions by an overworked group of laymen facing a vast quantity of incredibly complex problems.

This picture of House structure and outputs that emerges when we aggregate our preliminary findings on individual decision making is quite familiar to students of Congress. The theory of cue-taking does not lead to a view of the House drastically different from those already obtained through more standard analyses.

But our approach does provide a theoretical explanation of these empirical finds. This theory is quite comprehensive: it would seem to be applicable to a wide variety of legislatures (as well as other decision-making bodies) in any historical era. It can be operationalized and, at least for the House of Representatives, is highly predictive of actual outcomes. These are handy but rare attributes of most theories of political reality. The theory purports to explain the linkages between legislative inputs, structure, and outputs, the ultimate dependent variable of political research. Most theories about politics implicitly assume that political actors have all the information they want and need, as well as the time and capacity to process this information into decisions. Our theory, starting with the opposite assumption, shows how reasonable collective decisions are reached in a legislature despite the fact that most legislators know very little about most of the questions they help decide.

9

Interests and the Structure of Influence: Some Aspects of the Norwegian Storting in the 1960s

GUDMUND HERNES

I

INTRODUCTION

THIS chapter describes certain aspects of the functioning of the Norwegian Parliament, the Storting, in the 1960s. The most important data for this study were collected through interviews with all members of the Storting in the early part of 1966, just after a general election, and then again in the spring of 1969, just before the next election. However, I also have drawn on data that can be found in public documents and historical records.

The general analytical scheme within which the data will be interpreted is exchange theory, as it can be applied to the quantitative study of politics. It is hoped that the framework presented below can be of use in the analysis of other legislative bodies. To show how this can be done, I have quoted studies that give examples elsewhere of processes similar to those observed in the Storting.

II

CONCEPTUAL FRAMEWORK

AT the outset, before turning to the empirical investigation, it is necessary to outline the theoretical base for the analysis. The conceptual framework used here is the "theory of collective decisions," developed by the sociologist James S. Coleman, which I have attempted to adapt and to operationalize for legislative studies.

Coleman's theory of collective decisions falls within the general framework of exchange theory. The key units of his theory are *actors* and *events*. An *event* is an occurrence with two or more possible outcomes, which have different utilities for at least one actor, and which is under the control of one or more actors. An *actor* is any entity which has at least some control over at least one event, and for whom the possible outcomes of at least one event have differing utilities.[1] The

This chapter draws extensively on Gudmund Hernes, "Interest, Influence and Cooperation" (Ph.D. diss., Johns Hopkins University, 1971).

[1] The basic published sources are James S. Coleman, "Collective Decisions,"

274

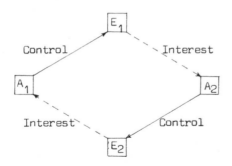

FIGURE 9–1.

A System of Two Actors (A_j) and Two Events (E_1)

simple dynamic assumption of the model is that an actor will try to exercise his control in such a way as to maximize the utility from those events that have different utility to him. If we define the interest of an actor in an event as the difference in utility the different outcomes make for him, we can say that actors and events are related in two ways: by the (partial) control the actors have over the events and by the interests the actors take in these events.

In a legislative setting, we can conceive of control as based on a representative's constitutional right to vote on all bills or on a committee assignment (or vote within a committee) or on a committee chairmanship. An event could be a bill and his interest in it could be the difference it makes to him whether the bill passes or not. The dynamic assumption of the model could be operationalized in the following way: a representative would cast his vote on bills of little interest to him in such a way so as to increase the probability that bills he favors pass and bills he opposes fail. This can be accomplished, for example, by entering into formal alliances (such as parties) or informal agreements (as in log-rolling).

Thus the key elements of the model are a set of actors and a set of events, and they are related by both the interests of the actors in the outcomes of the events and the share they have in the control over the outcomes. A simple system could be represented as in Figure 9–1.

Sociological Inquiry 34 (1964): 166–181; and Coleman, "Foundations for a Theory of Collective Decisions," *American Journal of Sociology* 71 (1966): 615–627. I have also drawn on some of Coleman's unpublished papers and on the manuscript of his book which has subsequently been published, *The Mathematics of Collective Action* (Chicago: Aldine Publishing Co., 1973).

Here we have two actors, A_1 and A_2 who each take an interest in an event, E_1 and E_2, different from the one that each controls. In a symmetric case like this, each would obviously be better off by exchanging control over what he has, which does not interest him, for what interests him but is controlled by the other.

Not all situations are as simple as this and not all are symmetric. As soon as the number of actors and events increases, a better means of representing the system has to be found. The simplest way to do this is by two matrices, with one row for each actor and one column for each event. In one of the matrices we could then enter the interest that each actor takes in each event, and in the other we could enter the amount of control each actor has over each event. An illustration of such a matrix is given in Figure 9-2.

One can now ask two types of questions: The first is: what are the sources of the interests of a representative in legislative outcomes? I will give an empirical discussion of this question below, but clearly we have to take into account such factors as constituency characteristics, on the one hand, and legislative career, on the other. The other question, to which I also shall return, is: what are the sources of control— and differences in control—over various issues? Votes and committee memberships and chairmanships already have been mentioned, but clearly voting rules (size of quorum, of majority needed to pass different types of bills, etc.) will also play an important role.

Thus we see the possibility of a systematic analysis in the sense of tying personal preferences to constitutional and organizational arrangements and investigating the consequences of their interaction. But such an analysis requires more precise concepts. Let us therefore pursue Coleman's theoretical analysis a step further.

I have already talked of exchange. But not all exchanges are symmetric. An individual who has a high degree of control over what others take a great interest in can extract more from them than they from him—an extreme illustration is blackmail. But politics abounds with examples. The representative controlling the pivotal vote in a ballot can obtain more IOU's. Loyalty is often the price of patronage. In diplomacy an ultimatum is intended to force an unfavorable exchange on a reluctant party. Thus, your control over that which is of interest to others gives you power. This control can manifest itself in a needed vote, a desired job, or an unwanted military attack. Somewhat paradoxically, we could say that events are valuable when actors take a great interest in their outcome, especially if these actors are powerful; and actors are powerful when the events they control have a high value.

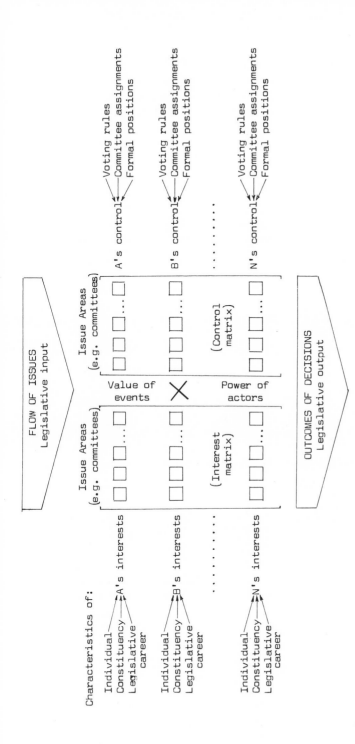

FIGURE 9–2.

Simplified Graphical Representation of the Paradigm. (The interests of the representative are a function of individual and constituency characteristics as well as his status and career in the legislature; his control over the various issue areas is a function of voting rules, committee assignments and formal positions. The matrices of interest and control determine the value of events and power of actors, which, in turn, modify the flow of issues and affect the set of outcomes of legislative decisions.)

Obviously, it is valuable to control an event if other actors take a great deal of interest in its outcome. But it is not irrelevant which of the other actors take an interest in it. To obtain a measure of the value of control of an event, we therefore have to weight the interest of each actor in its outcome by his power. Thus

$$\begin{pmatrix}\text{The value of control} \\ \text{of event } i\end{pmatrix} = \sum_j \begin{pmatrix}\text{The power of} \\ \text{actor } j\end{pmatrix} \begin{pmatrix}\text{The interest of} \\ \text{actor } j \text{ in event } i\end{pmatrix}$$

Similarly, one can argue that the more control an actor has over the various events, the more powerful he would be. However, it is not irrelevant which events he controls. It stands to reason that he should be more powerful if the events he controls are valuable. Thus

$$\begin{pmatrix}\text{The power of} \\ \text{actor } j\end{pmatrix} = \sum_i \begin{pmatrix}\text{Value of} \\ \text{event } i\end{pmatrix} \begin{pmatrix}\text{The control of actor} \\ j \text{ over event } i\end{pmatrix}$$

These definitions may at first look tautological, but it is no stranger than having two equations in two unknowns (value and power defined in terms of control and interest).

If we want to be more precise and express the same ideas in mathematical language, we have:

1. The *constitutional control* of an actor j over an event i is $c_{ij} \geq 0$, where the sum of the total control of all actors over the event equals one: $\sum_j c_{ij} = 1.0$.

2. The *interest* of actor j in event i, x_{ij}, equals the absolute value of his utility differences for that event, $-1 \leq y_{ij} \leq 1$. We have $x_{ij} \geq 0$, and the sum of all the interests of an actor in all events equals one: $\sum_i x_{ij} = 1.0$.

With these two primary concepts as building blocks, we can derive the following concept:

3. *Value of control* of an event in a vote market, or simply *value* of an event, v_i: In the basic theory, the equilibrium value of the sum of interests in the event, weighted by the power of the actor with that interest: $v_i = \sum_j r_j x_{ji}$, where r_j is the power of actor j. It is immediately seen that the more powerful the actors who are interested in i, the more valuable is control over the event: $\sum_i v_i = 1.0$.

4. The *power* (or resources) of an actor in the system, r_j: In the basic theory, power is the sum of control over events, weighted by their equilibrium value: $r_j = \sum_i v_i c_{ij}$. It is immediately seen that the more valuable the events an actor controls, the more powerful he is: $\sum_j r_j = 1.0$.

One important property of these definitions is that all actors and events are taken into account in the evaluation of the power of each actor and the value of control of each event.

It is fairly simple to solve for the vector of values of events or the vector of power of actors. For example, for the vector of values of events, we have, in matrix notation,

$$V = XC'V.$$

But there is no point in going any further into the mathematics of the model here. The definitions of value and power expressed mathematically above can be expressed verbally as follows:

> The value of control over action i is equal to the sum of interests in i of each actor times the total power of that actor. In turn the total power of actor j is equal to the [control] of j over each action k times the value of action k, summed over all actions k.[2]

Within this general framework, other concepts, potentially useful for political analysis, can be given a precise meaning and made amenable to quantitative analysis. For example, one can define "the final directed control of an actor over an event" as being proportional to his total power times his interest in the event and inversely proportional to the value of the event. The "directed power of the collectivity over an event" can be taken as the sum of the positive or negative interests the actors have in bringing about a specific outcome, weighted by their power. And "the value of the collectivity to an actor" is taken to be a function of how well his interests can be realized given the interests and power of the other actors. Concepts such as these make it possible to apply the model to coalition formation. Instead of taking individuals as actors, one could use parties, and calculate the values of these concepts for the various subsets of parties in the legislature. Obviously a political actor should join or seek to form a coalition which has a high degree of directed power over the various events, since such a coalition would have a high value to him in enabling him to gain control over events of great interest to him. However, in this chapter I will primarily use the concepts of power and value.

Let us therefore end this section by a graphical representation which can illustrate some of the analytical possibilities of the model presented above. In the middle of Figure 9–2 I have drawn an interest and a control matrix for a legislature.[3] This immediately raises the question

[2] Coleman, "Foundations for a Theory of Collective Decisions," p. 627.

[3] The figure is in part inspired by Figure 3 in Erik van Hove, "Collective Decision-Making in a Government Health Agency: The Regional Medical Program" (Ph.D. diss., Johns Hopkins University, 1971).

of what factors affect the interests of the representatives. Three sources of legislative interests have been illustrated on the left: personal characteristics, constituency attributes, and status in the legislature. Similarly, I have on the right illustrated sources of the distribution of control. In a legislature these have to do with both the formal organization and the constitutional rules, so I have listed such variables as committee assignments; formal positions like chairmanships; and voting rules. Input into the legislature includes the flow of issues, bills, resolutions, etc. Sets of outcomes of decisions made in these matters are affected by the structure of power generated by the distribution of interest and the distribution of control. The final product of this process is the legislative output: what finally passes or fails. As mentioned, the model also allows us to take parties or other collectivities as actors, and from the configuration of interests of the potential partners it is possible to predict what coalitions should be formed.

It is an advantage of this model that it not only includes both the institutional arrangements of legislatures and the distribution of preferences of legislators but also deals with the relations between them. It encompasses legislators and their social backgrounds and personal interests, as well as the rules of the legislature and its formal organization. In a certain sense it brings together the classic institutional approach to the study of politics and the more recent behavioral approach. To some degree, therefore, it can give a unified focus for empirical studies.

III
Sources of Legislative Interest

With Figure 9–2 as our point of departure, we can first ask how the interests of the representatives manifest themselves, how we should go about measuring them, and what factors affect them.

One way to proceed, in order to map legislative interests, would be to list all issues that have been introduced for consideration during a legislative session and ask the representatives how important passing or defeating each motion was to them. However, such a procedure would quickly defeat its purpose because of the sheer volume of issues.[4] For this very reason it also seems that the legislators themselves reduce cognitive and political complexity by dividing the issues into a much smaller number of issue-areas—though some bills or decisions may stand out and transcend these areas. (An example of the latter kind

---

[4] Another procedure would be to take presence during votes and participation in debates as a measure of interest, but such measures are not likely to be very reliable.

was the question whether Norway should join the European Common Market in 1972).

In the empirical analysis I therefore attacked the problem in the following way. In the Norwegian Storting, as in many other legislatures, a committee system has been set up to evaluate and possibly suggest modifications in bills before they are voted on in the plenary session. There are written rules about what classes of issues are to be treated in what committees, and the committees are named according to the issue-areas for which they are responsible: Agriculture, Defense, Finance, etc. The borders between these issue-areas remain fairly stable over time.

But this has an important corollary. Since the committees are the organizational delimitations of the various issue-areas, the interest that the representatives take in different classes of issues manifests itself in structural terms by their preferences for committee membership. Thus the organizational structure of the legislature itself contributes to reducing the cognitive and political complexity facing the representatives. In the questionnaire I therefore tried to establish what the committee preferences of the representatives were. They were not asked for a complete rank ordering, but only which three committees they most wanted to be a member of, and which three they least wanted to be a member of. Since there are 13 standing committees in the Norwegian Parliament, this leaves a residual of 7 not ranked either highly positive or highly negative. Note also that posing the question this way compelled the legislators to weigh the various issue-areas against each other. This is important for theoretical reasons: the reader will remember that in the previous section we required that, in the calculation of power, which we return to below, the interests of the actors be calibrated in such a way that they would add to one, which implies that they have to be weighed against each other. In fact, a representative can be a member of only one committee.

The representatives also were asked to rank the committees along other dimensions. For example, they were asked to evaluate which (three) were most and which (three) least prestigious among their peers, which required most and least special competence, which were most and least important for the nation as a whole, which were most and least important for carrying through the programs of their parties, on which ones they could accomplish most and least for their constituents, etc. It is an important fact about the Storting that, even though formally the committees are equal, they are in fact ranked on different dimensions. The aggregate results of five such rankings which will be

281

used below are given in Table 9–1. One, therefore, has to investigate what the interrelations and effects of these rank dimensions are.

By combining the responses to questions such as these one can try to evaluate the sources of the amount of interest that the representatives take in different issue-areas. Here are two examples of such investigations.

The first addresses itself to the following problem: whereas a bureaucratic motivational system is *monistic,* in the sense that its reward structure is set up in such a fashion that no external sanctions are presumed to affect the behavior of its members, the motivational system of a legislature is *dualistic.* Its members are elected to give expression to local interests, but at the same time are custodians of the common, national good. For the Storting it is possible to show not only that the representatives can be positively or negatively sanctioned in their constituencies but also that there has developed a latent reward structure within the Storting which confers prestige on those positions which enable representatives to influence decisions on nationally important issues.

It is necessary, therefore, to ascertain the relative impact of these two forces on the preferences or interests of the representatives. A useful point of departure for this analysis is the Davis-Moore theory of social stratification.[5] This theory states that the differential prestige associated with different positions directly affects the motivations of people to take these positions, while prestige in turn is determined by the importance of the tasks performed in these positions and the special competence needed to carry out these tasks.

In this case, we must consider not only the *national* importance of committees but also their *local* importance. In Figure 9–3 the model is represented by a path diagram.[6] As can be seen from the path coefficients, it is the national importance of the committees that most contributes to their prestige, while the direct effect of local importance on prestige is considerably smaller. The effect of needs for special competence on prestige is smaller still, which probably reflects the faith the legislators have in "on the job training" and their belief that it is

[5] Kingsley Davis and Wilbert Moore, "Some Principles of Stratification," *American Sociological Review* 10 (1945): 242–249.

[6] The national importance of the committees was measured by the question "Which three committees treat the three most important issues for the country as a whole, and which three treat the least important?" In a similar fashion the representatives were asked which three had the most and least prestige, which three required the most and least special competence, and which three they themselves most and least wanted to be members of. Since each of the 150 representatives evaluated 13 committees, the number of units analyzed was $(13\times150)=1950$.

TABLE 9–1. STANDING COMMITTEES IN THE STORTING RANKED ON 5 DIMENSIONS, 1966

	National Importance [a]			Local Importance [b]			Specialized Knowledge [c]			Prestige [d]			Preference [e]		
	Most	Neu-tral	Least	Most	Neu-tral	Least	Most	Neu-tral	Least	Most	Neu-tral	Least	Most	Neu-tral	Least
Administration (Adm)	–	14.0	86.0	2.0	27.2	70.9	0.7	34.7	64.7	–	13.3	86.7	1.3	28.0	70.7
Finance (Fin)	85.3	14.7	–	2.0	86.7	11.3	72.7	26.0	1.3	74.7	25.4	–	24.7	64.7	10.7
Justice (Jus)	1.3	48.7	50.0	–	45.0	55.0	38.0	59.3	2.7	0.7	58.0	41.3	8.0	50.0	42.0
Education (Edu)	49.3	50.7	–	34.0	66.0	–	32.0	60.0	8.0	43.3	56.7	–	36.7	62.0	1.3
Municipal Affairs (Mun)	22.7	74.7	2.7	58.6	40.7	0.7	6.0	75.3	18.7	24.7	75.4	–	45.3	52.7	2.0
Agriculture (Agr)	0.7	92.0	7.3	21.2	78.0	0.7	18.7	74.0	7.3	2.0	90.7	7.3	17.3	68.0	14.7
Defense (Def)	16.7	63.3	20.0	0.7	64.0	35.3	14.7	63.3	22.0	0.7	46.7	52.7	10.0	47.3	42.7
Protocol (Pro)	–	15.3	84.7	2.6	16.6	80.7	1.3	26.0	72.7	–	7.3	92.7	2.7	23.3	74.0
Communications (Com)	24.0	76.0	–	94.0	6.0	–	2.7	66.7	30.7	45.3	54.7	–	56.0	42.0	2.0
Seafare & Fish. (Fish)	–	92.0	8.0	31.3	68.7	–	20.0	69.3	10.7	0.7	90.7	8.7	13.3	69.3	17.3
Industry (Ind)	14.7	84.0	1.3	46.0	53.3	0.7	25.3	72.7	2.0	22.7	77.3	–	36.0	63.3	0.7
Social Affairs (Soc)	17.3	82.0	0.7	3.3	94.7	2.0	8.7	70.0	21.3	8.0	92.0	–	19.3	72.3	8.0
Foreign Affairs (For)	68.0	30.0	2.0	0.7	65.3	34.0	47.3	45.3	7.3	70.7	29.3	–	28.7	67.3	4.0

[a] National Importance (Which 3 committees treat the most important issues for the country as a whole, and which 3 the least?)

[b] Local Importance (On which 3 committees can one do most for local districts, and on which 3 the least?)

[c] Need for Specialized Knowledge (On which 3 committees is the need for specialized knowledge the greatest, and on which 3 the least?)

[d] Prestige (Which 3 committees have the greatest prestige among the representatives and which 3 the least?)

[e] Committee Preference (Which 3 committees would you most like to be on, and on which 3 least?)

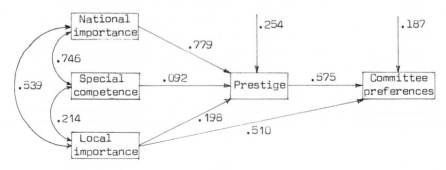

FIGURE 9–3.

Path Diagram for the Motivational System in the Storting as It Relates the National and Local Importance of Committees, Their Need for Special Competence, and Their Prestige to the Committee Preferences of the Representatives
(Aggregate Data)

their function to represent common sense rather than professional expertise. There is no significant direct effect of the need for special competence on the representative's choice of committees; its only effect is indirect through prestige. Prestige has the greatest effect on committee preferences, but it is not much larger than the direct effect of local importance, while national importance also has a direct effect on committee preference. About 49 percent of the variance in committee prestige and about 34 percent of the variance in committee preferences of the representatives is explained by the variables included in the model.[7]

[7] Scanning the articles in the *American Sociological Review* and the *American Journal of Sociology* that have employed path analysis indicates that few that have taken individuals as units of analysis obtain an R² of 0.50 or more, and several of the articles have R²'s below 0.2. Explaining 40 percent of the variance with individuals as units of analysis is, as a rule of thumb, a good result. In the present case, one also has to consider that a fairly crude measure 'of the values on the various variables is used. (It should be added that the amount of variance explained is not always the best test of a model). If aggregate data, instead of individual-level data, are used to describe the system, the amount of variance explained for prestige is about 94 percent and about 96 percent of the variance in committee preferences. However, one runs into the problem of multi-collinearity between national importance and the need for special competence. Nevertheless, this analysis at the aggregate level indicates that the model I have used to describe the sources of committee preferences not only is data-admissible, but also is reasonable. Other implications of the model, pertaining to changes in prestige and prefer-

Thus the reward system in the Storting, as in many other parliaments, is based on structural inequality. It is interesting to ask what motivational consequences this inequality (which stands in contradiction to the formal equal status of the committees) generates among the representatives. There are at least four possible reaction patterns. Some of those who feel insufficiently rewarded may want to leave "parliamentary life." Others may seek to change the rules for allocation of personnel to the various positions, as has happened, for example, in the struggles over the seniority system in the U.S. Congress. A third strategy would be to reallocate tasks between committees, thus removing the basis for the structural inequality. However, the most common reaction is the fourth: a desire to move out of committees of low rewards and into those of high rewards. In other words, committee changes can be conceived of as *promotions,* and series of transfers as *careers.* Most representatives see their situations as individual problems that can be changed by personal effort rather than as a problem of structural inequality to be altered by collective effort. We may therefore ask what functions this inequality has for the larger system.

Committee transfers are generally conditional on certain orientations. This implies that the unequal reward structure can be used to change the persuasions, preferences, and behavior of the representatives. To make its *incumbents* into *agents* is of course the explicit purpose of a bureaucratic motivational system. But the latent reward structure that has developed in the Storting functions in much the same way. And though all four reaction patterns listed in the previous paragraph can be found among the legislators, the last—desire for mobility—is the most common. This is mostly due to the relatively high subjective belief in the probability of moving ahead. Therefore the relative equality of opportunity in moving between structurally unequal positions has the latent consequence of undermining change toward greater equality by reallocating tasks between the committees or committee positions, and also has the consequence of creating party agents.

I shall presently return to the implications of this point for the analysis of legislative careers. But first I shall describe the interests of the representatives in a different manner.

Ever since Burke, it has been common to distinguish between two philosophies of representation: legislators acting on the instruction of

---

ences, are supported by available evidence. Cf. Gudmund Hernes, "Interest, Influence and Cooperation" (Ph.D. diss., Johns Hopkins University, 1971), chap. 3.

their constituents and legislators acting on an independent judgment of the national interest. One can conceive of "delegates" and "trustees" as qualitatively different roles.[8] But one can also consider the local-cosmopolitan dimension as a continuum and then ask what forces determine a representative's position on this continuum and what forces tend to change his position over time.

For this analysis I will assume that the representatives are self-interested actors who attempt to maximize their rewards from the two groupings that control the incentives in the dualistic reward system: their constituents and their party. In the Storting, as in most European legislatures, the parties are powerful organizations which control large parts of what is of interest to the legislators. What we want, therefore, is an estimate of relative effects of party and constituency rewards on the orientations of the representatives. I am, of course, aware that this formulation of the problem is not the only possible one and that it does not provide an exhaustive account of the relationships between constituents, party, and legislators.

To carry out the analysis, we need four things. First, we need as our dependent variable an index of localism-cosmopolitanism, by which we can characterize each representative.[9] Second, we need some way of characterizing the preferences of the representative—his "indifference map," to borrow a term from microeconomics. Here I have assumed that a measure of a man's general capacities and broad personal orientations is his socio-economic status. From other studies we know that men tend to pursue those activities which they have been rewarded for in their socialization period, that education tends to fixate preference structures, and that the boundaries of a man's political

[8] For a detailed analysis of such roles, see John C. Wahlke, et al., *The Legislative System: Explorations in Legislative Behavior* (New York: John Wiley & Sons, 1962).

[9] The index is based on three questions. The first is the question asked of the representatives in 1966 about the three committees in which they could do most or least for the districts. This gives us a measure of the local importance of a committee. The second is the question about which three committees the representative himself most and least wants to be a member of. The third is whether he considers himself primarily a spokesman for his district or for his party. The index is constructed by the following steps for each representative: (1) for each overlap "most important for districts" and "most wants to be on," add one to the index; (2) for each overlap "least important for districts" and "most wants to be on," subtract one from the index; (3) for each overlap "most important for districts" and "least wants to be on," subtract one from the index; (4) if all three choices of committees he wants to be on are among the six highest ranking district committees (Communications, Municipal Affairs, Industry, Education, Fisheries, and Agriculture, in that order), add one to the index; (5) if a representative considers himself foremost a spokesman for his district, add one to the index; (6) normalize it by adding three to the index value for each representative. The most locally oriented then get the value 8 on the index, and the most cosmopolitan the value 0.

horizon are affected by his location in the occupational structure. A compact summary of such biographical characteristics is a man's rank on an SES (socio-economic status) scale, so this is what was used. Third, we need some measure of the rewards a representative will get if he spends his time in the service of his constituents. Here I have assumed that the worse off his constituents are, the greater is the marginal effect of efforts on his behalf; and furthermore, the greater the effect, the greater the rewards that accrue to him. Since I have assumed that the representative will be rewarded more for activities on behalf of his constituents the more deprived they are in a national comparison, I will use an index of deprivation as an indirect measure of these rewards. I have used two indices: average per capita income in his constituency and the degree of urbanization in his home county. Finally, we need a measure of the rewards that accrue to a representative for efforts on behalf of his party. Here the most important general reward is influence, which I have measured by the influence attributed to a representative by the members of his party.

Having made the assumptions of the model explicit, we can turn to the empirical analysis. The results are summarized in Figure 9–4, which shows the path diagram from a multiple regression analysis. In short, this diagram tells us that high socio-economic status tends to reduce localism (or increase cosmopolitanism); that party influence has the same effect, but more strongly; that the better off the constitu-

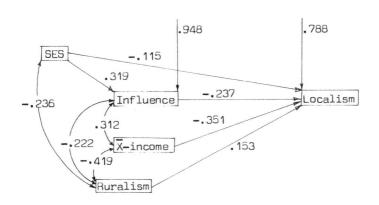

FIGURE 9–4.

Path Diagram for Determinants of Localism

287

ents of a representative are, the less locally oriented he is; and that the more rural his constituency is, the more locally oriented he is. Note that constituency characteristics seem to have the greatest impact. Note also that I have allowed for SES to have an indirect effect on cosmopolitanism through its effect on influence in the Storting. (More detailed analysis shows that this effect is greater in the larger parties). Thirty-eight percent of the variance in localism, as measured by this index, can be accounted for by the factors included in the model.[10]

Let us then turn to some implications of these results. I have argued that, in order to predict sets of outcomes of legislative decisions, we have to know what the broad orientations and interests of the representatives are, as well as the sources of change and stability of these interests. From the above path diagrams it can be argued that the most important sources of stability are characteristics of constituencies, while the most important sources of change are located in the reward structure within the legislature, notably in committee prestige and party influence.

Second, influence is a generalized reward that has the effect of modifying the amount of localism. Influential members of the Storting are forced to adopt national decision criteria by the conflicting demands for aids and assistance from locally oriented representatives.

Third, the above analysis, by indicating that representatives from deprived districts are more rewarded by their constituents, also suggests that they are more likely to exchange control over issues of national importance (such as foreign policy) for more control over issues of direct interest to their constituents. The political impact of an opinion depends on its location in the legislature, so to speak. For example, preferences with respect to agricultural policies have the greatest impact if they can affect the decisions on the Agriculture Committee, since the recommendations of the committee are unlikely to be changed in the plenary session. Therefore, constituency characteristics will have an impact on the legislative career of a representative in terms of his probability of gaining general influence. They should also have an impact on mobility between committees. In other words, it is necessary to tie the analysis of the distribution of policy interests to the organizational structure of the legislature. To this we now turn.

IV

COMMITTEES, CONTROL, AND CAREERS

So far I have stressed how the interests of the representatives manifest themselves in structural terms by being projected onto the committee

[10] As for the magnitude of R^2, cf. note 7.

system within the Storting. However, the committees are not just a delimitation of issue-areas on which the representatives can focus their interests. The committees are also, in the Storting, the first and most important stage in the decision-making process. It is here that bills are modified before being introduced for plenary consideration, here bargains are struck and compromises reached between the committee members—not only as individuals but also in their capacity as agents of parties. Only on rare occasions are bills changed after they have been reported from the committees. Therefore, the committee system is a way of formally distributing unequal control over the different issue-areas.

Assuming that the representatives are rational actors, the first corollary is that they will try to gain direct control over what is of greatest interest to them. If two such actors exchange what interests them little for what interests them more, the benefits of both are increased. The obvious implications for the distribution of control by committee memberships and chairmanships is that the representatives will attempt to obtain those formal positions that give them the maximum control over their greatest interests.

I am, of course, not arguing that all actions within a legislature should be interpreted as exchange. A legislature, for example, may have important symbolic or legitimizing functions. However, if one asks, why do the representatives engage in symbolic action or public rituals, one may be induced to adopt an exchange theoretical framework, though constituents need not be parties to such transactions (which they are not, for example, in Eastern European legislatures). Here I deliberately have chosen not to discuss other functions of or perspectives on legislatures, but rather to utilize the exchange theoretical framework as much as possible.

One may argue that the legislators in the Storting engage in a double exchange. "The transaction between the representative and his constituents is directly one of exchange: he works to obtain for them policies that will be most satisfactory to them, with the aim to induce them to reelect him. He has control (with his fellow legislators) of the creation of policies that are important to his constituents, and he in effect gives up to his constituents that control (by using it to further their interests), in return for which he anticipates their continuing to give him control over his seat in the legislature, which they can revoke at election time." [11]

Not everything the representatives do to please their constituents is a matter of policy output. However, this primary exchange between

[11] James S. Coleman, "Political Money," *American Political Science Review* 64 (1970): 1076.

constituents and delegates leads to exchanges between the delegates themselves within the legislature. When legislatures are organizationally differentiated into standing committees, some of the most important transactions are those leading to the committee assignments at the outset of the legislative session.

The empirical manifestations of these exchanges are easily established. To take but two examples from the Storting: From 1965 to 1969 one of the eleven members of the Seafare and Fisheries Committee was a shipowner, and the rest came from the leading seafaring and fishing districts in the country. Several had themselves been fishermen. Of the eleven-member Agriculture Committee, seven were themselves farmers, two were teachers at agricultural schools, one of the two women on the committee was married to a farmer and the other was the daughter of a farmer, representing one of the main agricultural districts. Charles O. Jones found the same pattern in the U.S. House Committee on Agriculture: all but one of its thirty-four members came from districts with significant interests in farm policy. Furthermore, members were assigned to commodity subcommittees on the basis of their constituency interests such as, for example, the dominant crop in the member's district.[12] Stanley Lieberson has established the same pattern in the U.S. Senate, where he finds a strong correlation between special interests of states and membership on Senate committees. He uses an index of interest of a state in the issue-areas delimited by the committees and finds, for example, that the Armed Services Committee is loaded with senators whose states rank above average in the amounts spent in them for military purposes. He also explicitly interprets these findings in terms of the collective decisions model: "a given group will not attempt to exert its influence on all issues to the same degree, but rather will concentrate on those that generate the greatest net gain."[13] Thus a constituency may develop a *vested interest* in having delegates on a specific committee. A representative from that constituency will try to obtain support for membership on it in exchange for supporting representatives from constituencies with different interests in their pursuit of a seat on committees controlling those interests. By such exchanges the benefits obtained by the parties to the transaction are increased. This process, whereby those who take the greatest interest in an issue-area gain control over it, is summarized in the colloquialism used in the Storting: "The goat gets to guard the

---

[12] Charles O. Jones, "Representation in Congress: The Case of the House Agriculture Committee," *American Political Science Review* 55 (1961): 358–367.

[13] Stanley Lieberson, "An Empirical Study of Military Industrial Linkages," *American Journal of Sociology* 76 (1971): 578.

grain." Since the data are readily available, this process also can be investigated in historical studies.

Let us then look at some of the political implications of this system of exchange of control. The first and most obvious is that those political groups who have their interest concentrated in a distinct issue-area will tend to have a greater impact on the decisions taken in that area than a group whose interests are more dispersed and only partly focused on that area. Clearly, consumers take an interest in the policies pursued, for example, by the Agriculture Committee or Fisheries Committee. But because their interests are dispersed, they have no effective agents on these committees.

Second, the amount of power wielded by a group in a legislature may not depend on its size. In a legislature with a strong committee system, the key political question is not *how many* representatives the group has as its agents, but rather *where* they are located. One may argue that, if the agents of a group *all* are located on the committee controlling its interests, the group is better off than if there also are interested representatives outside the committee, since there will be less know-how and expertise outside the committtee that can serve as a check on the recommendations of the committee. The general lesson is that, in a system of sequential decision making through subunits, with opportunity for mobility between them, the control of small groups over their interests can become much larger than in bodies which are not organizationally differentiated. Thus the division of labor, originally set up for coping with the extremely diversified and large flow of issues, has come to have a critical impact on political decisions and policy output.

Third, the biases that in this way are introduced into the legislative process obviously affect the rationality, from a national point of view, of the decisions taken. If organized groups with concentrated interests are able to enter into exchanges whereby they compensate each other by letting each gain control over what interests them most, more dispersed and less organized groups may have decisions made to their disadvantage, even if they constitute larger segments of the population. The way legislatures are organized therefore has direct implications for democratic theory.

Finally, this system may increase the differences of interest between constituencies over time. From American politics, the classical example could be the allocation of military installations. Once such an establishment has been located in a constituency for "accidental" reasons, the constituency is likely to develop a vested interest in it. Quite aside

291

from the vested interest in military spending this generates, it also generates the desire to gain control over the legislative committee making decisions affecting the installation. But this in turn is likely to lead to further allocations of military funds to the same constituency, so that a kind of positive feedback in the decision-making process is introduced. Thereby differences of interest between constituencies may increase over time, quite independent of differences in the location of natural resources. Thus one may get a concentration of interests over time within constituencies and a diversification of interests among them. One is reminded of the comment made to Mendel Rivers of the Armed Services Committee: "If you put more installations in your district, it will sink." Of course, such effects are not limited to the military sphere—prominent examples can be found in other issue-areas.

Since there is mobility between the committees, one can use characteristics of the flows of personnel to describe the committee system. By investigations of the official records it is simple to demonstrate that certain committees are used for "legislative apprenticeships," that the flows tend to lead from the less prestigious to the more prestigious committees, and that the average tenure in the legislature before obtaining membership on the various committees differs systematically between them. One can also investigate to what extent some committees are "absorbing states" in the sense that representatives, once they have obtained membership on certain committees, tend not to give it up.[14]

However, information on flows and tenures to characterize the committee system can be combined with the analysis of attributes of the representatives and can thus be used to characterize individuals by their typical career paths. For example, the Agriculture Committee is much more likely to become an "absorbing state" for a farmer than for the delegate of an urban district. I already have described the exchange processes that generate such results and connect career paths to constituency characteristics. Therefore I shall now carry

[14] For such analyses, see for example Donald R. Matthews, *U.S. Senators and Their World* (Chapel Hill: University of North Carolina Press, 1960), chap. 7; and Warren E. Miller and Donald E. Stokes, "The Structure of Representation," (forthcoming). For a more recent study of committee careers in Congress, see for example Charles S. Bullock, III, "House Careerists: Changing Patterns of Longevity and Attrition," *American Political Science Review* 66 (1972): 1295–1300; for a study of committee allocations, see David W. Rohde and Kenneth Shepsle, "Democratic Committee Assignments in the House of Representatives: Strategic Aspects of a Social Choice Process," *American Political Science Review* 67 (1973): 889–905.

out another type of analysis in which we first characterize the committees on two dimensions. By this means, it will be possible to describe what, from the structural point of view, are career paths and, from the individual point of view, what is a sequential maximization of control over key interests.

As mentioned before, formally the committees in the Storting are of equal status, but in fact they are ranked, and on more than one dimension. In connection with the discussion of local and national orientation, it will be useful to classify the committees according to the opportunities they give for promoting local and national interests.

I asked the representatives which three committees were most and least important in terms of decisions affecting the nation as a whole, and the same question was asked with respect to decisions affecting districts or constituencies. On the basis of the aggregate responses to these questions, one can rank the committees on two dimensions, their national and their local importance. The simplest way to represent the committees on these dimensions—which corresponds to the dualistic reward system (or "axes of representation" in classical political theory)—is by a coordinate system. On the horizontal axis, one can locate a committee in terms of its national importance—measured by the difference in percentage of the representatives who considered it among the nationally three most important and the percentage who considered it among the three least important.[15] In a similar fashion one can on the vertical axis measure the local importance of the committees. (Compare the percentages given as responses to these two questions in Table 9-1.) In Figure 9-5 the positions of the committees on such a coordinate system have been mapped.

As can be seen from the figure, six of the committees are distributed from left to right on the main diagonal: Protocol (mainly responsible for going through Government protocols and treating complaints about administrative decisions), Administration (mainly responsible for appropriations and laws regarding the administrative apparatus of the nation), Justice, Defense, Social Affairs and Education. Only the last two have positive ranks. Along the positive Y-axis we find the Agriculture, Fisheries, Municipal Affairs and Communications Committees, indicating that they rank high on local, but not so high on national importance. Finally, we find the Foreign Affairs and Finance Committee to the right and below the X-axis, indicating their high

[15] If, for example, 10 percent stated that the Defense Committee was among the three nationally most important, and 15 percent stated it was among the three nationally least important, it would get a score of —5 on this dimension.

293

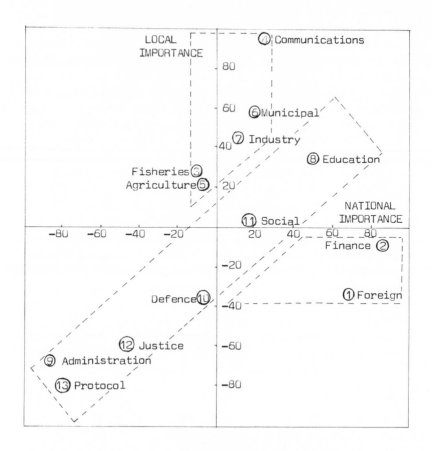

FIGURE 9–5.

Local and National Importance of Committees in the Storting. (The numbers in the circles represent differences in preferences between locals and cosmopolitans, from greatest [1] to smallest [13].)

rank on national but relatively low rank on local importance. The overall structure is therefore one of a "psi" or a trident.

Once the structural position of the committees on these two dimensions has been established, the next question is obvious: how does the system of potential impact on nationally and locally important decisions affect the flows of personnel, i.e., the motivations and careers of the representatives?

I cannot go into a detailed analysis of these processes here, but the

294

major results can be indicated.[16] The main finding is that there is a tendency for freshmen representatives to start in the stem of the psi. Over time the "locals" branch off into the locally important committees, while the "cosmopolitans" branch off into the nationally important ones. A group we can identify as "intermediates" in personal orientation has a greater tendency to prefer committees ranking high on both dimensions, though the evidence on this point is somewhat equivocal. Further analysis indicates that the "intermediates" serve another function: while both locals and cosmopolitans are generalists in the tasks they take on and the problems they address themselves to, the intermediates to a greater extent seem to be committee specialists.[17]

Two further points have to be made in this context. We have already seen that the orientation of the representatives may change after they have entered the Storting because of its internal reward structure and because of party influence. However, there may be systematic differences between the parties in the extent to which their goals correspond to the local interests (or constituency interests) of their representatives. To the extent that the goals diverge, the representatives may have alternative career paths: those who do not become nationally prominent can focus their energies on promoting constituency interests. And indeed there are systematic differences between the parties in the extent to which local and party interests of their representatives converge, and thus in the opportunity they give for alternative careers.

Second, the career paths of representatives may affect their orientations. By means of a mathematical model and by using data over time, it is possible to investigate the relation between the effects of interests and the effects of perceived influence. The main result of this analysis is that there is a positive feedback operating: the representatives tend not only to gain control over what is of interest to them but also to become interested in issue-areas in which they feel they can exercise influence. Specifically, a sense of control leads to and preserves interest in an issue-area, and, conversely, lack of experienced influence leads to abandonment of interest and avoidance of an issue-area. On the other hand, interest leads to a sense of control and also tends to preserve it; or, conversely, lack of interest leads to a sense of loss of influence and tends to preserve a sense of powerlessness in that issue-area.

[16] For this analysis, see Hernes, "Interest, Influence and Cooperation," chap. 5, "Career Differentiation."

[17] For an analysis of flows of personnel in terms of SES, see Ottar Hellevik, *Stortinget—en sosial elite?* (Oslo: Pax, 1969), chap. 10.

GUDMUND HERNES

This has an important corollary in the functioning of the Storting: whether or not a representative becomes fixated in his interests at an early point in his legislative career may depend on what committee he is assigned to. He may start out as a local or a cosmopolitan, and may remain so unless he is placed on a committee where he experiences a loss of influence in those issue-areas in which he originally took an interest. It also implies that changes in focus of interest can be engineered by reassigning a representative to another committee, and a history of "migration" between committees is likely to leave residuals of competence generating a cosmopolitan orientation.[18]

Some other consequences for the functioning of this Parliament also should be pointed out. First, the division of labor into committees itself creates resources that can be distributed among the representatives. It also generates power for the agents that control committee assignments, generally the parties and the party leaders. What has been said about the distribution of committee positions in the U.S. House of Representatives, is valid for the Norwegian Storting:

> The party leaders use their power over committee assignments variously, to reward members who have been loyal and cooperative, and to reinforce the strength of their own positions by rewarding members whose loyalty may be suspected but whose strength may no longer be safely disregarded.
>
> . . . . .
>
> Unfavorable assignments, of little political value to the recipients, are sometimes deliberately given by the powers that be as a mark of disapproval, or for reasons that might be described as "for the good of the order." [19]

Masters argues that aside from the major committees in the House, the most important single factor in distributing assignments "is whether a particular place will help to insure the re-election of the member in question." [20]

Though the Storting to some extent serves as a "mutual benefit and improvement society," it is also important for the party leaders to ensure effective representation on all committees, or, stated differently, an optimal allocation of personnel. In short, the division of labor

[18] See Hernes, "Interest, Influence and Cooperation," chap. 4.

[19] Nicholas A. Masters, "Committee Assignments in the House of Representatives," *American Political Science Review* 55 (1961): 351, 356.

[20] Ibid., p. 354. But see also Charles S. Bullock, III, "Freshman Committee Assignments and Re-election in the House of Representatives," *American Political Science Review* 66 (1972): 996–1007. See also Rohde and Shepsle, "Democratic Committee Assignments."

through the committee system not only generates a motivational system within the Parliament but also creates problems of personnel allocation and hence provides a source of power for those groups and individuals, mainly the parties and party leaders, who control the committee assignments. Furthermore, the fact that the committees can be ranked on more than one dimension, as, for example, local and national importance, creates a compensatory rather than a monistic reward structure, though to a varying degree in different parties. Those who either fail or cannot find their self-esteem as cosmopolitans may focus their talents on being effective constituency agents, or locals. This in turn reduces tensions and increases the job satisfaction of the representatives. It also gives the parties more flexibility in distributing personnel. Since influence tends to become specialized, conflicts may be reduced.

Two final consequences for the functioning of the legislature are so important that they deserve to be singled out. The division of labor through standing committees reduces the influence and overview of representatives outside their own committees. Since, to a large extent, they lack familiarity with issues handled in other committees, they must rely on the judgment of selected colleagues on these committees —colleagues whom they can trust. We may therefore suggest that the division of labor through the setting up of stable committees serves as a catalyst in the social organization of trust, for example, through political parties. Or, stated differently, organizational differentiation at one level generates the need for integrative organizations at another level. Substantiation of this hypothesis must await further research. One might argue that such a development would be stimulated by the fact that if a representative wants to affect the decisions of committees of which he is not a member, he is forced to enter into exchanges with those representatives who are. The most durable exchange relationships are those based on similarities of interest, and the most potent of these are parties, though regional alignments also play an important role.

However, exchange relationships not only serve as a catalyst in party integration. If a representative wishes to affect decisions on matters in which he takes an interest but which are under the control of other committees, what he can offer in return is his control over matters of interest to the members of these other committees that come before his committee. He has to employ his control over what interests others to gain control over what is of interest to him. However, the representatives take a great interest in the decisions made in some committees, while most of them take negligible interest in the decisions made in others. This means that the exchange positions of members of different committees systematically differ. I will now argue that this is the structural basis for the differentiation of power in the legislature.

V
THE STRUCTURAL BASIS FOR THE GENERATION OF POWER

LOG-ROLLING is discussed most often in connection with ballots in the plenary session, and refers to exchanges in which a legislator who cares a lot about the outcome of a ballot makes colleagues who care little about the outcome vote his way in the expectation of a similar return favor in the future.

In the Storting relatively few transactions of this type take place. However, the fact that each representative is a member of only one committee, even though he may want to affect the decisions taken in other committees, provides other opportunities for trading influence. Representatives not only interact in their capacity as voters in the plenary session but also can engage in log-rolling in their capacity as committee members.

In Section II I argued that the power of an actor is a function of how much control he has over decisions in which other actors take an interest. The greater his control and the greater their interest, the greater his power. I also have argued that one important way in which control of decisions is allocated is by committee assignments, and that the interests of the representatives materialize in structural terms by being projected on the committees. But since the amounts of interest focused on the various comittees are unequal, the structural bases for exerting influence for members of different committees should, according to the theory, also be unequal. It is the validity of this line of argument which I now want to explore.

In order to apply the model outlined in Section II, we first need a numerical expression for the interest that the representatives in each of the parties take in each of the committees. We also need a numerical expression for the relative share of each representative in the control of each of the committees. Once these have been decided upon, we can, by the definitions given in Section II, *calculate* the power of each of the representatives in each of the parties. But in order to test the model, we must have some *independent measure* of the power of members of each of the parties. We can then correlate the vector of *calculated power* with the vector of *independently measured power*. If the model is good, there should be significant correlation coefficients, they should be found for all partics, and they

298

should be higher than the correlations yielded by alternative simpler models.

The logic of the empirical procedure is as follows.[21] The numerical expression for the amount of interest a representative focuses on each committee has been taken from his response to the question: which three committees would you most like to be a member of, and which three would you least like to be a member of? One number was associated with the committees a representative most wanted to be a member of, a smaller number to the committees he did not mention either way, and an even smaller number to the committees he least wanted to be a member of. These numbers were calibrated in such a fashion that they added to one for each representative. As explained in Section II, this is required for the computation.

For the assignment of numerical values to the amount of control each party representative had over each of the committees, the following weighting was employed. Chairmen or vice-chairmen of committees were given larger numbers than the ordinary members of the committee, and the ordinary members larger numbers than the non-members. About half of the control of a party over a committee was assigned to members of the committee, the rest was evenly divided among the (larger number of) non-members.

Two exceptions were made from this last rule: the parliamentary leader of each party was assigned a higher number for each committee than that given to an ordinary member of his party; so was the vice-parliamentary leader, though the number assigned to him was lower than the leader's.

From these assignments of numerical values of interest and control, a vector of the power that accrues to each member of a party can be calculated from the model. This was done, not only for the matrix of "personal interest" described above, but also for a matrix of the perceived interests of the party in the various committees (based on answers to the question: which three committees are most important for carrying through the program of your party, and which three least?), and finally for a matrix based on the arithmetic average of personal and party interest. Table 9–2 illustrates what a control and an interest matrix look like. The first of the matrices is the control matrix for the Christian Democrats. The party has 13 members, one

[21] For full details, see Hernes, "Interest, Influence and Cooperation," chap. 6; and idem, "The Structural Basis for the Generation of Power" (Paper presented at the Mathematical Social Science Board Conference on Mathematical Models of Collective Decisions, Hilton Head, August 1971).

TABLE 9–2. Control and Interest Matrices for the Christian Democrats, and the Calculated Vectors of the Value of Control of the Various Committees and the Power of Each Party Member. (The interest matrix is the average of personal and perceived party interest in the committees.)

Adm.[a]	Fin.	Jus.	Edu.	Mun.	Agr.	Def.	Pro.	Com.	Fish.	Ind.	Soc.	For.
					Constitutional Control by Actor i (representative) in Event j (committee)							
.033	.033	.033	.033	.022	.033	.033	.033	.500	.033	.033	.033	.030
.033	.033	.033	.033	.022	.033	.033	.033	.033	.500	.033	.033	.030
.033	.033	.033	.033	.022	.033	.500	.033	.033	.033	.033	.033	.030
.100	.100	.100	.100	.067	.100	.100	.100	.100	.100	.100	.100	.600
.033	.033	.500	.033	.022	.033	.033	.033	.033	.033	.033	.033	.030
.033	.033	.033	.033	.022	.033	.033	.033	.033	.033	.033	.500	.030
.033	.033	.033	.033	.022	.033	.033	.500	.033	.033	.033	.033	.030
.033	.033	.033	.033	.667	.033	.033	.033	.033	.033	.033	.033	.030
.033	.033	.033	.033	.022	.500	.033	.033	.033	.033	.033	.033	.030
.067	.533	.067	.067	.044	.067	.067	.067	.067	.067	.067	.067	.067
.500	.033	.033	.033	.022	.033	.033	.033	.033	.033	.033	.033	.030
.033	.033	.033	.500	.022	.033	.033	.033	.033	.033	.033	.033	.030
.033	.033	.033	.033	.022	.033	.033	.033	.033	.033	.500	.033	.030

Directed Interest of Actor i in Event j

1	2	3	4	5	6	7	8	9	10	11	12	13
.046	.110	.046	.110	.110	.066	.046	.026	.110	.110	.066	.110	.046
.026	.110	.046	.110	.066	.066	.046	.026	.110	.110	.066	.110	.110
.026	.066	.046	.154	.066	.066	.026	.046	.110	.066	.066	.154	.110
.046	.154	.046	.154	.066	.066	.046	.046	.046	.046	.066	.110	.110
.026	.110	.066	.154	.066	.066	.046	.026	.110	.046	.110	.110	.066
.046	.066	.066	.154	.066	.026	.026	.046	.066	.066	.066	.154	.154
.026	.110	.046	.110	.110	.110	.066	.046	.110	.066	.066	.066	.110
.026	.110	.066	.090	.110	.090	.046	.026	.066	.066	.110	.110	.110
.026	.046	.066	.110	.066	.110	.026	.026	.110	.066	.066	.110	.110
.026	.110	.066	.110	.066	.110	.026	.026	.154	.046	.066	.110	.110
.046	.154	.066	.154	.066	.066	.046	.046	.066	.066	.066	.154	.066
.026	.066	.046	.154	.066	.066	.046	.046	.046	.066	.066	.154	.154
.046	.066	.110	.110	.110	.066	.046	.046	.090	.046	.090	.110	.066

The Value of Each Event

1	2	3	4	5	6	7	8	9	10	11	12	13
.034	.101	.059	.130	.078	.074	.040	.036	.088	.065	.073	.120	.101

The Power of Each Actor

1	2	3	4	5	6	7	8	9	10	11	12	13
.073	.063	.051	.148	.060	.088	.049	.082	.067	.112	.048	.093	.066

[a] Abbreviations are defined in Table 9–1.

for each row, each of whom has a numerical assignment of control over each of the 13 committees, one for each column. For example, the actor corresponding to the fourth row is the parliamentary leader of the Christian Democrats, and the last column represents the Foreign Affairs committee. It may be noted that the sum down the columns adds to 1.0. The second matrix is the arithmetic average of personal and perceived party interest of the same members in the 13 committees, listed in the same order. Here the sum across the columns adds to 1.0.

From these matrices we can calculate the value of control of each event and the power of each actor. It turns out that the most valuable event (or set of events, rather) to control in this party, is the fourth from the left, which corresponds to the Education Committee, in which decisions regarding education, religion, and cultural affairs are made— obviously a key concern to the Christian Democrats. But to arrive at this number I have weighted the interest of each of the Christian Democrats on the committee by his power.

However, if these two vectors were very sensitive to the actual assignment of numbers, then the vector of calculated power would be very unstable, and further analysis of little point. But it turns out that the test is fairly reliable in the following sense: as long as the basic rank order among the assigned numerical values in the interest and control matrices remains the same, the correlations between the resulting vectors of calculated power will be very high. We therefore can proceed to compare the vector of calculated power in each of the parties with an independent measure of the power of each of the representatives.

This independent measure is based on socio-metric choices by each party member of its three most influential representatives. The aggregate number of choices received by each member from his party colleagues was taken as an independent measure of his power. Needless to say, measurement error will be present; but by taking the aggregate number, it is reduced.

It turns out that the fit between the calculated and the sociometrically observed measures of power is quite good. The lowest correlation coefficient is found for the Liberal Party—0.46 for the matrix of personal interests and 0.49 for the matrix of perceived party interest. However, if one outlier is removed from consideration, these correlations increase to 0.63 and 0.61 respectively. For the other parties the correlations are 0.60 or higher, and the correlations tend to be higher for the matrix based on party interests than for the matrix based on personal interests. All correlations are too high to be attributable to

TABLE 9–3. CORRELATIONS BETWEEN AGGREGATE SOCIOMETRIC CHOICES RECEIVED FROM MEMBERS OF OWN PARTY AND CALCULATED POWER BASED ON PERSONAL AND PERCEIVED PARTY INTEREST

Party	Number of Members	Personal Interests	Party Interests
Center Party	18	0.80	0.84
Christian Democrats	13	0.80	0.82
Conservative Party	31	0.60	0.71
Labor Party	68	0.63	0.67
Liberal Party	18	0.46	0.49
(Lib. without outlier)	17	0.63	0.61

chance or measurement error. Their magnitude is the more impressive in view of the crudeness of the procedures for assignment of scores for the amount of interest and the amount of control of each representative. Moreover, the correlations are higher for this model, based on both the interest and control matrices, than for models of calculated power based on either the formal control of an actor or the aggregate interest focused on a committee alone.[22] Or, expressed differently, the model fits better than alternative simpler ones that, for the sake of simplicity and parsimony, might have been preferred. Various other tests of the model come out in its favor, though I shall not describe them here.

By the correlation analysis I have carried out a test of the construct or external validity of the concept of power as defined in the model outlined in Section II. The argument is that if the structural basis for the differentiation of power is, to put it simply, control over the interests of other actors, then this should have a direct effect on their subjective construction of reality. One would expect (though there is no necessary relation) that formal position, which I have used to operationalize control, affects sociometric choices. But the analysis shows that, if one weights this formal position as specified by the model, one obtains a better fit than one would for predictions based on formal position alone.

It is interesting to note that most of the representatives in the Storting tend to attribute differences in power to differences in *personal* capacities. I have argued that in order to get at the *structural* basis for the differentiation of power one has to ask *where* a man is located rather than *who* he is. However, it must be underlined that the vector

[22] For details, see Hernes, "The Structural Basis for the Generation of Power."

of calculated power (assuming no measurement error for the moment) in fact is an array of numbers denoting the *potential* power each actor has—i.e., the power he would have if the matrices of interest and control gave accurate representations of reality and there were perfect exchange. Therefore, one could take the vector of calculated power as a baseline for further study, and the departures from calculated power could be used as an estimate of differential skills, frictions on exchange, and control over interests not explicitly incorporated here.

It may be added that the representatives' attribution of differences in influence to differences in capacities serves to reduce tensions and conflict in the Storting, since the correspondence between personal effort and power establishes a kind of distributive justice between these two phenomena. Personal influence may also be incorporated into the theoretical framework by arguing that it is based on capacities (control) to perform tasks (events) which others want carried out (take an interest in).

On the other hand, if committees are an important structural base for the differentiation of power, this should, as stated before, have an impact on the representatives' subjective construction of reality. Richard Fenno writes about the House Appropriations Committee: "The most frequently mentioned source of Committee attractiveness is its power—based on its control over financial resources. 'Where the money is, that's where the power is,' sums up the feeling of the members. They prize their ability to reward or punish so many other participants in the political process—executive officials, fellow Congressmen, constituents and other clientele groups." [23] Manley argues that the major sources of attraction of the House Committee on Ways and Means are its power and prestige. "Ways and Means members share in the Committee's prestige and, at a more practical level, they are in a good position to accumulate political credit with their colleagues. . . . Newly elected congressmen are indebted to them from the first day they arrive and, as a member moves up the committee hierarchy, he is continually dependent on his representative on Ways and Means." [24]

Similar statements about the differential power of members of different committees in their interaction with fellow representatives, officials, constituents, and other clients are also frequent in the Storting.

[23] Richard F. Fenno, Jr., "The House Appropriations Committee as a Political System: The Problem of Integration," *American Political Science Review* 56 (1962): 314.

[24] John F. Manley, "The House Committee on Ways and Means: Conflict Management in a Congressional Committee," *American Political Science Review* 59 (1965): 935.

So, though the representatives primarily attribute differences in influence to differences in personal capacities, they also appreciate the structural basis for their power. What I have done is to incorporate these insights into a testable model. The model also fuses the traditional constitutional approach to the study of politics, stressing legal arrangements and formal organization, with the more recent behavioral approach, which often includes the investigation of personal preferences through survey analysis. In this model, the constitutional or organizational arrangement of the Storting is combined with the personal and perceived party interests of the representatives.

The above analysis also implies that the structural basis for the differentiation of power can change in two ways. One is by constitutional or organizational change, i.e., by reallocating tasks (or "events") between organizational units. Thereby the issue-areas (or interests) that actors control are changed. In a legislature this could come about by establishing a committee system where there was none before, by transferring certain kinds of legislation from one committee to another, or by dissolving old committees or setting up new ones. Thus one structural component of change in the basis for power is change in the organizational map. In most legislatures this can be done by the legislators themselves.

The other way of changing the structural basis for the differentiation of power is by changing the interests of the actors. It is here that the environment impinges most directly on relations within the legislature, since the flow of issues to it determines what the representatives take an interest in. Certain committees may have a temporary gain in importance when interest in the issues they control increases, as a Defense Committee does during a war. Others may show a fairly steady gain or loss in significance over time. The degree of stability of various issue-areas over time is an interesting question for historical analysis. However, even though the environment has a direct effect on the interests of the representatives, it must be underlined that the most important sources of changes in representatives' interests generally are due to processes internal to the Storting. We already have seen how orientations are modified by party influence and committee memberships.

As a matter of fact, this opens the opportunity for understanding the relationship between power, exchange, and cosmopolitanism. Being a member of a committee others take a high interest in is an important source of a representative's power. It also evokes initiatives and attempted exchanges from others. They will attempt to affect his stand in order to affect the outcomes of the decisions of his committee. But

305

many of the desired outcomes are bound to be conflicting, and the only way a representative on an important committee subject to conflicting demands can resolve and reasonably defend his position is by reverting to national decision-criteria or "the national interest." Thus I would argue that to some extent it is the same structural position which gives rise to both party influence and a cosmopolitan orientation.

VI

CONCLUSION

IN this chapter I have outlined a theory of collective decision making and have used it to analyze various aspects of the Norwegian Storting in the 1960s. The direct application of the model was facilitated by two conditions. First, interviews could be used to investigate the preferences and interests of the representatives. Second, the committee system provides a delimitation of issue-areas as well as of control domains.

However, the model is not limited to use on contemporary data. We saw how various interest groups tend to gain control over the committees that make the most important decisions with respect to their interests. The same can be shown to hold for political parties, at least in the Norwegian Storting. This kind of analysis also might provide an opportunity for historical research.

Nor is the model restricted to use on legislatures with a well-organized committee system. In order to operationalize the model for other settings, one has to ask: what are the events that the legislators take an interest in, and how is control over these events distributed among them? The same questions must be asked with respect to the relation between the legislature and its environment. The answers given to these questions will be determined by the characteristics of the specific legislature under study.

It should also be pointed out that the illustrations given above have not exhausted the analytical possibilities of the model. Since the processes described do not take place in a social vacuum, the next obvious question is how the transactions between the representatives are affected by the resources at their command. The concern would be, not so much with individual transactions, but with the proportion of these that have solidified into a pattern of exchange and cooperation, and with the ways in which the structure of power and the web of cooperation mutually affect each other.[25] Not only the relations among the representatives but also their interaction with local and central

[25] This topic is further pursued in Hernes, "Interest, Influence and Cooperation," chap. 8, "Influence and Cooperation."

administration as well as with other political actors outside the legislature would call for attention.

So far we have only treated representatives as actors. However, by the definition of actors in Section II, it is quite possible to regard collectivities of individuals as actors. Explicitly or implicitly this is often done in the social sciences. In micro-economics a theory of the firm is developed in which the firm is taken to be a unitary actor. In political science states are often treated as single actors, and terms like "national interest" are used.

If we are to treat collectivities as actors, we have to find a way of ascertaining their interests in the outcomes of events, and evaluating how much control they have over their outcome. For a party in a legislature, its share of the votes could be taken as a measure of its control, either in the legislature as a whole or by taking committees as event-sets. Interest could be measured by content-analyzing party platforms or by interviewing the legislators. Or one could take an *aggregate* of the interests of party representatives in different events as a measure of the *party's* interests in those events. In fact, one such aggregation is given by the vector of events, like the one in Table 9–2. In historical studies, biographies might be a source of information.

From an interest and a control matrix of this kind, one could then calculate, not only the relative power of the various parties, but also the "value of the collectivity," i.e., the value, to each of them, of being represented in the legislature. This might be of use in theorizing about constitutional sources of extremism. One could also use the model as a theory of coalitions by calculating the value of subcollectivities of parties to the members of such groups. A prediction would be that the coalition which will form is that for which this number is greatest. It is also possible to predict how the spoils, for example cabinet posts, will be split among the coalition partners.[26]

Thus the major advantages of the model, aside from defining central concepts in political studies in a mathematically precise manner, are that it combines constitutional arrangements with the personal preferences of political actors, and that the same basic theory can be used for analyzing not only the behavior of individuals but also that of collectivities or corporate actors. However, any model is an abstraction, and represents a perspective. Although it may give a certain unity to research endeavors, it also inevitably excludes certain aspects of reality.

[26] For a numerical illustration, see Hernes, "The Structural Basis for the Generation of Power."

List of Participants in the Conference at the University of Iowa, March 13–15, 1972

THOMAS B. ALEXANDER, University of Missouri
HOWARD W. ALLEN, Southern Illinois University
WILLIAM O. AYDELOTTE, University of Iowa
ALLAN G. BOGUE, University of Wisconsin
GEORGE R. BOYNTON, University of Iowa
JOHN R. BYLSMA, Augustana College, Sioux Falls, South Dakota
CLEO H. CHERRYHOLMES, Michigan State University
AAGE R. CLAUSEN, Ohio State University
JEROME M. CLUBB, Inter-University Consortium for Political Research, University of Michigan
ROBERT R. DYKSTRA, University of Iowa
JAMES Q. GRAHAM, JR., Bowling Green State University
CHARLES A. HALE, University of Iowa
BASIL D. HENNING, Yale University
GUDMUND HERNES, University of Bergen, Norway
PATRICE HIGONNET, Harvard University
SÖREN HOLMBERG, Göteborg University, Sweden
HENRY G. HORWITZ, University of Iowa
GEOFFREY HOSKING, University of Essex, Great Britain
WILLIAM J. IRWIN, Bowie State College, Maryland
CHONG LIM KIM, University of Iowa
ANTHONY KING, University of Essex, Great Britain
JOHN G. KOLP, Political Science Laboratory, University of Iowa
GERHARD LOEWENBERG, University of Iowa
WILLIAM C. LUBENOW, Stockton State College, Pomona, New Jersey
JOHN F. MANLEY, Stanford University
DONALD R. MATTHEWS, The Brookings Institution; now at University of Washington, Seattle
JOHN J. McCARTHY, Yale University
SAMUEL C. PATTERSON, University of Iowa
MOGENS N. PEDERSEN, University of Aarhus, Denmark; now at Odense University
NELSON W. POLSBY, University of California, Berkeley
DOUGLAS PRICE, Harvard University
ANTOINE PROST, University of Orléans, France
AUSTIN RANNEY, University of Wisconsin

CHRISTIAN ROSENZVEIG, University of Paris-X Nanterre, France

EDWARD V. SCHNEIER, JR., City College of the City University of New York

JOEL H. SILBEY, Cornell University

D. A. SMITH, Grinnell College, Iowa

PETER H. SMITH, University of Wisconsin

JAMES A. STIMSON, State University of New York, Buffalo

SANTA TRAUGOTT, Inter-University Consortium for Political Research, University of Michigan

DOUGLAS V. VERNEY, York University, Downsview, Ontario

HERBERT WEISBERG, University of Michigan

DAVID M. WOOD, University of Missouri

ROBERT ZEMSKY, University of Pennsylvania

The Contributors

William O. Aydelotte is Professor of History at the University of Iowa. He received his Ph.D. from the University of Cambridge, and taught previously at Trinity College, Smith College, and Princeton University. He was a member of the Board of Directors of the Social Science Research Council, 1965–1970. He is a member of the Steering Committee of the Social Science History Association. His publications include *Bismarck and British Colonial Policy* (1937; rev. ed., 1970), *Quantification in History* (1971), and a number of articles. He was a co-editor (with Robert W. Fogel and Allan G. Bogue) of *The Dimensions of Quantitative Research in History* (1972). He is a member of the National Academy of Sciences. He was a fellow at the Center for Advanced Study in the Behavioral Sciences, 1976–1977.

Aage R. Clausen has been since 1971 Professor of Political Science at Ohio State University. He received his Ph.D. from the University of Michigan, and taught previously at the University of Wisconsin and at the University of Göteborg in Sweden. His publications include *How Congressmen Decide: A Policy Focus* (1973), "The Measurement of Legislative Group Behavior" (1967), "State Party Influence on Congressional Policy Decisions" (1972), "Subjectivity and Objectivity in Dimensional Analysis: Illustrations from Congressional Voting" (1974), and other articles. He has served as Study Director of the Political Behavior Program of the Survey Research Center at the University of Michigan.

Gudmund Hernes is Professor of Sociology at the Institute of Sociology, University of Bergen, in Norway, where he has also served as chairman. He received his Ph.D. from the Department of Social Relations at Johns Hopkins University. His publications in English include "On Rank Disequilibrium and Military Coups d'Etat" (1969), "A Markovian Approach to Measures of Association" (1970), "The Process of Entry into First Marriage" (1972), and "Political Resource Transformation" (1974). He also has published extensively in Norwegian journals. He is currently director of a study of the distribution of power in Norway and recently has published a book laying out the theoretical framework for this study, *Magt og Avmakt* (1975). He was a fellow at the Center for Advanced Study in the Behavioral Sciences, 1974–1975.

Sören Holmberg is Assistant Professor in the Department of Political

Science at the University of Göteborg, in Sweden. He took his Ph.D. at the University of Göteborg. His principal earlier publication is *Riksdagen Representerar Svenska Folket: Empiriska Studier i Representativ Demokrati* (1974).

Geoffrey Hosking is Lecturer in History at the University of Essex, in Great Britain, and Director of Russian Studies for the University. He has also taught at the University of Wisconsin. He received his Ph.D. from the University of Cambridge. He is author of *The Russian Constitutional Experiment: Government and Duma, 1907–14* (1973), and has published a series of articles on the contemporary Russian novel.

Anthony King is Professor of Government at the University of Essex, in Great Britain. He took his D. Phil. from Oxford, and was a fellow of Magdalen College, Oxford, 1961–1966. He was co-author (with David Butler) of the 1964 and 1966 Nuffield College election studies, and has recently published *British Members of Parliament: A Self-Portrait* (1974). He is editor of the *British Journal of Political Science*.

Donald R. Matthews is Professor of Political Science and Chairman of the Department at the University of Washington, Seattle. He taught previously at Smith College, the University of North Carolina at Chapel Hill, and the University of Michigan. He has also served on the research staff of the Brookings Institution. He received his Ph.D. from Princeton University. His publications include *U.S. Senators and Their World* (1960), *Yeas and Nays: Normal Decision-Making in the U.S. House of Representatives* (with James A. Stimson, 1975), *Negroes and the New Southern Politics* (with James Prothro, 1966), and *Perspectives on Presidential Selection* (1973). He is a member of the American Academy of Arts and Sciences, and was formerly a fellow at the Center for Advanced Study in the Behavioral Sciences.

Mogens N. Pedersen is Professor of Political Science at the Institute of History and Social Science, Odense University, in Denmark. He taught formerly at the University of Aarhus, where he also did his graduate work. His publications in English include "Consensus and Conflict in the Danish Folketing, 1945–65" (1966), "Lawyers in Politics: The Danish Folketing and American Legislatures" (1972), and "The Geographical Matrix of Parliamentary Representation" (1975).

Douglas Price is Professor of Government at Harvard University, where he also received his Ph.D. He taught previously at the University of Florida, Columbia University, and Syracuse University. His publications include *The Negro and Southern Politics* (1957) and numerous articles on political parties and legislative behavior. He has a

312

book forthcoming which will be entitled *Causal Models of American Politics*. He was formerly a fellow at the Center for Advanced Study in the Behavioral Sciences.

Antoine Prost is Maître de Conférences (Histoire Contemporaine) at the Université d'Orléans and Professor at the Institut d'Etudes Politiques de Paris. He was formerly Assistant, then Maître-Assistant, at the Sorbonne. He holds the degree of Docteur Es-Lettres from the Université de Paris-IV. His earlier publications include, in addition to numerous articles, *La C.G.T. à l'Epoque du Front Populaire: Essai de Description Numérique* (1964), *Histoire de l'Enseignement en France, 1800–1967* (1968), *Vocabulaire des Proclamations Electorales de 1881, 1885, et 1889* (1974), and *L'Eclatement du Front Populaire: Analyse Factorielle des Scrutins de la Législature, 1936–1940* (1975).

Christian Rosenzveig is Assistant à l'U.E.R. de Sciences Economiques de l'Université de Paris-X Nanterre. He and Professor Prost, for some time, have been engaged in research together, and they are the joint authors of a number of articles reporting on their investigations.

Peter H. Smith has been a member of the Department of History at the University of Wisconsin since 1968. He taught earlier at Dartmouth College. He received his Ph.D. from Columbia University. His publications include, in addition to a number of articles, *Politics and Beef in Argentina: Patterns of Conflict and Change* (1969), and *Argentina and the Failure of Democracy: Conflict among Political Elites, 1904–1955* (1974). He has co-edited (with Richard Graham) *New Approaches to Latin American History* (1974).

James A. Stimson is a member of the Political Science Department at the State University of New York at Buffalo. He taught previously at the University of North Carolina at Chapel Hill, where he also received his Ph.D., and has been a Research Associate at the Brookings Institution. He was co-author (with Donald R. Matthews) of *Yeas and Nays: Normal Decision-Making in the U.S. House of Representatives* (1975), and "Decision-Making by U.S. Representatives: A Preliminary Model" (1970). He has published "Belief Systems: Constraint, Complexity, and the 1972 Election" (1975), and has several articles forthcoming that deal with models of Congressional behavior.

Index

Abram, Michael E., 53, 54, 57
"accidentalist" school, 137, 139–40,
    155–56
Adams, John, 32
Advanced Radical Committee, British
    House of Commons, 145
Alexander, DeAlva S., 29, 52
Andrade, Cayetano, 205
Asquith, Herbert Henry, 136–37, 139,
    154–55
Aydelotte, William O., 146–47

Bailey, Stephen K., 248, 250
Barber, James D., 91
Beer, Samuel H., 146, 153
Beer's "coefficient of cohesion," 146,
    153
Benson, Lee, 23
Benton, Thomas Hart, 34n
Benzécri, Jean-Paul, 16, 106
Berrington, Hugh, 230–31, 233
"Big Scale," 231–33
Bjurulf, Bo, 169–70, 178
Blondel, Jean, 3
Bojórquez, Juan de Dios, 193–94, 197,
    198–99, 215–16n
British House of Commons (1841–
    1847):
    Conservative Party, breaks within
        by type of constituency, 234–36,
        table, 235; party line, 231,
        234–36
    constituencies, classification of,
        227–28; extent of enfranchisement,
        244–45; influence on Parliament,
        237, 240–46; manipulation of,
        226
    constituency, and differences on
        issues, 230–33, 236–37; and
        party affiliation, relation between,
        229–30, 236, *table,* 229
    constituency variable, refinement
        of, 243–44

election contests, and breaks within
    parties (1841), 238–40, *tables,*
    239–40; incidence of, 237–38;
    constituency and party (1841),
    238, *table,* 239; re-election of
    incumbents (1847–1852), 241–43,
    246, *tables,* 242, 243, 244
Liberal Party, breaks within by
    type of constituency, 233, *table,*
    234; party line, 233–34
measure of voting on party (1841),
    231–33
party affiliations, identification of,
    227; in Ireland, 229; in England,
    Scotland and Wales, 230; and
    scale-type, 232–33
party line, liberals and Conservatives,
    231, 233–36, *table,* 235
British House of Commons (1906–
    1914), *see* British Labour Party;
    British Liberal Party
British Labour Party, Tribune Group,
    145
British Liberal Party, decline of,
    136–37, *table,* 137; division (roll-
    call votes), 145–46, *table,* 147;
    lack of ideological divisions in,
    140–43, 150, 154–55; party
    cohesion, 145–46, 153; Radical
    rebel votes, 149–53; 154–55;
    Whig rebel votes, 148–49
Brown, George Rothwell, 59n
Bryce, James, 3, 24
Buchanan, William, 46n

Calhoun, John C., 35
Campbell, Angus, 88n, 250
Cannon, Joseph, 49, 57, 58
career, objective vs. subjective, 64,
    93–94
Carranza, Venustiano, 188, 189, 193,
    205, 206, 208, 215–16, 217, 219
Chihuahua (Mexico), 215, 216
Clarke, P.F., 138n, 139–40
Clausen, Aage R., 14, 17

315

Library of Congress Cataloging in Publication Data

Main entry under title:
The History of parliamentary behavior.
  (Quantitative studies in history)
  "Papers were originally presented at a conference
which met at the University of Iowa, in Iowa City,
March 13–15, 1972."
    1. Legislative bodies—History—Congresses.
2. Legislators—History—Congresses. I. Aydelotte,
William Osgood. II. Series.
JF501.H57   328'.3'09   76–24290
ISBN 0–691–05242–5